READING ROMAN COMEDY

For many years the domain of specialists in early Latin, in complex metres and in the reconstruction of texts, Roman comedy has only recently begun to establish itself in the mainstream of classical literary criticism. Where most recent books stress the original performance as the primary location for the encountering of the plays, this book finds the locus of meaning and appreciation in the activity of a reader, albeit one whose manner of reading necessarily involves the imaginative reconstruction of performance. The texts are treated, and celebrated, as literary devices, with programmatic beginnings, middles, ends and intertexts. All the extant plays of Plautus and Terence have at least a bit-part in this book, which seeks to expose the authors' fabulous artificiality and artifice, while playing along with their differing but interrelated poses of generic humility.

ALISON SHARROCK is Professor of Classics at the University of Manchester. She is also the author of *Seduction and Repetition in Ovid's* Ars Amatoria *2* (1994) and *Fifty Key Classical Authors* (with Rhiannon Ash, 2002), and co-editor of *Intratextuality: Greek and Roman Textual Relations* (with Helen Morales, 2000) and *The Art of Love: Bimillennial Essays on Ovid's* Ars Amatoria *and* Remedia Amoris (with Roy Gibson and Steven Green, 2006).

THE W. B. STANFORD MEMORIAL LECTURES

This lecture series was established by public subscription, to honour the memory of William Bedell Stanford, Regius Professor of Greek in Trinity College, Dublin, from 1940 to 1980, and Chancellor of the University of Dublin from 1982 to 1984.

READING ROMAN COMEDY

Poetics and Playfulness in Plautus and Terence

ALISON SHARROCK

CAMBRIDGE
UNIVERSITY PRESS

CAMBRIDGE UNIVERSITY PRESS
Cambridge, New York, Melbourne, Madrid, Cape Town,
Singapore, São Paulo, Delhi, Tokyo, Mexico City

Cambridge University Press
The Edinburgh Building, Cambridge CB2 8RU, UK

Published in the United States of America by
Cambridge University Press, New York

www.cambridge.org
Information on this title: www.cambridge.org/9780521761819

First published 2009

A catalogue record for this publication is available from the British Library

Library of Congress cataloguing in publication data
Sharrock, Alison.
Reading Roman comedy : poetics and playfulness in Plautus and Terence / Alison Sharrock.
p. cm.
Includes bibliographical references and index.
ISBN 978-0-521-76181-9 (hardback)
1. Plautus, Titus Maccius – Criticism and interpretation. 2. Terence – Criticism and interpretation.
3. Latin drama (Comedy) – History and criticism. I. Title.
PA6602.S53 2009
872′.0109 – dc22 2009016622

ISBN 978-0-521-76181-9 Hardback

In memory of Edna Christine Wiegold 1932–2005
best of mothers

Contents

Preface

I hated Roman comedy as an undergraduate. Not only was it hard Latin, but also it gave little promise to be worth the effort, as being apparently a stereotype-ridden exercise in lamentable literary secondariness. It was only many years later when I was forced to teach the genre that I began to see that there might be some fun in it. Perhaps I should apologise for being slow, but anecdotal research suggests that I am not alone in my early experience, and that, apart from a select group of experts, most people, even professional classicists, are not avid readers. The less-than-avid readers of Plautus and Terence are first among those for whom this book is written. If the experts also find something here to amuse, if not to inform, I shall be well pleased.

From a career beginning in Augustan elegy, my entry into Roman comedy does not follow what might be thought the traditional route from the former to the latter. That there has been some degree of connection between the two genres has been known since antiquity, although not greatly exploited by modern critics, but the connections made have in any case been largely through what one might call the fictional worlds of the two genres. Insofar as one believes the imagined world of elegy to be that of a 'demi-monde', where the main players are slaves and freedwoman-prostitutes interacting with citizen men, that world can be seen to relate to the fictional world of the *fabula palliata*. This, however, is not my primary interest. I have been more concerned to consider how the *poetics* of Augustan poetry might find resonances in the artistry of republican comedy. Plautus and even Terence still labour under the calumny of baseness: their generic lowness, the immediacy of their performance, their early date in the story of Roman literary culture, the loss of so much other Latin literature from their period and their own self-deprecating self-display have contributed to an underlying prejudice about the playwrights as fundamentally different from respectable poets like Virgil, or even Ovid, and even as 'not really literature'. Their study has been the preserve of experts, who have done important work but who have not always evangelised effectively among a wider classical audience. Much of the recent non-philological work on comedy has been mainly concerned with performance; my primary concern, by contrast, is with reading, and with performance as it features in imaginative reconstruction by the reader. One of the aims of this book is to help in bringing Plautus and Terence into the mainstream of Latin literary studies.

The twenty-one plays of Plautus and the six of Terence all feature to some extent in this study, but the discussions are scattered throughout. Rather than burdening the text with multiple cross-references, I have attempted to use the index to guide the reader towards all discussions of a particular play.

All quotations from Plautus and Terence are from the relevant Oxford Classical Texts (OCTs), as are those of all other classical texts except where stated. I have translated all substantial passages in the main text, although not in the footnotes. All translations are my own unless otherwise stated: they make no claims to elegance or cleverness. Abbreviations for classical texts and authors are as in the Oxford Latin Dictionary (*OLD*) or, for Greek authors, Liddell and Scott (*LSJ*); abbreviations for scholarly journals are as in *L'Année philologique*.

This book began life far too long ago, when I was invited by the Department of Classics at Trinity College, Dublin to deliver the W. B. Stanford Memorial lectures for 1999. I am very grateful to the Department, and especially to Brian McGing, for the opportunity, their hospitality, and most of all their patience. I acknowledge with gratitude the support of the Leverhulme Trust and the University of Manchester for periods of research leave which contributed to the writing of this book. Many friends and colleagues have offered generous advice and invaluable moral support at various stages, among whom I would mention particularly Ruth Morello, David Langslow, John Henderson, Joanne McNamara, Emma Griffiths and Dorota Dutsch. I have been very fortunate in my dealings with the Press throughout, in Michael Sharp's acuity, flexibility and helpful advice and support, in the enormously useful reports from the readers, and in the expertise of the editorial team. I am particularly indebted to the care and expertise of my copy editor, Iveta Adams. The person without whom this book would never have reached its final form is Valerie Knight, my research assistant for the last couple of years, who kept me going when university administration threatened to overwhelm me, who insisted on precision when I would have been lazy, who went far beyond the call of duty in every aspect, and who always brought me a cup of coffee. It goes without saying that remaining errors are my own responsibility. Finally, I would like to thank my family, my husband Tim and our three boys who have all but grown up with this book, and my parents, Jim and Christine Wiegold, who have always supported me in every way. This book is dedicated to the memory of my mother.

CHAPTER I

Art and artifice

> Below art, we find artifice, and it is this zone of artifice, midway between nature and art, that we are now about to enter.
>
> (Bergson 1913: 66)

Bergson's tempting twilight zone where artifice rules is the domain of comedy.

Comedy is an art form which delights in its artificiality, glories in its artifice, and actualises its art – all with apparently effortless ease and studied avoidance of obvious studiousness. This study concerns the particular form of comedy which flourished as a performance genre in the late third and early–mid second centuries BC, the plays being first produced as part of festivals celebrating one of the gods, or on other religious, social, and political occasions, such as the dedication of a temple or funeral games for a great man like Lucius Aemilius Paullus.[1] The audience was on holiday and expecting a play to match,[2] but it was also, at least in part, a sophisticated theatre-going crowd with experience of different types of dramatic performance and of other forms of art. The plays of Plautus and

[1] Gruen (1992: ch. 5); Csapo and Slater (1995: 207–10); Leigh (2004b: 2–3); Marshall (2006: 16–20); Henderson (1999: 49).

[2] As a representative, see Beacham (1991: 21–2): 'while [the games were] quintessentially religious, to attend them was also to be on holiday, with the expectation of being entertained . . . Unlike the great theatrical festivals of the Greeks, at Rome the scenic games were only notionally competitive, with the emphasis not on a contest for artistic excellence (much less on free ethical debate), but on impressing and pleasing a crowd out for a good time.' Later (29), Beacham says that Roman comedians had to take care 'not to make excessive demands on the sophistication of their audience', although his position is softened (33) in response to the outright hostility of Norwood (1923). Wright (1974: 190–2) gives a nuanced assessment of the theatrical sophistication of the audience of Roman comedy. See also e.g. Beare (1964: 167): 'the increasing vulgarity of the Roman audience must have tended to degrade the status of those who performed to amuse that audience'. Polybius (30.22) tells us that in 167 BC the eminent Greek musicians assembled on the stage found that the readiest way to please the crowd was to indulge in a mimic battle. (Polybius, of course, could have his own rhetorical reasons for such a comment.) As Erasmo (2004: 29) says, it was the same audience for republican tragedy.

Terence flourished also as a textual genre which manifested itself in a much wider range of reading practices, including the scholarship of Varro, the rhetoric of Cicero, the epitomisation of the grammarians and moralisers, the exemplification of the schoolroom, and the imitation of the Western comic tradition.[3] If throughout this book I appear to privilege the performative audience, it is because the reading of scripted drama involves the imaginative construction of a performance context, even when the reader also makes use of the different interpretative resources available to him or her.[4]

ART AND DECEIT

Terence used his prologues to pursue literary debates which apparently (albeit misleadingly) had only tangential connection with the play at hand. This analysis of Roman comedy begins in the same spirit, with a reflection on art.

Crucial to ancient theories of art is the imitation of nature. So extreme is this code of naturalistic mimesis that its highest accolade is the capacity to deceive the viewer, as is demonstrated by anecdotes such as the famous contest between Zeuxis and Parrhasius. Zeuxis painted grapes which attracted birds eager for food, but Parrhasius tricked even his fellow artist by painting a curtain over his work.[5] The difference between Zeuxis and the birds is that he appreciates the curtain as a consummate work of art precisely when and because he realises that it is *not* real.[6] The work of naturalist art, then, is a pretence of deceit. The phrase 'pretence of deceit' is designed to evoke two different but related phenomena, on which depend the edifices of fiction. On the one hand, I suggest, the fictional construction of a pseudo-reality,

[3] In much of this textual flourishing in antiquity, it was Terence rather than Plautus who was most floriferous. See Reeve (1983: 412–13) on the early manuscript history. The story of how the plays of Plautus and Terence became literature is well told by Goldberg (2005b). The very notion of 'literature' has been deconstructed recently, for earlier Roman culture, by Habinek (2005). I remain convinced of its usefulness as a category.

[4] At a late stage in the revision of this work, I read Meisel (2007), one of very few works of scholarship on theatre which makes explicit its author's address to those who are reading plays, with an imaginative eye on the play in performance. He too often seems to privilege the live audience, no doubt for the same reason.

[5] The story is told by Pliny *Nat.* 35.65. See Isager (1991: 138) for this and for the aesthetic valuation of realism in Greek and Roman art theorists; Kris and Kurz (1979: ch. 3); Carey (2003: 109–10); Zanker (2003: 7).

[6] Elsner (1995: 17–18), apropos this story, says: 'At the heart of this anecdote, the genius of illusionism is ultimately defined by its ability to deceive.' He notes, additionally, that naturalism is not the only point at issue. Naturalism is 'inherently deceptive', and so opposed to the truth for which there was also an artistic drive in ancient theory.

whether in realist mode or fantastical, is predicated at some level on the deception of the viewer: or to put it differently, whatever kind of fiction is at issue, some part of our process of appreciation has to involve seeing the fictive creation as in some sense 'real'.[7] At the same time, however, art requires that the deceit be a pose, and be recognised, otherwise there is no art. Even at its most mimetic and representational, art only comes into being (as art) when there is a perceptible gap between the signifier and the signified. Otherwise the reader is too naïve even to qualify as a reader.[8] In another anecdote, Apelles used the reaction of real horses to his painted versions as proof of their realistic superiority (Plin. *Nat.* 35.95), but it is the discerning observers, not the horses, who appreciate the work as art. A naïve reader is like a bird pecking at painted grapes, a victim who is so much taken in by the fiction that s/he really believes it to be real, and does not recognise it as art. If someone looks at an Unswept Floor mosaic and sees an unswept floor, he is not a viewer of art, but someone who needs to tidy up.[9] Even at its most fantastic and provocatively anti-natural, art must use the pegs of our experience on which to hang its crazy ideas. It is this necessarily deceptive but also interactive relationship between reality and art which caused such anxiety for thinkers in the tradition of Plato, for whom Reality is a concept reified almost to divinity. Art must be treated with the utmost caution, precisely because it is parasitic on reality.[10]

[7] Useful in this regard, although his purpose is different, is Feeney (1991: ch. 1); also Newsom (1988) on interactions of belief and the suspension of belief in fiction; Hardie (2002: 180), '[o]urs is a knowing credulity, as we watch ourselves being duped by the art'.

[8] See Zanker (2003: 85) for a Hellenistic naïve reader, and Gill (1993: 48) for Plato on such naïve readers. For more on the pretence of deceit, and the need for the reader to be 'ignorant and wise simultaneously' (244), see Feeney (1993).

[9] The problem of absolute realism, if I might so call it, is perhaps what leads the scholars cited by Isager (1991: 137) to deprecate Pliny's artistic sense as too concerned with realism above all things. Halliwell (2002: 143–4) discusses the Platonic idea of perfect imitation as simply the same as the *imitandum* (Plato *R.* 3.395d–e). Many people's understanding of art would struggle to encompass such complete identification. Golden's Aristotelian reading of mimesis is helpful in distinguishing the specific cognitive aspect of the appreciation of art: '[t]he key to understanding Aristotle's aesthetic is to be found in this unambiguous emphasis on the fundamental intellectual pleasure and purpose of artistic representation – the quintessentially human delight in learning and inference, which is evoked by the mimetic structure of works of art' (Golden 1992: 64). The pleasure comes not from the thing represented but from the process of representation. Although made in a different context, Hunter's comment in Fantuzzi and Hunter (2004: 425) is important: 'both "drama" and "real life" are theatrical; failing to recognise that and assuming that they are theatrical *in the same way* are both mistakes which lead to truly comic results'.

[10] Halliwell (2001: 88) briefly discusses the largely positive connection in Aristotle between mimesis and fiction. Halliwell (2002: esp. 138) denies the validity of the commonly held interpretation of Plato's objection to mimesis as being 'copy of a copy'. Golden (1992: ch. 3) gives a clear account of the positive and negative aspects of Platonic mimesis: 'Plato held in delicate balance a philosophical contempt for *mimesis* – due to its essential alienation from ultimate reality – and a sober realisation

Of all fictional forms, it is drama which feels this deceit most keenly, because the fictive relationship is the more immediate as the dividing line between fiction and reality is the narrower, above all in the act of performance. In its pure, performative, form, to which all textual experiences of drama aspire, drama consists in embodied people, living, breathing, moving in front of us, but people who 'are' not what they 'seem', or perhaps, rather, whose 'being' is problematised by the relationship between their physical selves and their textual selves.[11] This is especially true in the ancient outdoor temporary theatre, constructed each time for the purpose in the Rome of Plautus and Terence, with actors and audience all involved in the same social and religious ritual.[12] Drama deceives us because it is so very like truth, and yet it depends for its force on our seeing through its tricks. To this deceit, which lies at the heart of drama, comedy has something extra to add. In comedy, a trick (a manipulation of identity, a lie like truth) is inherent. Deceit thus functions as a programmatic signifier of the play-making process itself: deceit is not just the manner and mode of art, but its substance as well, and hence the 'intrigue' which is the structuring device of very many comic plots is a metaphor for the play. Illusion and disguise are its essence, both as a play and within the play.

For all theatre is predicated on disguise.[13] An actor pretends to be someone other than himself. It may be that for ancient plays the personal identity of the actor (who will usually take several different roles within the performance) was less important than in the modern celebrity-obsessed culture, and that there was less opportunity for the kind of confusion between actor

that the skilled use of *mimesis* is an indispensable means for whatever approach we are able to make to that ultimate reality' (41). In ch. 4, and throughout, Golden develops a strongly cognitive and intellectual understanding of Aristotelian mimesis. For our purposes, what matters is the widespread acknowledgement of and anxiety about the relationship between art and nature. For Plato's almost overwhelming role in this debate, see Halliwell (2002: esp. 37–8). For the suggestion that a modern distinction between fictional and factual discourse does not correspond to anything in Plato's thought, see Gill (1993).

11 Aristotle famously used a distinction of medium as one of his ways of classifying works of literature, in which drama performs its representation by doing things (*Po.* 1448a–b1). Orr (1996), in a paper concerned with narrative as an act of mimetic repetition, stresses the especially direct status of drama in mimesis. On the peculiar narratological manner of drama, see Serpieri *et al.* (1981), and Laird (1999) for direct speech as a particularly mimetic form of narrative. See Duncan (2006: 9) on ancient and modern anxieties surrounding the inherent 'lying' of acting.

12 Goldberg (1998) is an important recent account of the performative context of Roman comedy. See also Moore (1991) on the *choragus* speech in Pl. *Cur.*, where the boundaries between the world of the play and the world of Rome are mangled. For a more detailed account of the *choragus*' and Plautus' Rome, see Sommella (2005).

13 Nelson (1990). Note in particular his comment (138): 'it is a commonplace of criticism that comedy thrives on disguisings, deceptions and mistakings: that is to say, on the provisional nature of our perceptions and interpretations of reality'. Particularly important for disguise in Roman comedy is Muecke (1986), and for the programmatic significance of lies, Petrone (1983: esp. 6).

and character which is so creative and yet so problematic in the modern performing genres. Celebrity actors were by no means unknown, even in the early years of Roman literature, as we can see from the comment about *Epidicus* and the actor Pellio in Pl. *Bac.* 214–15.[14] At the least, ancient theorists were acutely aware of the difference to the mimetic process which is produced by live performance, and were concerned enough about the psychological effects of acting a part to feel the need to hedge it around in various ways.[15] The very word *persona* is witness to the sense of an acted part as an identity, from its primary meaning as 'mask' through a 'dramatic role' to an 'individual personality'.[16] When the actor takes up his *persona* (mask and identity), he is also taking up the challenge of all literature, which is to explore the meaning of the self, or the meanings of selves, and is doing so in a very explicit way, both through the fact of acting and in the content of plays. The search for selves is paradoxically intensified in a medium which makes strong demands on the denial of one self and the acquisition of another.[17]

The ideal Aristotelian tragedy contains some mistake or misapprehension, the undoing of which brings or narrowly averts disaster; in some of the most influential classical tragedies, moreover, the matter is symbolised and intensified by horrific distortions of and misunderstandings about the nature, the very possibility, of seeing things clearly.[18] Sometimes the deep

14 Brown (2002: 232); Barsby (1986: 116); Garton (1972: 170–88) on known republican actors; Marshall (2006: ch. 2, esp. 87–90). The *Bac.* lines are deleted as a later interpolation by Zwierlein (1992: 204–12), following Mattingly (1960: 251): see below, n. 66. Celebrity actors in the later republic are attested by the relationship between Cicero and Roscius. The stigma attaching to acting in the Roman world is not an obstacle to celebrity status. See Csapo and Slater (1995: 275–7).

15 The Virgo in Pl. *Per.* clearly feels that acting the part of a prostitute in some worrying sense turns her into one. McCarthy (2000: 143) comments that the Virgo does not see any gap between appearance and reality (and so is functioning in a very different universe from that of comedy). For Plato's theoretical concerns about the psychological effect of acting, and of its near-relative reciting, see Halliwell (2002: esp. 52–3); Golden (1992: 41–3): 'Plato argues that the imitative process will encourage and accustom the imitator to *become like* that which he imitates' (43, his emphasis).

16 *OLD* s.v. *persona* 1, 2, 4.

17 Gill (1996) characterises the Greek conception of, as he puts it, '(what we call) "personality"' as being 'objectivist-participant' more than the modern 'subjective-individualist'. Possibly the weaker sense of boundaries around the self in Greek thought might contribute to the complexities involved in picking up a role as theatrical performer. Webb (2005: 7–11) discusses the anxieties expressed by late antique commentators on theatrical mimesis and the dangers it poses both to audience and to actor. On the wider history of ambivalence about the theatre from this perspective, see Goody (1997), who situates the anti-theatrical tradition alongside iconoclasm and other forms of anxiety about representation.

18 Sophocles' *Oedipus tyrannus* and Euripides' *Bacchae* are the most intense exemplars. The role of sight in deception will be considered in ch. 3. Fantham (2001) argues that although Plautus and Ennius did not know Aristotle's *Poetics*, Pacuvius (contemporary with Terence) may have done, either directly or through the lectures of Crates of Mallos in 168–167 and other Greek critics in

human question about personal identity is reified into specifics and is made tragic through the playing out of the possibilities for errors and mistakes to which human life is prone. All theatre, then, especially all Roman (and Greek) scripted drama, both in form and in content is concerned with identity, but identity perverted and manipulated. What in tragedy was *hamartia* – at least a part of which is a mistake based on an error about identity[19] – in comedy is renegotiated and replayed, but not fundamentally denied, by comic capers around the unstable identities of its characters (and ourselves). In this analysis, *hamartia* is the dark twin of the comedy of errors and ultimately of the intrigue as programmatic device, where pro-comic characters get away with deceit.[20]

Where tragedy played out the horrors of failures in the proper establishment and acknowledgement of identities, comedy manipulates. The humours of mistaken identity, disguise, intrigues, deceit, play-acting and recognitions all offer different but intimately connected ways of exploring the complexities, the possibilities, the limits, the difficulties of personal identity, and the control of knowledge about it, and so act programmatically for the action of the play itself.[21] Comedy jokes at us for wanting to hold onto ourselves, for thinking that our identity is stable, but also it offers us the opportunity to play through the comic possibilities of the instability

155 BC. Most of his plays have recognition bound up in averting disaster (cf. Euripides' *Iphigenia Taurica*), sometimes with a combination of recognition and intrigue. This plot-type is one highly favoured by Aristotle. In response to an interlocutor who suggested that Pacuvius was just making use of a successful plot-type, rather than being influenced directly by Aristotle, Fantham points out that Ennius did not use this plot-type, as far as we can tell. But if Plautus did? This binding-up of identity, intrigue and recognition seems to be Aristotelian as well as tragic, whether or not Plautus was directly conscious of it.

19 Else (1957: 378–9) argues for *hamartia* as a 'mistake about identity'. See Golden (1992: 80) for the view that *hamartia* is best understood as 'intellectual error'. (This is in keeping with his strongly intellectualist reading of Aristotle.)

20 The personified Agnoia (Misapprehension) in Menander's *Perikeiromene* could be called a direct descendant of tragic *hamartia*. Duckworth (1994: 140) makes clear the 'importance of being mistaken', as he creatively calls it, also linking comic misunderstandings and tricks with Aristotelian *anagnorisis* and *peripeteia*. Linking comic deceit to tragic *hamartia* is a stage further, and not one that Aristotle makes, but it seems a small step worth taking. Janko (1984), a defence of the Aristotelian nature of the *Tractatus Coislinianus*, reads comic errors as closer to 'flaws' than mistakes of knowledge. Else (1957: 379) also comes close to making the links which I am suggesting here: 'Recognition is a change ἐξ ἀγνοίας εἰς γνῶσιν; might not *hamartia* be the ἄγνοια from which the change begins?' Petrone (1983: esp. 101) takes the tragic connection in a different way, deriving comic deception in part from the tricks of tragedy, such as Clytemnestra's deceptive reception of Agamemnon.

21 Purdie (1993) reminds us that any attempt to say 'what comedy is' is liable to enact its own downfall, but that it is useful and perhaps inevitable nonetheless. As she points out, 'even at its simplest, joking is always overdetermined' (13, see also 36); Purdie uses the term 'joking' for all 'occasions of funniness' (12).

which we have a sneaking feeling might be inevitable (and hence, perhaps, not really too threatening).

PROGRAMMATIC PROLOGUE

It is a truth universally acknowledged that the beginning of a work of literature must be in need of an end, and that the edges of literary works are places where their artifice is particularly in evidence.[22] Beginnings and endings in comedy are sites of particular comic intensity, from the prologue's warm-up act posing as exposition, to the closing celebration of drink, sex and social integration, and the final call for applause, which both completes the stage-business and integrates the audience by allowing it to play its crucial judgemental role – and to dissolve itself along with the dramatic illusion. The end must finish what the beginning set out to do: sometimes it does so in ways we expect, sometimes – being comedy – it may overturn our expectations.[23]

At these liminal moments at the edges of the play, when the audience's power is at its greatest and the playwright's control is most vulnerable, the play must do two things: it must kick us into action (firstly listening, lastly applauding) by trumpeting its arrival and departure as pivotal moments in our perception of the world around us (i.e., moments which frame the play-world and the dramatic performance), and at the same time it must create an image that is greater than itself, one that stretches out into a wider fictional illusion, a social and ritual context, and a dramatic and literary tradition. Every beginning is a Big Bang, every end is *Finis*, Time, Apocalypse Now, but even the Big Bang tempts us to ask what went before, how it relates to everything else, whether it is *really* The Beginning, while The End always implies its own afterglow. Not wishing to overplay comic inversion, I begin with Beginnings (chapter 2) and end with Endings (chapter 5).

[22] Rabinowitz (1998: 58) opens his discussion of 'privileged positions' in the process of reading in a similar manner.

[23] For theoretical and critical discussion of beginnings, see Nuttall (1992) on narrative literature, and Said (1975) on both literature and wider culture. On beginnings and endings in Roman comedy, the most explicitly literary reading is that of Slater (1992a). The brief but rich discussion of beginnings and endings in Slater (2000: 122–7) touches on several of the same points that underpin the Plautine parts of my chs. 2 and 5. See also Duckworth (1994: 61–5) on Terence and Lanuvinus, (211–18) on Plautine prologues and exposition; Leo (1912); Abel (1955); Raffaelli (1984b); Anderson (1993: 137); Gowers (2004). The literature on literary ending is wide, among which Kermode (1967) is crucial. For comedy, important also are Frye's comments (1957: 163–71) on the generic significance of reintegration and re-establishment of the social order at the endings of comedies. Charney's comment (1987: 92) is worth repeating: '[i]n fact, the ending is likely to be the most artificial element in the entire action . . .'

No-one will be surprised to hear that Roman comedies involve plays-within-plays and deceitful plots hatched usually by clever slaves in order to achieve their goals.[24] Plautus, like Baldrick in the Blackadder series, has a Cunning Plan. In many Plautine plays, there is an intrigue which directs and constitutes the action: get money from the old man, pass off a prostitute as a matron, divert a letter which releases a girl from the pimp, persuade someone that his house is haunted, or that his eyes or ears deceive him, to give only a few examples.[25] Contrary to what is sometimes thought by the majority of Classicists who are not avid readers of Roman comedy, Terence also, albeit differently, plays with intrigue as an image for the process of playwriting.[26] Chapter 3 considers the games of plotting in both authors. That the deceits which constitute the plays come right in the end is an affirmation not only of the comic spirit but also more widely of the aesthetics of literary fiction.

Chapter 4 brings together a range of types and devices of repetition, seeking to present them as having something in common with each other in the generic self-positioning of comedy. This chapter attempts to capture a range of repeating devices used by Plautus and Terence, verbal, structural, thematic, metaphorical and intertextual. It seeks, moreover, to offer a holistic interpretation of them, by suggesting that they all partake in different ways in the same underlying phenomenon – the comedy of repetition. The holistic argument proceeds by accumulation, but is not essential to the reading of the chapter's parts.

And to finish: chapter 5. Here I return to the idea that edges are generically both intense and vulnerable. Its manner of ending, in particular, is integral to a play's identity as comedy: as Aristotle says (*Poetics* 1453a), it would be a travesty of tragedy for Orestes and Aegisthus to walk off arm in arm, and no-one to kill anyone at all. That would be for comedy. It is indeed what happens at the end of Plautus' *Rudens*, where the celebratory reconciliation and reintegration of society is so complete that even the

[24] See Benz, Stärk and Vogt-Spira (1995); Slater (2000); Moore (1998a); Muecke (1986); Petrone (1983); Blänsdorf (1982).

[25] Despite Bettini's (1982) argument for an underlying structure in Plautine (though not Menandrian or Terentian) plots in the manner of the anthropologists' 'six basic structures', comic plots show both huge variety and playful predictability.

[26] A commonly expressed classical non-specialist view of the Roman comic playwrights is that their plays are very similar, but that Terence is wet compared with Plautus. These two views would, of course, show some inconsistency. Wright (1974) makes a strong case for Terence's style as being very different from that of Plautus and all the other writers of *palliatae*. Even Wright's Terence can make explicit allusion to the standard style of the *palliata*, for all that he may not be chained to it.

pimp is invited in to dinner.[27] The prologue, spoken by the star Arcturus, threw that play into confusion at the beginning, nearly turning comic mess into tragic disorder with his tragic/epic shipwreck, but the play sorts itself out into civic order,[28] and moreover into dreams-come-true comic fantasy. Despite Arcturus' posturing about comeuppance for sinners, the deserving and the undeserving all get to celebrate in the end. The pimp goes in to dinner with the man whose daughter he was trying to sell into prostitution. To stop and think about how comfortable Daemones might be back in Athens, whether the pimp will continue his trade in women's bodies, whether the slave Gripus, who thought the chest was his salvation (not someone else's), will ever own anything, is to fall into the realist trap – the comic response is just a party, just the here-and-now. Or so it would have us believe. One of the clever tricks comedy pulls on us is to make us believe in the party – not literally, but emotionally and metatheatrically. Comedy also offers us the seeds of endlessness, however, and here too we see the artifice of the playwright.

WORDS AND MORE WORDS

> There may be something artificial in making a special category for the comic in words, since most of the varieties of the comic that we have examined so far were produced through the medium of language. (Bergson 1913: 103)

> The enormous sea of words represents possibilities of expression that can never be used. Words are gestural and have a life of their own available for comic exploitation. Once words and actions are separated from communicable meaning, they are freed of their utilitarian taint. (Charney 1987: 7)

Artificiality, however, is of the essence of comic art. Not all comedy is verbal, and indeed it is a *topos* of critical responses to Roman comedy to insist that the original performance would have been a lot more spectacular, more impressive, more visually funny, than the dry text left to us.[29] The

[27] Slater (1992a) feels some anxiety about the way in which the *Poen.* pimp is not so invited, such is the powerful expectation of comic integration. Perhaps it is *Rud.* which is remarkable in this regard, not *Poen.*: cf. *Cur.*, where the pimp is treated equally badly and excluded, by implication, from the dinner-invitation to the soldier-rival, now prospective brother-in-law. On the other hand, in *Per.* the pimp is also invited in.

[28] Konstan (1983: 73–95).

[29] Beacham (1991) is a sustained effort to offer more than a textual reading of Roman comedy. Beare (1964: 178), in a useful discussion of stage conventions, comments: '[t]he fact that an actor mentions some object is present may sometimes be evidence that that object was actually shown on the stage; at other times we know that the object was not and could not be shown to the eye, and therefore

words are the subject of this study, however, and are the primary vehicle through which the reader posits the performance.[30] Slater's discussion of Plautus' *Pseudolus*[31] is concerned with the power of Pseudolus' speech, and his ability to make things happen and run the plot by means of his clever words; my interest here is in vocabulary, in the clever words of Plautus (and Terence) by which *they* make things happen and run the plot. It will be argued in this book, particularly in chapter 3, that trickery is not only a crucial element in the workings of a play, but also programmatic for the nature of comedy. The rich specific vocabulary which Roman comedy employs for intrigue[32] consists of words for a trick, a trickster and a big mess.

As well as the great host of uses of *dolus* ('trick') and its variants, there are words stressing the artful cleverness of tricksters (variants on *astutus* and *doctus*, *callidus*, *versutus*/*vorsutus*, also *sycophantia* and cognates); the fictionality and makerliness of the trickster's skill (*fabr-* words, *machin-* words); its moral badness (*malum*, *facinus*) and dishonesty (*mendacium*, *fallacia*); playfulness (*lud-* words, which are of particular significance since performance is at *ludi*)[33] and artistry (*ars* and its variants). None of this is surprising per se, although the employment of this register of words can work interestingly in some contexts. For example, Tyndarus in *Captiui* (who both is and is not a slave) uses and has used of him the language of comic-slave trickery to describe his exchange of identity with Philocrates. When he rightly fears that his cover is about to be blown by the arrival of Philocrates' obtuse friend Aristophontes, Tyndarus sounds like any other comic slave:

had to be suggested to the imagination by words and gestures'. Fortier (2002: 12) puts starkly the point that the text is only part of the story: 'to discuss drama is to discuss a part of theatre'. See also Slater (2000: 3); Goldberg (2004: 385).

30 My interest in the words of comedy, although driven primarily by the desire to elucidate the text for a reader, finds some resonance in the case put forward by Purdie (1993) for reading all 'joking' (in her inclusive sense), whether verbal, visual or otherwise, as 'discourse', as a manifestation and instantiation of communication. Meisel (2007) also stresses the role of words, even though much of his interest is in modern dramatic forms of much more variable media than ancient theatre. See his comments at 44–5, including that 'a competent reader of plays will experience a *sensation* of visuality' (his emphasis). At the extreme verbal end of the reading of funniness is Chiaro (1992) on the language of jokes in popular media.

31 Slater (2000: ch. 7). The present section title is intended as an honorific allusion to that chapter title, 'Words Words Words'.

32 Brotherton (1978); Petrone (1983: esp. 94–8); Anderson (1993: 109–18, 131). Related is the important study of comic imagery by Fantham (1972).

33 For the connection between the action of the trickster in the play and that of the celebrants of the *ludi*, see Chiarini (1983: 215), who connects the phrase *ludos facere aliquem*, i.e. trick someone, with the festival *ludi*. Petrone (1983: 202–9) also connects *ludi scaenici* with games of deception.

> neque iam Salus seruare, si uolt, me potest, nec copia est,
> nisi si aliquam corde machinor astutiam.
> quam, malum? quid machiner? quid comminiscar? maxumas
> nugas, ineptiam incipisse. (*Capt.* 529–32)

And now Salvation can't save me, even if she wants to, and there is no help for it, unless I can manufacture some bit of cleverness in my heart. What cleverness, damn it? What should I plot? What can I invent? It's a pile of nonsense, of folly, that I've started.

By using this vocabulary, he is claiming comic status for the intrigue, a status which it never quite achieves, because of the nature of the trick, of the tricksters, and of their relationship with the 'dupe'. It is *trying* to be a comic trick rather than actually being one, and Tyndarus' words for it tell us so.[34] Similar is the use of *facinus* ('crime') to describe (*Bac.* 925) the capture of Troy, in Chrysalus' Troy metaphor for his triumph over the anti-comic forces. The capture of Troy is not normally a *facinus*, especially not from the point of view of the victors – but it becomes so when it is playing the role of a comic trick.[35]

In addition to these colourful but semantically predictable words, there are certain terms – ordinary words – which take on a peculiar significance for the genre, making them programmatic signifiers with a force beyond their ordinary semantic effects. Three comic words which signify comedy with particular intensity are *consilium*, *turbare* and *architectus*.

The ordinary basic meanings of *consilium* focus around notions of 'advice', 'deliberation', 'the act of taking a decision' etc., and hence a 'deliberate action', the 'exercise of judgement', and so both 'strategy' and 'intelligence'.[36] Cognate with *consul*, the word is much in demand in the arena of politics and the law. Plautus, typically, transfers the word from its highly respectable linguistic register into that of comedy, and gives *consilium* a programmatic force, signifying the cunning plan which is also the plot of the play.[37] The word occurs frequently in comedy, the highest count going to Plautus' *Miles gloriosus* at twenty-one instances, with Terence's

[34] See also 35, 47, 221–2, 250, 520–1, 539, 679: this list is not exhaustive. On Tyndarus' slave-like language here see Petrone (1983: 58–60).

[35] The notion of 'heroic badness' is important for the understanding of Roman comedy. See Anderson (1993: ch. 4), although I am not entirely convinced by his interpretation, which is in the tradition of Dover's (1972) reading of Aristophanes as arising from the pleasure of being naughty boys. See esp. Anderson (1993: 92) for the use of 'badness' language to express comic greatness. For the general concept of the slave's badness as a cause for celebration, see also Segal (1987: esp. 126–36).

[36] These words are all quoted from *OLD* definitions.

[37] It is the term that Donatus uses to refer to Davus' plot at Ter. *An.* 226 (Wessner 1962–3 1: 98).

Andria a close second at twenty instances.[38] Not every usage is remarkable, but both the frequency of the word and the significance it has in certain instances are telling. Often it comes to mean quite literally 'plot', and even when that is not its meaning it nonetheless retains a hint at self-reference (i.e. to the plot of the play).

In a passage in Plautus' *Bacchides* with strong programmatic significance,[39] the slave Chrysalus tells us how he despises weaker (Greek) comic slaves who defraud their masters of tuppence:

> non mihi isti placent Parmenones, Syri,
> qui duas aut tris minas auferunt eris.
> nequiu' nil est quam egens consili seruos, nisi habet
> multipotens pectus
> ubi quomque usus siet, pectore expromat suo.
> (*Bac.* 649–53)

I don't think much of those Parmenos and Syruses who carry off two or three *minae* from their masters. There is nothing worse than a slave in need of a plot – unless he has a powerful heart from which to find one when it's needed.

While it is true that *consilium* could just mean 'plan', its appearance here in one of the relatively few Plautine passages (outside prologues) which make near-explicit reference to Greek plays[40] must suggest a heightened programmatic force for the word in Plautus. There is a nice additional irony here: for once the audience is in a position to laugh at the scheming slave, because Chrysalus at this point does not know that Mnesilochus has gone and ruined his lovely plot!

Chrysalus uses the word again in his magnificent speech comparing the play with the story of Troy, at a crucial moment for Chrysalus as the controller, the mover and shaker, of this play:[41]

> ego sum Vlixes, quoiius consilio haec gerunt.
> (*Bac.* 940)

I am Ulysses, on whose devising all these things are accomplished.

[38] 108 occurrences in Plautus and 62 in Terence, therefore in fact relatively more common in Terence, despite the fact that Terence is conventionally seen as less interested in complex plotting. Even if one does not accept the meaning of *consilium* as 'plot', rather than 'plan' or 'advice', the high frequency of planning and advising in Terence is marked as an indicator of his 'Plautine' plot-orientation.

[39] See further ch. 4, nn. 88 and 89.

[40] References to the status of the speaker's own play as a play are common in Plautus, but direct external references to other plays are not, except in prologues.

[41] Jocelyn (1969b) and Skafte Jensen (1997).

He has also used it earlier, during his extraordinary piece of personalised plotting for his master Nicobulus, when Chrysalus discovered that *opus est chryso Chrysalo* (*Bac.* 240).[42] Thinking on his feet, he makes up a magnificent tall story to pull the wool over his master's eyes, and so avoid giving him the money which Chrysalus and the young master have been sent to collect. The tale goes round the houses, with first a refusal from the debtor, then a court case, then a pursuit by pirates (or rather, the aggrieved debtor and his friends). During this story, Nicobulus has been neatly trapped – by the power of plotting and storytelling. A perfect audience, he enters into the spirit of the story and even offers his own admiring interpretations of the principals' motives.[43] Chrysalus then relates the (fictional) trick which he played on the pursuers:

capimus consilium continuo; postridie
auferimus aurum omne <illim> illis praesentibus,
palam atque aperte, ut illi id factum sciscerent.
(*Bac.* 300–2)

We seize on a plan straightaway. The next day we carry off all the gold from under their noses, openly and overtly, so that they know that it has been done.

The master is totally caught, and echoes Chrysalus' last word as he responds *scite hercle* – 'that's clever' ('knowing') – and breathlessly asks: 'What happened next?' He does not realise that this is exactly how an audience of a fictional plot should react.

The trickster of *Miles gloriosus* and his team use the word *consilium* at almost every available opportunity. When Palaestrio is thinking up the plot of his first play-within-the-play, the one where he pretends that the girl has a twin sister,[44] he says something which could be paraphrased as 'Hush a minute, while I think up the plot':

paullisper tace,
dum ego mihi consilia in animum conuoco et dum consulo
quid agam, quem dolum doloso contra conseruo parem,
qui illam hic uidit osculantem, id uisum ut ne uisum siet.
(*Mil.* 196–9)[45]

[42] 'Chrysalus needs money', or, 'Golden Boy needs gold', as Barsby (1986: 43) translates the pun.

[43] See Nicobulus' comments at 293–4, 295, 297. Chrysalus comments on what he is doing in manipulating his audience at 286.

[44] Lefèvre (1984: 32–7) argues that this first plot is a Plautine invention.

[45] Palaestrio says something similar at *Mil.* 232–4: *tace, / dum in regionem astutiarum mearum te induco, ut scias / iuxta mecum mea consilia.* Clearly this playwright cannot work with noise around him, as Hofmann (1995: 217) says apropos 196.

Be quiet a minute, while I hold a mental convocation of plans and plot out what I should do, what trick I can prepare against my tricky colleague, who saw her here kissing him, so that he won't have seen what he saw.

There is an additional joke in the gap between the programmatic comic meaning of *consilium* on the one hand, and the import of the word in ordinary discourse and its good pedigree in legal and political language on the other.[46] A few lines later, when either Palaestrio is urging himself, or Periplectomenus is urging him, to get the play in motion,[47] the speaker tells the addressee (self or other): *reperi, comminiscere, cedo calidum consilium cito* ('invent, fabricate, serve up a nice hot plot quickly', *Mil.* 226). What is needed here is a 'piping hot plot'.[48] The plan to deceive the soldier by pretending that the (fictional) wife of Periplectomenus is in love with him is also a *consilium*, most intensely so in the plotting scene at 596:[49]

> PA. Cohibete intra limen etiam uos parumper, Pleusicles,
> sinite me priu' perspectare, ne uspiam insidiae sient
> concilium[50] quod habere uolumus. nam opus est nunc tuto loco
> unde inimicus ne quis nostri spolia capiat consili.
> nam bene consultum inconsultumst, si id inimicis usuist,
> neque potest quin, si id inimicis usuist, opsit tibi;
> nam bene <consultum> consilium surrupitur saepissume,
> si minu' cum cura aut cautela locu' loquendi lectus est.
> quippe qui, si resciuere inimici consilium tuom,
> tuopte tibi consilio occludunt linguam et constringunt manus
> atque eadem quae illis uoluisti facere, illi faciunt tibi.
> sed speculabor nequis aut hinc aut ab laeua aut a dextera
> nostro consilio uenator adsit cum auritis plagis.
>
> (*Mil.* 596–608)[51]

PA. You all stay inside a moment, Pleusicles, and let me first reconnoitre, to make sure that no one is laying a trap for the council that we want to hold. For we now need a safe place where no enemy can make a raid on our plans. For counsel is de-counselled, if an enemy gets use of it, and, if your enemy gets use of it, it can't

46 Likewise, in *Mos.* 687–9, Tranio draws aside in order to summon a senate in his heart – and think up the plot, as does another controlling slave, Epidicus, in *Epid.* 159, on which see Leigh (2004b: 49).

47 Some editions, including Lindsay, give the lines to Periplectomenus, but see e.g. Fantham (1972) for the attribution to Palaestrio. Whoever is the speaker, the lines also pick up the military and political vocabulary of 219–20: *uiden hostis tibi adesse tuoque tergo opsidium? consule, / arripe opem auxiliumque ad hanc rem.*

48 The metaphor from hot food is nicely brought out by Fantham (1972: 12).

49 See Fraenkel (1960: 226).

50 Punning here with *consilium.*

51 Scholars have suspected possible interpolations in this speech, as is an occupational hazard of Plautine verbal fireworks. See Zwierlein (1991a: 78–82). If some of the accumulation (e.g. 602) is the work of an imitator rather than of 'the man himself', that simply strengthens my interpretation of the programmatic force of the words.

not be an obstacle to you; for a well-planned plan is very often stolen, if the place for plotting is chosen with insufficient care and caution. Indeed, if your enemies have got to know about your plot, they fasten shut your tongue with your own plot and tie up your hands and they do to you what you wanted to do to them. But I'll spy out to make sure there is no hunter here, or on the left or the right, who can trap our plot with long-eared nets.

On seeing that the coast is indeed clear (with a wink at the audience), Palaestrio calls out his troops and makes sure that they are ready to carry through the *consilium* (612) that they have planned.

Terence takes up the programmatic force of *consilium* with gusto. A couple of choice examples here serve to anticipate my discussion in chapter 3 of the force and significance of Terence's games with plotting especially in *Andria*. The two main plotters of that play, Simo *senex* and Davos *seruus*, toss the word around between them, for example at 49, 159, (at 336 a contribution from Pamphilus), 589 (where Davos has to admit that the old man's plot is *callidum*),[52] 733. Likewise in *Heauton timorumenos*, in a metatheatrically suggestive passage (470–5) where the *senex* Chremes is proposing to his neighbour Menedemus that he should allow himself to become the 'victim' of a typical comic deceit plot, he offers his own slave Syrus as the main proponent of *consilia* for the young men who want to extort money from Menedemus (who wants to give, but secretly). In *Eunuchus*, the plan to smuggle Chaerea into the house of Thais in the disguise of a eunuch (a plan which is the central crux of the play) is hailed as the best plot ever by its enthusiastic actor (Chaerea himself): *dixti pulchre: numquam uidi meliu' consilium dari. / age eamus intro nunciam: orna me abduc duc quantum potest* ('you have spoken well: I've never seen a better plan produced. Come on, let's go in now: costume me and lead me off and on as quickly as possible', *Eu.* 376–7). The eponymous controlling, plotting parasite in *Phormio* knows exactly what to do to make the play turn out right: *iam instructa sunt mi in corde consilia omnia* ('now all my plans are drawn up in my heart', *Ph.* 321).[53]

The plan which is the plot of the play often involves a mess. Messiness is a defining feature of comedy, playing to its self-deprecating self-presentation as a 'low' genre.[54] Among the words used to signify comic mess are the

52 Could Davos' *callidum* ('clever') plot be a 'learned' correction of Palaestrio's *calidum* ('hot') plot from *Mil.* 226?

53 The line is quoted by Cicero (*N.D.* 3.73) in a passage replete with comic tricks and plots, just before he moves 'from the theatre to the forum' (3.74).

54 Gowers (1993: ch. 2) gives an astute and entertaining account of the role of food in Plautus' self-representation in this way. On the role specifically of cooks in the metatheatrical machinations of Plautus, see 87–93; on *turbare*, see 90–1.

variations on *turbare*, it being the job of comedy to throw everything into confusion, as Puck knew well. When applied to the plot, it is celebrated by the controlling characters. *quas ego hic turbas dabo!* says Chrysalus ('what turmoil I'll make here', *Bac.* 357), while Pseudolus makes a similar point when warning his master and the audience of his impending plot: *scis tu quidem hercle, mea si commoui sacra, / quo pacto et quantas soleam turbellas dare* ('but you know perfectly well, once I get started, what great storms I usually whip up, and how I do it', *Ps.* 109–10). Palaestrio also celebrates his comic power: *Quantas res turbo, quantas moueo machinas!* ('What great disturbances I make, what magnificent machinations!', *Mil.* 813). Epidicus, hearing in his programmatic opening scene with Thesprio that the rules of the game have changed under his feet and that he needs a new plot, exclaims *eu edepol res turbulentas!* ('By Hercules what a mess!', *Epid.* 72: the young man has come home but does not want to meet his father because he has bought a woman through financial irregularity – the stuff of comedy). And there are many more.[55] Variations on *turbare* can also apply to comic excess of other sorts, as when the parasite Ergasilus in *Captiui* makes his magnificent gastronomic goulash, having been given the freedom of the kitchen.[56] Although messiness is by no means confined to *turbare* and its cognates, we can see the programmatic significance of those words when they are repeatedly used of the 'mess' which Chaerea makes in Terence's *Eunuchus*, by entering Thais' house in disguise and raping a supposed slave girl he has just seen (and whom he will eventually marry).[57] Terence here satirises the comic convention of rape of a citizen girl leading to marriage, and the use of a typically comic term, which would otherwise be rather inappropriate and inadequate, to designate Chaerea's action helps make it clear that this rape-story is (ironically) just like any other comedy, made farcical by its excess.

An *architectus*, finally, is someone who makes and carries out the design, primarily of buildings. This technical term from the construction industry is an obvious candidate for metaphoric extension into the fields of experts in other arts, especially given the punning coincidence of sound in the first syllable with the word *ars*.[58] Surprisingly, perhaps, it is in fact

[55] For the programmatic celebration see for example Pl. *As.* 824, *Bac.* 988, 1057, *Cas.* 880, *Men.* 486, *Mil.* 334; or said in complaint about comic mess, Pl. *Am.* 1044, *Aul.* 405, 656, *Bac.* 1076, *Mos.* 1032, Ter. *Eu.* 649, 723, 868, 947. In Pl. *Rud.* 78, *deturbauit* describes the action of the storm and shipwreck that nearly brought tragic disorder rather than comic mess to that play.

[56] Similar is Syrus' reaction to the prospect of Bacchis and her entourage eating them out of house and home, Ter. *HT* 254.

[57] See esp. 649, 653, 723, 868.

[58] Cf. Cic. *Brut.* 118 regarding Stoics: *architecti paene uerborum.*

rare outside technical discourse.[59] Plautus' own lively development of the figurative potential of the word comes in *Miles gloriosus*,[60] in which it is used six times, all referring to Palaestrio and all contributing in one way or another to the building metaphor which signifies Palaestrio's production of his second play-within-the-play, in which a prostitute pretends to be in love with the eponymous soldier to trick him into sending the young master's girl away. The other strongly metaphorical use of the word by Plautus comes in *Poenulus*, when the slave Milphio admires what he believes to be the clever comic acting and plotting of Hanno. Like Pseudolus, he jokingly fears that his actor will prove a better comedian than himself:

> eu hercle mortalem catum,
> malum crudumque et callidum | et subdolum!
> ut adflet, quo illud gestu faciat facilius!
> me quoque dolis iam superat architectonem.
> (*Poen.* 1107–10)

My goodness what a clever man, bad, vigorous, shrewd and deceitful! How he weeps, in order to accomplish this task more easily! He even surpasses me, the architect, with his tricks.

I am going to take a hint from Palaestrio and use the term *architectus* to designate the controlling character, often a slave, who writes the plot with, for or against the playwright.[61]

All together, then, we have a self-referential plot, a clever plotter and a comic mess. Those are some of the essential ingredients of Roman comedy.[62]

[59] Of the 145 instances recorded by a full search of the Packard Humanities Institute (*PHI*) disc, 65 are from Vitruvius, and the vast majority of the remainder are also used in the technical sense. The second highest count goes to Cicero, at nineteen, the third to the Elder Pliny at thirteen (all technical) and the fourth to Plautus at ten. Cicero, interestingly, is the only author other than Plautus to make frequent (not very frequent) metaphorical use of the word. Cicero speaks of *omnium architectum et machinatorem unum . . . Chrysogonum* (*S. Rosc.* 132), in which he links the word with another good term for comic plotting, *machin-*.

[60] This play also shows the highest count for *consilium*.

[61] Ketterer (1986) uses the term in a similar way. There is a nice irony in the boast of the prologue speaker of *Truc.*, that Plautus proposes to build Athens in Rome *sine architectis* (3). I have been tempted to use the word *artifex* for the slave-playwright, since it would seem to fit so neatly with the penumbra of artful artificiality which I aim to express in this book, but in fact the word is not suitable. It is only used three times in Plautus, and once in Terence (*Ph.* 259, of Phaedria as a good actor), and refers to actors, not plotters. The Plautine occurrences are *Am.* 70, *Poen.* 37, *Cas.* 356.

[62] Henderson (1999: ch. 1), ostensibly a reading of *Poen.*, is a paradigm of messy play.

PLAUTINE PROBLEMS *OR* TROUBLE WITH TEXTS

This book offers what is primarily a literary reading of the plays of Plautus and Terence, its implied reader being a reader of texts who is a member of an audience only by projection and imagination.[63] The question is, of what texts? As Slater says, apropos Plautus, 'the texts themselves sometimes seem to be quicksand beneath our feet'.[64] Plautus, whoever he was, wrote something down; a troupe of actors at the initial performance said something which probably bore a close but not exact resemblance to what Plautus wrote; then the plays were tossed around between different sets of actors and written versions for over a century before late republican scholars undertook the editorial work which beat them into shape and gave them a chance similar to that of any other ancient text.[65] Maurach reminds us of the uncertainty which potentially underlies much of the Plautine corpus.[66] The armoury of scholarship in the last 150 years has been marshalled in various attempts to restore the original (that is, 'what Plautus wrote'), in which enormous progress has been made, either by the ousting of interlopers or by their naturalisation, and in the construction of a readable text. While acknowledging the importance of this work (at least in its more moderate forms), I must put down a marker with Slater, who says: 'it is useful, and indeed necessary to make the following assumption,

[63] Meisel (2007: 6), 'a script that becomes performance in the reading'.

[64] Slater (2000: 3). Of the many modern critics who have tried to express the problem and the non-problemacity of it, my prize goes to Gratwick (1993a: 3–4), in which 'Plautus' is implicitly elevated to the ontological status of 'Homer'.

[65] Tarrant (1983: 302–3); Goldberg (2004); Goldberg (2005b: ch. 2, esp. 60–4, 67–8, 83–6). For the role of actors' troupes in the early ownership of playscripts see Blänsdorf (1978). The twenty-five plays identified by L. Aelius Stilo, and the twenty-one designated as Plautine by his pupil Varro (almost certainly the same selection as we have today), were probably not the only genuine plays surviving into the classical period. Despite the early hiccups suffered by the text of Plautus, it is worth noting Tarrant's comments that the story of creative abuse by theatre companies ahead of the work of the philologists is a 'hypothesis' (1983: 302), and that the archetype of the extant manuscripts was itself a copy of an edition of high scholarly quality, including the signalled preservation of elements judged to be spurious, dating probably from no later than the second century AD (306). The text of Plautus that we read, therefore, is perhaps not quite the work of fiction that is sometimes implied. For a recent example of the 'fluid' school of early Plautine textual history, see Deufert (2002) and cf. next note.

[66] Maurach (2005: 62–7). Zwierlein's arguments for wholesale interpolation represent an extreme form of a common thread particularly in earlier Plautine scholarship, which is happy to excise lines on occasionally rather flimsy evidence or subjective reasoning. (Mattingly (1960) is a good example of a structured argument which assigns many lines, particularly from prologues, to the status of later interpolation, as part of his argument for a major Plautine revival which he dates to around 150 BC.) What is unusual about Zwierlein's hypothesis, followed also by Deufert, is the proposal that many such interpolations are the work of a single editor (who must have been a genius) as opposed to the 'many theatrical hands and voices' interpretation which had been more common previously.

even though it is patently untrue: we will consider Lindsay's Oxford text of a play to be the playscript'.[67] I hope it will not be considered too slippery if I suggest that my theoretical justification is in fact even greater than Slater's, since my primary interest is in a reader of a text, whether ancient or modern. Since it is likely that the most serious damage to what Plautus wrote occurred in the first few generations after the initial performance, what is read by a modern reader and by the majority of ancient readers is not wildly different.[68]

The other major Plautine Problem, which is also a Trouble with Terence and with which in both cases this book is not greatly concerned, is the nature of the relationship between the Roman plays and the Greek originals, neatly called the 'Homeric Question of Latin studies' by one scholar.[69] Or rather, this book is not much interested in hypothetical reconstruction, although I am conscious that where the evidence is available, the intertextual relationship between Terence, Plautus, Diphilus, Philemon and Menander (and Ennius, Naevius, Euripides, Aristophanes and others) is of enormous interest and potential fertility for a reader of the Roman comic texts. Only rarely is it possible to read that relationship without reconstruction,[70] such that one might be tempted to ignore the siren-songs of the 'Greek originals', but in this case we do not need to go so far as to say, to paraphrase Slater misleadingly, that 'even though it is patently untrue, we will consider the plays of Plautus and Terence to be their own inventions and not attributable to Greek originals'. I am subjectively sympathetic to the arguments of those who consider that this would be by no means patently untrue, but my interest is rather in the plays as they stand,[71] and the

[67] Slater (2000: 4).

[68] See Duckworth (1994: 52) for lists of the extant and lost plays of Plautus; Beare (1964: 49) for a suitably agnostic list of dates and Greek originals for the plays of Plautus. Gel. 3.3 offers the ancient testimonial to there being 130 plays attributed to Plautus in antiquity, although even in Gellius' day many were believed not to be authentic.

[69] Halporn (1993), who gives a brief but useful account of the literary history of the question: see esp. 191–3. Segal's comment in the introduction to his Oxford readings collection (2001b: xx) is nicely put: 'that he knew Greek well is unquestioned. That he translated faithfully is out of the question.' Throughout this book, I refer to the magisterial work of Fraenkel in its Italian translation of 1960. An English translation is now available (2007).

[70] Danese (2002: 134–6) offers a useful reminder of the paucity of hard facts, and the dangerous circularity in reconstructive arguments. The one famous passage of Pl. *Bac.* perhaps gives us a false sense of security about our knowledge: see Handley (1968). Barsby (2002) conveniently lists fragments of Greek comedies which either are or may be originals (perhaps it would be better to call them 'parallel passages') of lines of Terence.

[71] Among the strong claims for complete Plautine independence are Stärk (1989) on *Men.*, Goldberg (1978) on *Epid.* and Vogt-Spira (1991) on *As.*; Lefèvre, Stärk and Vogt-Spira (1991) *passim*. On the other side, which remains the dominant position, see Fantham (1981) and Lowe (2001). If in

relationship between the Latin plays and their Greek 'strong intertexts' is a crucial, though elusive, part of the plays.[72]

There has been in recent years an abundant critical outpouring, loosely centred around Eckard Lefèvre, which has stressed Plautine creativity and originality in part through the contribution of non-Greek elements in Roman comedy, including the rich native tradition of improvised theatre.[73] I have learnt much from criticism of this nature and from the related performance criticism which is particularly prevalent in America. It is perhaps attacking a straw man to say that I aim to avoid the tendency of this school to disparage literary criticism and to celebrate primitivism,[74] and I would certainly not want to set up an opposition between performance criticism and literary criticism, but nonetheless it is a major part of my aim in this book to (re)introduce the concept of the literary artist in these works and so to re-evaluate, for modern 'readers' rather than 'audiences', the study of texts on which sophisticated work in performance criticism has provided a basis for progress in literary analysis.

The problem of originality is even greater for Terence than for his rumbustious predecessor.[75] Terence has suffered in recent years, when many readers have stopped being so impressed with his lucid Latin, discovered

the last twenty to thirty years more books and articles have been published arguing for Plautine independence than the converse, that is perhaps because those who read Plautus as primarily an adapter of Greek models with 'Plautine elements' added on (the legacy of Fraenkel, the original drive of which was celebration of Plautine creativity in contrast to the standard nineteenth and early twentieth-century view which saw in Plautine texts only an opportunity to reconstruct Greek originals) have largely taken as read the existence and the hypothetical and partial reconstructability of the model. A good recent example of this kind of reading would be Lowe (2007). Gratwick (1993a: 16–30), in the introduction to his edition of *Men.*, is paradigmatic of this modern tradition, which uses Plautine relationship with and changes to Greek models, but is not enslaved to them. Also arguing for Plautine fidelity to Greek models, although by different means, is the work of Zwierlein (1990, 1991a, 1991b, 1992).

72 Danese's analysis (2002) of the state of play in the study of Plautus and his 'models' is particularly valuable, rightly stressing that we should think of the source for these 'models' much more widely than simply in the New Comedy of Greece. He comes close to treating models as intertexts, which is precisely the critical move that I think needs to be made. Several of the contributions to that volume, Questa and Raffaelli (2002), have useful reflections on the issue and its history, as does Maurach (2005).

73 See esp. Lefèvre, Stärk and Vogt-Spira (1991); Benz, Stärk and Vogt-Spira (1995); and Stärk and Vogt-Spira (2000). A somewhat different tradition, but of crucial importance to the Lefèvre school's emphasis on the earliest Roman drama, is the work of Wiseman (1998). At the other extreme on the question of Plautus' relationship with Greek New Comedy is the work of Zwierlein, who considers that by paring down the text which has been inflated by interpolations we can return to an original text which was much closer to the spirit of the Greek model. I am in agreement with Gratwick's review of the first volume (Gratwick 1993b) about the merits of this approach.

74 Vogt-Spira (1995: 71–2) comes close to doing so.

75 Although the standard view of Terence is that he remained closer to his models, other than in the matter of prologues and expository scenes, arguments for substantial changes in his plays have been made for example by Lefèvre (1978b) on *Ph.* and (1999a) on *Hec.*

that Plautus might be fun, and decided that Terence was a pale imitation of Menander, and an even paler one of Plautus.[76] Conventional wisdom, taking its cue in part from what is perhaps an overinterpretation of the case made by Wright for the 'stylistic unity' of the *palliata* tradition and Terentian difference from it, underplays the intertextual relationship between the two great extant exponents of Roman comedy. I aim to expose Terence as a subtle and playful playwright, self-consciously aware of his place in an established literary tradition. He is, I suggest, more artful, more artificial, more farcical than is generally assumed, as well as being (even) more literary. We will be looking at him through Plautus, and seeing how he approached the challenge which Ovid and Euripides faced also, that of writing in a well-established tradition.

[76] See, differently, Goldberg (1986: ch. 6); Beacham (1991: 47); Wright (1974: 127). Particularly important in this regard is the contribution of Henderson (2004), which stakes out the ground for taking the reading of Terence away from the 'wondrous simplicities of Terentian Latin as (if it were) cosiness designed for switched-off minds' (54) and towards something both more disturbing and funnier.

CHAPTER 2

Beginnings

How does anything ever manage to begin? There is an enormous burden of proof placed on the opening of any cultural act, be it literary work, religious ritual, public performance, educational session or indeed work of literary criticism. This is in part simply because the initial impression is crucial to the reception of the act and because mistakes at this point are among the hardest to repair, but, beyond that technical difficulty of creating a good impression apparently out of nowhere, the opening must bear an additional burden, which is a performative one. The beginning has to act as if it is doing something, causing something to happen, changing the world – when everyone knows that no beginning is ever really The Beginning. As Said says (1975: 50), 'a beginning might well be a necessary fiction'.

Yet for all this difficulty, it hardly needs saying that there is something very special about beginnings of all varieties, literary and social, and Roman culture is no exception to the pattern of strongly marking the opening, embodied especially in the cult of the god Janus. Our sense that every beginning is also an ending is symbolised by the very nature of the two-headed god, looking backwards even as he presides over novelty. Ovid, in the *Fasti*, has a discussion with Janus (*Fasti* 1.63–288) about the nature of the god and his jurisdiction over beginnings, in which the importance of beginning, and of starting as you mean to go on, is sanctified as essential not only to the poem thus initiated, but also to the Roman world and its relationship with the cosmos.[1] Although my primary concern in this analysis is literary, it is important to stress that the experiential effects

[1] See Hardie (1991) on this episode, including its programmatic force for the *Fasti* as well as the socio-religious importance of Janus and the art of beginning. It should be noted that Ovid's world is different from Plautus' and Terence's: the neat inauguration of the political year on the Kalends of January dates from 153 BC (therefore after the death of Terence). See Taylor and Holland (1952: esp. n. 22). The wider role of Janus as a god of beginnings, of thresholds and of time, is, however, ancient. See, conveniently, the rather lovely two-headed Janus-coin dating from 225–217 BC, illustrated as fig. 1.5 (e) in Beard, North and Price (1998: 33). On the extraordinary effects of the Julian reform of

of literary beginnings are not hermetically sealed from other kinds of initiation (the loaded word is apposite here), as Said's work amply shows.[2] Roman comedy, indeed, is itself at some level a 'ritual' act, and also a social and political act, not just a text. The beginning of a play has a literary life which can take written form and fly through time and space, and also a performative life which is integrated into the culture which produced it.

In Roman comedy (as in all performance), the particular stress placed on the opening is the need to settle the audience, grab their attention and engage their goodwill.[3] Whereas modern performance is generally aided in this task by semiotic means, such as lighting, music, curtains, the raised baton, etc., it seems likely that ancient theatre relied heavily on the visual effect of the first speaker(s) on entry, and still more on the very words of the text, to announce its beginning.[4] Many plays strike up with a request for attention:[5] some joke on the difficulty of getting the audience to settle down, using their slightly hectoring didactic stance of instructing members of the crowd on proper comic audience-behaviour as part of the *captatio beneuolentiae* which is the real, underlying 'instruction' to the audience. The performative problem of beginning has often been occluded to a lesser or greater degree in discussions of Plautine comedy by the long-held belief that the Roman audience was an unruly and ignorant mob who had to be coaxed or badgered into listening, like unwilling schoolchildren.[6] 'Grabbing attention' is something which all literature has to do: comedy is marked out by the way that it jokes with the idea, and puts its performance on show in a way which other literature is too decorous to do, or to admit to doing. In performance, the particular joke is with the audience, but

the calendar in 45 BC (and therefore between the time of Roman comedy and the time of Ovid), not only on Roman perceptions of the civic and natural worlds but also on our capacity to conceive the pre-Julian world, see Feeney (2007), esp. his final chapter.

2 Said (1975) is a deep and wide-ranging discussion of the connection between literary beginnings and other kinds of initiation, e.g. on origins and beginnings of thought, beginnings as originary thought.

3 Said (1975: 50): '[a] beginning gives us the chance to do work that compensates for the tumbling disorder of brute reality that will not settle down'.

4 Duckworth (1994: 84): 'In the later Roman theatre there was a curtain (*aulaeum*) which was lowered to reveal the stage at the beginning of the performance and raised at the close (cf. Cic. *Cael.* 27, 65), but there is no evidence for the use of such a curtain in the theatre in the days of Plautus and Terence.' Beare (1964: 179–80 and 267–8) is likewise clear that there was no curtain or other explicit mechanism for beginning and ending in the theatre of Plautus and Terence.

5 See Raffaelli (1984b).

6 Plautus has perhaps been too convincing! On the audience of comedy, see esp. Handley (1975), Parker (1996), Wiseman (1998) and Christenson (2000: 132). Beacham (1991: 39) is not the most ungenerous: 'The first thing we sense is the presence of a large, potentially unruly crowd whose attention and goodwill the playwright, acting through the speaker of the prologue, is concerned to obtain. Only once it has settled down can it be prepared for the entertainment at hand.'

other comic literatures also play with the process of opening, as can be seen in the famous example of Sterne's inimitable *Tristram Shandy* (see below, p. 51).

The most delightfully outrageous example of this game of instruction comes from the prologue to the *Poenulus*, which has been well analysed by Slater (1992a). The speaker begins as a drama critic, commenting on how a tragedy (Aristarchus' *Achilles*)[7] begins with a call for silence – a comment which then becomes simultaneously both a quotation and an instantiation of the *topos*. The prologue-speaker points out (supposedly at second remove) that the purpose of the *topos* is to settle the audience 'whether they are hungry or full' (*et qui essurientes et qui saturi uenerint*, 6): he not unreasonably suggests that they would be much more sensible to have dined before coming to the theatre, but then offers the play as food. The joke neatly slides us from the opening tragic quotation to the present comic reality, for food and eating do the programmatic work of comedy.[8] Next (11) he calls on the herald to make the audience shut up and listen – and then tells him to sit down and shut up. Since the herald has a real role which is preliminary to the play, his involvement here fudges the boundaries between the inside and the outside of the play.[9] These games pose as being preparatory to the beginning of the play, but it is not hard to see that they are only kidding – that they are really part of the spell by which the play works its magic.

A similar game opens the *Asinaria*, while Mercury, acting the prologue for *Amphitruo*, lays down the law about how the audience must behave. At *Captiui* 10–16, the prologue-speaker, after asking the audience if they get the plot so far, pretends that someone has said he doesn't. The offending audience member is blamed for skulking at the back (like students in lectures) and is invited to come forward so that the speaker will not have to shout so loud (understanding has turned into simple hearing, and the play is suddenly being acted for the benefit – cf. *Ps.* 720 – of the better

[7] Slater (1992a: 135) follows the view that Plautus is alluding to an Ennian version of *Achilles* ('probably a recent performance'). See Jocelyn (1967: 165–6), where he suggests the possibility of reading 'verses 3–49 of the prologue as a parody of commands given by Ennius' Achilles to the soldiers guarding his tent', although this view is modified in Jocelyn (1969a). For a dynamic metaphorical reading of this Achilles as a type for the 'Prologue as Generalissimo of another citizen-army camp', see Henderson (1999: 6–7).

[8] Gowers (1993: 60); Henderson (1999: 10–11).

[9] See Beare (1964: 169) for the *praeco* as a member of the team, along with carpenters, stage-hands, etc., but Beare is quite explicit that he has devised his account mainly on the basis of references in the plays. Likewise Beacham (1991: 40). Marshall (2006: 31) argues that the *praeco* 'was not in the company but was an official appointed by the magistrates'. He suggests the modern parallel of a 'front-of-house manager', which would contribute well to fuzzing the edges of the play world.

class of audience in the front rows).[10] The *Truculentus* Prologue[11] opens in grand alliterative style, asking deferentially on Plautus' behalf for a small space among the great walls of Rome in which to bring his bit of Athens:

> Perparuam partem postulat Plautus loci
> de uostris magnis atque amoenis moenibus,
> Athenas quo sine architectis conferat.
> (*Truc.* 1–3)

Plautus requests a little bit of space from within your great and pleasant walls, where he may bring Athens without builders.

Suddenly, the prologue-speaker turns on the audience – 'well, will you let him or not?' (*quid nunc? daturin estis an non?*, 4). The audience's acquiescence is then written in (*adnuont*), will-they, nill-they, followed by a similarly enforced refusal of Plautus' use of their private space, as opposed to the public space of Rome. For this, their traditional morals (*mores pristini*) are ironically praised, as the cause of their swift denial (or a sign of their private meanness): insult and flattery, audience-participation and actor-control all at once. The issue is not just one about Rome and Athens, but about actors and audiences, illusion and reality, and the question by whose leave the play can take place. The delicate balance of power relations between audience and play-folk is played out at the level of teasing pedantry.

The joking interaction here is between on the one hand dramatic text, which at least is planned and controlled by the actor-playwright, and at most is formally scripted, and on the other hand the actual instantiation of that performance together with all the regalia that go into it. And so the question arises about some preliminary: 'Is this bit part of the show, or not?' This joke partakes in general fuzziness about where things start, about the artificiality of any designation of something as the beginning.[12] For Roman comedy, further fuzziness lies in the wider ritual context, the *ludi* of which the dramatic production forms a part, and also, more directly (although perhaps less importantly), in the status of advance material such as announcements, and, for later readers, the plot-summaries (*argumenta*) and in some cases *didascaliae* attached to the beginning of texts.[13] 'Where',

[10] Marshall (2006: 77).

[11] The Prologue is a role which can be played by a named character or by an unnamed entity designated *prologus*. I use the capitalised title Prologue to mark this personified role.

[12] An easy example of this fuzziness is the status of a preface, which is the thing 'spoken before' the beginning of a modern printed book, and yet is also part of it.

[13] There is an interesting discussion in the extant fragment of Donatus, *De comoedia*, in which he considers why in some cases the play's title is announced before the author's name, while in others

as well as 'how', a play starts is not an easy question to answer. It is Terence who plays most creatively on this ambiguity with his literary prologues, which cut the line between performance and text, and that between inside and outside of the play, closer than ever before, and for a long time ever since.[14]

But when we go further into a play, we are constantly reminded that every play, even every new play, is to some extent always already a repeat. We see this in the case of supposedly 'necessary' exposition – where a great deal of what we are told we could have guessed anyway, from our knowledge of Greek New Comedy and Roman comedy – and we see it more generally in the formulaic and conventional nature of the genre. No play springs fully formed from the head of its author, but rather comes into existence in a network of other plays.[15]

Not only is the beginning jokingly undermined by the sense that the play is to some extent a repeat, but also we find that many plays have a great deal of trouble in actually getting on with it. Despite their obvious existence (cf. Said 1975: 43–4) and their initiatory performance, they mess around for ages before actually doing anything with the plot. This is because, although comedies are in some sense heavily plot-oriented, this is not in any very purposeful Aristotelian sense, but, rather, something of the comedy of Comedy is the struggle between the plot and the play for centre stage.

it is the other way round (a translation of this text is available in Sidnell *et al.* (1991: ch. 5); Latin text in Wessner 1962–3 I: 28). The passage in question is *De comoedia* 8.1 (Sidnell's translation): 'In most dramas the names of the plays were presented before those of the poets; in some, however, the poets' names precede those of the drama. The difference in this procedure has the sanction of antiquity. For when the dramas were first brought out, their titles were read aloud before the poets were named, to prevent them from being deterred from writing because of any hostility. However, when the poet had acquired a reputation by publishing many plays, the names of the poets again took precedence, so that the plays might gain attention through the poets' names.' It is not entirely clear exactly what confusions are at work here, but my point remains: announcement of the play is part of the total performance. So too are the preliminaries in written text: the reader is perhaps more powerful than the audience member in the degree of control s/he has over the role of preliminaries.

14 The literary prefaces of Henry James are fascinating in this regard. These prefaces, for the upmarket New York edition of his novels, are works of criticism which, as the author himself said in a letter to W. D. Howells, 'are, in general, a sort of plea for Criticism, for Discrimination, for Appreciation on other than infantile lines': Terence would have understood. See the introduction by Richard Blackmur to James (1934). Pearson's study of the prefaces (1997) analyses their importance in the history and theory of fictionality, and their purpose in constructing the ideal reader of James' text. Again, Terence would have understood.

15 My formulation here is simply a restatement of the Kristevan doctrine of intertextuality. The work I aim for it to do here is to stress the factoid that no beginning is *ex nihilo*, however much it may – and must – trumpet its opening.

PLAUTINE OPENINGS

Some of Plautus' funniest beginnings are the ones that mess around for ages before they make any real progress with the plot. Like Frankie Howerd's 'The Prologue', which never quite gets finished before the end of the show, there are Plautine beginnings which refuse to settle down and get on with the play. They are excellent examples of Said's 'hysterically deliberate' opening, those, as he says, in 'works that despite their existence cannot seem to get started; in each the beginning is postponed with a kind of encyclopaedic, meaningful playfulness' (1975: 43–4). Whether they begin with a couple of hundred lines of prologue, like *Amphitruo*, where the extraordinarily long prologue reflects the extraordinarily long night of Jupiter's pleasure, or come hurtling straight in like *Epidicus* with its aggressive 'hey you!', Plautine plays nearly always start with programmatic messing around, in which the play constantly gets in the way of the plot, which is always trying to shove the play out of the way so that it can say something and make things happen. This kind of opening is in contrast with what Said (1975: 44) calls the 'solemn-dedicatory' opening, more typical of grander genres, of which the almost overwhelmingly 'dedicatory' opening of Virgil's *Aeneid*, discussed in Nuttall's (1992) study, is an excellent example. Comedy occasionally flirts with this kind of impressive act of initiation – examples would be the opening lines of *Amphitruo*, *Rudens* or *Truculentus* – but such a pretension is almost immediately undercut.

First, this discussion needs to be set in the context of the extant corpus of Plautus. Doing so is already problematic, since its implicit claim to exhaustivity is undermined by the fact that the extant texts represent a drop in the ocean of republican Roman comedy, which was originally constituted by not only the significant number of other Plautine plays, but also all the *palliata* plays of his contemporaries and near-contemporaries, not to mention related genres such as the *togatae*, mime and Atellan farce.[16] I hope that this necessary compromise finds some justification in that my primary concern is with the reading of texts. On the one hand, we might say: happily, the genre is a highly homogeneous one, so we are likely to be making a fairly accurate description even on the basis of a small sample.[17]

[16] See Duckworth (1994: ch. 1) and Beare (1964: ch.2) for Italian performance other than the *palliata*. Wright (1974) gives a good account of the *palliata* playwrights other than Plautus and Terence.

[17] See Wright (1974) for the fullest expression of this point: the entire comic corpus, except for Terence, shows considerable uniformity of style. Wright is concerned with (largely linguistic) *style*, rather than with wider aspects of text and performance, although when discussing Terence he takes the matter further: '[i]n style, structure, characterization, and moral outlook Plautus (along with, I

On the other hand, we might reply: the very fact that Roman comedy presents itself as genre-bound, formulaic and in any case 'just a copy of Greek comedy' (that is a self-deprecating joke) encourages us to imagine that all plays start in the same way and that there is a standard formula for a Plautine opening. There are indeed standard *topoi* of opening, which could be held to add up to a 'formula' in the broadest sense, but (a) there are very many variations within that formula, and (b) the 'rule' is observed as much in the breaking as in the making. This is a general point about comedy: precisely *because* it works on the basis of parodic imitation of literature, life, itself and everything else, *because* this is our expectation in watching or reading a comedy, there does not need to be very much of a 'rule' for something to be created which can be played on, reacted against, inverted, parodied, etc.[18]

In this discussion, the *Bacchides* will be discounted because the opening is lost,[19] which leaves twenty plays either fully extant or at least presenting some part of their opening section. Of these twenty, thirteen begin with a prologue, while a further two (*Cist.*, *Mil.*) start with some other scene, but then offer a delayed prologue. This means, then, that the opening prologue accounts for 65 per cent of the Plautine openings (i.e., it is the norm, but the norm is not overwhelmingly followed). The remaining five (*Cur.*, *Epid.*, *Mos.*, *Per.*, *St.*) have no prologue at all in this formal sense.[20] *Mostellaria* contains a romantic monologue by the *adulescens* Philolaches, which performs some of the functions of a (delayed) prologue and plays with the pretence of being one, but since it is a *canticum* ('song') it should not formally be classed among the delayed prologues. Of the fifteen prologues, twelve are spoken by a character for whom this is the only role in the play, assuming that such is the case with the fragmentary *Vidularia*, of which only snippets – albeit juicy ones – of the prologue remain. The remaining three are spoken by characters otherwise involved in the play.

would argue, all the other Roman playwrights discussed thus far) and Terence are about as different as two poets working in the same genre can be' (127). It is, however, something of an unspoken *communis opinio*, among the majority of Classicists who are not specialists in comedy and among non-Classicists, that the plays are 'all the same'.

18 Take the example of the running slave scene – far more such scenes are 'parodies' than 'straight' scenes. See Dentith (2000) for an introduction to the theory of parody, although unfortunately he does not deal with ancient comedy.

19 See Gaiser (1970) for discussion of reconstructions of this opening.

20 Theatrical tradition has moved sufficiently far from Aristotle's definition of the prologue (*Po.* 1452b) as 'those parts of the play up to the entry of the chorus' into a convention of the prologue (formal address to the audience, in some way introducing the play and drawing the audience into its world, whether or not it includes explicit exposition of the plot or background) that we are justified in distinguishing formal prologues from any old opening to a play.

They are: in *Amphitruo*, the god Mercury, who is the crucial player in the play's deception; in *Mercator*, the *adulescens* Charinus, who combines his prologue with romantic monologue (unlike his colleague Philolaches in *Mostellaria*, Charinus just manages to slip into the category of 'prologue', rather than, or as well as, romantic monologue, because (a) he opens the play alone, (b) he speaks in iambic senarii, (c) he *tells* us he is playing the Prologue); and in *Miles gloriosus*, the clever slave Palaestrio, who controls the action.[21] All prologues use the spoken metre, iambic senarii, and all involve some direct address to the audience.[22] *Not* all involve exposition, a fact which we will discuss further below. Of plays that do not begin with a prologue: *Curculio*, *Miles gloriosus* and *Mostellaria* also open in iambic senarii; *Cistellaria* and *Stichus* have *in medias res* openings beginning with *cantica*,[23] while *Epidicus* begins with two lines of trochaic septenarii (so possibly recitative) and then launches into a *canticum*;[24] *Persa* opens with long iambic lines, the first designated ia_4 $tr_4^{\wedge}$ by Questa (1995: 279), followed by a mixture of iambic septenarii and octonarii, turning to trochaic at 13 and cretic at 17.[25]

Both formulae and variation can be seen also in the constitution of opening scenes, whether they follow, precede or replace the prologue. The most common constitution is some form of free + slave, a pattern going back at least to Aristophanes (for example, the memorable opening of *Frogs*), and particularly useful for giving exposition while also playing around with failing to get on with the play.[26] Four plays give us *adulescens* and *seruus* in the opening scene (*Cur.*, *Mer.*, *Poen.*, *Ps.*), and *Persa* has

[21] On Palaestrio's poet's-eye perspective here, see Frangoulidis (1996b).

[22] Moore (1998b: 248) states it as an 'almost universal' principle that plays open unaccompanied (i.e. in iambic senarii), apart from *Cist.*, *Epid.*, *Per.* and *St.*, none of which opens with a prologue in the sense implied here.

[23] Anderson (1993: 123). Arguing here on the basis of a relatively strong reading for the possibility of dating Plautus' plays, Anderson says that 'in the two remaining plays which Plautus wrote before the end of the third century, *Cistellaria* and *Stichus*, it is notable that he experimented with a lyric device that he did not adopt regularly thereafter: he opened the comedy with lyric conversation'.

[24] If indeed the distinction between trochaic septenarii and polymetric *canticum* is important, for which, and the history of the question of whether all metres other than iambic senarii were accompanied, see Moore (1998b: 245–7) and Marshall (2006: 204, 215), where it is argued that small numbers of iambic senarii mixed with other metres could continue with the music. Willcock (1995: 24) comments on these lines: 'here the first lines are trochaic septenarii, and they develop into a *mixtis modis canticum* of a peculiarly Plautine nature'. Questa (1995: 199), in his edition of the *cantica*, includes the lines in trochaic septenarii.

[25] See Marshall (2006: 204 and n. 7) on the designations of the longer iambic and trochaic lines.

[26] Silk (2000a: ch. 1) has an excellent discussion of 'Three Openings' of Aristophanic plays, including *Frogs*. Looking at (in reverse chronological order) *Plutus*, *Frogs* and *Acharnians*, Silk shows the programmatic nature of these scenes. It is worth noting that the two later plays both begin with master-and-slave routines.

two *serui*, one of whom is the lover and is therefore toying with the role of *adulescens*. Two further plays have *senex* and *seruus* (*As.*, *Aul.*), while three have two slaves (*Cas.*, *Epid.*, *Mos.*), in addition to which we must mention again *Persa*, plus also *Amphitruo*, where the opening scene is between a slave and a god pretending to be a slave. Three (*Capt.*, *Men.*, *Truc.*) have monologues (two of which are by parasites: *Capt.*, *Men.*) and then beyond that is a variety of other groupings.[27] This brief schema shows that, although there are patterns which can act as 'classic scenes', there is in fact a great variety of ways of opening a play.

I have sought to place the discussion in context, but inevitably, this being comedy, it is a context which is vulnerable to being sent up. In practice, a Plautine play is not required to position its parts in neat categories, and defining the beginning and end of the Beginning is even harder than doing the same job for the whole play.

Exposition: how much is enough?

Most Greek drama arises out of a context in which much of the information is available to the audience right from the beginning, so that the audience is in a position to appreciate the ironies of the drama, and to actualise its metaphorical position of superiority and power. In conventional tragedy, that information is already available because the Myth is part of the audience's cultural inheritance, although the prologue may nonetheless remind us of what we know, particularly in the metatheatrical hands of Euripides. Aristophanes is an exception to the norm of explicit scene-setting, probably because his plays are not so much plots as situations. Nick Lowe offers a powerful analysis of the role of Old Comedy and its descendants in the development (the 'invention') of fiction, which he attributes to its 'rivalry with tragedy'.[28] The real-world, if fantastic, situations of Old Comedy met the mythic plots of tragedy and became the realist fictive plots of New Comedy. For the Greek comedy which grew out of the comic and tragic drama of the fifth century, the standard way to recreate the effect of prior knowledge was by means of an expository prologue. One fourth-century Greek commentator actually made a joke out of the critical problem of comedy not having the ready-made material of tragedy, by complaining how much harder it is to write comedy than tragedy (contrary

[27] Three prostitutes (*Cist.*); soldier and parasite (*Mil.*); slave, soon joined by a *senex* and an *adulescens* (*Rud.*); two wives (*St.*); two *senes* (*Trin.*); too fragmentary to tell (*Vid.*, *Bac.*).

[28] Lowe (2000: 267).

to what might be implied by the accepted hierarchy of genres), because tragedies have their material already set up, whereas comedians have to invent theirs from scratch.[29] The primary purpose, or at least the pretext, of a comic prologue is to bring the audience up to speed on information which they do not already possess, but need in order to understand the play, such as prehistory of the plot and characters, plus occasionally some indication of what will happen in the play and how it will all turn out.[30]

But Plautine exposition is mostly a pose.[31] The nature and quantity of prologic (and other) exposition in Plautus is very variable, for comedy always treads a fine line between conventionality and the paraprosdokian. Almost half of the extant plays do not contain prologic exposition, either because they have no prologue or because the prologue refuses to expose the plot. This 'background information', which poses as being disseminated on a need-to-know basis, can be playfully refused or provided in super, if not always strictly necessary, abundance. In either case, Plautus is playing with the audience and with the control of knowledge, teasing with coy refusal or tempting with some snippet of information, which sometimes takes on a life of its own and conjures up a fictional world wider than the plot itself, the illusion of which is crucial to literary beginning. I shall consider first some examples of the refusal to tell, and then look at the opposite technique of creative storytelling.

Asinaria is keen to tell us about the Greek name of the play, its Greek author and about Plautus' 'barbarian' version, the name of which Plautus wants to be '*Asinaria*, by your leave' (10–12), but as for the plot – it's

[29] Antiphanes, *Poiesis* fr. 189. See Handley (1985: 411–12); Slater (1995: 37–9); Raffaelli (1984a). Gowers (2004: 150–1) reminds us that '[a]s far back as Euripides, and certainly as far back as Menander, dramatic poets seem to have used various devices to side-step the potential tedium of straight exposition'. This is true, but much work is being done by those words 'devices' and 'straight', which leaves room for substantial difference in the Roman style.

[30] Foretelling of the ending is seen (with outrageous disregard for dramatic cohesion) in Pl. *Cas.*; in *Capt.*, when the highly knowing Prologue tells us that Tyndarus will unknowingly enable the return of his unknown brother. *Cist.*, however, gives us lots of juicy background but then stops before telling us what will happen (197), though as in several other plays (e.g. *Men.* and *Rud.*) we could easily guess; the excessively knowing Palaestrio, speaking the delayed prologue of *Mil.* as if he were outside the play, tells us something of what will happen (which within character he would not know), though not the mechanisms for the resolution; *Poenulus*' Prologue does tell us the ending, although, as he says, he nearly forgets to after his complicated games with us (118).

[31] Slater (2000: 122–3): 'Plautus' prologues . . . have as their primary goal not information but induction' and (127): 'The jokes and banter that seem so irrelevant to a reader actually perform a vital function in alerting the audience to its role in the play and in the workings of the theatre.' See Duckworth (1994: 211–18).

just *ridicula res* (14). The Prologue playfully pretends that telling us the technical details is more important than introducing the plot:[32]

> nunc quid processerim huc et quid mi uoluerim
> dicam: ut sciretis nomen huiius fabulae;
> nam quod ad argumentum attinet, sane breuest.
> nunc quod me dixi uelle uobis dicere
> dicam: huic nomen graece Onagost fabulae;
> Demophilus scripsit, Maccus uortit barbare;
> Asinariam uolt esse, si per uos licet.
> (*As.* 6–12)

Now I shall tell you why I have come out here and what I wanted, which is for you to know the name of this play. For as to the plot, that's a trifle. Now I shall tell you what it was that I told you I wanted to tell you: this play is called 'The Donkey-Driver' in Greek. Demophilus wrote it, and Maccus translated it into barbarian. He wants it to be called *Asinaria*, by your leave.

Trinummus plays a similar game:

> sed de argumento ne exspectetis fabulae:
> senes qui huc uenient, i rem uobis aperient.
> huic Graece nomen est Thensauro fabulae:
> Philemo scripsit, Plautus uortit barbare,
> nomen Trinummo fecit, nunc hoc uos rogat
> ut liceat possidere hanc nomen fabulam.
> tantum est. ualete, adeste cum silentio.
> (*Trin.* 16–22)

But don't expect the plot of the play. The old men who are going to come out, they'll open it up. The Greek name of this play is 'The Treasure'. Philemon wrote it, and Plautus translated it into barbarian. He called it *Trinummus*, and now begs leave for the play to bear this name. That's it. Farewell, pay attention in silence.

Technical details, and contractual agreement on what the play's name shall be – but not any useful background or hints about the plot.[33]

The remaining scraps of *Vidularia*'s prologue suggest that a variation on this theme was used there.[34] There is apparently reference to the Greek name *Sc̣[h]ẹdị[a* (6), and to the Roman name, *nọṣṭẹṛ f[ecit] Ṿ[idularia]m*

[32] If Marshall (2006: 31) is correct in his surmise that the *praeco* might have announced the title of the play before the arrival of the prologue, then the presentation of these details in the prologue would be otiose – or a repetitious joke. See Henderson (2006: xi) on the prologue: 'The Prologue tells all | there's nothing to tell, so listen.'

[33] The formula *ne exspectetis* has considerable programmatic significance: see pp. 37, 71–2, 268–70, 280–1.

[34] On attempts to reconstruct a play out of these fragments, see Calderan (1982) and Dér (1987).

(7).[35] It is possible that in the next two lines the prologue plays around further with questions of knowledge (*ẹgọ fạ[x]o s[cibi]ṭịs*, 8; *p̣ṛịus noscịṭẹ [. . . . .]sc̣ịṭis*, 9: Calderan).[36] The line nearest to intelligibility acknowledges that the audience would be expecting a prologue, but probably then refuses to give one. I offer here the reconstruction as printed by Calderan (1982: 128):

> crẹḍo argumẹntum ụelle uọṣ [pern]ọs[cer]ẹ:
> ịṇṭ[elle]g[etis poti]ụṣ q[uid a]g[an]ṭ q̣[ua]ṇd[o a]gent
> (*Vid.* 10–11)

I believe you want to know about the plot, but you'll understand what's going on better when you see it acted.

It is unlikely that the prologue went on to give some hints of exposition, since the traces of 15–16[37] look closural; it is clear that even in this recognition comedy Plautus self-consciously plays around with the giving and withholding of information in the prologue. He teases us with what he knows we want and so brings us into the ambit of what he actually wants to give us.

For Plautus is bursting to tell us a tale. His storytelling powers are on show in the spectacular prologue to *Amphitruo*.[38] Mercury reminds us of his performative role as a storyteller early on, when he invites us to celebrate him as messenger of the gods (8–13) as well as through his other attributes. He is – jokingly – a dramatic messenger.[39] When Sosia wanders in rather anxiously for the first scene, he too whips himself up into the role of 'tragic messenger', with the speech that he rehearses before performing it to Alcumena. The touch is light, but if we are attuned to it, the implicit references to messenger speeches may draw to our attention the poetic role of storytelling in drama.

Many lines and metatheatrical jokes into the play, Mercury actually starts telling his story (97). The scene is set, the characters introduced: Alcumena is pregnant by her husband, and then Jupiter enters the story. The audience is invited to collude with Jupiter's adultery –

[35] Calderan (1982: 128) prints 6–7 thus: *Sc̣[h]ẹdị[a haec] ụọ[. . . . . . .]g[.]ae[. . . .]c[/ p]ọẹṭạ ḥạ<nc> ṇọṣṭẹṛ f[ecit] Ṿ[idularia]m.*

[36] Calderan (1982: 148) suggests that the prologue might be engaging in a joke quiz with the audience about guessing the name Plautus.

[37] *magis qu[. . . . .]ạḅẹọ[. . . .]ọṛtis nụnciaṃ/uọs ill[um a]ụḍịṭẹ [..]ṇọx p̣ṛọ ḥọc̣[* (*Vid.* 15–16 Calderan).

[38] It will be clear that I disagree with the reading of Gilula (1991) in downplaying the importance of reported stories.

[39] See Feeney (1998: 27) for Mercury's bilingual jokes on his name.

nam ego uos nouisse credo iam ut sit pater meus,
quam liber harum rerum multarum siet
quantusque amator siet quod complacitum est semel.
is amare occepit Alcumenam clam uirum
usuramque eiius corporis cepit sibi,
et grauidam fecit is eam compressu suo.

(*Am.* 104–9)

For I think you already know what my father is like, how free he is in these many matters, what a great lover he is once something has taken his fancy. He began to love Alcumena without her husband's knowledge and made use of her body for himself, and he got her pregnant again by his embrace.

In amongst all the complexity of Mercury's manipulation of the audience here, he is also 'just' telling us a story. Plautine prologues sometimes like to play a game of faux naïvety in their storytelling, and Mercury's account of the double impregnation of Alcumena is just that.[40] This can be seen for example in the overuse of the pronoun *is* (*ea id*), especially in 107–9,[41] in the magical quality of the double pregnancy and the extended night, and in the storyteller's careful insistence that we follow the thread. To paraphrase: 'Okay, have you all understood that? Alcumena is pregnant twice over, once by her husband and once by Jupiter – and funnily enough he's with her right now, and that's why this night is extra long.' Suddenly the story and the play merge, for now the story-myth which Mercury is telling us (while indeed also refusing to tell us) of how Jupiter pushed two nights together in order to engender Hercules is actually being played out (yet again) in the play, behind the scenes. The worlds beyond and within the play are brought into imagistic, illusionistic, but somehow convincing, congruence with each other.[42] Mercury makes us 'believe' there is more going on behind the scenes, both physically and temporally.[43] He continues with one piece

[40] Another example of simplistic storytelling appears below, apropos *Aul.*

[41] For the repeated pronoun *is* as a feature of archaic language, see Leumann, Hofmann and Szantyr (1972: 187). Courtney (1999: 153–5) gives a useful, though brief, account of the connections between Plautine narrative style and early Latin prose style. He appreciates the consummate artistry of Plautus ('a writer of great stylistic virtuosity'), but in my view errs in explaining Plautus' stylistic choices in his narratives from the desire for clarity rather than for the rhetorical effect of simplistic storytelling.

[42] The extra-long night is often considered a problem of this prologue, since the famous such night must surely have occurred nine months previously. The issue is discussed in Christenson (2000: 47) and Stewart (2000). Neither Plautus nor the gods require such realism.

[43] Likewise in *Captiui*, the Prologue carefully checks that we have understood (10), pretending to apologise for hitting us with so much exposition straightaway. That prologue also fudges the boundaries between inside and outside of the play, revels in its storytelling and conjures up a wider world. Franko (1995) indicates the likelihood that the play was staged either during or at least not chronologically far from the time of 'mutual antagonsim and *fides* disregarded, culminating with

of exposition that could be held to be fully necessary – the explanation of the trick of double identity, and of how we can tell the difference between Mercury and Sosia, between Jupiter and Amphitruo, even though no-one else can. We are gods.[44]

A share in the divine perspective is offered to us also by *Aulularia*, introduced by the Lar Familiaris who knows everything and has organised everything. This character is a great teller of stories, especially those where he is the hero. Again the level of storytelling is far greater than the requirements of the plot, and serves both to entertain the audience and also to create the greater world of the imagination. The Lar launches straight into his story, starting with its main character, himself:

> Ne quis miretur qui sim, paucis eloquar.
> ego Lar sum familiaris ex hac familia
> unde exeuntem me aspexistis.
>
> (*Aul.* 1–3)

In case any of you is wondering who I am, I will explain in a few words. I am the Lar Familiaris of this household, whence you have just seen me coming out.

He then moves back in time to relate his long association with the house, and its series of truculent owners, none of whom had the decency to pay their household god proper attention, although the first one, at least, had entrusted the Lar with the pot of gold which is the emblem and driving force of the play.[45] The Lar thus has the opportunity to display his own *fides*, and to use the ancient god's prerogative of aiding only those who honour him. The first owner of the treasure was a miser, and died without telling his son about the treasure. The second did the same, and the third would be going the same way, were it not for the dutiful daughter whose attention to the god invites him to make this play happen. (I am attempting, in the pedestrian way of the critic, to mimic the slippage between the inside of the play-world and the performance of the play, a slippage which is so crucial to Roman comedy and especially to its prologues.) This tale of atavistic miserliness is not of itself important information for the play: rather, it has the ring of a fairy story or fable, where repetitions of this nature are common, often as here grouped in threes. Irrelevant though it is directly to the plot, however, the series also has a programmatic effect, for this play

open warfare from 191 to 189' (167–8), between Rome and the Aetolian League. Franko argues that what we see in the play is the triumph of Roman moral values even in Aetolia. This adds a further layer to the interactions of inside and outside the play.

44 Just as the gods are slaves (*Am.* 26–9).

45 Konstan (1983) argues convincingly for the programmatic force of the pot.

will be about the proper movement of property between the generations – and it is that which was so sadly lacking in Euclio's ancestry.

But the Lar has not finished his story. It was he who made Euclio find the treasure, in order to enable the daughter's marriage (25–7); it was he who caused the old man next door to ask for the girl's hand, in order to nudge the young man who is her lover into action (31–3). We almost feel as if the young man's (conventional) rape of the daughter might also be the Lar's work, since he is such a controlling character for this play, at least in his own representation. One need-to-know piece of information, that the neighbour is the young man's uncle (35), appears in an offhand comment, hidden among the seamy details of the offending festival of Ceres at which the initiatory rape took place.

The Lar has given us, in effect, 'spare' information. In several of the prologues, the amount of strictly redundant exposition is so great as to create the illusion of enough material for a whole extra play going on in the background. This over-exposition is an artful device to trap us further into the play, to give us a sense of something bigger than we know about, something more, behind the stage house and beyond the play, that we cannot see but might imagine.

This device of over-exposition and playful storytelling is at work at the beginning and end of *Casina*, a play in which the love plot is displaced onto the two slaves who woo the same nubile slave-girl on behalf of young and old master severally.[46] The delightful prologue to this outrageous Roman romp is unusually generous in the production of exposition, including a promise of how it all turns out, but what is sketched out here is not so much the details of this play but those of the phantom recognition comedy which surrounds it. The prologue tells us about the exposed baby girl, the eponymous Casina, who grew up as a favoured slave of the house (41–6), about the young man and his father being in love with the slave-girl (48–9), and about how she will eventually turn out to be an Athenian citizen (81). At the end of the play, the young man's slave Chalinus,[47] who has been operative in the plot and has exposed the old man to acute embarrassment, turns into the speaker of an epilogue. He quickly whips through finishing off the background plot, reminding us that Casina will turn out to be the

[46] It seems apparent that the version we have is that written for a revival of the play, probably (although not necessarily) after Plautus' death. On the dates of original and revival, Beare (1934) argues for a date for the revival which would make the reference to worthless contemporary comedies a snide allusion to Terence; see also Abel (1955: 55–61). It is assumed by the commentators (see MacCary and Willcock 1976: 97) that lines 5–22 were composed for the revival, while the rest is Plautine. If this is correct, the later director was a clever reader of Plautus, this play and the dramatic tradition.

[47] Probably he is the speaker, see MacCary and Willcock (1976: 210).

daughter of the people next door, and the couple will marry. This offhand narrative is an outrageous denial of proper dramatic form, which conspires with the action of the prologue to create a wider world than just this play.[48] The quintessential moment of this device is the prologue's metatheatrical warning not to expect the young man's return during the play, using the *ne exspectetis* phrase which constitutes a signal of playfulness about the imparting of knowledge:

> is, ne exspectetis, hodie in hac comoedia
> in urbem non redibit: Plautus noluit,
> pontem interrupit, qui erat ei in itinere.
> (*Cas.* 64–6)

He, in case you were expecting it, today in this comedy won't come back to the city: Plautus didn't want to include him, so he broke down a bridge on the young man's route.

The young man never made the journey from that Greek play by Diphilus from which Plautus ('with barking name', 34) started out. With this neat slip between the play outside the illusion and the plot inside it, the prologue hints at a play that might have been and somehow always is behind this one, but cannot actually come on a stage that is crowded with the messing around of the *senex amator* and the cross-dressing pseudo-bride.

It is not only the skeleton of the recognition play that is contributing to the storyteller's powers of 'irrelevant' amusement. The story is embellished with jokey details that bring it to life in a way which is quite foreign to the needs of information. For example, we learn that the old slave who originally exposed the girl is lying ill in bed – or at least in bed (37–8). MacCary and Willcock (1976: 103) take this as a trace of the original recognition plot ('[t]he sick slave obviously played a key part in the recognition scene of Diphilus' *Kleroumenoi*') which Plautus has kept here, out of deference to his model, but not used. Be that as it may, the reference serves up the joke between different uses of the preposition 'in' with *in morbo* ('ill', 37) and *in lecto* ('in bed', 38),[49] and also offers the kind of false

[48] It is possible that a Greek play which is an important intertext for ours (maybe even Diphilus' *Kleroumenoi*) did indeed have such a scene. This is typical Plautine messing. Truncated ending like this happens in *Cist.* also. On the likelihood of Diphilus' play containing a recognition, see O'Bryhim (1989). O'Bryhim's case that Plautus has in this play made a blend of two Greek comedies with his own material to create a play which 'bears little resemblance to the prologue's description of the *Casina*'s Greek original' (81) does not place as much value as I would on the power of extraneous storytelling.

[49] Perhaps this is more than just a play on grammatical structures. The Prologue might mean to imply that the slave is either lazy or lascivious . . .

clue and playful messing which is so typical of the hysterically deliberate opening, setting up a series of more or less false trails throughout the prologue. The details of the exposed baby girl and her careful upbringing (*educauit magna industria*, 45) offer a broad hint that she will turn out to be freeborn and marriageable, although for most of the time the play is little concerned with this detail as other characters vicariously play out a much less respectable role for Casina; the formulaic *quasi si esset ex se nata* ('as if she were her [Cleustrata's] own', 46) might be a false hint, since Casina turns out to be the daughter of the couple next door, not Cleustrata. The girl's obvious nubility provokes both *senex* and *adulescens* to *amare ecflictim*, and to draw up their battle lines (49–50).[50] We now expect that this is going to be a comedy of generational conflict, like *Asinaria* or *Mercator*. Next the prologue explains that this is going to be a proxy battle, with both masters using their slaves as fronts for their own amatory intentions, the idea being that whichever slave marries Casina his master gets first access. Then suddenly the focus shifts from the father–son conflict when we hear that the mother is siding with the son, in order to punish the errant father, and indeed the son will not appear because of that 'broken bridge'. So this, then, is Plautus' play – not a romantic recognition but vicarious marital battles.

At the climax of his story, however, the Prologue employs another typical storytelling technique: he interrupts himself with a digression about the marriage of slaves. To his imaginary interlocutor's objection to the idea of slaves marrying, he replies that this is 'Greeking it up' (in Segal's happy phrase):[51]

> at ego aiio id fieri in Graecia et Carthagini,
> et hic in nostra terra in <terra> Apulia
> (*Cas.* 71–2)

But I say these things happen in Greece and in Carthage – and here in our own Apulian land!

After this piece of satirical nonsense, the Prologue returns (*reuortar ad illam puellam expositiciam*, 79) to the play and the plot and girl, Casina, who will turn out to be free and marriageable. Despite all this talk of slave-marriages and masters expecting to get in first with their slave's bride,

[50] Battle imagery: Franko (1999).

[51] Segal's account (1987; 1st edn 1968) of Romans laughing at Greeks in Roman *palliata* plays can be usefully combined here with that of McCarthy (2000), who reads the Plautine audience as free Romans laughing at slaves laughing at free Romans. For her, Plautus gives the Roman masters the possibility to identify with and to distance themselves from the slave.

he assures us this girl won't suffer any outrage during the play. After the play, however, it's another matter – she'll 'marry' anyone for the right price, and not wait for the ceremony (84–6). The naughty joke is a clever comment on what the Prologue has been doing throughout, which is to create the sense of a world beyond the play, and to blur the distinctions between imaginative world and performative world. Suddenly this girl who was to marry the young man in the romantic comedy which surrounds our play is turned into a prostitute who will enjoy her own *komos* at the post-play party. Since the actor of the girl – if there were one (in the 'reality' of performance there is not, since Casina does not appear, except vicariously as Chalinus) – would be a man, additional spice is added to the joke.[52]

In *Mercator*, the fuzzi-edging of the dramatic illusion is brought up front by the opening speech, which doubles as romantic monologue and expository prologue:

> Duas res simul nunc agere decretumst mihi:
> et argumentum et meos amores eloquar.
> (*Mer.* 1–2)

It has been decided that I should now do two things simultaneously: I shall tell both the plot and the story of my love.

Since he has this captive audience, the young lover very sensibly decides not to address his amorous complaints to the moon, as he says other comic lovers do,[53] but to these people in front of him, who might, after all, actually take some notice:

> non ego item facio ut alios in comoediis
> <ui>uidi amoris facere, qui aut Nocti aut Dii
> aut Soli aut Lunae miserias narrant suas:
> quos pol ego credo | humanas querimonias
> non tanti facere, quid uelint, quid non uelint;
> uobis narrabo potius meas nunc miserias.
> (*Mer.* 3–8)

I am not acting like I've seen others do in comedies under the influence of love, who narrate their sorrows to the Night or the Day, the Sun or the Moon – who I don't think care much about human complaints, what they want and what they don't want. Instead I'll tell you all about my sorrows.

[52] There is a nice paragraph to this effect in Beacham (2001).

[53] No doubt an extratextual allusion, whether to the comic koine or to some specific case: Barns and Lloyd-Jones (1964: 28).

Then the amorous and suffering young man interrupts himself to tell us the technical details of the performance: the Greek original is by Philemon, and is called *Emporos*, while in Latin it is the *Mercator* of Titus Maccus (i.e. Plautus).[54] The extraordinary intrusion of the technical details is hardly felt by the *adulescens*, so keen is he to tell his story.

Or at least to start it. He gives an account of how he was sent off to be the *mercator* in Rhodes, and that there he fell in love, but then he is sidetracked into a rambling disquisition on the pains of love, just when we thought we were going to hear the juicy bits of his story. Several self-referential jokes later, including a lot of nonsense about talking too little and too much (*multiloquium, parumloquium*, 31), the young man has another try at delivering the prologue and telling us his story (40). But this time, what we hear is not the story of *this* play, but of some complicated background which makes little difference to what happens in the play, and instead seems to offer a complete extra story.[55] When he first moved out of boyhood, Charinus fell in love with a prostitute (a separate affair from the current problem) and provoked his father into a typical display of the *pater durus*. After piling up the details of that story for a while, the storyteller moves even further back into the past, to reproduce at one remove his father's narration of *his own* youth, and his own *pater durus*, who kept him hard at work and far from any of the temptations of the city. This looks, then, like a second additional play in the background to the one we are eventually going to see. When the grandfather died, the father gave up on the city–country conflict, and instead bought a ship, thus becoming the original *mercator* (74–5: the reference to ships and trading gives the impression that the play is attempting to pull Charinus back onto the right narratological track). Charinus realised there would be moral mileage in offering to follow his father's example, despite his own love for the (completely irrelevant) prostitute, and rather to his surprise ended up on a successful business venture.[56] All this tells a good tale. Its purpose, perhaps, is to set the old man up as a hypocrite, since he will expose himself as a

[54] I paraphrase lines 9–10. The relationship of this play with Philemon's *Emporos* has been extensively explored by Lefèvre (1995: 9–59). See also Anderson (1993: 37–41).

[55] Leigh (2004b: 143–4) sees Charinus' tales as integral to the development of the play. There is a level at which nothing in literature is irrelevant because the very process of reading makes it relevant and encourages the telling of other stories, as indeed happens with Leigh's development of the story of what might have been.

[56] It is perhaps worth noting the moral ambiguities in the relationships of fathers and sons. Charinus tries to gain moral advantage by following in his father's footsteps as a merchant, but his father himself had started out as a merchant by rather outrageously flouting Grandad's good Roman advice, '*tibi aras, tibi occas, tibi seris, tibi item metis, / tibi denique iste pariet laetitiam labos*' (71–2), as soon as he died. See Leigh (2004b: 148).

senex amator at our first sight of him, but it is hardly essential information to the plot of this play. Amusingly, the one piece of information which the prologue does give us about the kind of play we are going to have is not made directly. Charinus tells us how he enjoyed the fruits of success, and was invited to dinner by an old acquaintance of his father, who provided not only food but also a woman for the night. It is this woman whom Charinus has brought home as his mistress, pretending she is a maid for his mother. So this is unlikely to be a recognition comedy (otherwise the girl would not have been provided to the lover as sexually available).

'The Prologue': another try at getting going

One of the most effective initiatory devices of comic openings is the 'hysterically deliberate' repetition of attempts to get going, which are sidetracked by all manner of delightful nonsense. In this section, I consider three different ways in which Plautus works openings of this nature: *Menaechmi* uses a formal prologue which is explicitly literary critical and openly metatheatrical; *Pseudolus* has an *architectus*-controlled scene which is implicitly metatheatrical; *Cistellaria* uses an *in medias res* opening which makes no acknowledgement of its status as a play until its second, and still more its third, attempt to get going.

Menaechmi is the most conventional:[57]

> Salutem primum iam a principio propitiam
> mihi atque uobis, spectatores, nuntio.
> (*Men.* 1–2)

First now from the beginning a propitious salutation I announce to you and to myself, spectators.

The play opens in dedicatory (and alliterative) mode, with a well-omened greeting (*salutem . . . propitiam*) surrounding initiatory inception (*primum iam a principio*), and developed in communitarian contract between audience, directly addressed, and play-folk (*mihi atque uobis*). Then the great announcement: 'I bring you – Plautus', undercut by the pedantic joke *lingua, non manu* ('in word, not in deed', 3), which is a sign of things to come.

[57] Gratwick (1993a: 30–4) analyses the difficulties involved in reading the prologue, and indeed any Plautine prologue, as 'authentic' in the straightforward sense of being an extant transcription of what was said in the first performance. As he rightly says: 'The very notions here of "definitive text", "authenticity", "revision", "interpolation" as they apply to the script itself seem here to dissolve and become confused' (31).

'So please listen' (4), and again more grandly 'pray open your attention to receive the argument':

> nunc argumentum accipite atque animum aduortite.
> (*Men.* 5)

The solemn declaration of intention to deliver the prologue is followed up by a barefaced lie:

> quam potero in uerba conferam paucissuma.
> (*Men.* 6)

I shall relate this to you in as few words as I can.

This is a signal, *not* for the beginning of the story, but for the first digression, a clever reflection on the nature of dramatic illusion and the relationship between Roman and Greek plays, in which, it is pointed out, the dominance of Athens should not be assumed. Or, to put it differently, the prologue tells us that 'the plot is Greeky, but it is not Atticy, rather it is Sicillily'.[58] And that (at least in the opinion of a copyist, if not necessarily of Plautus himself), he says with self-referential acuity, was the prologue to the prologue:

> † huic argumento antelogium hoc fuit †.
> (*Men.* 13)

Time for the plot: but the next three lines play teasing refusal. (I provide interpretative paraphrase rather than translation here.)

nunc argumentum uobis demensum dabo,	*I'll give you the plot*
non modio neque trimodio, uerum ipso horreo:	*No, I won't*
tantum ad narrandum argumentum adest benignitas.	*I might . . . okay, here it is.*
	(*Men.* 14–16)

Then the plot begins in pseudo-simplistic storytelling mode (17): 'once upon a time there was a Sicilian merchant . . .' and *ei sunt nati filii gemini duo* ('he had two twin sons', 18). Here is a piece of real information, which offers a broad hint that the play will be a twinning story, a comedy of errors, because even the twins' mother cannot tell them apart (19–20). We are diverted away from this crucial snippet immediately, however, by a digression on fictionality, truth and autopsy:

[58] See Fontaine (2006) for a clever suggestion of a pun here: this twinning plot is not only pertaining to Sicily but also 'is "double" or "counts twice" from the Latin noun *sicilicus*, a diacritical mark which served as a *nota* for gemination of consonants' (95).

> ut quidem ille dixit mihi qui pueros uiderat:
> ego illos non uidi, ne quis uostrum censeat.
> (*Men.* 22–3)

So someone told me who saw the boys: I never saw them, you know.

The same game will be played twenty-two lines later, when the Prologue comments on how he remembers well the name Menaechmus, given now to the second twin:

> propterea illius nomen memini facilius,
> quia illum clamore uidi flagitarier.
> (*Men.* 45–6)

That's why I can quite easily remember his name – I've so often seen him being drummed.

(We might pedantically note that this is inconsistent with his earlier claim never to have seen the boys – and then we might even more pedantically observe that the earlier claim referred to *boys*, plural, and *boys*, not adults.) These two diversions, together with the first digression on fictionality and illusion, move us further into the play-world. We started out thinking about how playwrights declare that the theatre space 'is' Athens, in order to make the whole thing Greeky; then we move onto the idea that the prologue-speaker is a storyteller recounting something 'real', but for which he cannot himself vouch; and finally we have reached the point where the prologue-speaker claims personal authority for the veracity of the world he is creating. Indeed, this passage is not the end of the sequence, for it culminates in the famous play with dramatic illusion and the construction of a play-world when the scene of the Prologue's story moves to Epidamnus, and he offers to take commissions for anyone while he is there (51–5).[59]

But to return to the plot. After the digression of 22–3, we hear the whole story about how the first twin became lost and the remaining twin was renamed – all this hardly in *paucissuma uerba*. Once the speaker is quite sure we understand about the double name,[60] he returns to Epidamnus, making his story (quasi-)physical in his imaginary movements around the Mediterranean/Adriatic. The speaker starts from Rome, to which he brings Plautus (3); moving to Athens to talk about how poets pretend that what they are presenting is Athens, to make it look Greeky (9); then to Syracuse because this is actually Sicillily (12 and 17); thence to Epidamnus to recount

[59] Anderson (1993: 137–8); Moore (1998a: 57–8); Marshall (2006: 28).

[60] This is another example, like those mentioned above in *Am.* and *Capt.*, of the pretended apology for this being all very complicated.

the abduction of (the Epidamnian) Menaechmus (32 and 49); from where he returns to – here:[61]

> nunc in Epidamnum pedibus redeundum est mihi,
> ut hanc rem uobis examussim disputem.
> si quis quid uestrum Epidamnum curari sibi
> uelit, audacter imperato et dicito,
> sed ita ut det unde curari id possit sibi.
> nam nisi qui argentum dederit, nugas egerit;
> qui dederit, magi' maiores nugas egerit.
> uerum illuc redeo unde abii atque uno asto in loco.
> (*Men.* 49–56)

Now I must take myself back off to Epidamnus, in order to reckon up this matter exactly for you. If anyone of you wants anything done in Epidamnus, speak up and give me your orders, but only if you give me the wherewithal to deal with it. Anyone who doesn't hand over the dosh will get peanuts; whoever does, will get – even less. But now I return to where I started, and yet I'm standing in the same place.

This is both a joke on the way in which the illusionary world can be anywhere, while always being the same stage, and also a play on the metaphor of a journey for the narrative line of a story. The 'return' is from the digression, and now we are going to get on with the plot. In Epidamnus. But – in another sense – we are in Rome. It is with this joke that the prologue will end:

> haec urbs Epidamnus est dum haec agitur fabula:
> quando alia agetur aliud fiet oppidum.
> (*Men.* 72–3)

This city is Epidamnus while this play is being performed; when another one is performed it will become a different town.

After the digression around the Mediterranean, we learn some useful information: the lost twin was adopted by his captor and is now rich and married. There is another broad but brief hint to the type of play we will see, in the word *dotatam* (61) describing the bride. This might sound good, alongside the other instances of the Epidamnian's wealth, but the wife-with-a-dowry, *uxor dotata*, is a stock character of Roman comedy who

[61] Gratwick (1993a: 140) suggests that the Prologue 'should descend to mingle with the audience during the narration of the Syracusan story . . . before making his way back "to Epidamnus"'. The scene could be made funny equally well by moving around as much as possible or very little.

always spells trouble (or, to put it otherwise, always gets a bad press).[62] The hint to the knowledgeable, then, is that this will be the kind of play in which a married man will try to cheat on his wife, who will punish him from her position of financial power. In fact, however, the wife is not a typical *uxor dotata*, being fairly young and seen in relation to a father as well as a husband, so the hint was slightly misleading. Unnecessary details of the death of the Epidamnian raptor (snatched away by a rapid river, 63–6) delay the progress of the play again, before we get a promise of what is going to happen – the travelling twin will turn up (as if we hadn't guessed). And then the prologue digresses again into a final disquisition on the dramatic illusion.[63] The prologue is thus nicely rounded off, the beginning apparently completed, but 'failing to begin' begins again with the opening scene, which is one of spectacular irrelevance, being the monologue of Peniculus about the nature of parasitism. It further delays the development of the plot, but also programmatically reflects the whole play, for Peniculus is the embodiment of irresponsible excess – just like the play.[64]

Just the opposite of the long *Menaechmi* prologue, and the similar extra-long versions in *Poenulus* and especially *Amphitruo*, is the extra-short one for *Pseudolus* – a two-line invitation to the audience to stretch their legs, because a long play is about to begin. But the self-deprecating tone of jokey artlessness sets up the studied artifice of the opening scene, which plays around with the difficulties of getting a play going. Pseudolus begins with a long speech about how (to paraphrase/interpret) if they don't have some dialogue the play can't actually do anything, because no-one will know what is going on. Instead of answering properly, Calidorus hands Pseudolus a letter.[65] In place of ordinary dialogue, then, there is a written script – in the form of this letter from Calidorus' beloved, a prostitute – which acts as a kind of go-between-cum-expository device. It also hints towards the plot, both the play-plot, which will depend on the use of another letter to secure the beloved's release, and the script-plot, which Pseudolus/Plautus,

[62] Wealth, in Epidamnus, comes with a verbal warning in any case. See Henderson (1998: 176); Gratwick (1993a: 139), who calls it 'Lossward', enhancing the pun at 51 by exposing an echo of an adjective in the proper noun.

[63] That is, according to the text as printed by Lindsay in the OCT. Gratwick (1993a) transposes 72–6 to after line 10, while noting that Watling (1965) prefers to have them between 56 and 57. Gratwick's view of the likely ending of the prologue is that a single line of 'farewell' followed the prologue's statement about the arrival of the Syracusan twin today. My overall reading of the prologue is not greatly affected by the position of these lines.

[64] Such a reading of *Men.* stands at the heart of Segal (1987).

[65] At the beginning of the second century BC, writing probably still had some aura of being clever, odd and special. See Jenkins (2005) for analysis of Plautine letters, scripts and the nature of reading.

as *architectus*, refuses to let us see.[66] Likewise with this opening letter, we can see it in Pseudolus' hands, but we are dependent on him to read it for us. He does so, eventually, after a lot of comic nonsense which purports to be highly relevant but which actually gets in the way of telling us what is going on. Living people, physical things and abstract things are all mixed up here: the individual letters are mating (they are trying to climb over each other, 23–4); this is writing from a Sibyl – it is incomprehensible (25–6); the girl is lying stretched out in the wax (34), a sophisticated, voyeuristic joke, in which the audience precisely cannot see the girl, cannot read the letter, does not know what the play is about; the formulaic *salus* (salvation and greeting: 41–6) of ordinary letter-writing comes in both wooden and silvery form. The reference to the silvery greeting is a broad expository hint that the young man needs money – which any halfway-skilled reader of comedy could have guessed already. But in the end, Pseudolus reads the letter out loud, and so we find out that the girl is to be sold to a Macedonian soldier that very day, unless something is done. So that was the prologue, written down.

My third example of the 'hysterically deliberate' opening, which makes several attempts at delivering The Prologue, is *Cistellaria*. This play begins *in mediis rebus* (a phenomenon which will be discussed in the next section), with a scene which does not acknowledge the audience although it gives a few hints of exposition; then there is a pseudo-prologue delivered by one of the characters from the first scene; and finally a delayed prologue (149), spoken by Auxilium, who complains that his fire has been stolen.[67]

The play opens with three women, two young, one older, in *canticum*. The first addresses the other two with an effusive expression of thanks, the only expository element of which is to make us ask, 'What is she thanking them for?' Her statement that Gymnasium (a prostitute name, as indeed we would expect in such a scene)[68] would not be dearer to her if she were her sister looks like it might be a hint at a plot element, but it is a red herring.[69] The two young women continue in this charming vein,

[66] See Sharrock (1996), and on *Ps.* and improvisation, see Barsby (1995). For this 'improvisation' as a literary artefact, see Goldberg (1995) on *Cur.*

[67] Anderson (1993: 31); Moore (1998b: 249). See Hurka (2004) for discussion of this unique double prologue.

[68] Cf. the cameo scenes of conversing prostitutes in Pl. *Poen.*, *Mos.*, and Ter. *Hec.*, but *St.* opens with two conversing women who are not prostitutes but respectable married women. See Auhagen (2004) for the *Cist.* scene, and Lowe (1988) for the *Poen.* scene.

[69] Except perhaps in the very complex sense as follows: it will turn out that the speaker, Selenium, was exposed, was picked up by the *lena*, Gymnasium's mother, who is the other agent in this scene, and was then given to another prostitute, who is now believed to be Selenium's mother. We might say, then, that the *lena* is a pseudo-mother to Selenium, since she picked her up as a tiny baby.

which is of itself unhelpful but looks as though it might be leading up to something informative, but they are interrupted by the older woman, who plays the role of comic clowning. Her first speech is a play on words leading to a formulation typical of Plautine jokers: an odd or paradoxical statement is made, clarification is requested by the naïve interlocutor and the punch-line is delivered:

LE. quod ille dixit, qui secundo uento uectus est tranquillo mari,
uentum gaudeo – ecastor ad ted, ita hodie hic acceptae sumus suauibus modis,
nec nisi disciplina apud te fuit quicquam ibi quin mihi placeret.
SEL. quid ita, amabo? LE. raro nimium dabat quod biberem, id merum infuscabat.
(*Cist.* 14–17)

LE. As the man said who sailed over a calm sea with a following wind, I'm pleased to sea[70] you, so sweetly have you received us here today – except that the training at your place leaves something to be desired. SEL. What's that, please? LE. They didn't pour enough, and what they did was watered down.

In this case, the resolution of the sequence is the *lena*'s conventional self-presentation as *multibiba.* She is upbraided for it by her daughter, but is unrepentant. The first young woman, Selenium, next attempts to resume the exchange of pleasantries which will, we feel sure, eventually lead us into getting somewhere with the play, but she is interrupted again by the *lena*, this time with a diatribe against the rich.[71] The *lena* is clearly playing the role of comic character, pursuing the agenda of the play-performance, rather than the plot, whereas the girls belong to the romantic plot which is having such a struggle to make its way onto the stage. It is in fact the *lena* who gives the first useful expository hint, slipping it in naturally on the tail of her diatribe. It may well be significant that it is at this point that the metre changes from the complex *canticum* with which the play opens, into a recitative metre, iambic septenarii:

quia nos libertinae sumus, et ego et tua mater, ambae
meretrices fuimus: illa te, ego hanc mihi educaui
ex patribus conuenticiis. neque ego hanc superbiai
caussa pepuli ad meretricium quaestum, nisi ut ne essurirem.
(*Cist.* 38–41)

Since we are both freedwomen, your mother and I, we were prostitutes: she brought you up, and I brought this one up, from fathers who were our clients. For pride's

[70] Such is my pathetic attempt to recreate Plautus' joke on *uentus* 'wind' and *uentus* past participle of *uenio*. Plautus flies this joke also at *Cur.* 314–16, on which see pp. 169–70.

[71] Cf. e.g. Periplectomenus on not having children, the evils of rich wives, etc. (670–722), which is a spectacular piece of delaying action to the progress of *Mil.*

sake I would not have driven her into the profession, except that otherwise I would starve.

Moore (1998b: 248) says that 'passages where the audience learns important information are usually unaccompanied'. In his argument about the musical structure of Roman comedy, in which the crucial distinction is between unaccompanied iambic senarii and all other metres accompanied, the change of meter at 38 would not be significant.[72] Although I would not suggest that the change here has a major structural effect, Moore's comment (249) that 'in a number of passages the music stops at the moment the informational section begins and starts again as soon as that section of the play is complete, thus creating a framed unaccompanied unit' (which he applies particularly to the double prologue of *Cistellaria* which is about to begin at 120), would seem to have some significance for the change of meter at 38.[73] There is not a correspondingly marked closure to the informative passage: the next change is to trochaic septenarii at 59, as is appropriate to the heightened emotion of Selenium's speech. Selenium now tries to nudge her way into the play, by attempting to distract the *lena* from her Plautine prostitute play, with a hint at her own, Selenium's, agenda, the romantic plot and marriage, but the *lena* responds with a mildly crude distortion of *nubere* which keeps the play away from its romantic plot:

> SEL. at satius fuerat eam uiro dare nuptum potius. LE. heia!
> haec quidem ecastor cottidie uiro nubit, nupsitque hodie,
> nubet mox noctu: numquam ego hanc uiduam cubare siui.
> nam si haec non nubat, lugubri fame familia pereat.
> (*Cist.* 42–5)

SEL. But it would be better rather for her to be given in marriage to a man. LE. Hey! She sure does marry a man every day, she has married one today, and soon she'll marry one tonight. I'll never let her sleep in a spinster's bed. For if she didn't marry, the whole household would perish horribly of hunger.

These jollities continue for a few more lines, until Gymnasium has her try at turning the tide. She notices that all this comedy is not pleasing Selenium, whose appearance is pale and sad (romantic, here, rather than tragic):

72 Marshall (2006: ch. 5) also argues for an operative musical structure of 'arcs', involving alternations of substantial passages of iambic senarii (which he describes as the 'rise' or 'inhalation' of the arc) and passages of mixed metres (the 'fall' or 'exhalation').

73 *Cist.* 38 does receive a mention in Gerick's list (1998: 140 n. 36) of marked changes of metre, under the category 'Bericht, Erklärung, Mitteilung, Drohung, allgemeine Sentenz', of which the second is most relevant.

. . . sed tu inter istaec uerba,
meus oculus, mea Selenium, – numquam ego te tristiorem
uidi esse. quid, cedo, te opsecro, tam abhorret hilaritudo?
neque munda adaeque es, ut soles (hoc sis uide, ut petiuit
suspiritum alte) et pallida es. eloquere utrumque nobis,
et quid tibi est et quid uelis nostram operam, ut nos sciamus.
noli, opsecro, lacrumis tuis mi exercitum imperare.

(*Cist.* 50–6)

But among all this talk, my dear Selenium – I've never seen you look sadder. Please tell me, why is this jollity upsetting you so much? You're not as clean and tidy as you usually are (look at that deep sigh!) and you're pale. Tell us what's the matter with you and what help you want from us, so that we can know. Don't, please, order an attack on me with your tears.

Her question is the one that is needed to get the exposition going: what's the matter? The answer, obviously, is love. While Gymnasium tries to convince her friend that, as a prostitute, she does not have the luxury of falling in love, she also inadvertently hints to the audience that this will be a recognition comedy. When she explicitly says that she has 'known' no man except her lover Alcesimarchus, Selenium is set up as a freeborn citizen who is accidentally in the position of a prostitute: she will therefore marry the hero in the end. There is another hint that the play is working towards a citizen marriage, in that it was at a religious festival, to which her (supposed) mother had taken her, that Alcesimarchus first saw her and fell in love with her. This *topos* belongs to the citizen affair. In place of direct exposition, then, we have occasional knowing hints.

The *lena* continues to interrupt Selenium's story with comic comments, but nonetheless we manage to learn that the lover is being forced by his father into a respectable marriage, and that the supposed mother of Selenium is insisting that she should return home, rather than stay in hopes that Alcesimarchus will come back to her. This, then, is the answer to the opening implied question about why Selenium is thanking Gymnasium and her mother profusely – she wants Gymnasium to keep house for her for a couple of days, while she goes to her mother. Selenium, embodiment of the romantic plot, leaves tearfully, and Gymnasium goes into the house, the final word of the scene being her *uale* to her mother (119). This scene has constantly ignored the presence of the audience, but perhaps this last word shows a trace of the *ualete* which conventionally closes a prologue.

Be that as it may, the next scene makes another, more explicit, attempt at giving us The Beginning of the Play. The girls having departed, the *lena* is left in control of the stage, and moves for the first time in this play into the 'normal' opening metre, iambic senarii, in which the play will continue throughout her speech and the delayed prologue by Auxilium which follows it.[74] The *lena* delivers her version of The Prologue, introduced by a pseudo-realistic self-justification, that women like her always talk too much when they have had a drink (which is most of the time). Now we hear the story of the exposing of baby Selenium, and how she, the *lena*, gave the baby to Selenium's supposed mother to bring up as her own. Like so many prologue-speakers, the *lena* spices her tale with unnecessary but entertaining details, and addresses the audience directly, in order to draw them closer into the world of the play, by letting them in on a secret:[75]

> id duae nos solae scimus, ego quae illi dedi
> et illa quae a me accepit – praeter uos quidem.
> haec sic res gesta est. si quid usus uenerit,
> meminisse ego hanc rem uos uolo. ego abeo domum.
> (*Cist.* 145–8)

The two of us are the only ones to know, I who gave it to her and she who received it from me – except for you. This is how it was done. If anything comes of it, I want you to remember this. I'm going home.

And finally.

After the *lena* has left the stage, perhaps again imitating the *ualete* of the end of a prologue by 'going in', the proper Prologue comes out. This is the deified concept Auxilium, who is greatly miffed that his help is hardly needed any more:

> Vtrumque haec, et multiloqua et multibiba, est anus.
> satin uix reliquit deo quod loqueretur loci,
> ita properauit de puellae proloqui
> suppositione. quod si tacuisset, tamen
> ego eram dicturus, deu', qui poteram planius.
> (*Cist.* 149–53)

That old woman is both – a drinker and a talker. She's hardly left any room for a god to get a word in. She's hurried to give you the prologue about the supposition of the girl. If she had kept quiet, I would have told you about it, I, a god, who can do so more clearly.

[74] After that, Alcesimarchus comes in, with a song in anapaests, for which see Marshall (2006: 233).

[75] Hurka (2004: 41–2) argues that Plautus developed the *lena*'s monologue in the original to give it prologic features in addition to an existing delayed prologue; but cf. Goldberg (2004) in the same volume. The *lena*'s speech has long been suspected of textual corruption in different ways: the disruptive, self-interrupting performance reflected in the manuscripts would accord well with her behaviour in the preceding scene and could be designed to reflect *flos Liberi*, as Goldberg (2004: 387) mentions.

But do the gods have more divine knowledge than comic characters in this play? Auxilium just has to make do with telling us the masculine and free side to the story.[76] His role as Prologue having been already usurped at least once, if not twice, he leaves the audience with a particularly fine example of a *ualete*, discussed further below. There has to be *something* left for the god to do.

in medias res*: doing it differently*

The wittiest of all openings is surely that of *Tristram Shandy*. Here the Horatian opposition between a despised beginning-from-the-egg and an admired plunge *in medias res* is joyously exploded. Tristram, the supposed teller of the story, begins indeed from his insemination, invoking as he does so, with crack-brained inverse scholarship, the authority of Horace. But Sterne simultaneously bewilders the first-time reader, who is pitched *in medias res*, into the middle of an ill-conducted marital engagement, which is simply unintelligible until we know the *previous* history of those concerned. (Nuttall 1992: 209)

Literature is full of the lore of beginnings despite the tyranny of starting a work *in medias res*, a convention that burdens the beginning with the pretense that it is not one. (Said 1975: 43)

Scholarship is historically so inimical to this kind of literary cleverness on the part of Plautus and his audience that it used often to be debated whether the Plautine plays which apparently begin without a prologue could really have done so, or whether in fact something is lost. Slater's discussion on the non-need for an expository prologue to *Epidicus* is exemplary in counteracting this tendency.[77] My concern is with how Plautus contrived this sophisticated alternative to the prologic opening. Although plays which begin *in mediis rebus* by definition formally ignore the audience, in several cases Plautus stuffs the scene with programmatic punches of a more or less explicit variety. In a few cases, however, the opening scene resolutely ignores the fact that it is a play, and that the audience might want to know what is going on, as was discussed above in the case of *Cistellaria*. No piece of theatre can be wholly immune to metatheatre, but occasionally even Plautus pretends to forget.

[76] Feeney (1998: 90), considering the (usual female) gender of personified abstractions, connects the comedy of Auxilium's lateness and bumbling complaints with neuter grammatical gender.

[77] Slater (2000: 16). See Duckworth (1940) for discussion of the older view (which he quietly opposes) that the play must have had a prologue which has since been lost; Slater (2000: 38 n. 9) for refutation of the argument for a lost prologue to *Per.*, and 28 for consideration of the question with regard to *Epid.*

Curculio has a delightful *in medias res* beginning that struggles to get going, while in the meantime playing programmatic games with the door, which must be coaxed into opening up, and later with the *lena* whose sensory perception of the scent of wine starts off the overdetermined physicality of this play.[78] There are other hints which foreshadow what is going to happen, such as the false lead about the beloved being a sister (51: she is *a me pudica . . . quasi soror mea sit* ('as pure from me as if she were my sister'), which might tempt us to think that such will turn out to be the case, as happens to Stratippocles in *Epidicus*, but instead she turns out to be the sister of the rival Therapontigonus), and the *oculissumum* door (15: where the 'eyes' are a term of endearment, as well as a joke with *occlusissumum*, 'most shut') which looks to the *monoculus* Curculio. The play starts with a classic initiatory move, a question from Palinurus (slave) to Phaedromus (master) as to where he is going, why he is dressed up like that and what the play is about. It both is and is not answered by Phaedromus' 'where love calls' (3): this tells us what we could have guessed anyway, that he is a lover, but not where we, and the plot, are going.[79]

Similar is the aggressively programmatic opening to *Mostellaria*, which comes hurtling in with one slave's thrust against another – *exi*, 'get out!' ('and get on with the play'):

> Exi e culina sis foras, mastigia,
> qui mi inter patinas exhibes argutias.
> egredere, erilis permities, ex aedibus.
> (*Mos.* 1–3)

Get outside, out of the kitchen, you rogue, you who show me your tricks among the pans. Come out of the house, bane of your master.

This may not tell us anything directly, but it indicates a great deal programmatically. This is going to be a rough and tumble play, in which a 'clever slave' is going to come in for abuse (*mastigia* is standard comic

[78] See Moore (2005); Fraenkel (1960: 97); Sharrock (2008).

[79] The old view that *Cur.*, and also *Epid.*, once had a prologue which is now lost, for which see Leo (1912: 196, 221), was already deemed most unlikely by Duckworth (1994: 230, 1st edn 1952), although in his commentary on *Epid.* (1940: 97) he is more circumspect. On the *Cur.* opening as a 'puzzling mime', see Arnott (1995: 187); also Arnott (1992). On the script versus improvisation of the opening, Arnott (1995: 188–9): 'It is a carefully constructed acting script for its characters, informing them not merely what they must say – keeping strictly to the words written, for otherwise there would be grave danger of unmetricality – but also what they must do in comic routines where the text provides a clear shorthand but the improvisatory skills of director and actors are needed to turn the written words into dramatically exciting action.' On this opening scene as a *paraclausithyron* which uses motifs found elsewhere rather than being dependent on a particular model, see Danese (2002: 143–4).

abuse) but get away with his cleverness (*argutias* is standard comic cleverness), causing trouble to his master, especially with regard to the house (*foras, ex aedibus*). In order to start any play, the actors have to 'come out', and that is what makes *exi* so initiatory a word for the opening of a drama, but in this case the emphasis on the house will turn out to have particular significance in this, the estate agent's play. The opening scene will continue with other hints, like the town/country opposition and the absence of the master (*sine modo adueniat senex*, 10). Despite opening *in mediis rebus*, and therefore nominally realistically, this play is not going to make much pretence of not being a play. Indeed, the fact that this opening scene is in the normal opening meter iambic senarii, rather than the trochaic septenarii that might be associated with this kind of aggressive scene, or song such as opens both the demure *Cistellaria* and *Stichus* and the equally aggressive *Epidicus*, may itself be contributing to the false-prologue feel. The opening of *Miles gloriosus* is another quasi-false prologue. The soldier's first line *curate ut splendor meo sit clupeo clarior* ('make sure the splendour of my shield is brighter . . .') shares several linguistic features with prologues, such as the second-person plural imperative, and the alliteration. But Pyrgopolynices is, at this point, spectacularly unaware that he is in a play. Both *Miles gloriosus* and *Mostellaria* have *in medias res* openings followed by monologues which play an explicitly prologic role.

One programmatic *in medias res* opening which does not use metre to pretend to be a prologue is that of *Epidicus*, referred to above, which opens with a complicated *canticum*, the first two lines of which are in trochaic septenarii (a metre often associated with agitated activity). In this beginning, as in the whole play, Plautus combines allusive and suggestive metatheatre with a refusal to be explicit, in contrast, for example, with the clearer cases of internal plotting and playwrights which will be considered in the next chapter. In *Epidicus*, Plautus projects himself into the *architectus*-persona without directly saying 'hey, guys, I'm the poet'. The opening is as programmatic as any direct address by a prologue, but the reader is expected to do some of the work. Epidicus rushes in shouting 'hey you!', and grabbing the cloak of his companion who is trying to get away. As in the case of *Curculio* and *Pseudolus*, a question is used as an initiatory device, but in this case the questioner is trying to resist the comedy that his question provokes. He asks (Epidicus has spoken first):

> quis properantem me reprehendit pallio?
> (*Epid.* 1)

Who is it who snatches me by the *pallium* as I hurry?

There are several programmatic elements at work here: first, a parody of the conventional comic meeting scene, when at least one of the principals requires an absurd amount of time and help to recognise the other, which is itself a parody of the comic convention of introducing characters by naming them; second, a parody of the epic and tragic scene where some god catches the hero from behind to stop him doing whatever he was bent on (originally in Hom. *Il.* 1.194, where Athene prevents Achilles from attacking Agamemnon, and parodied also at Pl. *Men.* 870); and finally, an admission that someone is trying to drag Thesprio into a comedy, for it is the *pallium* – the little Greek cloak which designates the *fabula palliata* – that Epidicus has caught. The word *pallio*, indeed, comes as something of a stylistic let-down at the end of Thesprio's rather grand line (the first line of the play, shared with Epidicus' opening *heus adulescens!*).[80] Epidicus' struggle to force his companion into comedy is continued a few lines later, when he complains with typical Plautine wordplay of Thesprio's *gradibus grandibus* ('big steps', 13).[81] Thesprio's name, nominally designating origin in Thesprotia,[82] may contain a jokingly comic version of a pretentious reference to the semi-mythical founder of drama, Thespis. Thesprio is forced into recognising Epidicus: *Epidicumne ego conspicor?* ('Is that Epidicus I see?', 4). The conventional recognition is almost certainly also designed to draw our attention to the eponymous status of Epidicus. If we know in advance that the play is by Plautus and it is called *Epidicus*, then we may interpret this programmatic naming of character and play as an *in mediis rebus* alternative to the formulaic production of technical details by the prologue.

After its spectacular bang of an opening, however, the (very complex) plot of this play has to work hard to get started. Once Thesprio has acknowledged that he is in a comedy with Epidicus, the two of them continue to mess around before Epidicus manages to extract the beginnings of the plot from his interlocutor. The first relevant interchange is at 20, *quid erilis noster filius?* ('What about our young master?'), which confirms the suspicion that there might be an *adulescens amans* in this play. It turns out, however, only to be a partial interchange, for Thesprio's reply is

80 Duckworth (1940: 101), while offering several parallels for the phrase *reprehendit pallio*, notes that 'it is surprising that Thesprio wears a *pallium* and not the *chlamys* usually worn by a traveller'.

81 The personified and poetically overdetermined Tragedy progresses *ingenti . . . passu* at Ov. *Am.* 3.1.13. It is perhaps optimistic to suggest that a similar metapoetic implication would occur to Plautus' first audience, but circumstantial support for the metaphor of size applying to tragedy could be gained from Aristophanes' *Frogs* and the comparison between Aeschylus and Euripides. Duckworth (1940: 110) gives parallels for the sound play and supports a military interpretation.

82 Duckworth (1940: 96).

entertaining but unhelpful – *ualet pugilice atque athletice* ('he's well boxerly and athleticly'). This is the cue for the dialogue to be sidetracked again, with a wonderful piece of comic nonsense about the young man's less than heroic exploits in war, and need for a bit of epic backbone in the form of some new weapons as a gift from Thetis (35–6). After this interchange, however, Epidicus manages to extract a bit more plot – the young man has brought home a girl, whose presence is something of an embarrassment before his father. Just when we think we recognise the typical New Comic plot, however, Epidicus pulls a fast one on us, with a bit of his own exposition which shows us that there was another plot going on in the background, before the beginning of the play:

> EP. qur eam emit? TH. animi caussa. EP. quot illic homo animos habet?
> nam certo, priu' quam hinc ad legionem abiit domo,
> ipse mandauit mihi ab lenone ut fidicina,
> quam amabat, emeretur sibi. id ei impetratum reddidi.
>
> (*Epid.* 45–8)

EP. Why did he buy her? TH. Because he wanted to. EP. How much wanting does this guy have? For certainly, before he went off to the legion away from home, he ordered me to buy from the *leno* the music girl he was in love with. And I obeyed the order.

This pseudo-prologue is in the hands of someone who is only going to give out the information he sees fit to divulge. In response to Thesprio's questioning about what the young master has done, and what Epidicus has done about it, our hero answers enigmatically: *quia cottidie ipse ad me ab legione epistulas / mittebat – sed taceam optumum est*... ('Since he himself kept sending me letters every day from the army – but it's best to keep quiet', 58–9). So he won't tell us either.

Most *in medias res* openings in Plautus, then, seem to have noticed that they are part of a play. The same can hardly be said for the extraordinary *Stichus*, which begins with a sung duet (*canticum*) between the two sisters:[83]

> PAN. Credo ego miseram
> fuisse Penelopam,
> soror, suo ex animo,
> quae tam diu uidua
> uiro suo caruit;
> nam nos eius animum
> de nostris factis noscimus, quarum uiri hinc apsunt,
> quorumque nos negotiis apsentum, ita ut aequom est,
> sollicitae noctes et dies, soror, sumu' semper.

[83] See Arnott (1972: 54–5) on the mixtures of conventionality and difference here.

PAM. nostrum officium
nos facere aequomst
neque id magi' facimus
quam nos monet pietas.
sed hic, soror, adsidedum: multa uolo tecum
loqui de re uiri.

(*St.* 1–10)

PAN. I think, sister, that poor Penelope must have been heart-sick, since for such a long time she was on her own without her husband. For we know how she felt from our own experience, since our husbands are away, and we are always worried night and day about their affairs in their absence, as is right, sister. PAM. It is right for us to do our duty, nor are we doing more than piety requires. But come and sit here, sister: I've got lots I want to say to you about this husband-matter.

The opening tableau might suggest two prostitutes, as in *Cistellaria* or *Poenulus*, but that possibility is quickly belied by the reference to Penelope, widowhood, *uiri*, *officium* and *pietas*. The scene does offer some crucial background information for the rather unusual plot – that the women are married, and devoted, and that their husbands are physically absent but not emotionally estranged. It tells us this, however, without for a moment acknowledging our presence. Instead, we seem to be privy to a nice little tête-à-tête between two young women who are erotically attractive but entirely unavailable.

Ritual initiation

Whatever their method of opening, Roman comic plays are religious acts: not in the manner of modern religious drama or medieval morality plays, which directly communicate the truths of the producing and watching faith community, but in the context of their performance as part of ritual *ludi*, irrespective of their content.[84] Recent developments in the study of Roman religion have enabled us to move away from regarding the plays' religious context as an empty shell filled with an independent work of literature or of entertainment, such as was expressed for example by Fraenkel.[85] Even so

[84] See Scullard (1981: 40 and 184) on the preliminary rituals involved in the *ludi scaenici*, apropos the *romani*; Csapo and Slater (1995: 207–20); Marshall (2006: 16–20).

[85] Fraenkel (1960: 365) says that a major difference between Greek comedy (esp. Old Comedy) and Roman was that in Greek comedy there was a great ritual sense, but not in Roman. Murray (1943), writing in the tradition of religio-mythic anthropology, allows religious significance to Roman comedy. On reading Roman comedy as part of the religious politics of Rome, see Henderson (1999: 18). On the role of theatre and the theatrical festivals in the political life of the middle republic, see Gruen (1992: ch. 5). Morgan (1990) argues for the personal religious importance of the *ludi* in the early second century. His interest is primarily in the *ludi florales*. Beard, North and Price (1998: 100–3) discuss the role of (real) priests in the rising importance of the *ludi*.

subtle a critic of religion and literature as Denis Feeney, however, regards Horace's *Carmen saeculare* as the only extant work of Latin literature which was performed as part of a ritual.[86] The plays of Roman comedy were indeed not ritual in the narrow sense, but they were religious and ritualistic in at least a secondary sense, and so perhaps might have the audacity to claim for themselves a role as works of Latin literature performed as part of rituals.[87] To this suggestion we could add the insight of a number of scholars that Roman religion is partly constituted by its own interpretation;[88] the contribution of ritual and religious behaviour within the fictional world of the plays themselves;[89] and the power of religious language to slip in and out of formal situations, between serious and comic or even parodic usage, within the community by which it is constituted. To this extent, the modern reader who decides to take account of the ritual context of Roman comedy is in a stronger position than the modern audience of performance, for whom that context is wholly lost. It is my suggestion that the religious nature of the act of comedy is sometimes explicitly played out in the relationship between the prologue and the audience, in which the Prologue acts as a kind of 'master of ceremonies' or, in the broadest sense, priest.[90]

When the Prologue calls for silence, he is using the metaphor of the ritual 'silence' or 'good speaking' which necessarily accompanies religious observance: *fauete linguis*. Plautus' cleverest coup in this regard is to use tragedy as a link between the comic prologue and ritual behaviour: *Poenulus* begins self-referentially with a literary critical comment on the beginning of a tragedy, 'Aristarchus' *Achilles*'. The Prologue dresses up his 'call for silence' in what is probably a quotation or near-quotation from the opening of that play:[91]

[86] See Feeney (1998: 37–8) on the complex sense in which the *Saec.* was and was not part of the ritual of the *ludi saeculares*.

[87] Cf. the fuzzy and contested boundaries of what constitutes proper parts of the ritual in an Andean village, as discussed by Bourque (2000).

[88] Beard (1990: 42); Feeney (1998: 127–31); Smith (2000: 136).

[89] Jocelyn (2001) gives a full account of religiosity and religious language apropos *Epid.*, with wider implications. He maintains an agnostic view of Plautus' 'policy on religious matters', which he regards as subordinate to the task of entertainment.

[90] I should stress that I mean the designation 'priest' in a very broad, metaphorical sense, not at all suggesting that the prologue-speaker is in any literal sense a priest. On Roman priests, see Beard (1990: esp. 44), where she argues that there was no straightforward category of 'priest' in the Roman world, no 'core of priestliness' in any easily recognisable sense.

[91] See Slater (1992a: 135); Jocelyn (1967: 165–6). Jocelyn (1969a), who suggests that it is not actually necessary to follow the general assumption that these lines are a direct quotation from the Latin tragedy, argues that the primary object of parody here (and of linguistic register in Ennius) is 'a real-life Roman *imperator*' (112). For the ritual call, see Scullard (1981: 24).

> 'sileteque et tacete atque animum aduortite,
> audire iubet uos imperator'.
>
> (*Poen.* 3–4)

Be silent and be quiet and pay attention; the general orders you to listen.

Jocelyn suggests that the line has 'a pompous tragic ring', but that *tacete* falls amusingly flat after *sileteque et*: such redundant repetition is, however, common in ritual language and need not undermine the ritual flavour. Ennius (assuming that he, rather than Aristarchus, is the author of the tragedy) may have himself appropriated the discourse of ritual for his equally 'religious' drama: the surprising part about the comic prologue's quasi-ritualistic behaviour is that it can be a parody (in the sense of a joking repetition, slightly askew, of a respected discourse) while at the same time drawing on a living sense of precisely that discourse.

The most common explicitly ritualistic behaviour in a Plautine prologue, however, is the prayer for divine blessing. When the prologue-speaker leaves the stage in order to allow the play finally to start, he often bids the audience farewell with formulaic and ritual good wishes for divine favour in war and peace, at home and abroad.[92] This happens especially in cases where the prologue is spoken by a divine character or a *prologus* who is not otherwise involved in the play. Such valedictions allude to the Menandrian tactic of ending a play with a prayer for victory,[93] in place of the *plaudite* and its variants which close Roman comedies. The difference in allusion is important: Menander prays for victory for this play in the competition (as do Aristophanes and Euripides) and for the favour of the audience; Plautus prays for military and patriotic victory, and the general favour of the Roman gods, for the Roman people as a result of their observance of the comic ritual. If the audience play their role properly, and perform the ritual of the play correctly, then the gods are pleased, and reward them not only with a great play, but also with all the other successes that show them to be favoured by the gods. In this sense, the play forms part of the Roman relationship with the gods, and as such could be loosely categorised as 'prayer'.[94]

[92] *As.* 15, *Capt.* 67–8, *Cas.* 87–8, *Cist.* 197–202, *Poen.* 128 (although the wish is just for the blessing of *Salus*, rather than specifically military safety), *Rud.* 82.

[93] As happens for example at the ends of *Dyskolos*, *Samia*, *Sikyonios*, *Misoumenos*. Aristophanic plays abound in victory songs of various types, but it is in the parabasis (which has affinities with the Roman comic prologue) that Aristophanes prays for victory in the contest.

[94] The Roman relationship with the gods is one of bargaining: *do ut des* (on which see Scullard 1981: 25). Beard, North and Price (1998: 34) argue that this relationship should be seen not as 'contractual' but rather as negotiation in which reciprocity played an important role. On the connection between Roman comedy and victory in the Punic wars, see Leigh (2004b: 37–8).

Despite the diversity of tone and pose of moral seriousness across the range of Plautus' plays, this formulaic prayer remains remarkably constant. We would expect the rather pompous divine prologue of *Rudens*, the star Arcturus who is very proud of his mission from Jupiter, to bless the audience with military success (82) as a result of the play, but elsewhere a very different prologue to a very different play makes a very similar point. *Asinaria* is a delightful piece of nonsense, a complete ass of a play about a *senex amator* with a ferocious wife, who says he wants to help his son's affair, but really wants to have it himself.[95] The prologue is jokey and informal, opening with:

> Hoc agite sultis, spectatores, nunciam,
> quae quidem mihi atque uobis res uortat bene
> gregique huic et dominis atque conductoribus.
> (*As.* 1–3)

Now then, spectators, please pay attention to this – which should turn out well for me and you and the troupe and the masters and hirers.

The tone is light and colloquial, and the speaker strikes a deal with us in very easy terms: 'you like the play, everyone benefits, you and us all'. The *praeco* is likewise playfully undertreated. He is asked to 'call for silence' – and in the next line told to sit down and shut up. That's quite enough bombast for this little play. No need for exposition either: 'You don't need to know the plot because it's just a bit of fun – *lepos ludusque . . . ridicula res* (13–14). So like it, and you'll be (guess what?) successful Romans, as you always have been.'

> . . . date benigne operam mihi
> ut uos, ut alias, pariter nunc Mars adiuuet.
> (*As.* 14–15)

Kindly oblige me, so may Mars, as on other occasions, aid you now also.

At the end of the play, the epilogue-speaker will invite the audience to release the *senex* from punishment, and therefore to return him to Roman status, by their applause. The message is: enjoy this play, sanction this piece of iniquity – and (remarkably) you will be upholding Roman values. I suggest that we should see this ironic message not as subversion of those values, but as an odd, inverted, comic affirmation of them. If a *ridicula res* about some asses sounds like an odd way to pray for victory, then we should expand our notion of what constitutes religious action.

[95] The entertaining and astute reading of this play by Henderson (2006) should be required reading.

The most extended of these 'good wishes' from the prologue is that in the (much-)delayed prologue to *Cistellaria*, where Auxilium takes six lines (197–202) to instruct the audience on how to be Romans, thus praising and rewarding them, by implication, in the same act. Be good spectators, be good Romans, perform this ritual properly: that's how you win the Punic wars. Auxilium's language is thick with the alliterations, repetitions, redundancies and duplications which are characteristic of both comedy and ritual language, topped up with an etymologising joke on the Prologue's own name in the phrase *augete auxilia*:

> haec sic res gesta est. bene ualete et uincite
> uirtute uera, quod fecistis antidhac;
> seruate uostros socios, ueteres et nouos,
> augete auxilia uostris iustis legibus,
> perdite perduellis, parite laudem et lauream,
> ut uobis uicti Poeni poenas sufferant.
> (*Cist.* 197–202)

That's how this matter has been done. Farewell and conquer by true valour, as you have done up to now; keep well your allies, old and new, increase your auxiliaries with your just laws, destroy your enemies, win praise and laurels, so that for you the conquered Punics may suffer punishment.

Instructions on how to behave, finished off with performatively prayerful good wishes, feature also in the prologues to *Captiui* and *Casina*, two plays which stand at opposite ends of Plautus' spectrum of respectability. The best-known example of the prologue-as-prayer, however, is the magnificently outrageous opening to *Amphitruo*, in which Mercury, playing the Prologue and playing the slave, keeps the audience entertained for a massive 498 lines, first on his own (the prologue), then with his dupe and double Sosia (first scene), then alone again (the prologue again), while Jupiter is (again) enjoying an extended night with Alcumena in the house, delaying dawn and the beginning of the play at his pleasure.[96] The prologue itself begins with 'the longest sentence in Plautus',[97] in which Mercury, in his capacity as god of the financial quarter, offers help with the audience's business affairs in return for their attention to the play. His highly entertaining

[96] See Christenson's (2000) discussion *ad loc.*, where he notes both the ritual and the legalist aspects of the prologue. See also Auhagen (1999) on features of the prologue as arising out of improvisatory drama. If we are to envisage that the oral/improvisatory influence is an intertext alongside others (including one or more particular Greek plays and/or the generality of Greek plays), then this is helpful; if as an alternative to artistic genius, less so.

[97] Christenson (2000: 134).

engagement with the audience is shot through with ritual and contractual linguistic features. We have, for example, the slow and strongly alliterative opening lines (*Vt uos in uostris uoltis mercimoniis / emundis uendundisque me laetum lucris*, etc., 'As you want me to be well-disposed to all your business affairs, in buying and selling lucre . . .'); the anaphora of clauses beginning *ut* (1, 4, 8, 9, 13 and 14 if that is genuine); formulaic reduplications like *quasque incepistis res quasque inceptabitis* ('things which you have undertaken and will undertake', 7);[98] listing of the deity's different capacities, which in this case include commerce, messages and perhaps the guiding of the dead (a hint of a joke in the call for *silentium*, 15),[99] although Mercury cleverly forebears to mention his sovereignty over trickery and lies;[100] the formulaic phrase *nam uos . . .* ('for you . . .', 11). There is a strong hint at a divine epiphany at 17–19 (*uenio . . . uenerim*, 17–19), which then slips into a piece of court oratory.[101] From here the way is opened for Mercury to lay down the law to the audience about how to behave, and to introduce a whole series of edicts about how the entire performance is to be run, by all those involved in the experience. The legalistic language which he now employs (67–74) shares many of the features of the prayer language which he has just used, and culminates in the alliterative *uirtute dixit uos uictores uiuere* ('he has said that you live as victors by your valour', 75), which hints towards that not-uncommon feature of the prologue's religious relationship with the audience, that good play-behaviour brings success in war and politics, enhanced on this occasion by the special divine authority of the speaker.

Christenson (2000, *ad loc.*) has rightly noted that the opening lines of Mercury's prologue constitute an inverted prayer. I would like to suggest that it is not just this opening but in fact the whole play which is – however comically, however playfully – a hymn, a hymn to Jupiter and to Hercules (never named but constantly sub-present – an absent presence

[98] In prayer formula, the need to cover all eventualities can encourage the repetition of a verb in different tenses, so that the other party cannot sneak out of the deal by hiding behind a linguistic imprecision.

[99] See Feeney (1991: 116) for how a republican audience, in that case of Livius Andronicus, might see Mercury 'in the role of Hermes, the escorter of dead souls'.

[100] Christenson's hint (2000: 134) that we should not trust this notoriously untrustworthy god is a nice touch. He says '[t]he comic irony in putting this contract in the mouth of a god known for lying and chicanery would not be lost on at least some of the audience'. See Feeney (1998: 27–8), esp. for the bilingual jokes on Mercury's name.

[101] On this prologue as an example of archaic rhetoric, see Auhagen (1999: 125–6); Jocelyn (1967: 43).

before its time, perhaps).[102] The 'hymn' celebrates the greatness and power of the Father of Gods and Men, and the birth of the hero-god who has been worshipped in Rome since early times. Narratives of the births of gods play a recognised part in ancient hymns, for example in the first Homeric Hymn (Dionysus), 3 (Apollo), 4 (Hermes) and 6 (Aphrodite).[103] We do not know at which festival *Amphitruo* was performed, but one of the possible occasions would provide a particularly neat counterpart to its content, as well as its performance. The Ludi Romani were a September festival in honour of Jupiter Optimus Maximus, and were in origin linked to the triumphal processions which culminated at his temple (dedicated 13 September 509 BC).[104] The play's internal occasion is Amphitruo's return home from his successful campaign, which will be accompanied by the birth of his son, and his acceptance of a special relationship with Jupiter. Mary Beard reads the *Amphitruo* as 'an in-your-face parody of triumphal *mimesis*', in which Amphitruo as triumphant general and double for Jupiter plays on the role of the triumphator as someone '"being", "playing", or "acting", god'.[105] Together with the aetiological account of the dual identity

[102] Hardie (2002): the Ovidian and other Augustan poetry with which he is concerned do indeed lend themselves well to the kind of allusive experience of non-presence which Hardie analyses, but even drama can play that game, especially in a case such as this where a well-known (and supernatural) story is at stake. For comedy and the absent presence, see Hardie (2002: 16, 107–9).

[103] Nesselrath (1995) argues that a concentration of plays about births of gods coincides with the movement from Old to Middle Comedy in the early fourth century BC; also Christenson (2000: 51). But see Csapo (2000: esp. 118) for objections to reading the development in a chronologically linear fashion.

[104] See Scullard (1981: 183–6); Beard, North and Price (1998: 40–1) on the Ludi Romani, and 43–7 on the symbolic connections between the games and the agricultural and military year. Scullard differentiates between the Ludi Romani as triumph-festival, and the 'October Horse' ritual on the Ides of October (193–4), together with the *armilustrium* which purified the returning army from the 'dangerous infection that it may have incurred from contact with bloodshed and strangers' (195), as religious marking of the end of the campaigning season. Since he later (213) describes the triumph as 'in origin . . . simply the king's return from a victorious campaign with his army and his thanksgiving offering to the god of the State', including the notion of purification of the returning army, Scullard's account could not be taken to negate the possibility that the Ludi Romani are connected with the celebration of the returning army. It is of course the case that at this period in Roman history the connections between the calendrical/festival year and the natural year were inaccurate in a way that seems extraordinary to the modern observer, but, as Feeney (2007: 198–201) shows, it bothers Varro's pre-Julian mindset not at all to describe a festival of grape-picking in association with the Vinalia of April. If *Amph.* was performed at the Ludi Romani, it matters less whether that festival actually took place in the autumn in that particular year than that the associations of the festival with a returning army should be active for the audience.

[105] Beard (2003: 41–3). She also suggests that identification of the Ludi Romani as the festival for this play would be deeply tempting, since the magistrate in charge of the proceedings would himself, in his triumphal costume, be playing the role of Amphitruo playing the role of Jupiter playing the role of a man. Halkin (1948) also associated the play with the Roman triumph, seeing Sosia's story of his master's success as a parody of Roman generals' claims for triumphs. Fraenkel (1960: 230) sees the triumphal language here as evidence for the influence of Roman life on Plautine plays.

of Hercules, such a reading enhances the parodic-cum-devotional religious role for comedy. The playwright's blessing on the Roman audience is just what we would expect: success in war, fertility and the favour of the gods.

TERENCE

> ille referre aliter saepe solebat idem.
>
> (Ovid, *Ars amatoria* 2.128)
>
> He often used to relate the same thing in different ways.

None of Terence's plays begins *in mediis rebus* – or perhaps all of them do. All six plays begin with a prologue offering variations on a theme of self-defence against hostile critics, apparently imparting very little information directly about the play in question – and then plunge (us) straight into the action.[106] What sort of an opening is this? How can we fit it into our theatrical experience, based now on at least half a century of *fabula palliata* and much more of staged performance? How did it work?

I am going to suggest that, whether or not Terence ever really argued with critics, what the prologues offer is a comic way of making a programmatic statement. When Terence opens play after play in almost identical terms, it is reasonable to suppose that this was a joke that worked.[107] Since the prologues are similar even to the point of closely repeated vocabulary,[108] it must have been a successful formula. We can well imagine that when we get the dark hint about *siquis . . . qui dictum in se inclementius / existumauit esse* ('. . . anyone who has thought something rather harsh has been said about him', *Eu.* 4–5) for example, or hear *Phormio* open with our old friend the *poeta uetus*, the theatre would immediately erupt into the applause of recognition, as when a popular singer begins a favourite golden oldie unannounced. Terence's colleagues (another word for rivals), if they had any sense, will have joined in the applause. Indeed, if Terence were just abusing the opportunity afforded by the situation (as he claims in the *Andria* prologue), if these are nothing more than 'straight'

[106] The exception, on a straightforward reading of the manuscript tradition, would be the first performance of *Hec.*, but it is highly unlikely that this play was performed first without a prologue.

[107] The alternative view, of 'unpopular Terence', is thankfully now becoming outdated: see Parker (1996: 602–4). Habinek (1998: 56) offers a slant on the prologues in keeping with his view of the elitist nature of Roman literature.

[108] Donatus *ad Eu.* 1: SI QVISQVAM EST QVI PLACERE STVDEAT BONIS *attendenda poetae copia, quod in tot prologis de eadem causa isdem fere sententiis uariis uerbis utitur* (Wessner 1962–3 I: 270). Terence's variations in vocabulary are about as varied as *uariis uerbis*.

representations of a personal fight with a rival, then they would not be likely to make a successful comic introduction to a play, especially when repeated ad nauseam. The remainder of this chapter will consider how these openings might have entertained the audience with something more than personal nastiness disguised as petty bickering about dramatic technique.

Terence's prologues have aroused much critical interest for the imaginative reconstruction of his embattled theatrical career and for their tempting hints about what *palliata* authors may have thought they were doing with Greek originals, but not so much interest as ways of opening plays.[109] Our habits of reading may be inimical to Terence's intratextual dynamics in this respect, for modern readers tend to detach Terence's prologues from his plays, in a way which performance would make impossible: so, before entering into the (endlessly fascinating) question of what the prologues are about, I examine what they are doing, how they function as openings. In performance, in the theatre which is moulded in the tradition of Plautus and Naevius and Caecilius, a play begins when the prologue-speaker comes out and commands the attention of the audience, to exercise his primary prologic role of drawing the audience into the play.[110] Readers have the option of skipping prefatory material, but a reader of the text of comic drama does not. Whatever Terence may pretend (*An.* 6) about the requirements of exposition, he captures his reader/audience not by provoking our imaginative collusion in the creation of a fictional plot, but by stimulating our involvement in the entire world of the play – composition, performance and all.

109 Beacham (1991: 48–51), for example, offers a conventional 'straight' reading of the prologues, as does Brothers (2000: 16–20). 'Straight' also, but unusual in taking the part of Luscius Lanuvinus, is Dér (1989). See also Segal (2001a: 226). Goldberg (1983) is excellent on their rhetorical nature, as is his discussion of their relationship with oratory and especially Cato in his 1986 book, at 40. Pohlenz (1956) is remarkable in placing the prologues within a literary tradition; Taliercio (1988) makes a good, if brief, case for a programmatic role for the prologues; Gilula (1989) is a valuable reading of the metatheatrical role of Ambivius Turpio; brief discussion in Slater (1992b), also Lada-Richards (2004) on the *Hec.* prologue. One of the most important readings of the prologues in conjunction with their plays is Gowers (2004), which argues that '[t]he plays can be read in sequence as constructing a particular image of Terence the playwright, while conversely the prologues can be read between the lines as mirroring the plays they present but apparently sideline' (151). Smith (2004) in the same volume also suggests a programmatic function in the prologue (esp. to the *Ph.*), making particular use of the language of economics at work in prologue and play, on which see Gowers (2004: 158).

110 My discussion above has suggested that exposition is a device of the true primary prologic function, creative beginning. Pohlenz (1956: 434) describes Terence's refusal of exposition as 'ein programmatischer Bruch mit der Tradition', which at some explicit level remains correct. Dér (1989: 283) and Gilula (1989: 106) also make strong claims for the originality of Terence's activity in the prologues.

Beginning at the beginning

As noted above, the semiotics of opening places a huge burden on the crucial initiatory moment, a burden which is carried by the prologue-speaker who has to command attention from the audience – and to *make things happen* – simply by the power of his own presence. Plautus used a variety of speakers for this task, including gods, internal characters and anonymous prologue-speakers whose only role (Janus-like, Terminus-like) is to oversee the entrance to the play. Terence takes up and develops the last of these Plautine possibilities, using only 'external' *prologi*, who speak on behalf of the poet. But he makes a daring innovation, which is to put a name and an identity to the anonymous *prologus*, and one which comes not from the world of the play, but from the world of the performance.

In two of the six plays (*Heauton timorumenos* and *Hecyra*) the prologue-speaker explicitly identifies himself as L. Ambivius Turpio, the actor-manager who had previously worked with Caecilius and now with Terence. In the remaining prologues, the speaker is not formally identified, but he speaks in such a way as to suggest a close relationship with the poet and also a significant personal authority for himself. It is possible that Turpio spoke all the prologues,[111] and that it was in some way obvious to the audience that this was the case. The opening line of *Heauton timorumenos* indicates that the audience would see that he was an 'old man': and it would seem that the audience would be able to recognise him, since, although we say 'he is clearly identified', he does not actually name himself. The alternative possibility is that the prologues of plays other than *Heauton timorumenos* and *Hecyra* 'were delivered by young members of [Turpio's] troupe'.[112] This use of a member of the cast, not of the *dramatis personae*, as *prologus* is remarkable. It cuts the line between play and performance closer than ever before, and brings the mechanics of play-production alive before our eyes, thus glazing over the divisions between play-world and 'real world' in which performance takes place. Turpio's job is to draw the audience into the play, constructing them into the 'ideal readers' of Terentian comedy.

The prologue-speaker – whether Turpio or a sidekick – puts Terence the poet, rather than the particular play, to the forefront of our thoughts.

[111] The *didascaliae* indicate that it was believed at the time of their composition that Turpio produced all the plays. Mattingly (1959) argues forcibly against the reliability of the *didascaliae* and of most of the extratextual data available to us, suggesting alternatives to the conventional ordering of Terence's plays, which would make not *Ad.* but *Eu.* the final play. These views have not all been accepted, but the reliability of the *didascaliae* is certainly not unassailable. See Goldberg (2005a: 17–18).

[112] Gilula (1989: 97).

Terence could have gone one stage further towards replacing the material of the play with the techniques of poetic composition by presenting the prologues in his own person, but to do so would have lost a crucial element of his self-presentation: an advocate can say things in praise and defence of the poet which would be unacceptably hybristic coming from the poet himself. Terence uses the arrangement, moreover, to play around with the notions of scripting, of 'who speaks', which are at issue in drama generally.[113] In the prologue to the *Heauton timorumenos*, Terence/Turpio play/s on the idea of control:

> oratorem esse uoluit me, non prologum:
> uostrum iudicium fecit; me actorem dedit.
> sed hic actor tantum poterit a facundia
> quantum ille potuit cogitare commode
> qui orationem hanc scripsit quam dicturu' sum?[114]
> (*HT* 11–15)

He wanted me to be an orator, not a prologue-speaker. He made the judgement yours, and gave me as the 'actor' [i.e. the one who acts in court]. But will this actor be able to do as much by his eloquence as he who wrote this speech which I am about to deliver did through his clever cogitation?

Here, and whenever Turpio speaks of his own actions, his own history, his own hopes, Terence fudges and so highlights the question of authorship.

To return to the beginning: how do the prologues manage their initiation of the play? Plautus uses the opening line or few lines to grab the audience's attention with his poetic pyrotechnics; Terence's prologues are doing something similar, as well as something different. I quote the three opening lines of each here:

> *Andria*
> Poeta quom primum animum ad scribendum adpulit,
> id sibi negoti credidit solum dari,
> populo ut placerent quas fecisset fabulas.
> (*An.* 1–3)

When the poet first turned his mind to writing, he believed that his only business was that the plays he made should please the public:

[113] Henderson (1999: 44–5): 'The threat [of Terence's new type of prologue] is to annul performance, the difference of actorial mediation, the material significance of the rendition.' Gilula (1989: 101): '[w]hat we have here, then, is Ambivius Turpio himself acting the part of Ambivius Turpio, who acts the part of *orator*'. Leeman (1963: 25) refers to 'some scholars' (unnamed) as considering that the prologues might actually be the work of someone other than Terence, perhaps even Ambivius Turpio himself, but no-one now believes that.

[114] There is a nice play on the double meaning of *actor* – one who *agit* in court is an *actor*, as is an 'actor' in our sense: Fantham (2002).

Heauton timorumenos
Nequoi sit uostrum mirum quor partis seni
poeta dederit quae sunt adulescentium,
id primum dicam, deinde quod ueni eloquar.
(*HT* 1–3)

First of all, let me say that none of you should be surprised at how the poet has given to an old man a part usually taken by a youth, and then I shall tell you what I have come to say.

Eunuchus
Si quisquamst qui placere se studeat bonis
quam plurimis et minime multos laedere,
in is poeta hic nomen profitetur suom.
(*Eu.* 1–3)

If there is anyone who aims to please as many of the good people as possible, and to hurt as few as possible, this poet proclaims that his name is among them.

Phormio
Postquam poeta uetu' poetam non potest
retrahere a studio et transdere hominem in otium,
maledictis deterrere ne scribat parat.
(*Ph.* 1–3)

Since the old poet cannot drag the poet from his career and hand the man over to unemployment, he is preparing to deter him from writing by slander.

Hecyra (2)
Orator ad uos uenio ornatu prologi:
sinite exorator sim eodem ut iure uti senem
liceat quo iure sum usus adulescentior.
(*Hec.* 9–11: opening of second extant prologue)

I come before you as an orator in the guise of the prologue: allow me to gain your indulgence such that I may make use of that right as an old man which I used as a younger man.

Adelphi
Postquam poeta sensit scripturam suam
ab iniquis obseruari, et aduorsarios
rapere in peiorem partem quam acturi sumus . . .
(*Ad.* 1–3)

When the poet realised that his writing was being watched by unfriendly eyes, and that enemies were denigrating the play which we are about to produce . . .

Of the six prologues (including the *Hecyra* prologue to only the 'third performance'), three explode with the letter 'P' (*An.*, *Ph.*, *Ad.*), while five (all except *Hec.*) contain the magic word *poeta* in the first three lines. Several are highly alliterative, in an only slightly more restrained version of the Plautine manner. Five plays (again, all except *Hec.*) open with a subordinate clause. Aristophanes famously poked delightful fun at a similar practice in Euripides' prologues (*Frogs* 1207–45), no doubt in part because he saw the point, and saw how effective such a construction may be in drawing the listener forward, towards the grammatical resolution of the sentence and into the world of the play. In three Terentian cases (*An.*, *Ph.*, *Ad.*), the subordination is one of time, as is appropriate to the beginning of a story and to the creation of a world which is greater than the world of the play. Two prologues throw the play and its issues out into the world, most explicitly in *Heauton timorumenos* with the implied question (on which more below) about the identity of the speaker, but also in *Eunuchus* with the universalising *si quisquamst qui*... These are the mechanics of getting started. But what *is* starting here?

Plautine elements in Terentian prologues

A Roman comic play: these prologues are more Comic than one might think, more 'Plautine' than the long history of critical appraisal of them might suggest. As such, the prologues do what Terentian plays as a whole do – innovate within a tradition, for they both deviate and also derive from their poetic Uncle Plautus. Terence's drama may be shockingly different, but, like all good Roman cultural acts, the prologues are steeped in their past and only make sense within the context of *mos maiorum*.

In the discussion above, I referred to Terence's use of 'Plautine' alliteration. Playful alliteration of this nature is of course not only Plautine, being a feature of archaic style generally,[115] but when Terence uses it in this context, the strongest intertexts must be to the fore, especially since he does not generally make a great deal of use of archaic alliteration throughout the plays. The particularly plosive power of much of Terence's prologic alliteration might even tempt us to hear an echo of the name of his great predecessor. But the connections between the two go much further. The very idea of the 'advocate' who speaks the prologue, although never developed by Plautus in the literary critical or quasi-juridical ways of

[115] See e.g. Coleman (1999: 47–8) and my ch. 4. On elements of Plautine style in Terence see Karakasis (2005: ch. 7). Deufert (2002: 25–9) denies that there is any requirement to believe that Terence was intimately acquainted with the text of Plautus, a view supported by his and Zwierlein's arguments that a later editor inserted many lines into the text of Plautus, using Terence as a helping hand, which would mean that the references work in the opposite direction. I do not find it plausible that a literary artist of Terence's skill, who appears to have had access to many works of literature both Greek and Roman, would not have read and closely studied the works of his illustrious predecessor.

Terence, is inherent to the notion of the formal prologue. Plautus (or rather, the Plautine author) even jokes with the idea of putting the presentation of himself/his play into the hands of another.[116] Moreover, Terence uses his prologue-speaker for a very similar purpose: the Plautine prologue tells the story, more or less, of the play, while the Terentian prologue tells the story, more or less, of its production. Both are ways of using storytelling to create the illusion of a greater world beyond the play.

Another Plautine element in Terence's prologues is the relationship with the audience. Terence uses traditional formulae for calling the audience to attention, for telling them (and not telling them) the technical details of the play's ancestry, and for instigating the 'contractual' relationship between playwright and audience which is so crucial to Plautus' *captatio beneuolentiae*. For Plautus, the deal he offered his audience was one which encompassed not only the enjoyment of the play in return for attention to it, but also grandiose promises about military success and the favour of the gods. Terence is more demure, but along the same lines. The audience can be promised a good play if they behave, but they are also promised (and thereby flattered by) the honour of doing justice and upholding the right order of things in the ludic world. On their part, they must pay attention and like the play, and the terms in which they are invited to do so are clearly evocative of those of Plautus. Their reward will be good plays. Each of the prologues (again, taking only the second extant prologue to *Hecyra*) ends with a formulaic promise similar to the Plautine *ualete*:

> *Andria*
> fauete, adeste aequo animo et rem cognoscite,
> ut pernoscatis ecquid spei sit relicuom,
> posthac quas faciet de integro comoedias,
> spectandae an exigendae sint uobis prius.
> (*An.* 24–7)

Be favourable, pay just attention and adjudge the case, so that you may know what hope there is for the future, whether his further comedies are to gain a hearing or to be driven off the stage from the start.

> *Heauton timorumenos*
> exemplum statuite in me, ut adulescentuli
> uobis placere studeant potiu' quam sibi.
> (*HT* 51–2)

Take an example from me, so that young men may strive to please you rather than themselves.

[116] *Men.* 3: *adporto uobis Plautum – lingua, non manu.*

Eunuchus
date operam, cum silentio animum attendite,
ut pernoscati' quid sibi Eunuchus uelit.
(*Eu.* 44–5)

Pay attention, and apply your minds in silence, so that you can come to know what the Eunuch wants for him/itself.

Phormio
date operam, adeste aequo animo per silentium,
ne simili utamur fortuna atque usi sumus
quom per tumultum noster grex motus locost:
quem actori' uirtus nobis restituit locum
bonitasque uostra adiutans atque aequanimitas.
(*Ph.* 30–4)

Pay attention, attend with just mind in silence, lest we should suffer similar fortune as we did when our company was driven by a riot from the stage, where the valour of our producer ['actor'] and your helpful goodness and justice have now restored us.

In this case, the contract is even more Plautine in the description of the play's pedigree just before this *peroratio*. Terence has said that the play is called *Phormio* because the character of that name has the main part, *per quem res geretur maxume / uoluntas uostra si ad poetam accesserit* ('through whom the play is most of all waged, if your will acceeds to the poet's request', 28–9). So it is '*Phormio*, by your leave', just as, for example, Plautus says in Trinummus: *nomen Trinummo fecit, nunc hoc uos rogat / ut liceat possidere hanc nomen fabulam* ('he made its name *Trinummus*, and now requests that you allow this play to bear that name', 20–1, there being only a one-line *ualete* left to come in that prologue):

Hecyra (2)
mea causa causam accipite et date silentium,
ut lubeat scribere aliis mihique ut discere
nouas expediat posthac pretio emptas meo.
(*Hec.* 55–7)

For my sake accept the case and grant it silence, so that others will wish to write and it will be worthwhile for me to stage new plays bought at my own expense.

Note here the Plautine-sounding anaphora *causa causam*,[117] to help fix this contract in the Roman *palliata* tradition. Crucial also is the issue of

[117] Donatus *ad loc.* is a nice comment: *oratorie: sic enim fit, cum persona pro persona ad commendationem affertur* (Wessner 1962–3 II: 202).

silence: Terence places the Plautine call for ritual 'silence' (cf. above) into the specific context of a play which, he says, has suffered from the wrong sort of noise:

Adelphi

... facite aequanimitas
poetae ad scribendum augeat industriam.
(*Ad.* 24–5)

Make it such that your right-mindedness will spur the poet onto greater industry in writing.

In this final play, Terence makes a particularly challenging reference to the Plautine prologic tradition, and to his own innovations within it. Just before the closing contractual formula, he says:

de(h)inc ne exspectetis argumentum fabulae,
senes qui primi uenient i partem aperient,
in agendo partem ostendent.
(*Ad.* 22–4)

But don't expect the plot of the play. The old men who come out first, they'll open up part of it, and they'll show another part in the acting of it.

The joke is that here, in the sixth (and, as it turned out, last, except perhaps for the final performance of *Hecyra*) Terentian play, the last thing the audience would expect from the prologue would be an exposition of the *argumentum*! Terence must be alluding here to a favourite metatheatrical device of Plautus'. The closest parallel is in the prologue to Plautus' *Trinummus*:

sed de argumento ne exspectetis fabulae:
senes qui huc uenient, i rem uobis aperient.
(*Trin.* 16–17)

But don't expect the plot of the play. The old men who will come here, they'll open it up.

Deufert (2002: 28) claims that the Plautus passage is an interpolation based on the Terentian passage, but the spread of the phrase *ne exspectetis* elsewhere would seem to belie the suggestion. It occurs on four occasions in Plautus other than the *Trinummus* example above, all highly metatheatrical: *Cas.* 64, where we are not to expect the young man to appear in the play because of Plautus' sabotage of the bridge; *Cist.* 782, the epilogue, where we are told not to expect anyone to come out again (i.e. any more of the play); *Truc.* 482, where the soldier Stratophanes, in an uncharacteristic fit of self-awareness, tells us *spectatores* not to expect him to perform like a *miles gloriosus* (although he does in fact do so, so his metatheatrical moment was a bluff); and *Ps.* 1234, where Ballio, acknowledging defeat by Pseudolus, uses the phrase to refer to stage conventions about entrance and exit. Terence makes just one use of the phrase other than the passage under consideration, which is a metatheatrical ending comment at *An.* 980, in the manner of the *Cistellaria* ending. Terence uses the phrase to place his prologue in a Plautine tradition, differently.

No exposition here, then, but a promise of 'old men' to offer an expository scene by way of compensation. In fact, only partly will Demea and Micio expound the background to the Terentian plot, crucial elements of which they do not at this stage know, while also partly the exposition will come through the play itself (*in agendo*), which is so great a dramatic development on Terence's part. Here too, however, he may be acknowledging, or indeed proclaiming, that in making this development he is working innovatively within a tradition, for he too may have noticed that the old men of *Trinummus* actually *don't* tell us very much about the plot.

It is a commonly held pretence in ancient theatre that the main purpose of a prologue is *narratio*, the exposition of the *argumentum*.[118] Plautus' prologue-speakers are forever getting distracted from doing so, even in those plays where the prologic expectation of exposition is fulfilled. They are inclined to signal their attempts to get on with The Prologue with one of those traditional formulae for calling the audience to attention. Terence never tells us the *argumentum* of a play in his prologues, but he does use the formula and he does tell stories. In *Andria*, for example, we are invited to listen to the story: *nunc quam rem uitio dent quaeso animum adtendite* ('now please pay attention to the charges', 8). This would lead us to expect something about the play, perhaps a bit of background information or hints towards a future recognition. What we get, however, is not anything explicit about its *argumentum* or about what happened to the characters the night before, but rather a bit of its literary historical ancestry, and hints at an argument about the status of the Roman *palliata*, leading to implicit

[118] As Donatus comments on *An.* 6: *quod uere prologi est officium* (Wessner 1962–3 I: 43). On the prologue to *HT*, Eugraphius has developed the thinking slightly: *ad Hau.* 11, ORATOREM ME ESSE VOLVIT NON PROLOGVM *uti apud uos agerem causam potius, non officio fungerer prologorum: prologi enim, sicuti iam dictum est (Andr. prol. in.), aut argumentum narrant aut poetae personam commendant aut audientiam postulant* (Wessner 1962–3 III.i: 155). Barsby (2002: 269): 'The consensus of scholarly opinion is that in almost all of his plays Terence suppressed a divine prologue which stood in his Greek original. This prologue is assumed to have conveyed to the audience certain important facts which are unknown to some or all of the characters on stage.' He suggests that the situation is not so simple, but none of the arguments against Terentian originality in the manner of exposition seem compelling to me.

praise for the audience's knowledge of literature. Utterly different from Plautus' practice, and yet, in a sense, deriving from and alluding to it.

This Plautine behaviour is perhaps most apparent in the prologue to *Heauton timorumenos*. The play opens with the speaker announcing, obliquely, who he is. 'In case any of you are wondering who I am and what I'm doing here, I'll tell you.' So we might paraphrase the opening, and so likewise begin a number of Plautine plays, such as *Aul.* 1–2: *ne quis miretur qui sim, paucis eloquar / ego Lar sum familiaris*. Terence has picked up *ne quis* (as *nequoi*) in the opening word, *eloquar* in line 3 and *paucis* (understand, *uerbis*) in line 10.[119]

The Prologue continues with the simplistic structure 'first I'll tell you who I am, then (*deinde*, 3) why I have come [in the manner of the epiphanic divine prologues of conventional New Comedy]; next I'll tell you the details of the play (*nunc qui* . . . , 7–9), and then what it's all about (*nunc quam ob rem* . . . , 10). The primitivistic narrative style continues through the narration: *nam quod* . . . (16), *tum quod* . . . (22), culminating in the resolution of the whole story, *quare* . . . (26). This pseudo-naïvety about the role of the prologue to perform these services for us comes out of Plautus (where, of course, it is no more genuinely naïve than it is here), but Plautus' occasional flirting with a refusal to behave like a proper prologue is taken to extremes.

At one level, Terence is quite genuinely constructing his prologue in the manner of Plautus. Likewise, *Phormio* pretends to get back, after a digression, to telling us The Prologue, using the conventional formula (*nunc quid uelim animum attendite*, 'now pay attention to what I want', 25), and he does indeed give us the technical details in proper Plautine fashion. But the difference is in the refusal. Turpio tells us, in *Heauton timorumenos*, that he has come before us in order to introduce the play (1–5). Immediately, the apparently straightforward introduction is problematised, however, by a question of numbers; he has come to present *ex integra Graeca integram comoediam*, which looks like a straightforward and wholesomely traditional contribution to the issue of *contaminatio*, but the integrity of the play is undermined by the introduction of a particularly Terentian plot element, duplicity: *duplex quae ex argumento facta est simplici* ('which

[119] Other plays beginning with an implied question from the audience which the prologue is set to answer: *Capt.*, and also *Trin.*, in which Luxuria uses a similar formula (*nunc, ne quis erret uostrum, paucis in uiam deducam* . . . 4) to explain who she is and what the play is about. The delayed prologue to *Cist.* has the speaker start by saying who he is. An opening identification of this nature is usual where the prologue is spoken by someone other than the anonymous *prologus*. Mercury tells us who he is at *Am.* 19, although he hints at it broadly in the opening mega-sentence. Arcturus opens *Rud.* similarly, though with rather less theatrical self-awareness.

has been made double out of a single plot', 6). The point here is not how Terence changed the Greek original in order to make it *duplex*, but how the claim destabilises the traditional purity of the *integra* and *simplex* play.[120] Indeed, Eugraphius, who believes in the law against *contaminatio*, takes this as a claim that Terence has translated precisely one Greek play to make precisely one Latin one.[121] It is a lucky convenience that 'comedy' is feminine in Latin, since it makes this whole issue take on a suggestively sexual aura.

The next move is a delightful piece of refusal: 'I have told you that I am here to present a Roman *palliata* play. Now as to who wrote it and what it was called in Greek – I won't tell you, because being clever spectators you know already.' (I paraphrase *HT* 7–9 here.)[122] Again a Plautine motif, of the telling (and non-telling) of technical details, is alluded to and developed by Terence. The sequence continues with what looks at first as if it is going to be an introduction to the play itself (10). Before he can actually say anything about the play, however, Turpio goes off into a digression about the relative effectiveness of playwright and performer in the production of theatrical eloquence (13–15), only after which does he get back to the story, which, as ever, is about the argument with critics, not background to the plot. This digressive structure, teasing us with the (im)possibility of getting on with it, is again typically Plautine.

A final point on the Plautinity of Terentian prologues. The elderly Turpio goes on to complain about the 'work work work' that playwrights and audiences demand of him, his ancestry in this respect going back perhaps to Xanthias in the opening of Aristophanes' *Frogs*.[123] Not only is this generically comic, but also in this particular case it links the prologue closely to the subject matter of the play, which figures an elderly man who works like a slave, even though he need not – not that the audience know that yet.[124] Still more important in what Turpio says is that, according to this prologue, Terence's plays are more lively, more challenging, than those

[120] See Brothers (1980: esp. 95–7) and Dunsch (1999) for extensive discussions of the meaning of these lines. I find it hard to accept Dunsch's suggestion that the reference is to a technical discussion of style, rather than anything to do with the plot.

[121] *quoniam Andria e duabus comoediis uidetur esse confecta, quippe illic et Perinthia et Andria continentur, quod quidem criminis loco aduersarius dederat, ideo hic 'ex integra' inquit 'comoedia integram comoediam acturus sum', ne uideatur ab aliquo tacta aut ipse alteram tetigisse, sed unam comoediam et integram ad Latinum sermonem interpretatione mutasse.* (Wessner 1962–3 III.i: 154).

[122] Cf. Henderson (2004: 56).

[123] Cf. Sosia's muttered complaints (166–9) as he approaches Mercury, who feels that he himself has more justification for complaining! Most complaints, however, come from women, who after all do the work.

[124] This point is made also by Gowers (2004: 155–6).

of his contemporaries. It is significant that the terms of self-advertisement that he uses are not those of the delicate aesthetic which we are inclined to associate with Terence, but something rather more full-bodied and Plautine.[125]

The intertexts

Plautus and the *palliata* tradition are not the only contributors to making the Terentian prologue effective both as comedy and as literature. There are three other areas which should be explored for an understanding of what Terence is doing here: oratory; comic agonism (including Aristophanic and sub-literary manifestations); and Callimachean poetic programme. All these three intertexts have something in common: they are structured according to a reciprocal, confrontational paradigm which gives a conventional framework in which to explore issues that of themselves may be but need not inherently be confrontational. The prologues are full of arguments over the rights and wrongs of comedy and of particular comedians. The constant reference to arguments about the nature of the play serve (a) to create a sense of something greater, something beyond what we can see and (b) to provide a suitably comic vehicle for a programmatic exposition of the nature of Terence's comic art.

In 'arguing with his critics', Terence places his prologues squarely into the tradition of 'comic agonism', in which some degree of conflict and confrontation has always played a crucial role, both in the ancient understanding of how comedy developed, and in manifestations of it from early times. Probably following Varro, Horace constructs an ancestry for comedy which has it born out of light-hearted ritualised slanging-matches performed by good solid *prisci* once the work was done and the harvest gathered (*Ep*. 2.1.139–55).[126] He reports a (to Augustan sentiment) rather more disturbing development of this tradition, into a sharper, harsher,

[125] The interpretation of Gilula (1989: 101–3) is slightly different, in that she presents Turpio as saying (being made by Terence to say) that he is tired of doing that role and wants the opportunity to show what he can do with something gentler, i.e. this play. The two possibilities are not wholly incompatible: Terence both is and is not like Plautus, is and is not boisterous.

[126] See Brink (1982: 179–86) for a clear account of this passage and its likely literary relatives, including Virgil and Tibullus as well as Livy. He favours Varro as the most important source, although he reads Horace's 'historical judgements on early Roman drama' (183) as quite different from Varro's (for whom Ennius and Plautus mark a climax in 'classic status'). It seems likely, and Brink does not discount this, that there is also a role for possible Greek theoretical models in both Varro and Horace. Strictly speaking, the passage in the letter to Augustus talks more generally of drama, though comedy is clearly a major player, whereas the *Ars poetica* passage is concerned explicitly with comedy.

personal satire, which 'happily' was then curbed by law and returned to playful teasing. It is no accident that this is said in a letter-poem addressed to Augustus. Horace must be alluding to 'fescennine verses', those originally impromptu, responsorial songs which are associated with fertility and happy celebration, but which are themselves distinctly rude. What matters particularly for understanding the programmatic prologues of Terence is that Horace saw comedy as developing out of the mutual hurling of insults. On the closely related passage in *Ars poetica* 281–4, Brink (1971) implies, rightly, that Horace is using a quasi-historical story about the legal suppression of comic outspokenness as a literary critical vehicle for comment on the changes between Old and New Comedy.[127] Livy's account (7.2.3–7) offers a genealogy for comedy which is less 'organic' and more deliberate, in that he attributes the beginnings of dramatic performance to a conscious decision on the part of the state's leaders, as a religious response to a national crisis, but it too stresses the quasi-fescennine element in early drama.[128]

Whatever the status of these aetiological stories as literary history, as literary criticism they are very acute. Conflict is comic.[129] One extreme manifestation of the phenomenon is the Roman practice of *flagitatio*,[130] the abusive demands designed publicly to shame a debtor into paying up, and performed for laughs in both dramatic and real-life contexts. A colourful example is provided by Plautus' *Pseudolus*, when the eponymous slave's young master invites him: *onera hunc* [Ballio] *maledictis* ('pile him up with curses', 357), while the literary manifestation of the practice is well known from Catullus.[131] It is perhaps worth noting that Cicero and his friends on a number of occasions use *flagitare* and its associates to joke about literary friends' importunate demands for pieces of writing.[132] Satire and its close relative invective also play the programmatic game of conflict,

[127] See Brink (1971: 316–17). Beare's account (1964: 10–14) is also useful on the (ancient belief in the) agonistic origins of comedy, although (see Beard, North and Price 1998: 43–8) he is surely wrong to doubt the connections between fertility, agriculture, warfare, magic and religion. On fescennine-type altercation in comedy, see Vogt-Spira (1995: 77).

[128] See Goldberg's important study (2005b) of how early Roman literature was received and indeed 'constructed' by later republican and imperial Romans. On Livy, see Goldberg's p. 8 and the literature mentioned in his nn. 19 and 20.

[129] Gowers (2004: 156–7) connects the conflict between Terence and his older rival with that between fathers and sons within the play (apropos *HT*). On 'bitching in the theatre' as something that should not entirely surprise us, see Henderson (1999: 46).

[130] See Usener (1901: 1–28), on *flagitatio*.

[131] E.g. poems 42, 55, 103. On the comic–dramatic connections of Cat. 42, see Fraenkel (1961); Goldberg (2000).

[132] E.g. *Leg.* 1.5, *Q. fr.* 2.9.1, *Fam.* 3.11.4, 12.30.2, 15.17.1, *Rep.* 2.23, *De Orat.* 2.188.

even in such supposedly eirenic hands as those of Horace.[133] Terence's prologues are clearly not literally *flagitationes*, but they do belong to the same conceptual world. In *Eunuchus* (17–19) Terence threatens that there will be plenty more where that came from, if his opponent does not cease his behaviour.

The quintessence of comic agonism is Aristophanes. Not only is Old Comedy replete with insults and arguments both within the play itself and directed out of it into the world of the Athenian audience, but also the very structure of the plays depends on the confrontational 'agon' which will be the source of humour, the driving force of the play and the 'problem' to which the great celebration at the end will be the 'solution'. The essential comedy, then, is confrontational. Moreover, Aristophanes provides Terence with a more specific intertext for his argumentative, literary critical prologues when he uses the parabasis as an opportunity to celebrate his own play by attacking other people's.[134] Remembering also the forensic-rhetorical nature of Terence's prologues, we should note that several of Aristophanes' agons have a forensic base (e.g. *Wasps*, *Acharnians*) or a closely related political base (e.g. *Knights*). Closer still to Terence's situation is Aristophanes' ongoing quasi-external battle, that with Cleon (the symbolic anti-hero of *Knights*), who is said to have prosecuted Aristophanes for slander after *Babylonians*.[135] Aristophanes' legal battle with Cleon provides a good model for Terence's quasi-legal quasi-battle with, as it might be, Luscius Lanuvinus – the more so if, in fact, Aristophanes is making it up.[136] But perhaps the perfect model in Aristophanic comedy are the hilarious and spectacular battles the Old Comedian waged with his own poetic rivals, including his own 'malevolent old poet', Cratinus[137] (and, of course, Euripides). Aristophanes and his mates were indeed engaged in a real competition of the highest symbolic importance, in a sense that is not true of Terence and *his*, but the presence of any real conflicts, competitions or other forms of opposition does not undermine the possibilities for comic

[133] On this subject, see Schlegel (1999).

[134] See Hunter (1985: 30–3); Ehrman (1985); Dobrov (1995b). Arnott (1985) argues convincingly for the connection between Terence's programmatic prologues and Aristophanes' programmatic parabases. The literary affinity between the comic prologue and the Aristophanic parabasis is made explicit by the opening statement of Hubbard (1991: 1) and his extensive n. 1.

[135] See Dover (1972: 99–100). For a reading which stresses the historicity of that event and of some degree of later restriction of comic satire on persons (the 'Syracosian law'), see Atkinson (1992).

[136] Halliwell (1991); MacDowell (1995: 42–5); Silk (2000a: 10).

[137] The very title of a recent book on the practitioners of Old Comedy other than Aristophanes is telling of this agonistic relationship – *The Rivals of Aristophanes* (Harvey and Wilkins 2000). Of particular interest in that volume is the essay of Luppe (2000: 15–21), which depicts the explicit rivalry between Aristophanes and Cratinus as both mutually exploited and highly creative.

mileage: explicit rivalry was funny, and was effective as a way of plotting out one's space in comedy.[138] Was this intertextual relationship conscious on the part of Terence and (at least some of) his audience?[139] Even if it was not conscious, the parallel indicates the generically conflictual aspect to comedy, which suggests that what Terence is doing in the prologues is comic generically, and would almost certainly also have been funny.

Twentieth-century theorists would take the question of conflict further, and make its role into something universal in drama. Frye (1957: 167) says: 'It is hardly possible to imagine a drama without conflict.' Huizinga's famous essay on 'Homo ludens' places the 'agonistic principle' as a driving force for play at the heart of civilisation. It may no longer be intellectually acceptable, but Huizinga's comment (1949: 96) at the end of his discussion of the Greeks and Romans implies a high valuation for our subject: '[d]uring the growth of a civilisation the agonistic function attains its most beautiful form, as well as its most conspicuous, in the archaic phase'. T. S. Eliot's *Sweeney Agonistes: Fragments of an Aristophanic Melodrama* is, like Terence's prologues, a work of literary theory couched in agonistic, dramatic form.

But it is not only drama that uses conflict as a structuring device for the exposition of an idea. It is a wider trope of literature. The technique of couching literary critical statements in terms of arguments between proponents of opposing schools is an old one, going back at least to the agon of Euripides and Aeschylus in Aristophanes' *Frogs*, and reaching its zenith with the Hellenistic poets. Most famously, Callimachus used, or possibly even invented, an argument between poetic practitioners as a vehicle to display his own wares and to introduce his great work. I suggest that Terence is writing in the tradition of such arguments, even directly alluding to the opening of the *Aetia* and other crucial programmatic passages such as the end of the *Hymn to Apollo*.[140]

138 Heath (1990) sees the abusive interactions between the Old Comic poets as a kind of 'ritual game'. Sidwell (1995) makes a case for Aristophanes' highly developed rivalries and allegories in his politics and poetics, specifically Aristophanes' *Wasps* as a complex parody of Cratinus' *Pytine*. Ruffell (2002) offers a sustained reading of the comic competition between Cratinus and Aristophanes. It is notable that many of the accusations thrown around by the fifth-century Greeks are similar to those supposedly levelled at Terence: collaboration, plagiarism, inadequate or inappropriate innovation.

139 See Pohlenz (1956: 441). Pohlenz places the prologues of Terence in the tradition of the poetic sphragis going back to Hesiod, and ranging through the lively violence of Aristophanes, the poetic self-consciousness of Callimachus and the theories of the rhetoricians.

140 Hunter (1985: 32) hints at such a possibility, as does Taliercio (1988), esp. at 54, when she mentions Terence's use of programmatic terms such as *studium*, *labor* and *ars*. Ehrman (1985: 375) raises the possibility, but dismisses it immediately on the grounds that 'it is extremely difficult to detect influences upon Terence's works from genres other than those within the range of ancient comedy',

There are several passages which bring this Callimachean possibility to the fore. In the *Andria*, which almost certainly opens Terence's career on stage, the playwright's very first word to the public sets the programmatic tone: *poeta*. The word is not unusual of itself, being a standard term for a playwright, but such an explicit emphasis within the play on the playwright himself is almost unknown. Plautus may create internal playwrights in the sense of metaphorical substitutes, but of himself he is far more self-effacing. Another important word in this line is *scribendum*, 'writing', Terence's preferred term for the activity of the playwright, much favoured in the prologues.[141] Terence, then, sends a man out on stage to tell the audience about his writing. Contrasting with this highly literary and self-conscious opening line, the sentence finishes with the statement of purpose: *populo ut placerent quas fecisset fabulas* ('that the plays which he made should please the public', 3). With appropriately archaic and Plautine alliteration, the stated aim is public service.[142] Self-conscious literary sophistication and popular approval are held in balance. Terence then says: 'when I first directed my attention to writing comedy, I intended to go about it in a certain way, in service of your good selves, but Someone forced me to do things differently'. There is an echo here of Callimachus, couching his programmatic statements in the *Aetia* prologue in the form of an early interview with Apollo: 'when I first put my tablet on my knees, Lycian Apollo said to me . . .'. Not only is there a close conceptual parallel between these two prologic histories of poetic production, but also there may perhaps be a slight verbal echo, in the stress on the mechanics of writing (*scribendum*, δέλτον (*Aet.* 1.21), the writing tablet), and in the emphatically placed designation 'poet' (*poeta* opening Terence's play; ἀοιδέ opening Apollo's speech to Callimachus, *Aet.* 1.23).[143] As is well known, the programmatic scene between Apollo and Callimachus had huge progeny

an objection which I suggest, here and in ch. 4, should no longer hold. Objections to the suggestion that Terence is directly alluding to Callimachus would probably take these two forms: in a play, a literary allusion of this understated nature, and to a non-dramatic text, would be lost on the audience; and anyway they were not well-educated enough to know Callimachus. The second of these surely needs little answer: indeed not all of the audience would know Callimachus, but there is no reason why a sizeable minority might not, since this is a time of great interest in and influx of Greek literature. The first is a more serious matter, although it is worth remembering that dramatic works also have a textual life outside the performance. I suspect that this kind of allusion is given with a light touch precisely so that it should not be essential to enjoyment of the scene – it is there for those who can see it, but does not get in the way for those who do not notice it.

[141] *An.* 1, 5, *HT* 43, *Eu.* 7, 36, *Ph.* 3, *Hec.* 27, 56, *Ad.* 16, 25. Plautus self-deprecatingly attributes the action of *scribere* to another, calling his own action *uortere barbare* (*As.* 11, *Trin.* 18).

[142] Ehrman (1985: 373) links this claim for public service to that in Ar. *Ach.* 655–8.

[143] This suggestion is not intended to deny the connection with Aristophanic programmatic practice here: Arnott (1985: 2–3).

with a great many variations.[144] Terence says that the interference occurred when he *animum . . . adpulit* (1) towards the idea of writing comedy. The phrase contains a similar idea to that of the opening of Ovid's *Metamorphoses*: *in noua fert animus mutatas dicere formas / corpora* ('The mind leads me to speak of forms changed into new bodies'). Terence could not be conscious of a connection here (I am not suggesting any particular 'common source' for Terence and Ovid, apart from the general pervasive influence of Callimachus), and Ovid may well not be conscious of it either, but the parallel can help to point up the programmatic force and the generic differences. Ovid is (at least posing as) writing epic, in which the power of poetry, the gods, the muse, flows through the poet and draws him he knows not where.[145] By contrast, the fiercely independent comic playwright presents *himself*, not divine inspiration, as the driving force of his poetry.

The hint from this allusion to Callimachus and his writing tablets is that Terence's opponent, the *uetus poeta*, is playing some odd sort of Apollo role, as many other variant figures will come to do as Latin poetry develops.[146] In the prologues as a whole, however, the opponent's role is much more like that of the Telchines, those half-mythical, half-contemporary critics of Callimachus, who complain about the kind of poetry he writes – and thus conveniently give him the opportunity to defend himself.[147] In Terence's case, Donatus identifies the *maleuolus* as the comic poet Luscius Lanuvinus (Wessner 1962–3 1: 43); for Callimachus, the *Scholia Florentina* on the opening of the *Aetia* supply names of contemporary poets who, it is claimed, are lurking behind the Telchines figures. Both sets of ancient commentators may, in a sense, be right about the identifications, but we should be wary of taking this identification too far and interpreting it too literally. These 'opponents' serve an important programmatic purpose, and so are constructs of the two texts. Terence refers several times to his

[144] See Wimmel (1960); Sharrock (1994: 206–10). Hunter (2006), while stressing the extended Hellenistic family in the Roman poetic diaspora, nonetheless foregrounds the powerful Big Brother which is the first fragment of the *Aetia* (ch. 1).

[145] I have tried to unpack this issue in Sharrock (2002).

[146] See esp. Wimmel (1960) and the widespread progeny of the advising Apollo in Augustan poetics.

[147] See Cameron (1995: ch. 8). His whole book, of course, takes rivalry as the entry-point for consideration of Callimachean poetics and Latin criticism. Interest in the biographical 'identity' of the Telchines is noted as an obstacle to interpretation by Schmitz (1999), who gives additional references. Schmitz's reading of the poetological programmes of the *Aetia* prologue, and indeed other passages of Callimachus, as being designed as *captationes beneuolentiae* is obviously relevant to my argument here, although I would not want to undermine the poetic programme of either Callimachus or Terence.

opponent(s), but never by name. The *uetus poeta* appears four times (*An.* 7, *HT* 22, *Ph.* 1 and 13); a singular *maleuolus* is mentioned twice, but both these are as glosses on the *uetus poeta* (*An.* 6, *HT* 22). On four occasions, the critic actually enters in the plural: they are *maleuoli* in *HT* 16 and *Ad.* 15, and *iniqui* in *Hec.* 54 and *Ad.* 2. The move into the plural not only serves to make the whole affair more cryptic, mysterious, but ultimately unchallengeable: it also should direct us towards the Telchines.

Moreover, the Terentian *maleuoli* act in a similar way to the Callimachean Telchines. Not only do they object to the poet's kind of poetry (ἐπιτρύζουσιν, *Aet.* 1.1, *accusant* etc.), but also they spread rumours against the poet and try to poison the thoughts of the powerful against him (as do the personified Envy in Callimachus' *Hymn to Apollo*, and the *maleuoli* who *rumores distulerunt* in *HT* 16). There are similarities also in each poet's defence: for example, the opponents' own poetry is attacked in *Eunuchus* and in the *Aetia* prologue (whether or not it is the *Lyde* of Antimachus that is the subject of Callimachus' criticism); counter-accusations of stupidity are made (*Aet.* 1.2 and the braying donkey of line 31, and *An.* 17). There might be a link also in the stress on age, since Terence presents himself as the bright young thing being persecuted by an envious has-been, just as Aristophanes contrasted himself with the elderly Cratinus, and Callimachus uses the idea of being 'like a child' as an image in his poetics: that is, he is a child at poetic heart, even if not literally so.[148]

One of the most interesting and indeed surprising passages where this programmatic intertext seems to be relevant comes in the prologue to the *Phormio*, where the terms of supposed abuse against Terence are very close to terms of Callimachean approbation, at least as developed later by the Augustans: *quas ante hic fecit fabulas / tenui esse oratione et scriptura leui*[149] ('that the plays that he made previously are thin of speech and light in writing', *Ph.* 4–5). Both *tenuis* and *leuis* will become significatory motifs of the Roman–'Callimachean' poetic programme. Donatus (Wessner 1962–3 II: 351), as often, is both enlightening and somewhat confusing on this line. He remarks that the objection shows the accuser's lack of skill, because this *leuis* style is appropriate to comedy. Under the influence of the term *oratio* and the rhetorical colouring of the prologues generally, he is probably

[148] See Morgan (2003) for an account of the poetological metaphor of Callimachean childlikeness in Ovid's *Metamorphoses*.

[149] We might notice what a beautifully structured line that is, close to a golden line.

thinking of the great rhetorical debate between different levels of style. Donatus claims that Terence is defending himself against a real accusation, which is that his style was less sublime than that of Menander, arguing that such a style is suited to tragedy: *Reuera autem hoc deterior a*[150] *Menandro Terentius iudicabatur, quod minus sublimi oratione uteretur; quod ipsum nunc purgat dicens in tragoedia altiora posse transire* ('but indeed Terence was judged worse than Menander, because he used less sublime speech; an accusation which he denies, saying that in tragedy higher speech can cross over', Wessner 1962–3 II: 351, *ad Ph.* 5).[151] The accusation is the vehicle for a valid critical point. The *maleuolus* objects, because Terence does not bring on *insanum . . . adulescentulum / ceruam uidere fugere et sectari canes / et eam plorare, orare ut subueniat sibi* ('a mad young man who sees a deer fleeing and dogs following, and the deer crying and begging him to help her', *Ph.* 6–8). It is likely that there is something in a recent play, perhaps even a play of Luscius Lanuvinus, which is being parodied here.[152] Whatever the original play was like, in Terence's version it is clearly some kind of tragic parody. I suggest that the 'mad young man' is not 'lovelorn' (as in Radice's 1976 Penguin translation), but rather refers to the maddened subjects of tragedy, such as Orestes, Hercules or Ajax. The diminutive of the classically comic term *adulescens* is parodic: Donatus (Wessner 1962–3 II: 351) indicates that it refers to a comic person inappropriately placed in a tragic situation.[153] It would be typical of tragic parody to call (e.g.) Orestes an *adulescentulus.* The deer could hint at Iphigenia, and the dogs at the Furies, or both of them at Actaeon and his hunting dogs. It is a mishmash of tragic scenes, jokingly thrown together as the opposite against which Terentian comedy defines itself. In saying something akin either to 'because I did not write tragedy', or to 'because I did not use an obvious over-the-top tragic parody or inappropriate tragic scenes in a comedy', Terence is using a ploy similar

150 *a* is omitted by *O* and *V*, according to Wessner's apparatus. As Flickinger (1931: 687) says, it is 'manifestly an error'.

151 It is not absolutely clear what Donatus is saying here. If we were to amend the text to *in tragoediam* then the meaning would be straightforward: 'saying that higher things can cross over into tragedy'. I am not aware of any manuscript support for such an emendation, but in any case the critical point seems clear enough.

152 Traina (1977: 159 n. 223) describes *plorare, orare* (*Ph.* 8) as the parodic echo of Luscius Lanuvinus. Since it seems likely that his *Phasma* contained some sort of a 'mad scene', a parody here seems plausible. That Terence was inclined to parody the language of his contemporaries is shown, for example, by the strong likelihood of parodic quotation of Caecilius in *Ad.* 985 (Caecil. 215) and *Ph.* 686 (Caecil. 91). See Deufert (2002: 26 n. 49).

153 Donatus, according to Wessner, actually quotes the final word as *adulescentem* in his initial lemma, but then in his sub-comment specific to the word he quotes *adulescentulum* and remarks: *ut comicam personam ostenderet, artificiose imminuit 'adulescentulum', quo magis persona a sublimitate tragica discessisset.*

to that of Callimachus when he says that the Telchines complain 'because I did not compose one continuous poem of many thousands of lines on kings and heroes'.[154]

There is one way, however, in which the Terentian programme might seem wholly at odds with the Callimachean: its attitude to the crowd.[155] Whereas Callimachus poses as despising the ignorant masses who cannot understand his poetry, and speaking only to those few who can follow his complex syntax and recondite allusions, Terence plays to the gallery. His only concern is that his performance should please the Roman People (*An.* 2–3, *HT* 52, *Eu.* 1–2). Nonetheless, Terence uses something similar to Callimachean flattery of his audience's intelligence when he declines to tell them anything about the play because they know already, and especially when he praises them as good judges of comedy, in contrast with the ignorant crowd who could not understand the *Hecyra* on its first two airings. The audience is flattered into thinking of itself as above such things – even if its actual makeup is little different from that of the 'mob who ran after tightrope walkers'.

Oratory: captatio, *accusation and defence*

Scholars from antiquity to the present day have seen that Terence's prologues are modelled on the style of forensic oratory.[156] This is more than just the conventionality of a rhetorical training which permeates so much of (later) Roman literature: it is an explicit and highly marked strategic ploy. What is at stake in the adoption of the oratorical pose to introduce a comic drama, in 160s BC Rome? Why do it, especially since, according to my argument, the 'quarrel with critics' was invented or at least noticed for the very purpose, as Terence seems jokingly to admit? As he hints in *Phormio*, we might wonder whether, if the old poet had not attacked him, Terence would have had no material for his prologues:

[154] It is possible that Terence's scene might allude also to the attack on drama, epitomised by Orestes, in Callimachus, *Epigram* 59, on which (and Callimachus' interaction with comedy) see Thomas (1979: esp. 187–8).

[155] The reading of Habinek (1998), mentioned above, p. 63 n. 107, would better suit the Callimachean programme in this regard.

[156] As Donatus says of the second surviving prologue to *Hec.*: *magna arte hic prologus scriptus est et nimis oratorie* (Wessner 1962–3 II: 195). Goldberg (1983) gives a clear account of both the originality and the intertextuality of Terence's rhetorical prologues, linking them with oratory and specifically with Cato. See also Goldberg (1986: ch. 2); Leeman (1963: 24–5); Gelhaus (1972); Barsby (1999a: 81–2); Arnott (1985); Fantham (2002); Anderson (2003–4). Aristophanes' comic style, also, is intimately bound up with that of rhetoric: on this, see Hesk (2000: esp. ch. 5).

'uetu' si poeta non lacessisset prior,
nullum inuenire prologum po[tui]sset nouos
quem diceret, nisi haberet cui male diceret,'
(*Ph.* 13–15)

If the old poet had not harassed him first the new one would not have been able to find anything to say in his prologue, unless he had someone to abuse.

This joke is framed in exactly the comic manner of – posed – improvisation and antagonism.

One reason is simply that drama and public rhetoric have a great deal in common in the ancient world,[157] where so much of the public culture depends on performance, persuasion and public entertainment. Even without Terence making it explicit, (forensic/political) speeches and (dramatic) prologues share crucial features: the *captatio beneuolentiae*, through which the speaker grabs the attention of the audience and draws them into the world of the play/speech, encouraging them to see things from a point of view which he creates; and the *narratio*, through which the speaker entertains the audience with storytelling, whether it is about the plot of the play, the history of the play's production or some juicy incident from the background of one of the players in a court case, or some moment of Roman history which should inspire the contemporary audience to live up to *mos maiorum*, all of which in some way works to manipulate their attitude to the speaker's case (whether forensic or dramatic).

It is possible, also, that Terence's pose involves some degree of parody: not indeed any kind of vicious satire such as that in Aristophanes' *Wasps* or Kafka's *The Trial*, but a joking, allusive technique in which a non-serious activity (comedy) apes a serious one (oratory), and where the joke is on the parodist as much as on the parodied. One of the greatest orators of the time, Cato, may perhaps offer a parallel for Terence's mix of genres here: it has been noted that the prologue to Cato's *De agricultura* is written in a style distinctly different from that of the main body of the work, and Leeman (1963) has suggested that Cato's prologue is structured according to the

[157] The relationship between drama and oratory in republican Rome is a subject of considerable importance, especially given the implications for the status of theatre in public life. As Stanford (1983: 4) said of Greek drama: 'Oratory was highly histrionic, just as parts of tragedy were highly rhetorical.' Goldberg (1983) is excellent here. Leigh (2004a) makes important points about the connection between comedy and oratory, esp. 326–7. Although his primary interest is with late republican (i.e. Ciceronian) oratory and its games with mid republican comedy, by now a literary text as well as continued or revived performance-genre, he also argues for the likelihood of considerable continuity in rhetorical theory between the two periods (esp. 330–2). On the wider connections between oratory and acting, see Duncan (2006: 58).

norms of rhetorical theory (although this is not universally accepted).[158] It is possible, then, either that there is some specific interaction between Cato and Terence,[159] or that this practice of opening a literary work by pretending to 'stand before an audience of judges' was a popular device of the day. Terence's 'great friends', Scipio and Laelius, were themselves (to become) important orators. The tone of Terence's prologues, then, is one of playful parody of serious oratory, which offers not criticism but honour to a great Roman institution.[160]

The relationship with Roman institutions is another 'purpose', or rather 'effect', of the rhetorical nature of the prologues. By posing as an orator, Terence brings his *fabula palliata* into the heart of contemporary Roman culture, for all that his performance is in some ways closer to the tone of Greek comedy than is most of the *palliata* tradition,[161] and that it constantly takes issue with the questions of translation, transculturation, tradition and originality, while offering the Romans something new and strange in the comic world. The rhetorical prologues, which even critics who read Terence as a window onto Greek New Comedy will admit constitute free composition by Terence, give a Roman immediacy to the 'translated' Greek play, which Terence will subtly and quietly exploit throughout his dramatic career.

Moreover, the rhetorical pose gives Terence licence. Precisely because the theatre is not the forum, and because Turpio is not a *patronus* and Terence is not Cato, precisely because Terence/Turpio speaks in metaphorical inverted commas, he can get away with behaviour which would potentially be offensive, off-putting, or just plain uninteresting, if it were presented 'straight', *in propria persona*. Why should we be interested in Terence's battles with his critics? Because Terence makes a performance of it. If the quarrel had been wholly serious, silence might have been a better policy, but as a pose it is presented for the sake of entertainment and programmatic introduction of the play.

158 Von Albrecht (1989: 11–20) gives a balanced account of the debate.

159 Leeman (1963: 21) suggests that the *De agricultura* should be dated to Cato's old age, to around the time of his death in 149 BC, which would rule it out as a direct model for Terence. If the late date is correct, the alternative direction of influence would not be impossible. Astin (1978: 190–1) considers the argument for a late date for *De agricultura* to be 'plausible but not securely established'.

160 Leeman (1963) suggests that Terence is influenced more by Greek rhetorical theory than by anything indigenous. Whatever Terence may have read in preparation for writing the prologues, however, the audience will have received these performances as playful copies of the entertainment provided by public speakers in other areas of their public culture.

161 Wright (1974) has surely a strong point in this regard.

And so, finally, to the substance of the 'accusations'. Under all the rhetorical hot air, most of it boils down to variations on a theme of plagiarism.[162] One other element is easily dispensed with, which is that Terence claims to have been accused of making use of the help of his great friends in the composition of his plays.[163] This is clearly just *honoris causa* – an entertainingly original way of giving acknowledgement to powerful friends and artistic patrons, and of offering a kind of literary dedication. As a bonus, the honourable mention also allows Terence to flatter the audience for their own relationship with the great friends (*Ad.* 19), and to situate the performance of his Greek *palliata* squarely in contemporary Roman society.[164] Apart from the 'great friends' ploy, all the other supposed accusations relate in some way to questions of translation, plagiarism, intertextuality and literary tradition, and it is these that we must take seriously, because it is clear that Terence wants to keep an intense focus on questions about the relationship between dramatic texts.

Of the six prologues (again, I am including the prologue only to the third performance of *Hecyra*), four centre their literary critical debate on the issue of the 'proper' relationship between plays. The exceptions are *Hecyra*, which is unusual in other ways also, and *Phormio*, in which the critical issue is style, as discussed above. In *Andria* and *Heauton timorumenos*, the pseudo-accusation is that Terence 'spoiled' several Greek plays in order to make one Latin play. In *Eunuchus* and *Adelphi*, the focus is marginally different: that Terence is acting as a 'thief' in his manner of taking elements from certain plays. Terence has thus caused the invention of two wonderful comic-critical metaphorical terms for talking about the relationship between dramatic texts: *contaminatio* and *furtum*.[165] Despite

162 There is, in addition, the small point about 'style' to which I have referred above.

163 Very briefly at *HT* 24; more expansively at *Ad.* 15–21. It is probably no accident that the compliment to his backers comes in the play performed at the funeral games of Lucius Aemilius Paullus, put on by his natural sons Fabius and Scipio: see Henderson (1999: 49–50). See also Gruen (1992: 202) on this.

164 *Vita Terenti* (4) recognises that this defence is a calculated compliment: *uidetur autem leuius* <*se*> *defendisse, quia sciebat et Laelio et Scipioni non ingratam esse hanc opinionem* (Wessner 1962–3 I: 6).

165 On *furtum*: Simon (1961); Russell (1979: 11–12) on [Longinus]'s use of the term κλοπή and on the (largely rhetorical) charge of plagiarism in ancient literary criticism. Also Barsby (1999a: 16): he nicely points out (87) that Plautus 'would have been guilty of the same charge of *furtum* which T. now faced' if the Colax plays of Naevius and Plautus are both adaptations of Menander. See, briefly but usefully, Gowers (1993: 101–2) on the metaphor of the thief. On *contaminatio*, Beare (1959), who favours the meaning of *contaminare* as 'to spoil, sully', is an example of the high-running feelings that the notion has generated in the past; Fraenkel (1960: ch. 9) discussed the issue in detail, it constituting one of the areas on which, so he says in the preface to the Italian edition, he has changed his mind since 1922; Kujore (1974) continues the argument in the old manner, the failing of which (in my view) is a literalist reading of what should be seen as a remarkable piece of literary

the best efforts of scholars from Donatus to the present day to force Terence's prologues to tell us in what sense the *palliata* plays were 'translations' of Greek New Comedy, and thus to allow us to know what those elusive beauties were really like, the only lesson Terence teaches in the prologues is that clever readers of his drama must look out for the weaving together of many plots and plays (both external and internal to the present performance): that is, that we must watch out for intertextuality. He tells us (to misquote another famous thief) that it would be easier to steal his club from Hercules than a line from Menander, but he doesn't really tell us what the stolen goods look like and whether he has given them a respray.[166]

Prologue to Eunuchus

As Terence says of Menander's *Perinthia* and *Andria*, if you've seen one Terentian prologue you've seen them all. Terence has to qualify his statement immediately, of course, and so do I, since each prologue would repay close attention. Analysis of one, the *Eunuchus*, is offered here as an exemplum, since the fact of being 'variations on a theme' is part of the prologues' charm. Barsby (1999a) has briefly outlined the schema of the prologue and its rhetorical structure (81–2); we shall be more concerned with the effects of some details.

As was noted above, the *Eunuchus* prologue begins, in the Plautine manner, with a *captatio beneuolentiae*. Terence presents himself as *quisquam* who wants to please all good men (flattery of the audience) and hurt as few as possible.[167] Another *quis*, the poet hints darkly, might think that he has been treated a bit roughly by Terence, but only because the opponent damaged the speaker first. He, Terence, is simply responding to the unprovoked and undeserved attack. The idea, then, as in the *Andria*

criticism and simultaneously of comic rhetoric. Dér (1989) takes the accusations at face value and constructs out of them, by negative implication, a poetic programme for Luscius Lanuvinus and other contemporaries which would eschew all such messing. See Goldberg (1986: ch. 4); Sharrock (1996); Wright (1974: 99); also Gratwick (1982: 117): 'If *contaminatio* as a technical term is to be used in future, it should be redefined to denote all those ways in which a Roman playwright might "mess about" with his model.' The term is remarkably resistant to erasure, however. A good way forward is that suggested by Oniga (2002: 209) apropos *Am.*: 'una volta ammessa una pluralità di fonti e il procedimento della contaminazione, individuare un modello principale diviene un problema tutto sommato secondario'.

166 On the significance of 'translation' in Terence in the context of the engagement of Latin literature with Greek, particularly Hellenistic, predecessors, see Fantuzzi and Hunter (2004: 467). McElduff (2004) argues that Terence himself was aiming at 'translation' in the sense of rivalling or surpassing his models, rather than copying them, thus 'in the mould of other Roman thought on translation' (126).

167 In this he is like Aristophanes, as Barsby (1999a) points out.

(where Terence says 'I'm sorry, but I'm afraid I simply can't tell you what this play is about, because I have to respond to the unjust attacks on innocent me'), is that 'I wouldn't speak if I were not forced by the behaviour of my adversary'. This introduction offers *captatio* to the audience both *a persona* and *a persona aduersarii* – that is, both by presenting the speaker as being on the side of the angels, and by offering a negative picture of the adversary.[168]

But the ploy of offering a *responsum* rather than a *dictum* is not used just in order to make Terence look good and his adversary look bad: it also has a connection with some of the specifics (although, in keeping with the elusive style, never *very* specific) that Terence uses in counter-attack. Terence claims that Luscius *laesit prior* ('hurt me first', 6). He has already made this claim several times, including, most outrageously, in his first play, *Andria*. The new twist offered by *Eunuchus* is that the question of who should speak first is made into an issue in a (very obscure) attack which Terence makes on his adversary. He claims that Luscius' recent rendition of *Thesaurus* is an absurd piece of folly, because in it he has a legal case in which the defendant speaks before the plaintiff, in contradiction of proper practice and all rational sense (so Terence presents the case). Commentators all note not only that this is really rather a trivial accusation, but also that, since Terence has just accused Luscius (apparently) of being a slavish translator, the fault must lie with the Greek original.[169] More important is the possibility that there is some hint at a metaphorical connection here with the quasi-legal altercation between the two playwrights, where the issue of 'who speaks first' and 'who damaged whom' is important. We might note the linguistic connections between the lines describing the contest of Terence and Luscius, and those describing the content of *Thesaurus*:

> responsum, non dictum esse, quia laesit prior.
> (*Eu.* 6)

It's an answer, not a speech, because he attacked me first.

[168] See for example *Ad Her.* 1.8.

[169] So Barsby (1999a: 84), who mildly describes Terence's criticism as 'less than telling', on the grounds that in, for example, Menander's *Epitrepontes* 'it is similarly the man in possession who speaks first', and that the fault should presumably be ascribed to the Greek original. It might be worth noting that Donatus (Wessner 1962–3 1: 271) interprets *bene* as *ualde*, meaning that Luscius is said to have translated 'a lot' rather than 'closely' or 'well'. This would iron out a few problems but remove a large plank from the basis of modern scholars' interpretations of the argument between Luscius and Terence. Unfortunately it looks a bit forced on the ancient commentator's part. See Garton (1971) for an account of what can be known about the play, and an attempt to identify its Greek original. He inclines towards Menander.

scripsit causam dicere
prius unde petitur, aurum qua re sit suom,
quam illic qui petit . . .

(*Eu.* 10–12)

He wrote that the man from whom the gold was being sought pleaded his case as to why it was his before the man who was seeking it . . .

More significant still, perhaps, is that in the next few lines Terence jumps out of the context of the *Thesaurus* play back into discussion of himself and Luscius so abruptly that it is initially hard to see what is going on:

. . . aut unde in patrium monumentum peruenerit. [play]

(*Eu.* 13)

. . . or how it came to be in his father's tomb.

de(h)inc ne frustretur ipse se aut sic cogitet . . . ['real life']

(*Eu.* 14)

From now on let him not delude himself or think . . .

It might even be possible to make the play match the 'reality' quite closely. Luscius has the Pot of Gold which is Comedy (it is hard not to hear a reference to Plautus here, especially remembering the metaphorical work done by the Pot in that play);[170] Terence seeks to get it from him because he is the true heir of Comedy, of Plautus. But Luscius spoke first to defend his possession, of something which should not rightly be his. It was Terence who was cheated out of his inheritance, which he now rightly claims back, but the usurper abused him still further by speaking first.[171] Be that as it may, it must be significant that Terence constantly stresses the age difference between himself and his adversary. A conflict between a young man and an old man, which the young man must win, is obviously a good programmatic image for the content of Comedy.[172]

170 I am not here entering into the old debate about whether Menander's *Thesaurus* could have been the original of Pl. *Aul.*, on which see Garton (1971: 24–5).

171 Garton (1971: esp. 33–4) suggests that Terence has manipulated our understanding of Luscius' play, to imply that there was an actual court scene, whereas, he argues, there must have been only an arbitration-type scene. Thus Terence makes Luscius' action in the timings of the speeches seem more out of place than it would have done in its own context. Such a view would support my programmatic reading of the altercation.

172 See Sutton (1993) for an account of the conflict of generations as an integral structuring device of comedy. Note that Segal (2001a) claims that most comedy involves the triumph of youth over age, but that in the beginning, with Aristophanes, it was the other way round. One might say that the rejuvenation of the old Aristophanic hero is itself a form of the triumph of youth over age, but with typically comic 'having it both ways' and cashing in on the nostalgic force of the great past without compromise of vigour.

In this prologue, Terence, unusually, refers to two plays by his adversary. The other is the *Phasma*, about which Terence says precisely nothing, except that *siquis* (Someone) recently produced it, and that it was by Menander. (The mention is made just after the strange insinuation about 'Luscius' being a good translator but a bad playwright.) The ancient commentator Donatus kindly tells us the story (Wessner 1962–3 I: 272).[173] It concerns a young man who falls in love at first sight with a girl whom he sees when she appears in the hole-in-the-wall which her secret real mother, the young man's stepmother, has made in order to allow them to meet. (As usual, they live next door.) The theme of sudden, overwhelming 'love', and of illicit intrusion into the house, will be crucial to Terence's own play about to begin, in which a young enthusiast will see a girl in the street, dress up as a eunuch in order to get into her house, and rape her. Is it possible that Terentian 'thieving' – that is, 'intertextuality' – actually extends to contemporary intertexts like the plays of his rival?

Luscius himself next plays the intruder's role. Having dispensed with analysis of his rival's own plays, and made suitably vague threats about future counter-accusations if his adversary does not cease from his inappropriate behaviour, Terence settles down (again) to (not) telling us The Prologue. 'We are going to act the *Eunuchus* "of Menander"' (19–20). Then he is sidetracked into telling another juicy story of the history of the production. After the aediles had bought the play, 'he' (meaning 'Luscius', but actually, in Terence's Latin, just an unexpressed subject) arranged to see a preview. Again, Terence teases the poor drama critic, who desperately wants to know what he means by *emerunt* (20), what kind of preview this might be, how Luscius might be in a position to get *inspiciundi... copia* (21).[174] But what is happening here is that Luscius has got 'inside' the play, intrusively, deceitfully, in order to attack it. This may hint at the central point of the play we are about to see, which is the intrusion of Chaerea into the house of Thais, in order to rape Pamphila. At the least, the story serves to draw the audience into the world of the play, offering a skilled

[173] Why does he choose to do so this time, rather than the 101 other times when we would have liked to know what was in a now-lost play? Perhaps this time *he* happens to know. We should not assume that the late antique commentators had full copies of the Greek and Roman plays that they discuss. Garton (1971: 19) takes it as 'highly doubtful' that Donatus would have been in possession of a play text by Luscius, and ascribes the plot summary to an earlier commentator.

[174] Barsby (1999a: 85–6): 'This is our only record of a preliminary performance of a Roman play before state officials. Since the play had already been bought, the performance cannot have been part of the normal selection process. T.'s account rather implies that Luscius had demanded a preview of the play in order to voice his criticisms of T.'s methods.' The idea that such a demand, of itself, would be met with an obliging personal preview is unlikely.

viewer – if a 'hostile' one – who gives them the crucial lesson. Look for the intertext.

Luscius exclaims that a thief, not a poet, has produced this play. His purported reason for this accusation is that the characters of the soldier and the parasite are claimed to have been taken from earlier Latin plays by Naevius and Plautus (necessarily *two* plays, as Barsby and others have seen).[175] But Terence denies the charge, claiming that his soldier and parasite come from Menander's *Kolax*, not that of either of the Latin poets. Critics from antiquity to the present have rationalised this, and Terence's claims in e.g. *Andria* (16) about his adversary's objection that *contaminari non decere fabulas* ('plays ought not to be contaminated'), into a system in which *contaminatio* is the mingling of material from more than one Greek play, while *furtum* is the use of material which had already appeared in a Latin play.[176] The argument goes: these characters come not from Naevius and Plautus but from Menander (which is tantamount to an admission of *contaminatio*, as the commentators note); the poet did not know that Plautus and Naevius had used them before (probably lying, but in any case, would this mean that at least one of Plautus or Naevius is also 'guilty' of *furtum*?); but all comedy uses conventional characters anyway. This is like a court case in which *argumentatio* involves subtle sleights of hand, in which precise logic is less important than effective rhetoric. Summing up the case for the defence, Terence asks for indulgence: that the new poets should be allowed to do what the old poets had done. Donatus notes the rhetorical force of this *peroratio*: *cum magna defensione*, he comments, on the principle of *mos maiorum* which is the emotive basis for the argument.[177] A logical basis it does not have, since the original 'accusation' was that of taking material from earlier Latin poets.[178] The whole disingenuous hoax is introduced in order to offer the audience a little hint about what the play will be like, a somewhat lively romp with soldiers and parasites

[175] Barsby (1999a: 86–7). Brown (1992: 106) expresses the view that Plautus' play is a revision of Naevius'.

[176] Donatus (Wessner 1962–3 I: 267) comments: *non sine crimine, quod multa in hanc translata sint ex multis poetis Latinis*, which I take to mean 'and not without crime, because many things are in it transferred from many Latin poets'. (*Not* that the things had already been translated by the other Latin poets.) See n. 169 above, and, on Terence's claim for relationship with earlier Latin comedians, esp. Kujore (1974: 41), who hints that Terence may be deliberately manipulating the term *contaminare* in order to refer to his own, and Plautus', originality with regard to Greek originals.

[177] Donatus (Wessner 1962–3 I: 277, *ad Eu.* 43): *cum magna defensione Terentii semel facientis id, quod saepe ueteres.*

[178] Unless Terence means that he should be allowed to take from an earlier Latin poet, just as Naevius or Plautus took from Plautus or Naevius (see n. 175). But since Terence's argument was that he was taking from Menander anyway this hardly helps.

(but – typically – not telling us anything about the really interesting, extreme and unusual elements of this play), and in order to play with the whole question of tradition and originality.[179]

Terence follows up the piece of nonsense about *furtum* by making a general statement about comic conventionality, originality and intertextuality. His ostensible purpose is defence of his 'use' of particular characters from particular plays, and so it must have some implications for what Roman playwrights thought they were doing when they 'used' an existing character: such a use was not very different from what we would call 'conventionality', or the use of 'stock' characters, or possibly even 'intertextuality', rather than specific 'translation':

> quod si personis isdem huic uti non licet:
> qui mage licet currentem seruom scribere,
> bonas matronas facere, meretrices malas,
> parasitum edacem, gloriosum militem,
> puerum supponi, falli per seruom senem,
> amare odisse suspicari? denique
> nullumst iam dictum quod non dictum sit prius.
> (*Eu.* 35–41)

But if he is not allowed to use the same characters as others do, how is it more permissible to create a running slave, to make matrons good and prostitutes bad, a parasite greedy, a soldier boastful, to sneak in a baby, to have an old man deceived by a slave, to love, to hate and to suspect? In sum, nothing is now said which has not been said before.

This highly conventional list actually highlights the ways in which Terence's construction of character and plot in fact deviates from the norms at the same time as depending on them.[180] Even in this play, supposedly his most 'Plautine' and conventional, the character-descriptions do not fit very precisely: no running slave, no *matrona* of any description, a *meretrix*

179 Likewise in *Ad.*, Terence uses the *furtum*-wheeze in order to hint to the audience about a rough-and-tumble scene between an *adulescens* and a *leno*, over which he initiates a critical question for the audience to consider: Plautus left it out when he created his play *Commorientes* out of Diphilus' *Synapothnescontes*, and so Terence introduced it into his *Ad.*, based on that of Menander. Problem: he claims that he ought not to be accused of *furtum* in this act, but rather be praised for having reinstated the poor, neglected little scene. But in that case he is guilty of *contaminatio*, not *furtum*. Again, however, we have a taster of a 'strong' scene, but again, the taster is actually of something rather insignificant in the play as a whole. When the thus-marked scene comes, we spectators are fooled by the dramaturgy as much as Demea is onstage, because we read it straight as an account of a young man's violent theft of his prostitute girlfriend.

180 As Barsby (1999a: 88) says: '[b]ut T. is oversimplifying to make his point: it was an important part of his technique (and of Men.'s before him) to play on the audience's expectations by offering subtle variations on the stock characters and situations'.

but hardly *mala*, a parasite who is conventional in some ways but not really *edax* (no grand comic mess of comestibles, for example, like Plautus' Ergasilus), likewise a soldier who tries to be *gloriosus* but isn't very good at the part, no substituted child (actually rather rare in extant comedy) and most of all no old man deceived by a slave – though there will be a slave deceived by a slave. Parmeno indeed plays some elements of the role of 'cunning slave', but ends up deceived himself by an even more cunning slave woman, and actually confesses to the master, who is neither *pater durus* nor *iratus senex* in any case. Terence makes us feel comfortable with the conventions of comedy – and then destabilises them.

In sum, Terence's prologues are six meditations on the question of what it means to write a play in the *palliata* tradition, in Rome in the 160s BC. Their primary effect is not dry critical analysis or cheap voyeuristic vision of artistic in-fighting, but a highly original way of drawing an audience into the world of the play, and teaching them to watch with an eye to convention and difference, to allusion and intertext.

The Prologue (again)

All of Terence's plays begin by entering *in medias res.*

One of the best-known aspects of Terence's dramaturgy is the effect which his replacement of the 'conventional' prologue with literary polemics has on the position of the audience, dramatic suspense and exposition *in agendo*.[181] As we have seen, there is some exaggeration and simplification at work here, since many of Plautus' plays also avoid the expository prologue, but it remains true that Terence's bold innovation with beginnings has repercussions throughout his plays, not least on his 'opening' scenes. We noted above that beginnings, especially comic beginnings, are constantly subject to delay. Terence's programmatic prologue, which displaces something of the burden of opening onto the first scene, is a supreme act of deferral which allows him a teasing 'refusal to begin' even without the antics of Plautine clowns. The first scenes thus become another try at delivering The Prologue.

The opening scene has to offer some degree of exposition of the plot, in order to kick the play into action and make things happen. Many of the techniques Terence uses are familiar from Plautus: storytelling for its own sake (especially in *Hecyra* and *Adelphi*), the creation of a 'greater world' beyond the play, which almost makes us feel as if there is an extra play

[181] See Duckworth (1994: 233–4); Lefèvre (1969); Goldberg (1986: 183–6); Barsby (1999a: 89–91).

in the background that we cannot see (especially in *Andria* and *Phormio*). But there is also something especially Terentian going on, which we might characterise as a kind of challenge to the audience, a challenge to get at the 'true' information among all the slightly insecure pieces of communication that we are offered. This feature is not exclusive to the beginnings of plays, but it is here that it is most striking since it is most innovative.

Andria offers Terence's first experiment in exposition *in agendo*, with a dialogue between the *senex* Simo and his freedman Sosia, a character brought in for the purpose.[182] The scene, and indeed Terence's use of protatic characters, has come in for some criticism. 'Terence deserves praise for the laudable desire to substitute dramatic dialogue for the monologue of the Greek original but he has not been entirely successful with his protatic characters; there is no harm in the fact that they do not appear later in the play; the fault is that they are colourless and have no personality . . . Such scenes are not really dialogues but monologues which pretend to be dramatic.'[183] Only with regard to Sosia does Duckworth's accusation of colourlessness seem valid: Philotis and Syra in *Hecyra* are both entertaining characters in their own right, and reflect interestingly on the play's feminine agenda, while Davos in *Phormio* plays a startling role – the honest slave, who thus shows up the horrible dishonesty of the free characters in that play.[184] Even Sosia, or at least his scene, has important programmatic functions: the theme of plotting comes in even ahead of the plot, and the idea that Simo is drawing Sosia aside in order to give him a highly confidential account of the 'truth' (as he sees it), in denial of the presence of the audience, is a clever way of drawing the audience closer in, eavesdropping.

But note that although Simo tells us a great deal of background information, he does not tell us the crucial facts about the plot. He can't – because he does not know them. The same is true with all the apparently expository opening scenes: in *Phormio*, the protatic Davos and the slightly more dramatically important Geta tell us about the situation of the *adulescens* and the parasite, but nothing of the crucial plot details to do with the double marriage of the uncle;[185] in *Hecyra*, Parmeno tells Syra and Philotis all about his young master's premarital, marital and extramarital activities,

182 Boyle (2004: 17): 'the first freedman in Latin literature'. Protatic characters are indicated by Donatus also for *Ph.* and *Hec.* (Wessner 1962–3 1: 36, 49).

183 Duckworth (1994: 108).

184 His role is particularly surprising for someone with the name 'Davos': cf. *An.*

185 If Lefèvre (1978b) is right that the bigamy did not occur in the Greek original, it is noteworthy that Davos and Geta, whose opening scene most people would regard as a Terentian invention for the purposes of exposition, do not explain details of the double marriage.

but nothing about the pregnancy and premarital rape which are crucial to the plot; in *Adelphi*, Micio speaks in a monologue which is nearest of all Terentian openings to a conventional prologic exposition, but he only gives us part of the picture about the younger generation of brothers (he does not know why Aeschinus has not come home, or anything very much about either boy's activity). All this, because the characters simply do not know. Incomplete exposition is, of itself, nothing new, as we have seen in discussion of Plautus: what is remarkable about Terence is the extent of the gaps in our information, and the potentially misleading and unreliable nature of the early hints we are offered. For example, the opening of *Hecyra* with two prostitutes in conversation might make us expect a courtesan-play, not a citizen-play. Moreover, when Parmeno apparently tells them all the gossip, we might wonder whether he really knows what he is talking about, since he spends all the rest of the play being kept out of the way and not allowed to fulfil his 'proper' role.[186]

Terence's replacement of the Plautine prologue with an 'extra-dramatic' one does not remove from Terence the opportunity to tell a story and expound the plot, but it does release him from the expectation that he should do so in a way that is true, reliable, or anything like complete. He chose to keep the audience guessing right up to the end.

186 See Barsby (1990).

CHAPTER 3

Plotting and playwrights

μέγιστον δὲ τούτων ἐστὶν ἡ τῶν πραγμάτων σύστασις... ἔτι ἄνευ μὲν πράξεως οὐκ ἂν γένοιτο τραγῳδία, ἄνευ δὲ ἠθῶν γένοιτ' ἄν· (Aristotle, *Poetics* 1450a)

The putting-together of the actions is the greatest of these... without action there could not be a tragedy, whereas without characters there could.

The plot's the thing. It is not, of course, the only thing, for Aristotle perhaps means little more (or less) than a point about medium (that drama only comes into existence when some action happens), while Anglophone critics use the term 'plot' in different ways for different purposes, not all of which can automatically be said to reflect on each other.[1] It is nonetheless possible, I suggest, to make a claim for a particular kind of plot activity as integral to the workings of Roman comedy: that internal plotting is a programmatic sign for comedy; that internal and external plotting (that is, the best laid plans of the characters *in* the play, and the plot *of* the play) are mutually reinforcing; and that instability of identity within a play slides into the precarious construction of identity in the production of a play. This means not just that there is a lot of deceit and a lot of instability of identity in Roman comedy, but specifically that these issues work together, and that they constitute a programmatic metaphor for the dramatic performance.[2] I do not intend to imply, let it be stressed, that 'metatheatre' is the 'answer' to what is going on in the plays,[3] but that the metatheatrical and the

[1] As Lowe (2000: ix) says of the word 'plot', 'it remains for many theorists a suspect term, worryingly slippery to define, and tangled up with lines of theory that have not fared well in the history of post-war criticism'. His major interest in this important and dense book is in what might be called 'storyline', which sometimes but not always connects with the activity of plotting with which I am more concerned.

[2] Such a metaphor is hinted at by Lowe (1989).

[3] Rosenmeyer (2002). I find it difficult to comprehend Rosenmeyer's polemic against the practice and terminology of metatheatre. While agreeing that 'the manufacture of a new encompassing genre

intratheatrical interact. As Nelson says (1990: 151–2), 'it is clear that the comedy of many times and places has successfully exploited techniques for teasing, cajoling, or disorienting readers and auditors, for exchanging back-chat with them, and even for drawing them into the performance. It has played tricks based on illusion; it has made a joke out of the tenuousness of the grasp human beings have on reality. It has turned the world upside down. Metafictional techniques, which lend themselves to such procedures, are for that reason peculiarly suited to comedy.' Indeed, this metafictionality which suits comedy so well seems to be bound up in the very complexity of the comic plot, for, as Frye (1957: 170) says, '[t]he plots of comedy often are complicated because there is something inherently absurd about complications . . . comedy regularly illustrates a victory of arbitrary plot over consistency of character'.

Would it be right to say, then, that Roman comedy is plot-driven? It is often true that the complexities – which are by no means always rational – of plot are what make the comedy (Plautus' *Epidicus* and Terence's *Andria* are good examples), but on the other hand it is also the case that there is great comic power precisely in the plot-stopping irrelevance of jokes, verbal fireworks, flights of fancy, running slave routines and suchlike bits of stage business. In Plautus' *Rudens*, for example, the comedy is in the way of the plot until Trachalio, after many lines of irrelevant squabbling, eventually says (1090–1) that the chest belongs to the *leno* and contains the solution to the plot's problems, as he could easily have said straightaway.[4] Plot makes comedy, but paradoxically plot is funny precisely when it fails to make progress; or, perhaps, we should see comedy as divided into plot and anti-plot, each of which requires the other.

PLOTTING IDENTITY

Comic plots are not all the same.[5] What is remarkable, in a genre which is by no means as uniform as convention would have it, is the extent to which the plots of comedy revolve around manipulations and instabilities of identity. A very high proportion of the extant plays involve at least one

[might be] an obstruction to enlightenment' (107), I cannot get away from the sense that the term 'metatheatrical' is well placed to express the moments of heightened and marked awareness, on the part of play, players and people, of the theatricality of the act in which they are involved, a primary point of which, in comedy at any rate, is fun.

[4] These plot-stopping irrelevances played a crucial role in the development of Fraenkel's theory of 'plautinische im Plautus'.

[5] There are of course certain 'stock' patterns, and much creative effect and humour can be derived from manipulation of those patterns.

element of deceit, disguise or recognition (which is the resolution of a kind of accidental disguise).[6]

Out of twenty-six plays under consideration (discounting the fragmentary *Vidularia*), twelve plays (on a fairly conservative reckoning)[7] contain internal acts of deliberate disguise, while a further two (*Bacchides* and *Menaechmi*) are so bound up in mistaken identity as crucial to their plots and performances that they can be categorised in the same way. This means that half the extant plays of Roman comedy involve an element of disguise.[8] In addition, seven plays involve an act of recognition (as indeed do several of the 'disguise' plays). That leaves only five plays unaccounted for. Of those, *Mercator* could be classed as a disguise play (the girl is disguised as a maid for the mother, rather than as a concubine; the father and son each take on the imagined persona of a 'friend' who wants to buy the girl; the monkey-dream sets everyone's identity into fabular form); *Mostellaria* is a highly tricksy play, which is nearly all deception of the returning *senex* by the clever slave. These two, then, fit neatly into the same category as the bulk of the plays. What remains is a group consisting of *Stichus*, *Aulularia* and Terence's *Adelphi*. In the first of these, the father starts out by trying a trick on the girls, pretending that he is thinking of getting married, but it does not amount to much of a deception. *Aulularia* feels as though it ought to involve both trickery and recognition, but if there is any trickster at work here it is the Lar Familiaris who has caused Euclio to find the pot of gold by means of which he will be able to marry off his daughter. And the 'recognition' is not a new identity for the girl (thus allowing her to marry the young man), but rather the finding of the pot, and the pseudo-recognition that the pot and the girl are 'the same'. *Adelphi*, probably the last play of Roman comedy as we know it, is an oddity, because it alone appears not to have either disguise or recognition, or any intrigue, and so perhaps not to be concerned with the questions of identity which have dominated the genre. The impression is misleading, however, since as a play about adoption it must inevitably raise questions of identity. It might, perhaps, not be a comedy: but in fact the play depends on a series of mistakes about identity, in a broad sense. Micio is deceived about the meaning of Aeschinus' initial abduction of the prostitute; the family of Sostrata are likewise mistaken about his motives and intentions; Demea is

[6] Anderson (2002) analyses 'resistance to recognition' as a driving force particularly in Terentian plays, where that resistance forms part of the complexities of plot which delay the ending.

[7] *Am.*, *As.*, *Capt.*, *Cas.*, *Epid.*, *Mil.*, *Per.*, *Poen.*, *Ps.*, *Trin.*, *HT*, *Eu.* Less conservatively, also *Cur.*, *Men.*, *Mer.*

[8] See Muecke (1986) for a groundbreaking discussion of disguise in Roman comedy.

deceived about the identity of the lover of the prostitute, and about the characters of both his sons. If there is a trick, or a play-within-the-play, it is that played by Micio on Aeschinus, when he pretends that a stranger has come to claim Pamphila in marriage. Finally there is the extraordinary and incomprehensible scene where Demea undergoes a 'change of heart' (if so it is), and decides to (pretend to) play out the alternative stock role for a *senex*. If Demea is cheating, however, then the play is performing the most outrageous piece of manipulation of identity.

Comedy is predicated on the manipulation of identity because it makes a joke of our anxieties and renders them less painful through laughter, so that we can not only enjoy a jocular look at what it means to have an identity, but also admire and join vicariously in the plotter's divine standpoint. Sometimes, the plotter comes clean and acknowledges his own identity as the playwright: when that happens, there is often the kind of explicit playfulness with selfhood and knowledge that we call a 'recognition', often played out in a 'recognition scene' but also not infrequently achieved off-stage. Around half of the extant plays of Roman comedy (five out of six for Terence) contain an explicit manifestation of the motif in which someone, usually a girl, turns out to be someone else, in such a way as to enable the desired resolution of the plot.[9] As is well known, the motif was exercised in Greek tragedy, particularly by Euripides among the authors of extant plays, and was much admired by Aristotle, as a satisfactory resolution to the hamartic complication of the plot. A modern realist plotting-aesthetic might criticise the motif as an oversimplified, 'convenient' device to extract the plot from the hole of its own making, but such a criticism misses the point. The point is that a character finds her or his identity, and hence new life, not only in order to resolve the plot, but also in order to give substance to our desires about stability of the self. These desires take concrete form in the traditional tokens which throw a physical lifeline to the plot of recognition plays (cf. particularly *Cistellaria*, *Rudens* and *Hecyra*). The recognition plot and the intrigue plot (which are not mutually exclusive) are two sides to the same coin: a play does not simply *include* a recognition

[9] Golden (1992: 74): 'Aristotelian reversal (περιπέτεια), a change of fortune from one state of affairs to its opposite, and recognition (ἀναγνώρισις), a change from ignorance to knowledge, are features of both tragic and comic *mimesis*. Both must arise "out of the structure of the plot itself so that they developed from events that have previously occurred" because for Aristotle, as we have seen, "it makes a great difference if something happens *because* of something else or merely *after* it" (1452a 18–21)'. Cave (1988) is an extensive discussion of recognition in literature, the main interest of which is in modern European literature, but which reflects interestingly on the artificiality, literariness and cognitive significance of recognition for Roman comedy also.

scene or a trick, but rather it is constituted by these features because it is ultimately about identity and the artful manipulation of it.

VISION AND CONFUSION

Theatre is a visual art, in actuality when performed and in potential when read or spoken. 'Re-cognition' of events in a play is not a matter of 'just watching', but of reading as active spectatorship. Theatre requires its audience to be aware of the gaps between that vision and the normal processes of perception. When the comic trickster tries to convince us that we are seeing something contrary to all the evidence of our senses, his action is a miniature analogue of the work of the playwright.[10] Stage convention draws metatheatrical attention to the process of vision and its connection with understanding and with identity, in various games of seeing between the characters themselves. The ridiculous convention that when two characters meet in a play it takes them some time and quite a bit of stage business to recognise each other is a symbol of the work theatre has to do, and is often self-parodied.[11] Moreover, it is common for one character to be ahead of the other in recognition, such as in the scene in *Miles gloriosus*, to be discussed further below, when the weak Sceledrus comes out talking about his knowledge of what he has seen: he cannot see the strong Palaestrio, who *can* see him, and can recognise that this is the man he wants. Vision is power. There are eavesdropping scenes where from a realistic point of view the characters (or perhaps we should say, the actors) are clearly neither invisible nor inaudible to each other.[12] There are humorous cases of outrageous failure on the part of characters to see what is blatantly obvious to the audience, for example at *Cist.* 671–704, where the maid Halisca hunts for the lost eponymous casket, watched by Lampadio, who is holding it. She follows its tracks in the dust (698), Pooh and Piglet-style, so intent on her search that she neither sees nor hears her quarry until it is shoved in front of her nose. A similar visual joke on perception and the

[10] Mercury, the prologue-speaker of *Am.*, and Palinurus, who introduces *Cur.*, conjure up night in the midst of a bright Roman feast day. See Arnott (1995: 190) on mimed stage business in *Cur.* On the general point about the deceptiveness of vision, there is also a brief discussion in Slater (2001: 192), apropos *Epid.*

[11] Examples: Pl. *Cur.* 111–26, *Epid.* 1–5, *Rud.* 228–43 and many a running-slave routine. Failure to recognise runs into refusal to acknowledge, as in the first interaction between Pseudolus and Ballio at *Ps.* 243–65.

[12] Marshall (2006: 167) usefully describes eavesdropping scenes as 'split-focus'. Goldberg (1986: 78–9) says that eavesdropping 'often suggests for the audience's benefit which of two characters in confrontation will eventually triumph'. See also Bain (1977: 105–17); Slater (2000: 134).

senses informs the follow-the-wine scene at *Cur.* 96–109. In this section, I examine the self-conscious comic playfulness about the control of vision and its connection with personal identity.

To take a simple example first: *Mostellaria.* The young man Philolaches and his dissolute friends are living a life of dissolution, when the father suddenly returns. The slave Tranio packs them off inside, and undertakes to hold off the old man. This he does by convincing him that his house is haunted, and that the noises he can hear coming from it are not, contrary to appearances, the drunken shouts and raucous singing of a bunch of dissolutes, but the screams of angry ghosts. The next part of the trick involves the house next door, which Tranio pretends that Philolaches has bought at a very good price.[13] The *senex* Theopropides is delighted at his son's good business sense, and wants to look around the property. Tranio now plays one old man off against the other, by telling the real owner of the house that his master is thinking of building some new women's quarters and would like to look at his house as a model, and by telling his master that the supposed vendor of the house is unhappy about having to sell it, and so likes to act as if he were not doing so. The scene of particular relevance to the issue of sight is that in which Tranio shows off the house to his master, its own owner and the audience.[14]

Vision is highlighted straightaway, with the request and invitation *inspicere* (772, 806, 807). Then Tranio deceptively invites Theopropides not only to look at the house, but also to look at the man who is supposedly selling the house, and to *see* how unhappy he looks at the prospect. 'I see', replies Theopropides:

> TR. ah, caue tu illi obiectes nunc in aegritudine
> te has emisse. non tu uides hunc uoltu uti tristi est senex?
> TH. uideo. (*Mos.* 810–12)

TR. Ah, make sure you don't cast it in his teeth that you've bought the house, since he's so down. Don't you see how sad-faced this old man is? TH. I see.

In fact (that is, the play's first-level fiction), the supposed vendor is not unhappy at all, but Tranio has made Theopropides think that he is, simply by inviting him to look at the situation in a certain way.[15] Master and slave

[13] For the play's basis in the Greek law of property transactions, see Lowe (1985a: 14). For its strongly Plautine spirit, Stärk (1991: esp. 122–3) on the house-viewing scene.

[14] There are brief references to this scene in Slater (2000: 172–3, 142). See also Leach (1969b).

[15] Tranio follows it up by inviting the old man to be careful to avoid appearing to tease the other *senex*: *inridere ne uideare* . . . (812). The quasi-deponent usage *uideare* is, in context, visible in its original role as the passive of *uideo.*

enter (*quin tu is intro*, 815), or rather, somehow appear to enter and inspect the property. We must assume that in fact all three men stay outside the house.[16] Even with the best props a Roman play can muster, what we 'see' of the insides of houses in comedy is mostly in the words, words often unrealistically but entertainingly spoken from outside the house.[17] So it is for Theopropides:

> TR. uiden uestibulum ante aedis hoc et ambulacrum, quoiusmodi?
> TH. luculentum edepol profecto. TR. age specta postis, quoiusmodi,
> quanta firmitate facti et quanta crassitudine.
> TH. non uideor uidisse postis pulchriores.
>
> (*Mos.* 817–20)

TR. Do you see the vestibule in front of the house and the walkway, what they are like? TH. Very excellent indeed. TR. Come on, look at what the doorposts are like, how strongly made and thick they are. TH. I don't seem ever to have seen finer doorposts.

When Simo remarks on the price he once paid for them, Tranio directs Theopropides' hearing and sight again:

> TR. audin 'fuerant' dicere?
> uix uidetur continere lacrumas.
>
> (*Mos.* 821–2)

TR. Do you hear him say '*had* paid'? He seems hardly to be able to hold back his tears.

Astute viewers might already guess that the sight being presented to us, these two old men and two old doorposts, is a bit more complex and funnier than the sight presented to the old men themselves. This house is going to come to life through Tranio's words and through the creative power of drama: the process is simply an exaggeration of the coming-to-life which is the action of all drama. In this case, however, we have already been prepared for the metaphorisation of the physical by the physicalisation of metaphor in the *adulescens*' description of his degenerate state as being like that of a house originally well built but falling into ruin (84–156).[18]

[16] Marshall (2006: 49) considers that the *postes* of 818, for example, could be part of a painted stage set, but that it is more likely that 'all such details were supplied by audience imagination'. Beare (1964: 279–83) refutes the arguments of those who propose a porch in front of the house, on which such indoor scenes might be played: 'there is much obvious make-believe in Tranio's description of what he sees' (282). See also Milnor (2002).

[17] The pedantic realist Simo in Ter. *An.* scoffs at such behaviour, as is discussed below.

[18] See Milnor (2002) on the house metaphor. The humour of literalisation is part of the stock in trade of comedy.

Surprisingly, it is Theopropides who begins the process of bringing the house to life. In response to hearing that the doorposts originally cost *tris minas pro istis duobus praeter uecturam* ('three *minae* for the two of them besides delivery', 823), the old man remarks: *hercle qui multum inprobiores sunt quam a primo credidi* ('good heavens, they are much more worthless than I thought at first', 824). This provokes a typically Plautine joke-routine, with Tranio's question *quapropter?* ('Why?': usually such a question signals the acknowledgement that the previous speaker has made a joke, but one which the current speaker does not understand, or pretends not to understand, so that the joke can be explained). We expect the old man's line at 824 to be a response to the statement of original cost, and so we interpret *inprobiores* as having some relation to financial irregularity, and a general lack of moral soundness.[19] Perhaps the joke will be something like 'because they stole so much money', thus making a fairly predictable anthropomorphism of doors and doorposts (which is indeed happening). Theopropides, however, replies *quia edepol ambo ab infumo tarmes secat.* The doorposts are being undercut by woodworm.[20] On a straight reading, we should see this as typical Plautine abuse-humour – it is funny to disparage the quality of things, even when such disparagement and the actual quality of the thing disparaged are largely irrelevant to what is going on (here, they would be not so much irrelevant as antithetical, since the speaker is in fact pleased with what he sees – that is the magic of Tranio, to make his dupe/the audience see what he wants them to see, even against the evidence of their eyes). But is there more to this joke? The word *tarmes* is almost a hapax legomenon, since the only other occurrence (according to both *OLD* and *PHI*) is the explanation at Paul. *Fest.* p. 358M (*tarmes genus uermiculi carnem exedens*, 'tarmes is a type of flesh-eating worm'), but the *OLD* makes it cognate with *tero*, the meanings of which are rich: it is hard not to suspect a hint of a sexual joke (e.g. *OLD* s.v. *tero* 1b), though probably more immediate is a hint that the 'doorposts' are being worn down by the action of the *tarmes* – who must, when we look back at it, be Tranio, just as the parasite Curculio is a weevil in the play of that name.[21] What might be pure humour in the intention of Theopropides, or even

[19] The word *improbus* and its cognates are extremely common in Plautus, usually applied to people, with moral implications. It is a standard insult. A search in *PHI* of *improb-* scored fifty-three, plus two for *inprob-*. The other occurrence in *Mos.*, at 626, *danista qui sit, genu' quod inprobissumum est?*, comes in a financial context.

[20] See Lowe (1985a: 24) for the joke here on Roman methods of execution.

[21] Strong (1906: 68–9) notes the manuscript reading *tramis* for *tarmes* at (Lindsay's) 825, and says that 'the poet certainly plays upon the name *tramis* which is meant to recall Tranio'. It is indeed tempting to see a nominal connection here, as in *Cur.*

such fussy disparagement as is typical of business transactions, becomes the first stage in the identification of the doorposts with the two old men, and of Tranio as the 'worm' who 'eats away' at them before their very eyes.

Tranio takes control back into his hands in his next reply. He pretends to an expert discussion of the techniques of carpentry (*intempestiuos excissos credo*, 'I think they were cut at the wrong time', but they are alright now *si sunt inducti pice*, 'if they are dipped in pitch'; they are a good piece of work, not done by some *pultiphagus* barbarian workman – such as Plautus?),[22] but it is becoming clear to the audience that he is talking about the old men, who have been around far too long, arrived at the wrong time, are being cut down and having a bad time (from their own point of view), and need to be dipped in pitch. The word *excido* is a straightforward expression for cutting down trees (*exciditur ilex*, Enn. *Ann.* 176 Skutsch), but it also has military usages, to destroy, lay waste, etc. (military imagery is common in Plautine deceits), and is used elsewhere explicitly for the artful extraction of money from old men (*Bac.* 668). It also has the specialist meaning 'to castrate'.[23] Pitch would be an appropriate substance to prevent wood from rotting, but it is also used in slave-torture (*Capt.* 597).[24] Construct it how you like – that's the power of metaphor.

The scene being now firmly in the hands of Tranio, it is sight (both the old men's and the audience's) which he manipulates. *uiden coagmenta in foribus?* ('do you see the joints in the doors?', 829), he asks, introducing a repetitious run of words of seeing: *uideo, specta* (829), *contemplo* (831), *uiden* (832), (*non edepol*) *uideo*, (*at ego*) *uideo* (833), *specta, conspicere* (835), *uides, intuor* (836), *optuere* (837), *conspicari, contui* (838), *conspicio* (839), *optuerier* (840). He invites Theopropides to note how neatly the doorposts 'sleep' (829): the reference, as Slater notes, is clearly to the old men as sleeping dupes, and Tranio and the audience as wakeful tricksters, but the image is also nicely fitted to the pseudo-technical comment on the joinery.[25] Then Tranio, still playing the role of technical expert, begins to expound the

22 The disparaging joke on Roman barbarians is of course metatheatrical and celebratory. See Owens (2000: 397); also Fraenkel (1960: 99), Lowe (1985a: 24–5), Gowers (1993: 53–4).

23 The word's meaning as 'castrate' is first attested in Ovid, at *Fast.* 4.361, and may therefore not be active for Plautus. That specialist meaning must, however, relate to the next specialist meaning recorded in the Thesaurus Linguae Latinae (*TLL*) (1242), which is the medical sense of amputation. In view of the likely medical connotations of pitch, it seems reasonable to suppose a pseudo-medical (and possibly mildly obscene) register here.

24 Drinking pitch is used as an insult posing as medicinal advice at *Mer.* 140.

25 Slater (2000: 142) refers *dormiunt* directly to the old men, and not to the doorposts at all, but this is because it is only an aside in an illustration of the way that the trickster and audience are 'awake' while the dupes are 'asleep' in Roman comedy. For the technical language, cf. Tac. *Hist.* 3.47.15: *camaras uocant, artis lateribus latam aluum sine uinculo aeris aut ferri conexam.*

pictures at an exhibition: 'Do you see the picture of a crow deceiving two vultures?' His master completely fails to see, which Tranio eventually puts down to his old age and failing eyesight. After all, old men in comedy are never allowed to see what is going on. The audience 'see' perfectly well, in that they understand that the crow is Tranio and the vultures are the old men, that the picture is a fable and the ecphrasis is a reflection on the power of drama to control our vision. They might, however, if prone to self-examination and self-irony, note that they too cannot *really* see a picture of two vultures and a crow, even if they look directly at Tranio and the old men.[26]

An even more able trickster than Tranio calls the shots in *Miles gloriosus*, a play structured around spectacle and disguise. After the opening scene in which the eponymous *miles* is paraded for us in all his bombastic glory, while the parasite tells us how to look at him, the original *architectus doli* (Palaestrio) comes out to deliver the prologue and establish his control over what we see and how we see it. His peroration piles on the language of Plautine deceit, and links it explicitly with sight – ours and that of his dupe:

> ei nos facetis fabricis et doctis dolis
> glaucumam ob oculos obiciemus eumque ita
> faciemus ut quod uiderit non uiderit.
> et mox ne erretis, haec duarum hodie uicem
> et hinc et illinc mulier feret imaginem,
> atque eadem erit, uerum alia esse adsimulabitur.
> (*Mil.* 147–52)

We'll cast dust in his eyes with crafty wit and clever tricks and we'll make it so that he hasn't seen what he's seen. So that you don't soon get confused, today this woman will be wearing two different faces, here and there, and will be the same, while she pretends to be the other.

Palaestrio is going to throw the dust in someone's eyes, to change what he sees.[27] We, however, are to be immune to this deceit, because of our superior knowledge. We are to enjoy the error, but not be subject to it (*ne erretis*), because we will understand that the woman is going to bear

[26] Lowe (1985a: 25), whose major interest is in ascertaining Plautine additions to the play: 'we may doubt whether in the *Phasma* Theopropides would have gullibly accepted Tranio's account of an invisible picture'.

[27] Strictly speaking, it is *glaucuma*, 'cataract', which he is going to throw in Sceledrus' eyes, but the English idiom seems a justified slippage here. For the metaphorical use of medical terms, see Langslow (1999) 198–200 on Latin poetry generally, and 202–5 on Plautus specifically, including the current passage.

two *imagines* and, while actually being one person, will pretend to be another (and two). If Palaestrio really means us to attain his godlike level of understanding, then this is rather a confusing way of going about it (as usual).[28] Doubling, duplicity, distortion of vision, deceptive identity and a close shave with Error (as ever, comic error is the flipside of tragic *hamartia*): such will be the stuff of this play.

Another scene, this time between the trickster and his aid, furthers the preparations for the intrigue, building up our picture, our sight, of the slave and the monkey on the roof, looking inside at the lovers kissing – scenes which we can never observe directly in ancient drama. When the watcher (*qui uidit*, 266) finally comes out to give his side of the picture, he is lost even before he starts, for his opening gambit is to place himself in the position of the sleeper:[29]

> Nisi quidem ego hodie ambulaui dormiens in tegulis,
> certo edepol scio me uidisse hic . . .
>
> (*Mil.* 272–3)

Unless indeed today I have sleep-walked on the roof, I certainly know that I saw here . . .

His insistence on his own certainty, his own self (*ego*, *me*, plus first-person verbs), protests too much, for it is this certainty, this knowledge of self, which will be undone by Palaestrio's trick. Nonetheless, Sceledrus makes another attempt to impose his own control on his visual capacities with the claim *egomet duobus his oculis meis* ('I myself with these two eyes of mine', 290), in response to Palaestrio's (conventional) question *tutin?*[30] The conversation continues in this mode for some time: Sceledrus' insistence on knowledge of what he saw comes to loom larger than any other knowledge he might have about himself (*quid fuat me nescio: haec me uidisse ego certo scio*, 'I don't know what will happen to me: I certainly do know that I saw these things', 299). As Palaestrio insists that it would be in Sceledrus' interests to change his eyes and what he says about them (327), the dupe insists on the connection between sight and knowledge of the self: *mihi ego uideo, mihi ego sapio, <mihi> ego credo plurumum* ('for me I see, for me I know, <me> I trust most of all', 331). Palaestrio's Plautine response is a unique insult about sight and knowledge – *stultiuidu[s]* (335).

28 Marshall (2006: 104–5) suggests that Plautus insists so much on explaining the trick to us in order to display the connection with 'twin' plays, in which, it is suggested, the same actor plays both twins. This may be so, but I would stand by the opinion that the laboured explanation is intended to give us the sense that we are being let into something terribly complicated and clever.

29 See Slater (2000: 142) for sleep as a characteristic of the duped.

30 Palaestrio metatheatrically questions the realism (*ueri simile*) of Sceledrus' story. See the final section of this chapter, pp. 156–62.

The comic answer to the problem of someone who has seen something he should not have seen is to change his perception of his own experience and make him see things differently. Palaestrio hatches a plan to claim that Philocomasium's twin sister has recently arrived from Athens, and that it was the double, not the girl herself, whom Sceledrus saw.[31] Because of a backstage hole which Palaestrio has had made between the two houses, Philocomasium can pass from one house to the other without Sceledrus (or the audience) seeing her. *We* of course take Palaestrio's word for it that there is such a hole, and that the two girls are the same person. Sceledrus is forced to see the 'two' girls popping up from one side then the other and back – in a childish game of doubles, of peek-a-boo behind a pillar[32] – until he is so confused that he has to admit that there are two of them, and that he misinterpreted what he originally saw. It is no coincidence, in this play of sleep and knowledge, that Philocomasium introduces her fake twin by way of a prophetic dream (382–93).[33] Sceledrus starts to doubt himself, though he still tries to hold onto his sense of self:

> nescio quid credam egomet mihi iam, ita quod uidisse credo
> me id iam non uidisse arbitror.
>
> (*Mil.* 402–3)

I don't know what I should believe for myself now, because what I believe I saw I now think I didn't see.

And then:

> nihil habeo certi quid loquar: non uidi eam, etsi uidi.
>
> (*Mil.* 407)

I haven't got anything certain that I can say: I didn't see her, even though I saw her.

When the 'real' girl goes into the soldier's house, to expiate the dream, the 'twin' comes out of Periplectomenus' house, and not only pseudo-conventionally does not see (pretends not to see) the other characters on stage, but does not recognise them (i.e. pretends not to recognise them, in her persona as new arrival). It is at this point that Sceledrus, under the

[31] Lefèvre (1984) argues that Plautus invented the 'twin-sister' trick.

[32] This is a remarkable scene of doubles, with extensive linguistic echoing (e.g. *haec hinc huc* at 418 and 377, and the repeated *ea uidetur* in the knowing mouth of Palaestrio at 417 and 419). Linguistic repetition is discussed in detail in ch. 4.

[33] Comic dreams include a disproportionate number of monkeys: see Connors (2004). After all the excitement, Sceledrus is overcome, so he goes off to hide for a bit, and drinks himself into a stupor. Palaestrio and another slave, Lurcio, have a scene of fun about it.

influence of Palaestrio, starts to doubt not just his knowledge of what he has seen, but his very identity:[34]

> Sc. metuo maxume,
> Pa. quid metuis? Sc. enim ne <nos> nosmet perdiderimus uspiam;
> nam nec te neque me nouisse ait haec. Pa. persectari hic uolo,
> Sceledre, nos nostri an alieni simus, ne dum quispiam
> nos uicinorum inprudentis aliquis immutauerit.
> Sc. certe equidem noster sum.
>
> (*Mil.* 428–33)

Sc. I'm very afraid. Pa. What are you afraid of? Sc. That we have completely lost ourselves, for she says that she doesn't know you or me. Pa. I want to investigate this here, Sceledrus, whether we are ours or belong to someone else, just in case some neighbour has changed us while we weren't looking. Sc. Well I'm certainly ours.

Finally, the double exposure of Philocomasium and her 'twin' on stage is redoubled by a twofold entry of Sceledrus into the houses, to see and report on the girl inside. Thus he brings both scenes imagistically onto the stage: we see Philocomasium embracing her lover in one house *and* asleep alone in the other house at the same time – even though we know it is a trick, we still enjoy (and enjoy in safety) the experience of the dislocation of reality and reason.

The next time we see Palaestrio, he is looking around to check that no-one is watching while he and his aids think up the ultimate plot:

> sed speculabor nequis aut hinc aut ab laeua aut a dextera
> nostro consilio uenator adsit cum auritis plagis.
>
> (*Mil.* 607–8)

But I'll spy out to make sure there is no hunter here, or on the left or the right, who can trap our plot with long-eared nets.

Such a statement can only be made with a massive wink at the audience, who are allowed to see and hear the secret machinations – although in fact all we get for some time is veiled hints (*sed uolo scire, eodem consilio quod intus meditati sumus* . . . 'but I want to know, that plot which we hatched out inside . . .', 612), and a long distraction into Periplectomenus' comic philosophy. Eventually, however, we hear the plot: Periplectomenus will provide a client of his, who will pretend to be his wife and in love with the soldier. She will give Periplectomenus' ring (which Palaestrio demanded

[34] The language of identity used by the slaves reflects their status: *nostri* 'ours' encompasses both belonging to 'our household' and being owned.

from the old man before he would even tell him the plot) to her maid to give to Palaestrio, so that he can give it to the soldier as an introduction and pledge of love from the false matron. Palaestrio will then persuade the soldier to let Philocomasium go, using the faked arrival of the mother and sister from Athens as a convenient excuse. Pleusicles will dress up as the sailor who is to take the women back to Athens. The later parts of this ploy we do not hear in the plotting session, only as they unfold, but we already know enough to encourage us to entrust ourselves to Palaestrio.[35]

The joke about there being 'no-one' around is repeated later (955), when Palaestrio is preparing to tell the soldier about the supposed wife of Periplectomenus and her 'overwhelming desire' for him, and asks him to look around and check there is no-one who might overhear. Pyrgopolynices, proving his vision already clouded, replies: *nemo adest* ('no one is here', 957). He falls for the plot immediately, because he has such a false vision of himself as universally desirable and desired. When the maid Milphidippa comes out to play her part (*Iam est ante aedis circus ubi sunt ludi faciundi mihi*, 'now here in front of the house is the circus where my games need to be played', 991), she makes explicit use of the stage convention about not seeing the other characters on stage: *dissimulabo, hos quasi non uideam neque esse hic etiamdum sciam* ('I'll pretend that I can't see them and I don't know that they're here yet', 992). She has picked up the hint from Palaestrio, in his introductory comment on her, in which he controls the soldier's vision: *uiden tu illam oculis uenaturam facere atque aucupium auribus?* ('Do you see her hunting with her eyes and bird-catching with her ears?', 990) – more truly than the soldier realises.

The scene between the maid, the soldier and the *architectus* is a classic piece of deceptive acting. The principals even keep drawing attention to their game, and the fun they are having, privately asking each other *ut ludo?* (1066a, 1073), and encouraging the audience to laugh at the soldier's folly and their own cleverness. After Milphidippa leaves, the soldier starts on Palaestrio's plan to 'get rid of' his concubine. Palaestrio nearly slips up, by overplaying his visual hand, when he tells the soldier about the twin sister: *quia oculis meis / uidi hic sororem esse eiius* ('since with my own eyes I saw her sister to be here', 1104–5), which causes Pyrgopolynices to wonder about a casual affair with her as well – but he is swiftly diverted by Palaestrio's information about the mother, and the sailor, in whom the soldier also expresses sexual interest, so that he has to be diverted again.

[35] In this discussion, I am not making much mention of the metatheatrical effects of Palaestrio's control of the plot, especially the highly expressive vocabulary of plotting, as I am taking these features for granted while concentrating on the interactions of sight and (false) identity.

This play is obsessed with the issue of sight, and who sees, and who is tempted to see. Again at 1137, when Acroteleutium, Milphidippa and Pleusicles come out to join Palaestrio to plan the next 'act', they look around to check *ne quis adsit arbiter* ('that there isn't any eyewitness around'). Milphidippa replies *neminem pol uideo, nisi hunc quem uolumus conuentum* ('I don't see anyone, except him whom we want to see here'), meaning Palaestrio. The audience, of course, know that they are there too, but they also know that they are being allowed to piggyback on Palaestrio's part. (Or rather, that is the effect on them of the trick of sight – and on us, since the reader is taking a second-level piggyback on the live audience.) Either she cannot see us because we are thick as thieves with Palaestrio, giving us magical invisibility, or she can see us because she is in league with Palaestrio, who has let us into the charmed circle. Pleusicles is to dress up as the sailor, complete with eye-patch (the conventional disguise draws attention to vision), and to threaten to set sail without her, if Philocomasium does not board immediately. All goes according to plan, and Philocomasium is taken away in front of the very eyes of Pyrgopolynices. There is a moment when the disguise nearly slips, when Pleusicles gets too close to Philocomasium (1334–5), but Palaestrio draws attention away from his less-skilled actors onto himself, who can maintain a part to the end. In fact, he almost overplays it (again), and the soldier becomes so convinced of Palaestrio's sincere love for him that he nearly refuses to let him go after all.

Escape they do, however, and the play goes into its denouement. Periplectomenus plays his part as injured husband; then Sceledrus makes a surprise late return to the play, in order to act as (tragic) messenger, with the news that the man with the eye-patch has two eyes, and was not a sailor after all (1430). For the final time, Sceledrus is able to say that he saw Pleusicles and Philocomasium *osculari atque amplexari* ('kiss and embrace', 1433), just as he had seen at the outset. Sceledrus' presence thus links together the two tricks of the play, and the interactions of sight and disguise. With the undoing of the disguise and the restoration of proper sight, the soldier realises his mistake. The 'recognition' is not the typical 'lost-daughter motif' of comedy, but is if anything rather closer to tragic *anagnorisis*.

The strongest case in Roman comedy for the interactions of disguise, duality, sight and identity is the 'hapax' play, *Amphitruo*. In this play, the trick through which the *architectus* (Mercury) helps the rather unusual lover (Jupiter) to enjoy his beloved is to steal the identities of her legitimate husband and his more conventional slave. Being gods, who can change the bodies of things into different forms, their disguise is absolute, and their appearance identical to that of their dupe-doubles, except for the little flags which signify 'true' identity (i.e., false identity) to the audience. Only we are able to see these signs:

> ea signa nemo <homo> horum familiarium
> uidere poterit: uerum uos uidebitis.
>
> (*Am.* 146–7)[36]

No-one in the household here will be able to see these tokens: but you'll see them.

This, then, is the first trick of sight, to make us believe that we alone have the clue to stable identity. (For it is only true that the other characters 'cannot see' the tassels because the *architectus* says so.) The play's humour pulls out all the stops: the inherent comedy of twins, mistaken identity, audience-superiority over the ignorance of the dupes, vicarious illicit sexuality made 'safe' by the divine authority of its perpetrator, confusion, violence to person and to logic, outrageous imagery and lively language. Yet, as many commentators have sensed, there is a serious dimension to this odd play, with its potentially nightmarish exploration of the loss of personal identity.

The facts of stolen identity, intrigue as play-acting, disguise as deceit – all these and more are probably too obvious in this play to require detailed analysis here.[37] Our concern is the interaction between perversions of vision, the assuming of a role and personal identity. Mercury himself is the first to speak explicitly about the effects of role-playing on the character – though he says so in jest:

> quando imago est huiius in me, certum est hominem eludere.
> et enim uero quoniam formam cepi huius in med et statum,
> decet et facta moresque huius habere me similis item.
> itaque me malum esse oportet, callidum, astutum admodum,
> atque hunc telo suo sibi, malitia, a foribus pellere.
>
> (*Am.* 265–9)

Now that his image is in me, I'm determined to trick the man. And indeed since I have taken on his form and condition, it is appropriate for me to have also his deeds and morals. And so it's right for me to be bad, clever, completely cunning and to repel him from the door by his own weapon, badness.

[36] The motif occurs in a similar position to its parallel in *Mil.* 150–2.

[37] See Stewart (1958) on vision and identity in *Am.*, esp. his comments on madness and drunkenness at 354; Christenson (2000: *passim*, and esp. 165) on the role of Mercury's asides in manipulating the vision of the audience; Muecke (1986); Bettini (1991); Bond (1999). Slater's metatheatrical reading (available at Slater 2000: Appendix IV) also offers some useful comments on illusion in this play (see esp. 188).

The implied psychology is that playing a role habituates the actor to certain forms of behaviour. Mercury (god of thieves) nicely here steals not only Sosia's appearance, but his very self. On reflection (the one great privilege of the reader), we might note that the terms Mercury uses to describe Sosia actually apply rather closely to himself already – *malum, callidum, astutum* – both as god of thieves and business deals, and as *architectus doli* of this play. Could it be, then, that his *pose* of stealing an identity along with an appearance in fact hides the *reality* of doing so? Mercury and Sosia are always already each other's double. And yet, surely these terms in fact apply less well to the human slave than to his divine Other: Sosia shows himself neither clever nor astute, and hardly even 'bad', in the course of the play. Mercury's assumption of his identity seems now to be daylight robbery, rather than mirror-imaging. In view of this point, Mercury's comment (aside) to (or rather, to the audience about) Sosia takes on a particular irony: *ain uero, uerbero? deos esse tui similis putas?* ('What's that, you wretch? Do you think the gods are like you?', 284) – which of course in his case they are.

Everyone knows that night and fear can increase the size of an adversary. It is particularly amusing, however – or scary – for this phenomenon to be experienced by someone looking at his own double. Sosia's reaction to his first sight of the Sosia-Mercury is that he doesn't like the look of him (292), and then that this adversary looks excessively big and beefy (299). Whatever the physical size of the two actors, and whether or not the original production team aimed at making the two of them literally look as similar as possible (as 441–6 would imply), the audience are meant to laugh (perhaps uncomfortably) at Sosia's exaggerated fear of his own mirror image.[38] It is worth remembering that, at this point, Mercury can see Sosia but pretends not to and yet is in control of the scene and of knowledge about the characters, while Sosia thinks he is eavesdropping on Mercury although in fact he cannot really 'see' him and is not directing our gaze at him (as the commentator would usually be doing in such scenes), and moreover that he thinks that Mercury cannot see *him* (*perii si me aspexerit*, 320 – to which Mercury 'replies' that he can smell someone . . .).[39] Rather, our gaze is directed back at Sosia himself, through the mirror of Mercury. As Mercury plays to Sosia's fears (the sleep image, which is recurrent in this play, and a culinary metaphor[40] for violence are active here), Sosia's response

[38] Zanker (2003: 65): 'it is in this discovery of the huge potential of the mirror image for multiple perspectives, for paradox, and for the light it can shed on emotional states that the origin of the new, specifically Hellenistic interest in mirrors is most reasonably located'.

[39] See pp. 178–86 for discussion of this type of comic echo.

[40] See Gowers (1993: 88).

furthers the destabilisation of his personal identity, this time in the form of his name, which will come to be important again later. Mercury's fists are hungry because they have not eaten today, although they put four men to sleep yesterday: Sosia fears *ne ego hic nomen meum commutem et Quintus fiam e Sosia* ('that I might change my name and become Quintus (= the fifth) instead of Sosia', 305).[41] And again, when Mercury is pretending to track Sosia by smell and sound, the human tries out the old Odysseus trick in the hopes of escaping from his Cyclops. Mercury feeds him the cue: *certe enim hic nescioquis loquitur* ('for certainly Someone is talking', 331). To which Sosia 'replies':

> saluos sum, non me uidet:
> 'nescioquem' loqui autumat; mihi certo nomen Sosiaest.
> (*Am.* 331–2)

I'm saved, he can't see me. He says that 'Someone' is speaking; my name is certainly Sosia.

Unhappily for him, Mercury is neither one-eyed nor blind, but is in fact Sosia's own double. As the human tries to insist on his identity (I'm not 'Nobody', I'm Sosia), his words echo Mercury's own introduction of himself, *nomen Mercuriost mihi* ('my name is Mercury', 19)

At last comes the confrontation towards which this scene has been working. Both characters insist that they are Sosia. One of them has the advantage of knowing that he is lying, and of a divine perspective which enables him to tell a deceitful tale of the contested identity (Mercury can relate to Sosia how Sosia secretly drank up a jar of wine in the tent, 426–32). The other ought to have the advantage of telling the truth, but in this play, 'identity' (and the truth about it) is less something absolute pertaining to a person than it is an act of power. A crucial moment comes when Sosia asks who he is, then, if not Sosia. Mercury's reply is *ubi ego Sosia nolim esse, tu esto sane Sosia* ('when I don't want to be Sosia, then you by all means be Sosia', 439) – but now he must take himself off and leave Mercury room to be Sosia. Mercury is Sosia because he wants to be, in defiance of conventional reason but in the spirit of comic logic. It is at this point that Sosia takes a serious look at the situation, and notes how the other really does seem to be his mirror image, which he knows because *saepe in speculum inspexi* ('I've often looked in the mirror', 290).[42] What is ridiculous (literally, funny, as well as stupid) about the situation is the very idea that someone could be tricked into doubting himself. And yet . . . It is hard for Sosia not to accept

[41] See Fraenkel (1960: 21, 28).

[42] This is a joke on the moralistic *topos* of introspection and self-knowledge.

the evidence of his eyes. There is something scary as well as funny about this loss of self. He leaves, muttering to himself:

> ubi ego perii? ubi immutatus sum? ubi ego formam perdidi?
> an egomet me illic reliqui, si forte oblitus fui?
>
> (*Am.* 456–7)

Where did I perish? Where was I changed? Where did I lose my shape? Or did I leave myself behind there [sc. at the harbour], if perhaps I've forgotten?

All this play's scenes of confused confrontation engage with sight and identity.[43] There is one point in particular which suggests a connection between sight, identity and deliberate deceit as comic descendants of tragic *hamartia*. When Jupiter, as Amphitruo, has made peace with Alcumena in front of Sosia, he sends them both off and then remarks to the audience that his plan is progressing nicely. He describes their state as a form of error: *errant probe* (975). He will deliberately intensify the state of error in the family in order to achieve the resolution. The greater the error, the more satisfying the resolution.

Moreover, Jupiter, like Mercury, has control of identity:

> Ego sum ille Amphitruo, quoii est seruos Sosia,
> idem Mercurius qui fit quando commodumst,
> in superiore qui habito cenaculo,
> qui interdum fio Iuppiter quando lubet.
>
> (*Am.* 861–4)

I am that Amphitruo, whose servant is Sosia, the one who becomes Mercury when it suits him, I who inhabit the upstairs attic, and from time to time become Jupiter when I feel like it.

The speech is funny for its own sake, and for the sake of all the delightful ironies of the disguised god and the semi-divine knowledge of him on the part of the audience. But it also acts as a comment, possibly ironic, on the power of the stage to produce an identity when it is wanted: 'I can be Jupiter when I want to'. *Possibly* ironic, however, because such a situation would imply a greater stability of identity, a clearer gulf between a fixed fictional identity and a fixed real identity, than the whole story of ancient

[43] When Amphitruo tries to get a grip on the question of whether Sosia saw Alcumena seeing Amphitruo the previous evening, he instructs the slave to look at him in order to establish the truth (750–1); Sosia picks up the idea that they are seeing double when he notes explicitly that he and his master have each given birth to a twin, and that they could reasonably expect the cup to have been doubled as well – although that expectation is cheated (785–6); Amphitruo doubts his self-knowledge (844); in the Mercury-Amphitruo scene which matches the first Mercury-Sosia scene, Amphitruo opens with the words *ego sum* (1021). And so on.

drama allows us to experience. Jupiter's identity, after all, has been the first to be undermined by this play, when he was presented in the prologue as both king of the gods and an acting slave (27–9).

'But they are gods,' someone might say, 'gods can take up and put aside other identities at will.' It is certainly true that Greek and Roman myths are thick with stories of gods disguising themselves as mortals for various usually nefarious purposes, themselves suffering no adverse consequences. In this regard, comedy enables its favoured characters to share in divine power and divine carelessness. When pro-comic characters dress up as other people in order to perform a trick, they too can act without regard for ordinary logic, as for example the false eunuch in Terence's *Eunuchus* and the false bride in Plautus' *Casina*. In the extremely complex *Epidicus*, the hired girl who has been pretending to be the daughter of the *senex* defends herself when her cover is blown, in terms reminiscent of the divine unconcern of Jupiter and Mercury.[44] The (false) father, Periphanes, thinks he is effecting a recognition scene between his daughter and her mother, whom he seduced many years ago. He is shocked to find that the older woman does not recognise the girl, and when he confronts the girl with Philippa's claim that she is not Acropolistis' mother, her reply is *ne fuat / si non uolt* ('she doesn't have to be if she doesn't want to be', 584–5). She continues the same game for several minutes:

> equidem hac inuita tamen ero matris filia;
> non med istanc cogere aequom est meam esse matrem si neuolt.
> (*Epid.* 585–6)

Nonetheless even if she is unwilling yet I will be the daughter of my mother; it is not right for me to force her to be my mother if she doesn't want to.

And then:

> ubi uoles pater esse ibi esto; ubi noles ne fueris pater.
> (*Epid.* 595)

Be my father when you want to; don't when you don't want to.

Identity becomes something to be picked up and dropped at will. A joke is thus made of something which not only is not normally subject to arbitrary choice (one either is or is not the parent or child of another), but also is normally central to the comic righting of wrongs and the resolution of plays.[45]

[44] See Meisel (2007: 24) on release from logic in comedy.

[45] Slater (2001: 201) suggests that Acropolistis is here making a risqué joke, implying an erotic relationship in place of the filial tie which has just been blown. Simia has a similar play on the idea

PLOTTING AND PLAYWRIGHTS IN PLAUTUS

Most scholars now agree that the clever slave, who designs and directs the intrigue of many plays, is closely identified with the playwright himself.[46] His Cunning Plan to cheat the master (conventionally, though in fact by no means always, he outwits his master *maior* in order to help out his master *minor*: the terms come from *Asinaria*) thus becomes a metaphor for the plot of the play, as well as the actuation of it; his action in putting on the performance cuts deep into the realist illusion, in order to extol the anti-naturalistic theatricality of the play and his own power over it. The consummate artist in this respect is Pseudolus, whose directing of the plot and its complexities catches and binds us as surely as it does his dupes, tricking us into thinking it's a brilliant plan – both plot and play – (which, in another sense, it is) and even warning us in advance that we are going to be tricked, all in order to prove his control of the fictional world.

The close identification between slave-*architectus* and playwright creates a kind of first-person voice, similar to that of more subjective genres. This does not mean that the slave-character says what the man-Plautus thinks, but that the slave projects the 'poet's voice', becoming the playwright's persona.[47] Pseudolus directs the play as if it were about the money for gods' sake, but artifice for its own sake. When he needs to think up the plot, he tells us his poetic status clearly, in the great *quasi poeta* speech (401–5) in which he celebrates his intention to invent those twenty *minae* and make them real. This *is* the invention of the plot,

of knowledge and self-knowledge at *Ps.* 925: *numquam edepol erit ill' potior Harpax quam ego*, and 928–30: *in timorem dabo militarem aduenam, / ipsus sese ut neget esse eum qui siet / meque ut esse autumet qui ipsus est.*

[46] Slater (2000: originally published in 1985), is the *locus classicus* for the metatheatrical reading of the slave, which was proposed by Wright (1975). The idea of the controlling slave as a particularly Plautine invention goes back at least to Fraenkel (1960: originally published 1922, ch. 8).

[47] Dobrov (1995b) explores the Aristophanic 'poet's voice' ('the unstable partial identity between protagonist and playwright in comedies such as *Acharnians* and *Wasps*, for example, as well as direct self-presentation in the parabases', 50) and its legacies. He suggests that in Middle and New Comedy the poet's voice retreats 'leaving the characters in the play world that insists on its autonomy through the dramatic illusion' (50–1): in this regard Plautus certainly and Terence arguably are closer to Aristophanes than to Menander. Dobrov's comment (50) that '[t]he dialogism of Old Comedy is thus not yet rigidly structured by the identity of character and voice' implies a narrative of development through ancient comedy. I suggest, however, that his analysis could apply to Roman comedy: '[r]emarkable here is the facility with which a given speaking subject may be distorted and overshadowed by the "poet" beyond the limits of consistent character'. This is what I will suggest is happening, albeit subliminally, with the Roman poets.

and it is more than that – it is also the actualising of art into material reality.[48]

Pseudolus is the greatest example of the 'clever slave' as controller of the action and metaphorical playwright, *architectus* in my terminology, but he is not the only one. Palaestrio, Tranio, Epidicus and Chrysalus, at least, will give him a run for his money.[49] Although the thematics of deception and questions of identity are near-universal in Roman comedy, however, the 'pure' form of the play-type (if we may so call it) exists in just under half the plays of Plautus, and – remarkably – the majority of the plays of Terence, although always with a dose of irony. This 'pure' form we might characterise as the 'Pseudolus' form, that is, one where the poet's voice is closely identified with a clever slave who controls the action and directs the play. Other 'pure' plays include *Miles gloriosus*, *Epidicus*, *Mostellaria*, *Persa*, *Amphitruo*, *Asinaria* and *Poenulus*, although the extent of the *architectus*' control is variable. Then there are plays where the controller is not a slave, such as *Casina* (a woman, working with a slave), *Truculentus* (a prostitute) and *Trinummus* (a group of *senes*!). In *Curculio*, the *architectus*-role is shared between the parasite who directs the action and the slave who directs the audience's view of the play; something similar happens in *Poenulus*. Some plays have confusion and deception but no real controller, such as *Menaechmi*.

Not always does Plautus make it easy for us by having his slave-*architectus* tell the audience directly how clever he is. One play with an extremely complex plot, in which we are totally in the hands of the *architectus*, is *Epidicus*, although the eponymous slave ignores us much of the time. He is too busy managing a horrendously complicated plot in a mere 733 lines to have time to engage in a lot of banter with the audience, although he certainly does celebrate his triumph and insidiously let us feel as though we

48 Petrone (1983: 6) takes the speech as programmatic for her study of metatheatrical deception in Plautine comedy. Hunter (2006) also uses it as a programmatic introduction, and comments: 'behind the comic passage lies allusion to serious ideas about literature' (82).

49 Pseudolus represents an extreme case of the playwright's control of mimesis. His deceit of his master is all the more magnificent precisely because he had already warned the old man to beware. Comparable is Mnesilochus' report of his father's response to hearing of Chrysalus' first deceit (the one about the court case, the shipwreck, the rich man in Ephesus): *si tu illum solem sibi solem esse diceres, / se illum lunam credere esse et noctem qui nunc est dies* (*Bac.* 699–700): to which Chrysalus replies (701): *emungam hercle hominem probe hodie, ne id nequiquam dixerit*. An interesting additional twist here is that not only does Mnesilochus celebrate the power the cunning slave has over belief and reality, but also he in doing so tricks Chrysalus, previously resistant, into helping him. The trapper is trapped. (There are many connections between *Bac.* and *Ps.*, including a letter scene in each, and a warning that is itself part of the trick.)

are getting into the charmed circle of his control.[50] Nick Lowe has rightly described the play as having 'the ancient world's most mind-boggling plot'.[51] It is one in which Epidicus is by no means always comfortably in control. Like Pseudolus, Chrysalus, Palaestrio, Tranio and his other partners in crime, he has to improvise, or at least, like Plautus, to play at doing so.[52] This is an exceptional play, the primary purpose of which is to give Epidicus something to stand on while he displays his powers of trickery.

The plot itself looks like a massive piece of *contaminatio*, as if Plautus/Epidicus had thrown several plots together, and shaken them up to see what came out – and then squeezed about four plays' worth of action into the space of half a play. The resulting mishmash has encouraged a minor industry of investigation and speculation into the nature of the play's relationship with its (or, any) Greek original, and the consequent possibilities for the reconstruction of that hypothetical Greek play.[53] My own analysis of the play will have to admit to agnosticism in this regard, which perhaps is a position not so different from that of at least some members of the original audience. We may be able to assume that a few members of the audience knew a lot of Greek plays very well, and that they were in the enviable situation of appreciating many of the intertextual jokes that are lost on most of us. A significant proportion of the audience, however, may not have been intimately acquainted with the texts of Greek New Comedy, but were very well aware of the koine of the comic theatre, which they may have divided into 'Greek' and 'Roman' for some purposes but not

[50] Slater (2000) overplays the extent of the relationship between Epidicus and the audience (19, 21), but since his primary purpose is to illustrate the metatheatrical force of Epidicus it is perhaps not unreasonable to play up Epidicus' role as the audience's friend. He is on stronger ground when he notes (20): 'For a moment Epidicus may seem not equal to the audience but superior, because he seems to have a plan he does not share with us.'

[51] Lowe (2000: 219). He has a table, although I do not find that it leaves me any less confused. It may be that every reader has to write his/her own table in order to make sense of this plot. Willcock also has one: he points out that all four of the possible comic categorisations of girl/woman are present in this short play (1995: 24). See the essays in Auhagen (2001a), particularly the contribution of Moore, who shows how the metrical and musical complexity of the play contributes to its frenetic pace.

[52] See on this subject the essays in Benz, Stärk and Vogt-Spira (1995). Improvisation is a major element in Slater's important discussion of this play (Slater 2000: 15–29), which has several points in common with mine, and indeed my discussion is perhaps just footnotes to Slater's. The play is taken by Slater (2000: 15) as 'the type against which the variations we will find in other plays play'. I would be inclined to give that honour to *Pseudolus*, but the two are clearly close allies.

[53] Goldberg (1978) famously argues for the play as free Plautine composition. Fantham (1981) argues against this case, as do Arnott (2001) and Lowe (2001), all three incidentally extricating the complexity of this strange play.

for others. A certain confusion about what exactly Plautus is doing with the traditions of Greek comedy is, therefore, not entirely inappropriate.

Epidicus uses his first scene alone with the audience for a debate about control of the play. Epidicus' performance at 81–103 is a delightful *canticum* in which he considers the problems (briefly giving us some background information in the process) and admits he has no idea what to do about the situation. Such deliberative soliloquies are not rare (Arnott 2001), but the following little exchange is priceless, even though it is so close to the koine of comic diction:

> nequam homo es,
> Epidice.
> qui lubidost male loqui? quia tute te<te> deseris.
> quid faciam?
> men rogas?
> tuquidem antehac aliis solebas dare consilia mutua.
> (*Epid.* 96–9)

This is typical comic dialogue, except that usually there are two speakers. Every reader will see that this passage involves an 'imaginary speaker' in pseudo-dialogue with Epidicus.[54] Slater reads the interchange as taking place between the actor and the mask-character, in which the actor might even take his mask off and talk to it.[55] A slightly different way of reading this would be to understand the 'two' speakers as 'Plautus' and 'Epidicus'. Since they are so closely related to each other, as 'authors' of this play, the slippage is easy – it is just a split into the persona's two halves. On this reading, the dialogue would go like this:

> [PLAUTUS] You're a waste of time, Epidicus.
> [EPIDICUS] Why do you take pleasure in abusing me?
> [PLAUTUS] Because you are giving up on yourself.
> [EPIDICUS] What should I do?
> [PLAUTUS] You're asking me?

Then he (one of them) says 'you indeed used *dare consilia mutua* to others'. The basic meaning of this is something like 'you used to give advice to others',[56] but *dare mutua* also means 'to lend'. The implication, I suggest, is that Epidicus is accusing Plautus (or, possibly, the other way round) of not sharing the plot as he usually does with his slave-*architecti*. But

[54] Duckworth (1940: 163) on 99; Auhagen (2001a: 207–8).

[55] Slater (2000: 17–19). Later (21), he hints briefly at a possible interaction between Plautus and his characters.

[56] As Duckworth (1940: 163) notes, 'the typical intriguing slave should be *plenus consili*'.

a way must be found: *aliquid aliqua reperiundumst* (100).[57] One of them (Plautus/Epidicus) finds a way of controlling the play a few lines later, when the young men come out to give a bit of innocent exposition. Epidicus takes up the role of audience within the play, which itself signals his control of the situation: *huc concedam, orationem unde horum placide persequar* ('I'll withdraw over here, from where I can follow their conversation in peace', 103).

There is no prologue to give early exposition of the plot and its background. To stand a chance of picking up on what is going on, we have to pay very close attention to the dialogue, but as good Plautine readers we know that hints and leads may not always be what they seem. The play is also extremely elliptical (so much so that critics have wondered whether it has suffered textual violence), with the result that we have to accept that we might have missed something when we blinked (metaphorically). Part of our pleasure has to be in surrendering ourselves to Epidicus' brilliance and letting him lead us – while at the same time trying our best to run fast enough to keep up with him. This is a play in which story and narrative move in very different ways – that is, we hear about events out of their chronological order. To make up for the fact that the modern reader of literary criticism has so many disadvantages compared with the original audience of the play, and for the fact that I am not Epidicus, I offer a bit of pedestrian background exposition.

Periphanes is a widower whose son Stratippocles is away fighting in an Athenian war in Thebes. The old man also has a daughter (Telestis), by a woman whom he seduced years ago in Epidaurus, who then brought the girl up in Thebes. Telestis has been taken prisoner and bought by Stratippocles, without his knowledge of her identity. Periphanes knows that she has been bought (though not the identity of the buyer) and has wanted to find her. He is also thinking of marrying her mother. Before leaving for the war, Stratippocles had been in love with a music girl, and had asked the slave Epidicus to buy her. Epidicus told Periphanes that he had found the lost daughter, so Periphanes gave him the money to buy her. Epidicus buys the music girl (Acropolistis) and installs her in the house as the daughter of Periphanes. In the meantime, however, Stratippocles has transferred his affections to the Theban captive (who, unknown to him,

[57] This is ironically echoed in the delightful piece of 'something' nonsense between Stratippocles and Chaeribulus at 331–4, noted also by Slater (2000: 19 n. 7): ironically, because the boys are floundering around and not realising that it is Epidicus who is in control. It might be worth noting that Epidicus' complaint at 97 about his interlocutor's pleasure in abusing him is also echoed by Chaeribulus in that scene, at 333: *qui tibi lubet mihi male loqui?*

is his half-sister Telestis).[58] He bought her with money borrowed from a banker, which now needs to be repaid. Stratippocles returns to Athens, and demands that Epidicus find a way of paying off the banker. That is the Question, the Goal, of the plot: unusually, the achievement of the Goal does not result in either marriage or its alternatives for the young lover. He can neither marry his beloved nor have her as a concubine because she turns out to be a citizen, but his half-sister; there is no mention of him marrying anyone else, although (as we will see) such a marriage is plotted for by the older generation; he cannot console himself with his former beloved because she left the house and the play when her cover was blown.

The play is overdetermined with plots, which look like they are coming from different directions, but in fact are skilfully woven together by Epidicus/Plautus. The distinctions between levels of fictionality, between reality and disguise in identity, between internal characters and playwright break down when the internal plot merges with the external. The critic is inevitably tempted to try and sort it out. To begin with identity: there are three girls at issue in this play, all of whom either are or are presented as the beloved of the young man Stratippocles, and all of whom have at least two fictional identities. There is one girl (Acropolistis) in the house, believed by the father to be his lost daughter, but actually the first mistress of the young man. Then there is the second girl (Telestis), who is the current beloved and actually the daughter of Periphanes. And there is the third girl (the *fidicina*), who is pretending (whether she knows it or not) to be the mistress of Stratippocles, and therefore the first girl (or, in a sense, the second). To put it another way: Epidicus produces a third girl, hired, who pretends to be the second one (who is actually the first one – the one in the house and appearing to be the daughter . . . who is actually the remaining one, the first, in a sense, or the last, in another). Or we could consider the matter from the point of view of the money. Periphanes pays once 'for Telestis', but actually for Acropolistis; and a second time 'for Acropolistis' but actually (according to one trick) for the *fidicina* and (according to the other, real, trick) for Telestis, in that the money in fact goes to pay the banker for her. There is only one young man to balance these three girls, unless we count the *miles* who throws in a quick spanner about halfway through. There is only one father also, but he has his own complication in that, now a widower, he is interested in marrying the woman whom he seduced some years ago in Epidaurus (that is, Philippa, the mother of

[58] A flirtation with the edge of incest is surprisingly common in ancient comedy. See Segal (2001a), although I think he overplays the point. See also Slater (2001).

Telestis). Each generation is supported by a friend, but they are not integral to the plot. To confuse the identities further, the father himself had played the roles both of *adulescens* and *miles gloriosus* in his youth, as he reminds us and the internal characters.[59]

Before the play begins, another play had been plotted out by Epidicus, the one in which he procured the music girl for his young master by tricking his old master into thinking that she was his long-lost daughter. At this point, since we do not know the father's story and that there really is a lost daughter, we think this daughter-plot is something Epidicus had just concocted for the occasion. When Stratippocles comes back from the war, and it transpires that he has changed his mind about the kind of play he wants to be in, his change of affections, with its resultant second round of financial need, which on the part of the *adulescens* is extremely unusual, puts Epidicus in a very awkward position. In his monody mentioned above (it comes just after the opening scene in which Epidicus finds out from his fellow slave that Stratippocles has returned with a new girl), Epidicus says: *neque ego nunc / quo modo / me expeditum ex impedito faciam, consilium placet* (85–6). 'No plan is pleasing now as to how I might extract myself from these intricacies.' The implication is that the original *consilium* (plot) he had is no good any more. Not only is the old plot no good, but moreover in the next scene the young master demands a different one. Epidicus overhears his master's wish for the *operam Epidici* (120), which he proposes to extract by threats of violence. The hidden Epidicus' wry response is *salua res est* ('the matter is saved', 124), in allusion, perhaps, to the proverbial saying about the old actor and the show which must go on.[60] It might seem odd that Epidicus responds to the threat of punishment with an expression of relief and hope, and at one level his comment is indeed ironic.[61] On the other hand, this is a moment of movement, where Epidicus starts to see the way to salvation, even if no-one else can do so, so the matter is indeed saved.[62]

After Epidicus' monody, the next section of the play consists of two parallel movements.[63] First, Epidicus overhears the young master and his friend discussing the situation, then makes his presence known and joins in their plans; second, the older generation come out for some exposition, which Epidicus also overhears before going through the same process of

[59] See Slater (2000: 24 and n. 14). [60] See below, p. 233. [61] See Slater (2000: 20).

[62] There is a nice ironic echo in his last word, *symbolae* (125), of Stratippocles' last word, *syllabam* (123).

[63] In fact, the whole play up until the first moment of crisis follows a similar pattern: introduction with Thesprio; Epidicus alone; Epidicus overhearing then joining the young men; Epidicus alone; Epidicus overhearing then joining the old men; Epidicus alone; the young men waiting for Epidicus, who joins them; the old men, with Periphanes waiting for Epidicus to do the trick, and then Apoecides arriving to report it; then the entry of the soldier, which is the moment of *peripeteia*.

greeting and planning. He thinks up two cunning plans, one for the young master and one for the old, each acting as a variant on the other and playing with the instabilities of artifice. We will look briefly at each one.

As soon as Epidicus is persuaded to take on the new plot, Stratippocles asks 'what is to be done with the music girl', to which Epidicus replies that he'll think of something, echoing his resolution at 100 after the interchange with 'Plautus':

> aliquid aliqua reperiundumst
> (*Epid.* 100: Epidicus to Plautus, or vice versa)

A way must be found someway.

> aliqua res reperibitur,
> aliqua ope exsoluam, extricabor aliqua.
> (*Epid.* 151–2: Epidicus to Stratippocles)

Some way will be found, by some means I'll sort it out, I'll extricate us somehow.

'Yes, you're full of plots', says Stratippocles: *plenus consili's* (152). At this, Epidicus launches into yet another plot, one about a soldier who is also in love with the girl and will buy her:

> est Euboicus miles locuples, multo auro potens,
> qui ubi tibi istam emptam esse scibit atque hanc adductam alteram,
> continuo te orabit ultro ut illam tramittas sibi.
> (*Epid.* 153–5)

There's a rich Euboean soldier, made of money, who when he finds out that that one has been bought for you and that you've brought another one back, will keep on begging you of his own accord to transfer the first one to himself.

Mention of the soldier here could be a lead for us into another thread of the plot, but in this scene it is presented in such a way that it looks like a false lead, something Epidicus made up for the purpose. Having placed the plot in the hands of Epidicus, the young men go inside to enjoy themselves at leisure, while Epidicus holds a *senatum . . . consiliarium* in his heart (159) and urges himself on to greater heights of trickery. Although we are not privileged to know what the trick will be, we are heartened by our hero's determination: *senem oppugnare certumst consilium mihi* ('my plan is fixed to war down the old man', 163), before he makes a somewhat undermotivated exit to leave the stage open for the old men. He will go inside to tell his young master not to step outside Chaeribulus' house *neue obuiam ueniat seni* ('in case he should meet the old man', 165, end of scene). Cue *senex.*

Periphanes enters with his friend Apoecides, continuing their conversation about Periphanes' desire to marry the woman he had seduced, and his anxiety about his son's reaction to this idea. Epidicus returns (if he ever really left) just in time to hear Apoecides suggest that getting Stratippocles married would help, and Periphanes agree, expressing his distress at the rumours about his son and the music girl. Irony: the rumours *were* true, and the girl he thinks is his daughter in the house is in fact that beloved of his son, but the son has transferred his affections to someone else, who really is Periphanes' daughter. Periphanes' acceptance of his friend's suggestion is nicely ironic too, with Epidicus lurking in the shadows: *laudo consilium tuom* ('I approve your plan', 190).

Epidicus makes his presence known by acting the part of a running slave.[64] After a suitable amount of horseplay there comes the prologue to Plot 2: Epidicus tells the two old men a false but nearly true tale about the arrival home of the army. He claims to have overheard two prostitutes talking about the girl Stratippocles loves, and about their envy at her prospect of being set free by the rich young man who dotes on her. Warming to his theme, Epidicus re-enacts (or rather, invents)[65] a conversation in which the prostitutes report that a letter had come that day from Stratippocles, saying that he would buy Acropolistis with money that he has borrowed from a banker in Thebes (251–2). This is another nicely ironic near-truth, since Stratippocles really has borrowed money from a banker in Thebes in order to buy his beloved. Epidicus now manipulates the old men into persuading him to suggest what their plot might be, since they realise they need one:

> PE. quid ego faciam? nunc consilium a te expetesso, Apoecides.
> AP. reperiamus aliquid calidi, conducibilis consili.
> nam ille quidem aut iam hic aderit, credo hercle, aut iam adest. EP. si aequom siet
> me plus sapere quam uos, dederim uobis consilium catum
> quod laudetis, ut ego opino, uterque – PE. ergo ubi id est, Epidice?
> EP. atque ad eam rem conducibile. AP. quid istuc dubitas dicere?
> EP. uos priores esse oportet, nos posterius dicere,
> qui plus sapitis. PE. heia uero! age dice. EP. at deridebitis.
> AP. non edepol faciemus. EP. immo si placebit utitor,
> consilium si non placebit, reperitote rectius.
>
> (*Epid.* 255–64)

[64] He tells himself (194–5): *orna te*, 'put on your disguise', and *palliolum in collum conice*, 'pile up your little Greek cloak on your neck' [act the part of a running slave from a New Comedy], and *adsimulato*, 'pretend' [that you have been looking for the man all over the city . . .]. He ends his self-addressed pep-talk *age, si quid agis* (196). Slater (2000: 21 and n. 10).

[65] Slater (2000: 22): Epidicus almost overdoes it, for love of play-acting and 'the music of names'.

PE. What shall I do? Now I need a ploy from you, Apoecides. AP. Let's find some piping hot, useful plan. For he will be here soon, I expect, if he isn't already. EP. If it were right for me to be more knowledgeable than you, I could give you a clever plan which, I think, you would both approve – PE. Where's that, then, Epidicus? EP. And just what you need in this circumstance. AP. Why do you hesitate to speak? EP. It is right for you to go first, and for us to speak afterwards, since you know more. PE. Get on with it! Come on, speak. EP. But you'll laugh. AP. We certainly won't. EP. If you like my plan, use it; if you don't, find a better one yourselves.

The passage is full of delicious ironies and echoes. It contrives to find (*reperire* repeated from 100 and 151) and replace the inadequate *consilium* of Apoecides with a much more praiseworthy (259 ~ 190) one from Epidicus. This passage marks the beginning of the resolution of Epidicus' original problem about the *consilium* that [*non*] *placet* (264 ~ 86). For the playwright (Plautus/Epidicus) and his accomplice the reader, there may be an additional irony in this *conducibile* plot (lit. 'hireable', 256, 260) which will in fact involve the hiring of a girl (Girl 3, the second *fidicina*, on whom more below), although the old men are not to know about that.[66]

Epidicus suggests that Periphanes should pretend that this is the sort of play, like *Asinaria*, *Casina* and *Mercator*, in which the father and son are rivals for the prostitute: he should arrange to buy Acropolistis himself. In this case, however, the rivalry would be a trick, since once he had bought the girl, Periphanes should send her away. Once she is out of the way, it will be easy enough to get Stratippocles to marry and 'not to give any trouble about what you want' (282–3). Periphanes walks straight into it. He does not even quibble when Epidicus mentions the already high price[67] of forty *minae*, with the suggestion that a bit extra would come in handy to clinch the deal. As Epidicus will say just after this scene, there is no more fertile field for a fraud in the whole of Attica than old Periphanes, who just keeps on paying (306–9). For good measure, Epidicus throws in a variant of the 'soldier-rival' story (quite unnecessarily, because Periphanes was not complaining anyway). He says that the old man will be able to recoup his money because Epidicus knows a man who wants to buy the girl:

66 As Petrone (2001) notes, Epidicus' interaction with the old men is couched in terms of a debate in the senate, with its rules about who should speak before whom. She shows how the various legal references in the play are puns on the name of Epidicus (esp. 181–3). The invitation to 'use the plan if you like it, or otherwise look for a better one' sounds formulaic in that context.

67 The slave-prostitute in *Ps.* costs twenty *minae*. The drunken waster Philolaches in *Mos.* paid thirty for his girlfriend (300).

> quia enim mulierem alius illam adulescens deperit,
> auro opulentus, magnus miles Rhodius, raptor hostium,
> gloriosus: hic emet illam de te et dabit aurum lubens.
> (*Epid.* 299–301)

Because another young man is desperate for that woman, and he is made of money, a great big Rhodian soldier, hostiraptor, a braggard: he will buy her off you and give the money happily.

The story is much the same as it was to Stratippocles (and looks equally fictional) except that this time he is Rhodian rather than Euboean, which is probably because now he needs to be in a position to take the girl far away.[68] A particularly nice twist of interplay between fictional and intratheatrical reality might go like this: the Euboean soldier is real, while the Rhodian one is made up (even though they both seem made up when they are introduced), but when the Euboean soldier gets real and gets into the play, Periphanes thinks he is the Rhodian soldier about whom Epidicus had told him. In that case, Epidicus' story is a tricksy lie which is so close to truth that even the critics are caught in his web.

The other twist to the plot which appears to have more to do with the pleasure of artifice than with strict necessity is the involvement of Apoecides. Epidicus says that there needs to be someone else to take the money to the pimp for the music girl (287), because if Periphanes went himself the pimp and/or the girl might suspect that he wanted to separate her from his son (in Epidicus' false tale to the old men). Apoecides is elected. It is true that Epidicus cannot afford for Periphanes himself to negotiate with the pimp, because he isn't *really* going to buy Acropolistis – having already bought her. It will be Epidicus himself who will do the negotiation, however, and to do it he will have to hoodwink Apoecides just as much as Periphanes. Perhaps he reckons Apoecides will be even more of a push-over. Or perhaps he just wants another scalp.[69]

So, all Epidicus has to do now is to provide a third girl. As luck – or the playwright – would have it, a girl is already to be hired to perform at Periphanes' house that day. Epidicus will pretend that she is the beloved

[68] See Faller (2001) and references there to earlier scholarship on the 'riddle'. Plays with heroic slaves and heavily deceptive plots tend to produce a lot of 'problems' for the critic: see Sharrock (1996) and, differently, Lowe (1999) on *Ps.*, and the bibliography referred to there. Faller comments: '[e]s scheint daher, als sei das Rätsel um den euböischen und den rhodischen Soldaten des *Epidicus* nur für die späteren Philologen ein solches'. The difference between us, perhaps, is that he would see the discontinuity as not mattering to Plautus' audience, whereas I would see the game with the critic, ancient or modern, as part of the power of the text.

[69] Slater (2000: 23) says that Epidicus wants Apoecides to go because Periphanes is proving 'a little sharper than he should be'.

of Stratippocles. Epidicus' rare interlude with the audience between the old-men scene and the next young-men scene gives us a glimpse of the process of plot-making:

> sed me una turbat res ratioque, Apoecidi
> quam ostendam fidicinam aliquam conducticiam.
> atque id quoque habeo: mane me iussit senex
> conducere aliquam fidicinam sibi huc domum,
> dum rem diuinam faceret, cantaret sibi;
> ea conducetur atque ei praemostrabitur
> quo pacto fiat subdola aduorsus senem.
>
> (*Epid.* 312–18)

Just one thing is bothering me, what hired lyre-player I can show to Apoecides. Ah, I've got it: this morning the old man ordered me to hire some lyre-player to play for him at home, while he performs the rites. I'll hire her and explain to her in advance how she can deceive the old man.

We later readers should be careful not to confuse this true story of a hiring for a *res diuina* with the later false story about hiring for a *res diuina* to celebrate the return of Stratippocles.[70] Most of Epidicus' lies are so like truth that they confuse the critic. Here, within the level of reality at which Epidicus interacts with the other characters on stage, Periphanes really has told him to hire a music girl for the evening, and the slave is now improvising with this piece of luck. At the level at which Epidicus metaphorically stands for Plautus, the playwright is putting together the plot, mostly for the fun of plotting.

The following young-men scene is an orgy of plotting and triumphant celebration. It is also so elliptical that past readers have found it necessary to suspect that bits have dropped out of the text.[71] Undoubtedly there are textual problems in the scene, which are intensified in the crucial lines about the various tricks. What happens, more or less, is that Epidicus arrives on the scene where the young men are waiting and worrying. On giving the money to Stratippocles, our hero launches into an incomprehensible

[70] Duckworth (1940: 277–9) is good on this.

[71] See Duckworth (1940: 298) on the state of play at his time, which has not to my knowledge been surpassed. He takes a conservative view, printing without lacunae but bracketing 353. The first part of 359 he considers *desperatus*, but interprets lines 358–9 as a reference to 'the precautions which the *senes* have taken to avoid deception'. See also Stärk (2001: esp. 100–1). Duckworth punctuates 352 thus: *Nam leno omne argentum abstulit pro fidicina; ego resolui.* Either version makes the same degree of sense (or nonsense). Duckworth's reason for bracketing 353 is not for the sake of sense, but because of an 'accumulation of difficulties' (p. 299) regarding the line. If 353 is indeed an interpolation, then the overall meaning of the speech is the same, but the presentation is even more elliptical than it would otherwise be.

joke (349–51) in which the father flashes in and out of metaphor as the money that comes from him, and which is dead (cf. 339) and/or kills him. It's all tied up in a sack (i.e. the money bag). Stratippocles does not really understand it any better than we do, as is shown by his response to the word *parenticidam* (349) – 'What sort of a word is that?'[72] After such a beginning, Epidicus then shows off his tricks:[73]

> nam leno omne argentum apstulit pro fidicina (ego resolui,
> manibus his denumeraui) pater suam natam quam esse credit;
> nunc iterum ut fallatur pater tibique auxilium apparetur
> inueni: nam ita suasi seni atque hanc habui orationem
> ut quom rediisses ne tibi eiius copia esset.
>
> (*Epid.* 352–6)

For the pimp took all the money (I paid it, I counted it out with these hands) for the lyre-player, whom your father thinks is his daughter. Now again I have found a way to deceive your father and help you: for I have persuaded the old man and used all my rhetoric on him so that when you return you won't be able to enjoy her.

Whether or not we accept the authenticity of 353, we can, with some effort, make out the sequence of thought. The pimp has taken the money for Girl 1 (Acropolistis, bought on the false premise of being Telestis); Epidicus was the one who handed over the money (which will matter later); now he has devised and carried out the second plan, which – and here there is switch of focaliser to the old man – 'will stop Stratippocles having access to his beloved music girl when he gets home'. That, then, is the first part of the second plot. Stratippocles responds with an exultant *eugae!*, either because he really understands, having been told about the second plot off-stage,[74] or because he does not understand but can see that 'hurrah' is the appropriate response. Epidicus' next statement, *ea iam domist pro filia* ('she is now at home as his daughter', 357), must refer back to the first girl, thus switching the focalisation back to 'reality'. So it goes something like: 'they think that I'm going to buy Acropolistis in order to

[72] This is exactly the kind of moment when the heroic power of the *architectus* is displayed, in a nutshell. Epidicus says that *nil moror uetera et uolgata uerba* (350), just as Pseudolus responded to his young master's confusion at the slave's creative use of proverbial language by saying *at hoc peruolgatumst minus* (*Ps.* 124). Better to make up a proverb than use a conventional one. (Part of the joke of this, of course, is that proverbs only work because they are conventional.) The organising idea of the moneybag might have an obscene meaning, but more important is its reference to the sphere of the traditional punishment for parricide, which involved being tied up in a sack with various unpleasant objects, hence the point of the word *parenticidam*.

[73] I have printed here as Lindsay. See n. 71 above.

[74] '[F]or even if we delete 353, there is no reason to assume that Stratippocles does not know the details of the first deception.' Duckworth (1940: 300).

stop you getting access to her, but actually Acropolistis is in the house right now, posing as Telestis'.

Epidicus reports how the old men think they have appointed Apoecides as a minder to Epidicus, to make sure that the purchase of 'Acropolistis' goes through without either exposing Periphanes or trusting Epidicus (357–9). But our hero says: *nunc ego hanc astutiam institui* ('now I have set this cunning in motion', 363). He will go to the pimp on his own, and tell him that if he (Epidicus) brings a man along to talk about the sale of the music girl, he (the pimp) should say that he has received the money – fifty *minae* – for her. Since the pimp did indeed receive money from Epidicus only a few days ago, he does not have to tell the pimp anything about either the second or the third girl, but simply encourage him to bump up the cost a bit. Duckworth (1940: 304), who well understands that there is no real problem in these lines (just a lot of cleverness), suggests that the pimp will simply assume that Epidicus has made a profit on the deal. When the pimp swears that he has been paid for the girl, he will believe he is talking about Girl 1, whereas the old men will understand him to refer to Girl 3 (whom they think is Girl 1). No problem. There is a question over whether this bit of deceit ever happens. If it does, we are not told so explicitly, but in such a compressed play it is not surprising that plots are not gone over twice. As Epidicus says, we don't have time to sit around discussing it: *sed nimi' longum loquor, diu me estis demorati* (376).[75] It hardly matters whether the trick actually happens, off-stage, or whether Apoecides never in fact meets the *leno* and so the plan is not needed.[76] Epidicus quickly sketches out the plan to organise Girl 3 (the hired music girl) into her role, and then leaves, amid general applause.[77]

With the next scene ends the outward movement of this tightly structured play. Apoecides comes back with the music girl, and is full of admiration for Epidicus' ploy of telling her that she has been hired to play for a sacrifice in honour of Stratippocles' return (so she is thought to be the dupe of Epidicus, since Apoecides believes she has actually been bought).

[75] Epidicus makes a similar observation at 665: *abeo intro, nimi' longum loquor*. There is a lot to get through in this play, no time for standing around chatting. Pseudolus is more specific about the metatheatrical import of the point: *sat sic longae fiunt fabulae*, 'these plays are long enough as it is', *Ps.* 388.

[76] So Duckworth (1940: 305), comparing Palaestrio's readiness to use the twin-sister trick against the soldier, although it turns out not to be necessary.

[77] On the question of whether the music girl is tricked by Epidicus or is in on the plan, see Slater (2000: 25), who is agnostic on the matter, but ends with the comment that she 'simply joins in the spirit of Plautine fun by also deluding the old man'. The alternative possibility, that he duped her as well, would sit easily with the extreme control of Epidicus in this play.

The music girl's arrival heralds the beginning of the pigeons coming home to roost. To cut a long story short (or rather, to simplify a complex but short play), the various tricks start to fall apart, when first the soldier (he was real after all) and then the mother of the real daughter (and so was she!) turn up and disabuse Periphanes of the various tricks. It looks like the play is going to fall apart in Epidicus' hands, until the banker brings along the captive beloved, whom Epidicus immediately recognises as really the real daughter of Periphanes. Because Epidicus actually has now found the daughter, the old man has to forgive him, and all is well. All is not well for Stratippocles, who loses the current beloved when she turns out to be his sister (while he goes into the house to get the money to pay for her), but perhaps that should be a lesson to him not to mess with the playwright's plotting. Epidicus is not only freed and given financial support but is also able to require his master to beg to be allowed to release him.[78]

After all its twists and turns,[79] this play turns out to have a recognition plot. Perhaps the oddest aspect of this play is that the recognition scene itself is so easy, so trivial. There have been two failed recognitions already, between Periphanes and first the soldier (with Girl 3 offered for Girl 1) and then the mother (with Girl 1 offered for Girl 2), but the final 'real' recognition scene simply involves Epidicus saying: 'Is that Telestis I see?' (635).[80] For a second, it almost looks like this is yet another piece of opportunism on the part of the *architectus*. On the purely internal, naturalistic level of the play (insofar as such a play can be said to have a 'naturalistic' level), the recognition is genuine, and is confirmed as such by Telestis' response, in which she agrees to the proposition that she remembers Epidicus coming with gifts for her birthday when she was little. The acid test, a meeting with Philippa, is not shown. At the metatheatrical level, Epidicus is in a position to confirm and stabilise the identity of Telestis because he is 'really' the playwright, and knows the script, and has the power to decide who's who. The power that we, as readers, have is in letting him get away with it all. The release which Epidicus achieves against the odds at the end is a powerful metaphor for the successful production of the play itself. We, along with the master, release the playwright and his slave-*architectus* when we applaud.

[78] See Segal (1987: 109–10) on this ending as saturnalian.

[79] *uorsutior es quam rota figularis*: Chaeribulus to Epidicus, 371.

[80] Slater (2000: 27) acknowledges the problems that other critics, including even Goldberg (1978: 87), have had with this ending, but considers that it is 'perfectly in keeping with the improvisatory nature of the action so far'.

PLAYWRIGHT AS SLAVE

The fact of the playwright's identification with a slave is fairly well established, but what is the meaning of it? Answers have been sought to this question, even before it was formulated clearly, in terms historical, psychological and sociological. Ancient tradition, followed by many critics in the early years of modern scholarship, makes Plautus himself a former slave, who describes servile sufferings from first-hand knowledge, and (for some critics) offers to a predominantly lower-class audience a figure with whom they can identify. Since recent understanding of ancient literary criticism allows us to read the biographical details primarily as acts of interpretation of the works themselves, while it is now generally accepted that the audience was socially mixed, and that Plautus had at least one eye on the elite, we must look somewhere other than in personal biography for an answer. The suggestion of Fraenkel, one of the first critics to see the importance of the controlling slave's role, was that the reason for the greatly developed role of the slave in Plautine comedy, by comparison with anything in Greek comedy, was not only for rumbustious humour but also to create a good part for the boss, the *dominus gregis*, who was a very powerful person.[81] This may be true, although it sits slightly uncomfortably with the common idea that the clever slave's closest identification is with Plautus himself, and in any case it does not answer the question of what it might mean. If in relation to recent slave societies an author were to identify his or her voice with that of a slave, the meaning would be direct social criticism, as for example in Toni Morrison's novel *Beloved*. It would surely be anachronistic, however, to suggest that Plautus takes on the voice of a (powerful) slave in order to criticise the very institution of slavery.[82] Rather, when ancients think about slavery they are not interested in human rights: they may be interested in the defining of in-groups and out-groups, but they may also be inclined to think about questions of identity and the instability of fortune, and the precariousness of social distinction. Plautus might be giving his audience a prod about the precariousness and instability of their own identity as the men in togas – or, indeed, of their identity as the men, and possibly women, *not* in togas.[83]

81 Fraenkel (1960: 239–41).

82 Henderson (2006) comes nearest to finding direct social criticism in *As.* See also Anderson (1993: 141) for a response to earlier accounts of comedy as protest.

83 McCarthy (2000) has an excellent discussion of Roman attitudes to slavery. She points out that Plautine characters differentiate between slaves by condition and 'real' slaves, implying that 'the knowledge of one's own susceptibility to such an accident does not necessarily inspire fellow feeling

But this is not enough. Two insightful responses are particularly worthy of mention. Segal (1987) reads the triumphant slave as the embodiment of carnivalesque inversion which is a hallmark of comedy; while for McCarthy (2000) the clever slave offers powerful Roman men the opportunity both to identify with a despised but subversive character and also, ultimately, to despise him. Without wanting to detract from these valuable psychological and sociological explanations of Plautus and the slave, I would suggest the addition of a rhetorical, poetic, generic motivation for the poet's servile voice, which contributes to explaining not just the presence of clever slaves, but specifically the connection between the slave and the poet's voice.[84]

When Plautus presents his own image through the persona of the clever slave, he is playing out the problem of relationships of power which is crucial to all literature, and especially to drama. He is doing so in a way which is appropriately modest (*sic*), and calculated as a goodwill gesture, a *captatio beneuolentiae*, towards the audience. It is not uncommon in other genres for an author to present himself humbly, and to do so half-genuinely, half-ironically, the hexameter Horace being the classic example, but it is particularly effective in comedy, where a pose of lowness is programmatic. Comedy, as a genre, is characterised and defined by its baseness, and a slave is the most base of characters. But Plautine comedy is cleverer than it pretends to be; its 'playwright' is a slave who is cleverer than everyone else, and is licensed to show off about his cleverness, his control of everyone else, precisely by his servile status. The triumphant slave is self-celebrating, certainly, but also ultimately self-deprecating. This is the essential irony, like that of Socrates who knows that he knows nothing. Cicero understood this well when he placed together Plautus and Old Comedy and Socrates as his prime examples of sophisticated humour (*Off.* 1.104). Roman comedy poses as being just something the playwright threw together, but actually it is artful, subtle and sophisticated. The playwright-as-slave is a way of telling us all that, politely.

The playwright is the god of his fictive world. Although he is the creator and controller of that world, to play out the role with any degree of

with the once and future slave' (170 n. 7). While this does seem right, I would suggest that the more subtle and complex destabilisation of identity in the corpus militates against the rigidity in practice which the 'natural slave' idea would embody in principle. Duncan (2006: 162–73) reads *Capt.* against the background of the point that some actors are slaves.

84 See also Anderson (1993: 141); Leigh (2004b: 26–37), who suggests that the prominence of the clever slave, especially his celebrations, has some connection with the situation of slave armies in the Punic War, and that there is an on-going subliminal allusion to Hannibal as trickster; Fitzgerald (2000), who analyses the 'peculiar position and ambiguous status of the slave' (11) as playing out the fantasies and fears of the audience (see also his ch. 2).

specificity would be offensive and rhetorically off-putting. The playwright has (an illusion of) total control, such that, if we saw only the triumphant moments of *Pseudolus*, *Bacchides*, *Epidicus* and others, we might start to feel a bit threatened by his control. His self-presentation also as (our) slave allows him to get away with it, because we are allowing him to get away with it. Despite the enormous power of the slave-as-playwright, his position is not always wholly comfortable. His masters, both within the play and in the audience, demand of him that he please them, that he control the world for their pleasure and purposes. This is why the *architectus* is sometimes subjected to unreasonable demands, threats and abuse by his masters. In some plays, certainly, the controlling slave is treated with inverted, saturnalian respect by those who need him.[85] In *Epidicus* in particular, however, the young master and his friend are very demanding and quite rough with the slave-hero. There is approval eventually for Epidicus, together with freedom and other delights, but there is also the threat of punishment if he does not succeed.[86] Plautus is examining the relationship of playwright and audience (and masters and slaves) from a different perspective, looking at the stresses and anxieties which the playwright suffers and overcomes in successful performance. The power relation is delicately balanced.

The playwright has to be a slave, then, precisely because he is in some sense 'really' a god.[87] Like a god and a slave, the playwright both controls the play and also is dependent on the audience's response. The character who plays this role closest to the line is Mercury in *Amphitruo*, whose status literally as god and slave allows him to reflect the playwright particularly closely. Throughout the play, and especially in his spectacular prologue, Mercury tempers his displays of divine power (themselves offering us a share in the divine perspective) with self-deprecating irony and familiar chattiness. Mercury, like Plautus, controls the world: he directs the sight and self-knowledge of Sosia and Amphitruo (as discussed above); he turns day into night (strictly speaking, it is Jupiter who extends the night, but Mercury is in a position to compliment Night on doing a good job); he controls not only the plot of the play, but also the genre of the play, changing it with a divine wave of the pen from tragedy to tragicomedy to comedy (51, 63, 96); he controls also the performance, not only by running

85 For example, wheedling masters call their slave *patrone* at *As.* 689, *Capt.* 444, *Cas.* 739, *Rud.* 1266.

86 Davos in Ter. *An.* suffers in a similar way.

87 Cf. the situation in Greek tragedy and myth, where 'man' famously exists 'between the beasts and the gods', and the hero constantly risks slipping out of the central category into one of the two inhuman extremes.

the show and directing our vision as regards the plot, but also by laying down rules about the behaviour of audience and actors (64–85). Yet he also addresses the audience as a suppliant, and expresses his own fears about the performance. The expression of fear is bound up in a jokey paradox about the gods Jupiter ('born from human parents', 28: for a second the actor peeps through the mask) and Mercury fearing *malum*, the trouble which comes to slaves in comedy, and to slave-actors whose performance is not up to scratch (31). But the fact remains: Mercury-Plautus has come to plead the cause of his play, and to engage the audience's attention by his delightful mixture of divine hybris and humble anxiety to please. Reminding the Romans of past services to the State (40), Mercury fudges divine military and economic favour with previous dramatic success. Explicitly he says (39–49) something that we might paraphrase: 'My father and I have deserved well of the State, but I won't remind you of all our past services, as I've seen divine characters in tragedies do, because my father knows you are grateful and doesn't need to remind you of his benefactions.' By interposing into the (non-)claim about divine benefactions a disparaging reference to other, non-comic, dramatic performances with less rhetorically effective *captationes beneuolentiae*, Mercury-Plautus shows his divine and his poetic power – without explicitly saying so.

The anxiety of the divine playwright shows us that power relations with the audience do not always go one way in a comedy. The relationship is neither straightforward subservience nor simple power, but rather an odd mixture of the two, in equilibrium. He deceives us, because we give him power to deceive. We are like Callipho in *Pseudolus*, happy to put aside our work and watch the slave's antics all day – in admiration, yes, but also insisting that he perform. The release which many slaves achieve at the end of the play is a metaphor for the resolution (release of tension) which the playwright experiences in the successful production of the play.

If the playwright-as-slave works so well, then, why does Plautus not use it all the time? It is always risky to argue for a generality on the basis of surviving plays, but my suggestion is that the *architectus*, the controlling slave, the slave-as-playwright, is a Plautine comic type which is sufficiently strong to be active in the background, as an interpretative effect, even when absent in person. It can become a norm of typology, against which other characters can measure themselves.[88]

[88] This will become particularly important in my discussion of Terence, below. The case is difficult to make with any degree of certainty without clearer evidence than we possess about the relative dating of the plays, but for what it may be worth several scholars date both *Mil.* and *Am.*, both

In *Casina*,[89] for example, the part of controlling character is played by the *matrona*, who organises the action and sets in motion the play-within-the-play, with its tricky disguise and feigned identity.[90] The other issue of identity in this play – the off-hand reference to a recognition which allows Casina to be married to the *adulescens* – barely seems integrated with the farcical games of vicarious lust. Such an impression might be mistaken, however: Mother knows best, and it is her champion who will win the play.

Another play which does not have an ordinary slave-*architectus*, but which is very much bound up in disguise, deceit, slavery and identity, is *Captiui*, the 'serious' play which self-righteously avoids the usual comic roguery. (A young master and slave have been captured in war. They are bought by a *senex* who is trying to find someone he can exchange for his own son, a prisoner of war on the other side. The old man also had another son, stolen by a runaway slave twenty years previously. The 'slave' of the original duo turns out to be this lost son, but only after he and his master had exchanged identities, in order to allow the master to return home to set up the exchange of prisoners, the old man thinking it was the slave he was sending. We know better, because the prologue has told us what is going on.) The play is by no means lacking in comic capers around stable identity, but it engages with them in rather unusual ways. There is a kind of intrigue from the master-and-slave couple, Tyndarus and Philocrates, in their prince-and-pauper exchange of identities, but despite Hegio's worry that he looks like a comic deluded *senex*, that 'trick' never really makes it to the status of comic *consilium*.[91] The credit for driving the plot goes as much to Hegio himself as to the play-within-the-play which Tyndarus and Philocrates try to perform in earnest. This, I suggest, is why Hegio is such an unusual *senex*. He is not the stereotypical angry father of

of which have powerful slaves, relatively early. Duckworth's review (1943) of Buck (1940) contains (350) a convenient table listing the datings of Buck and Enk (1953), both of whom date these two plays between 207 and 204 BC.

89 Generally thought to be late: see Franko (1999) for the lively imagery of this play, in which both antagonists take on some of the characteristics of the 'clever slave', but the success of each is clearly demarcated by semantic means, including their names and associated imagery.

90 See Anderson (1993: 105).

91 Muecke (1986: 227–9) is doubtful as to whether the exchange between Philocrates and Tyndarus can be classed as 'disguise' according to the terms of the discussion. McCarthy (2000: 173) takes the view that 'the superficial similarities of Tyndarus' and Philocrates' trick with the disguise schemes of other plays serves as a defining aspect of the play': she is right to call the similarities 'superficial', because for all their language of deception and comic badness and their plays with identity the young men's ploy is not really comic. On the uncomic tensions and questions left hanging at the end of this play, see Konstan (1983: 69); Thalmann (1996); Ketterer (1986: 131).

New Comedy, nor indeed the indulgent father.[92] Rather, he is more like a controlling character, organising his actors in various directions. He has a plot in action before the play even opens, and despite the impression that it is slipping from his control at one point (when he discovers the sub-plot of the captives' exchange of identity), it does at least produce the desired result in the end. Hegio is the only Plautine father who opposes the young people, but gets what he wants at the end of the play.[93] True, the actors do not sustain the roles he sets out for them, but they could not manage the plot without him. This may help explain why Hegio indulges in comic banter, particularly but not only with Ergasilus the parasite – behaviour which does not seem to fit easily with the comic stereotypes of old men. His unacknowledged son Tyndarus is the image of his father in character. Both try to manipulate what happens, both play around with identity, both use a kind of style which comedy associates with slaves.[94] The other exceptional aspect of this play is Tyndarus: the only slave in comedy actually to be sent to the mill, actually to suffer – presumably because he is not really a slave.[95]

But who is really a slave? As *senex*, Hegio represents a crucial figure in the audience – the chaps in togas. If he has a trace of the role of *architectus*, he becomes a kind of honorary comic slave, and so represents the poet more closely than any other socially elevated character. This daringly close identification of the poet with slave and with *paterfamilias* forbids any easy reading either of the play or of the slave as playwright. Oddly, it is finally the 'villain' Stalagmus, whose role in the play has been tiny, who is left playing out the defiance of the clever slave. Perhaps this is in order to take the edge off the worryingly slave-like characterisation of Hegio.

If the '*senex* as *architectus*' is odd, however, then the '*architectus* as *adulescens* (*amans et egens*)' is even odder. This is the scenario which Plautus plays out in *Persa*, a play in which he experiments with the furthest

92 McCarthy (2000: 176–7) analyses his character, seeing him more as a variation on the blocking character than as a type of trickster.

93 Daemones in *Rud.*, for example, gets the daughter he wants, but out of the blue, and not through his own plotting, and in any case he had never opposed the young people.

94 McCarthy (2000) discusses how masters in several plays act in some ways like slaves, particularly in *Men.*, *Cas.* and *Capt.* The suggestion that Hegio is taking something of the role of *architectus* in this play would not be incompatible with the case made by Frangoulidis (1996a) for reading the culinary creations of Ergasilus as metaphors for the poetry of Plautus. This is the play in which all identities, all roles, are messed up and shared around.

95 Leigh (2004b: 57) points out that the slaves of *Capt.* are exceptional in the Plautine corpus for having a history, and the geography that goes with it. His whole ch. 3 is an important reading of the play in conjunction with Roman legal issues surrounding the status of those who have been captured in war and then returned.

reaches of the subversion of status-identity and power.[96] The play has a clear *architectus* – Toxilus – who directs the action, sets in motion and stage-manages the play-within-the-play which constitutes the act of deceit, and ultimately triumphs over agelastic forces. He also celebrates his success and comments metatheatrically on the action (although not to the same extent as the greatest *architecti*). But he is doing it all for himself. He is the lover whose beloved must be extracted from the pimp; he needs the help of his friends;[97] it is his 'father' (actually, master) whose absence allows a space of licence in which the affair, the deceit and the play can take place. But he is and remains a slave. Moreover, one of his helpers is a free parasite, who outrageously supplies his own (virginal, marriageable) daughter to be the prima donna of Toxilus' tricksy internal play.[98] McCarthy (2000) has an excellent chapter on this play, in which she analyses the multiple roles of Toxilus as lover, civic defender and master, while still being a slave.[99] Her discussion also highlights the effects of the *puer delicatus* Paegnium and the virgin daughter of the parasite Saturio as being rebels (albeit perhaps failed ones) against the forces of rebellious farce (see esp. 158–61). To this sociological reading I would only add a poetico-sociological footnote. This is the play where the ultimately powerless get some sort of a voice, some sort of power: the passive Virgo gets to play tricks *and* state her own objections;[100] the normally useless lover gets to plan his own trick-solution;

96 Slater (2000: 31) nicely brings out the shocking effect of slave as lover. Lowe (2000: 196) describes the setup as 'entirely bizarre'.

97 Crucially, the 'help' he gets is a piece of luck which he can turn to his advantage. Toxilus started out bemoaning his need for money. His friend, a slave in another family, came along and was duly asked for help. The friend, Sagaristio, thus clearly plays the role of peer-friend, *sodales*, as well as having a go at usurping the 'clever slave' role. Sagaristio does indeed provide money (and celebrates like an *architectus* at 251), by diverting money given to him by his own master in order to buy some bulls. But when the money arrives, Toxilus has already made his plans for the disguise-trick, in which Sagaristio is going to be an actor (462–6), and although he does indeed use the money to get the girl from the pimp quite straightforwardly, he still needs his own (much cleverer) trick in order to pay Sagaristio back, to take the de rigueur vengeance on the pimp, and to give the play something to do.

98 Lowe (1989) argues that Plautus has greatly expanded the role of the Virgin, and given her a speaking, tricksy part which she would not have had in the Greek original.

99 I am not quite convinced by McCarthy's (2000) argument for the triumph over the pimp as being an assertion of civic, rather than comic, values, but the difference is perhaps one of emphasis. (It is interesting that 'subversive' comedy so often seems to end up apparently upholding conventional societal values.) It is indeed true that Toxilus is promoting citizen-identity and the civic value of *fides* in the face of the perjured and foreign pimp who traffics in citizen women, but he does so with so heavy a dose of irony that I cannot see his actions as primarily 'moral' (see e.g. McCarthy 2000: 125). Slater (2000: ch. 3) is a metatheatrical reading of the play. See also Chiarini (1983).

100 See McCarthy (2000). Chiarini (1983) suggests that the Virgo is already acting in the first scene, and is only posing as a 'modest girl', a view opposed by Lowe (1989). I would note that the 'modest girl' oppositional stance which the Virgo seems to adopt, and which McCarthy (2000) offers as

and the *architectus* gets to work on his own behalf. This might, then, be the most subversive of Plautine plays, in which the poet subliminally expresses his irritation and frustration at always having to work for someone else, to respond to the demands of the master, the convention, the audience, rather than his own desires and wishes. What a shame that it doesn't work.

Clever slaves, like poets, must not act in their own interests.[101] Although Toxilus is the *architectus* of his play, he somehow fails to draw us with him in the way that Pseudolus, Chrysalus, and Epidicus and the rest, succeed in doing, especially when (as McCarthy 2000 points out) he acts more like a master than a free-spirited slave. This, perhaps, is the final trick of the *architectus*-tradition: making us like the heroic slave for his subversion and his free spirit, but only when he is altruistic and nice. Real freedom, now, that's another matter entirely. We will not let the playwright pursue his own dreams, as Terence acknowledges twice (*An.* 3, *HT* 52). We insist on him conforming to our expectations and demands. We insist that he remain a slave.

Could it be that Plautus wrote *Truculentus* in bitter response? This late play[102] has rightly been seen as an experiment in a satirical mode and as an ancestor, if not by direct lineage, of the verse satire of later Latin literature.[103] There is no reason to suppose that it was other than popular, but that does not rule out satire directed at the audience.[104] It is an extraordinary piece which has 'very little plot'[105] but no lack of plotting, monologues in excess but no lack of characters interacting with each other, and classic set pieces of the comic world put together in surprising ways. While it might be true that very little actually happens during the course of the play, there are so many plotlines (each lover has his own story) and such an air of deception that the play manages to give the appearance of being busy. This play contains a grasping courtesan at its centre, and a trick based on a supposititious baby, both of which are often thought to be quintessential

her rebellion against the farcical mode, is a highly conventional one, and so perhaps not much of a rebellion. At least she gets to say it herself, I suppose. Hardy (2005) reads the Virgo as a metatheatrical tragic figure who (comically) does not fit in the comic world.

101 McCarthy (2000: 123–4) notes how this point limits the subversive power of the clever slave, and that Plautus' experiment in *Per.* is in working with a clever slave without the 'legitimating framework' of the young master's affair (158).

102 Discussion in Enk (1953: 28–30), who opts for 189 BC.

103 Dessen (1977) and Konstan (1983: 142–64) develop the reading of the play as satire; Anderson (1993: 82–7) concentrates on the replacement of romantic notions with satirical ones; Moore (1998a: 140–57) shows how deeply embedded the play is in its Roman context, and therefore how far the audience is implicated in the satire as a satiric butt.

104 Indeed, Cicero says that Plautus in his old age rejoiced in *Truc.* and *Ps.* (*Sen.* 50).

105 Konstan (1983: 142), and references there. Enk's account (1953: 22–8) of judgements on the play from the sixteenth century to his own day make entertaining reading.

comic motifs, although neither of them is in fact common.[106] It ends with the three equally deluded and disreputable lovers (independent young man of the city, foreign soldier, country boy eager to cheat his father) all still vying for the attention of the central courtesan, but none of them sure of their continued access. A bolt from the blue has meant that the city boy, Diniarchus, has to marry the baby's mother, whom he seduced while he was previously engaged to her, but even he seems intent on keeping open a refuge in the brothel.[107] The harsh satire is directed by no means only at the vices of the grasping courtesan, but more especially at the idiocy and profligacy of all three lovers, with all of whom the audience is made to identify.[108] The play has only one trickster, one plotter, one controlling character, and that is the courtesan Phronesium. If *Persa* was an exploration of an *architectus* as lover working for himself, *Truculentus* takes the experiment a stage further, making the love-object into a kind of *architectus* whose domination of all around her is complete. Phronesium is the only plotter in the play, and she has a quite absurd degree of control over her victims, who shout about her wickedness and their awareness of their own depravity, and then melt at her slightest word.[109] No-one else really gets much of a look in: Phronesium's servants are extensions of herself, the cook who brings the presents from Diniarchus is entertaining but has as his only act of initiative a bit of personal diversion of his master's resources, while the title character Truculentus, whom we might expect to

106 Not surprisingly, Phronesium is always put forward as the prime example of the grasping courtesan, for example by Duckworth (1994: 258). The back story to *Cist.* also depends on a (highly illegal) supposition of a freeborn baby to a prostitute who uses it for financial gain (*Cist.* 135–44). There are of course many other women who are in it for the money (i.e. survival), but they are not central: the Bacchis sisters are roundly upstaged by Chrysalus in *Bac.*, just as Acroteleutium is an adjunct to Palaestrio in *Mil.*, and the interest in *Men.* (as indeed in *Bac.* and to some extent *Mil.*) is primarily in the humour of duality and mistaken identity, not in the grasping ways of the courtesans. Gilula (1980) also treats Phronesium as the 'indisputable example' (151) of the bad prostitute; her main interest is in demonstrating that all Terence's *meretrices* are *malae*, which requires rather exacting standards of goodness. The motif of the supposititious baby, especially when used as a deliberate trick, is in fact rare. There is an allusion to it in Ter. *An.*, and it can serve as an accusation and an insult, especially towards midwives, but this is the only case in Roman comedy of it being used within the play as a trick. It is perhaps not surprising that it should be associated with on the one hand midwives, and on the other hand prostitutes, since both categories of women are associated with insecurities about legitimate transmission.

107 This situation is unique in Roman comedy. The young man who has raped or seduced a citizen girl always wants to marry her. Those whose marriage is a part of the play do not also consort with prostitutes within the immediate span of the play.

108 See Moore (1998a: 143).

109 One example among many: Diniarchus has a bitter and self-aware speech at 335–51, but as soon as Phronesium comes out and teases him that her door doesn't bite (which it does!) he does not even make a show of resistance but helplessly exclaims: *uer uide: / ut tota floret, ut olet, ut nitide nitet!* (353–4). See Duncan (2006: 147).

be a worthy adversary to Phronesium, turns out to be completely hopeless (and also self-serving).[110] In this case, then, the playwright is hidden in the most unlikely guise of the scheming prostitute, whose lovers make constant demands and yet are pathetically easy to control as long as she feeds them the right stuff.

PLOTTING AND PLAYWRIGHTS IN TERENCE

Even his detractors credit Terence with major dramaturgical developments in the double plot,[111] the effect of which is not only the production of plays tightly structured around doublings of various kinds, but also, especially when combined with his innovative use of prologues and consequent positioning of the audience, an unprecedented foregrounding of interweaving plot elements.[112] When Terence came to write, the persona of the 'internal playwright', the *architectus* who drives the plot and play, and who is quintessentially a clever slave, was already well established. One might expect, then, that a double plot would either have two such slaves or perhaps would give one plot to a clever slave and the other to some alternative controlling character. This is almost what happens in Terence's *Andria* (slave versus father), but in fact the relationship which Terence develops between the playwright and the slave-*architectus* is nothing like so neat and co-operative. One of the games Terence plays with Plautus is to take the earlier playwright's greatest invention, the controlling clever slave, use him, but then confuse him.[113] In the plays of Terence, there is a constant battle for authorial control, with competing plots jostling for attention. Instead

110 One of the worries of the play for critics is why Truculentus gives in to Astaphium's blandishments before they have even happened: Konstan (1983: 154–5).

111 Norwood (1923: 146). As Levin (1967: 301) says, virtually every critic from Donatus on has commented on this aspect of Terentian dramaturgy. His own interest is in the balance of the two plots between two different kinds of romantic relationship, one leading to marriage the other not. He does not consider either *An.* or *Hec.* to be genuinely double-plotted (305). Wiles (1991: 31–2) is more in keeping with most modern readers in seeing all Terence's plays as, to a greater or lesser extent, double-plotted, and briefly though usefully indicates the contrast with Menander that the situation creates in the position of the audience. Goldberg (1986: ch. 5) is a good example of modern reading of Terentian duality. Gilula (1991) argues for playing down the significance of double-plotting. Dunsch (1999) takes the view that many Menandrian plays were also double-plotted, as does Zagagi (1994: 46–50).

112 Cf. Menander's famous remark, reported by Plutarch (*Mor.* 347e), that once he has got the plot sorted out the rest is simple. Plautus certainly (e.g. *Am.*, *Men.*, *Bac.*) also wrote plays with structural dualities, but that is not the same as interweaving plotlines.

113 It is a gradual process: Kruschwitz (2004) also sees chronological development at work here. McCarthy (2004: 101) does not contest the 'general consensus . . . that Terence pruned back the functions of slaves', but argues that the later playwright 'normalised it to a surrounding framework of naturalism'.

of identifying the authorial voice closely with one character, Terence offers various characters the chance to plot, but also allows his own presence as playwright, separately from any cipher, to intrude more directly on the plot. In narrative terms, the focalisation is much more widely spread than in Plautus.[114] In this section, I examine some of the ways in which Terence shares out (and denies) the authorial voice among his characters; in the following section, my primary concern will be with the manipulations of realism. There is some inevitable slippage between the two sections.

Already in *Andria*, Terence creates complex interplays between various levels of fictionality, albeit in a less flamboyant way than is Plautus' style. There are four plotters (or groups of plotters) at work: Simo *senex*, Davos *seruus*, Glycerium and Pamphilus (*amantes/adulescentes*), and Terence, who perhaps might be termed *poeta*, as if that were a stock character also. Some of the plotters make explicit their suspicion that plotting is itself an overriding value: Simo expresses the opinion that Davos is plotting for the *adulescens* more to spite Simo than to help his son (162–3), while both Simo and Davos use the language of plays directly to refer to other people's stories.[115]

Simo *senex* wants his son to marry the daughter of the man next door; Pamphilus *adulescens*, however, is in love with Glycerium, the supposed sister of a courtesan from Andros, and has made her pregnant; the girl is in fact the long-lost daughter of the man next door, but we will not know that until almost the end of the play. In the end, then, Pamphilus *does* marry the 'daughter of the man next door', as his father wanted. A somewhat similar plot pattern occurs also in Plautus' *Cistellaria*, where Alcesimarchus is in love with the supposed prostitute Selenium, but is being forced to marry the daughter of the Lemnian Demipho. It turns out that Selenium is also a daughter of Demipho, born as a result of rape of the woman who is now his wife, the other daughter having been born to an intervening wife. As far as we can tell from the fragmentary state of that play, there is no sign of a matching match for the other daughter, as Terence contrives in *Andria*. The motif of marriage to an earlier rape-victim, after an intervening marriage to someone else, occurs also in *Epidicus*. For all their complexity, neither of these Plautine plays shows the duality of Terence's play, nor do they show the same degree of battle for authorial control, although there is perhaps

114 For the narratology of drama, and in particular the manner of mimesis, see the essays in the first section of Ferroni (1981a).

115 Goldberg (1986: 78–9), apropos a comment that overhearing indicates power, sees Simo as being given the edge over Davos in their early interaction at 128–9, in that the old man has overheard Davos talking about him and has a trick up his sleeve.

the germ of such an idea in the 'interaction' between Epidicus and Plautus discussed above.

Chremes (the man next door) has heard about the affair and so breaks off the planned marriage with his known daughter. But Simo hopes to put his son in an awkward position, and test him out, and even rather confusedly to get the marriage to happen anyway, by pretending that the wedding is going ahead this very day. Davos discovers Simo's deceit, and gets Pamphilus to pretend to agree to the marriage in order to wrong-foot the old man. But after Pamphilus has acquiesced so obediently, Chremes is persuaded, and the marriage is really set up again, so Davos and Pamphilus are stuck. There is an extra complication, which never quite manages to get a proper look-in,[116] that another young man, Charinus, is actually in love with the (known) daughter of Chremes; he now believes that Pamphilus has fallen in love with the girl himself, and is suitably distressed. A second plan involves the baby, who is born during the play. Davos is just about to make use of the baby, when along comes Crito, a relative of the Andrian and an old friend of Chremes, who can say Glycerium is a citizen; he is brought out to tell Simo the truth, and is recognised by Chremes. It turns out that Chremes' brother went on a journey years ago, along with his niece (Chremes' own daughter), was shipwrecked, was received along with the niece by the father of Chrysis, *adfinis* of Crito, but died. Chremes to this day has not known what happened to his brother and daughter. It is Pamphilus who is able to supply the original name of Glycerium (Pasibula), so it all slots into place.

It is in the activity of the individual plotters that it is possible to see how internal playwrights interact in a Terentian play. The play begins and ends with a marriage between the son of Simo, the first plotter, and the daughter of Chremes, who is only ever an audience. The only difference between the two potential marriages is that the opening one is false, and involves the wrong daughter. In fact, Simo is only pretending that this is a marriage; he is trying to direct the plot by an additional level of fiction and deceit, aiming to turn the fictional into the real. This will be achieved eventually, but not by him. In the early stages of the play, Simo makes a show of being in control, and it is he who gives us the exposition of the plot which the

[116] Donatus tells us (Wessner 1962–3 I: 118) that Charinus is an invention of Terence's and is not in Menander. On the possibility that this might mean 'not in Menander's *Andria*', but possibly imported from the *Perinthia*, see Barsby (2002: 254). What I am describing as the failure of the Charinus' plot 'to get a proper look-in' is what leads Levin (1967) to consider this play not in fact to have a double plot.

prologue has lacked, in the form of dialogue with his freedman Sosia.[117] He even offers us his own 'proper' expository prologue – *rem omnem a principio audies* ('you will hear the whole story from the beginning', 48) – in place of the literary one provided by the playwright. In the process of his explanation to Sosia, Simo produces a long narrative of the arrival of the Andrian, Pamphilus' involvement with her, her death, the funeral and Glycerium's grief, which exposes Pamphilus as her lover when he saves her from going too close to the flames. As a narrator of other plays Simo is effective; it is with creative fiction that he gets in a muddle, as we will see shortly. This day is set for the wedding (102) and even though it is now false, he is going ahead with the pretence in an attempt to order the plot. Before he finishes, however, Simo lets slip that there is a Davos in the case, when he worries that Davos might have an alternative *consilium* which he tries to forestall with his own:

> simul sceleratu' Dauo' siquid consili
> habet, ut consumat nunc quom nil obsint doli
> (*An.* 159–60)

At the same time if that troublemaker Davos has some plot, then he'll use it up now when tricks are no trouble.

Donatus (Wessner 1962–3 1: 35) gives the protagonist role to Simo, which would perhaps surprise the modern reader who would expect either the scheming slave or (what a modern might call) the 'romantic lead' to take that position. If one takes the central idea of the play to be the interactions of plotting between Simo and Davos, however, the ascription makes good sense.[118]

So to Davos' attempts at plotting. Davos, the first controlling slave in Terence, comes into the play with on the one hand all the expectations formed by the *architectus* tradition, and on the other his milder Menandrian name. Simo has set him up as a Plautine trickster, but will Terence let him play that role? Pseudolus is metaphorically looking over his shoulder to see what sort of a job he makes of it. Simo tries to forestall any deception on Davos' part, by warning him off (190), but Davos pays him back with a clever metatheatrical joke. Simo is dropping hints about the possible negative effects of Davos on Pamphilus, which Davos refuses to understand. You don't understand? No, *Dauo' sum, non Oedipus* (194). Davos cannot

117 A protatic character whom Donatus (Wessner 1962–3 1: 36–7) says Terence has invented, on which see Anderson (2004).

118 On the balance of the play and its domination by Simo, see Goldberg (1981–2).

guess what his master means, because he is Davos (a new comic slave)[119] not Oedipus, the proverbially clever tragic hero, whose cleverness was instrumental in his tragedy. For anyone even slightly acquainted with tragedy, in a few words there is a subtle generic game, in which Davos points to his role as comic clever slave, and to the fact that such a role is an inversion of the cleverness of the tragic hero.[120] Donatus (Wessner 1962–3 I: 91) comments that Davos thus turns Simo into the Sphinx. That would indeed be one point to Davos, but in fact control is balanced between him and his master: Davos may throw the riddle back in Simo's face, but he does not succeed in answering it. Perhaps Davos is not as much in control as he would like (us) to think. At the end of the scene, the master tries to snatch back the initiative:

> sed dico tibi:
> ne temere facias; neque tu haud dicas tibi non praedictum: caue!
> (*An.* 204–5)

But I'm telling you: don't do anything rash, and don't say I didn't warn you. Watch out!

With these words, Simo could perhaps be alluding to Pseudolus, who sets up his trick precisely by warning his master that he *will* deceive him. Simo warns Davos not to try to be Pseudolus, using the clever slave's own language.[121] It should not escape our notice that the old man in this play, Simo, shares a name with his counterpart in the *Pseudolus*.

Is Davos playing Pseudolus or not? A few lines earlier, when Simo demands an acknowledgement that Davos understands his point, the slave replies with an ironic *immo callide* ('very clever', 201): yes, he understands very clearly that he is to play the role of the *seruus callidus*. When Davos is left alone, his self-addressed soliloquy wondering about what his plan ought to be (*nec quid agam certumst*, 209) reflects with a difference the deliberations of Pseudolus when he will become a poet and invent those twenty *minae* (401–5):

> Postquam illic hinc abiit, tu astas solus, Pseudole . . .
> (*Ps.* 394)

Now that he has gone away from here, you're standing alone, Pseudolus . . .

119 MacCary (1969), examining the possibility that Menander's slave names may be indicative of their characters, suggests that Daos is a slave who tries to trick but fails at everything he does. If this is right, then there would be an additional irony in Davos' claim here.

120 See Fraenkel (1960: 12).

121 At almost the other end of the play, Simo again reflects the Pseudolesque structure when he mentions Davos' forewarning: *credo et id facturas Dauo' dudum praedixit mihi* (840).

Enimuero, Daue, nil locist segnitiae neque socordiae . . .
(*An.* 206)

Well then, Davos, no room for laziness or inactivity . . .

The difference for Davos is that he is not at all sure whether he can live up to the expectations of the tradition (209: should he help his young master or not?). We come to see not only that he does not have a plan – that after all is not unusual for the great improvisers of the *architectus* tradition – but also that other people do.

This takes us to the third group of plotters, Glycerium and Pamphilus. They, according to Davos, have concocted a story in which Glycerium is a citizen: 'Once upon a time there was a merchant, who was shipwrecked off the island of Andros . . .'. So Davos parodies their plot.[122] His response is *fabulae!* Those would be *fabulae palliatae* presumably, since this story sounds like a typical plot-background of New Comedy. It is presented to us here as a complete fiction, but Terence's audience would hear the description as precisely the kind of plot they are always being offered, maybe even as the plot of a particular play which is an important intertext for this one. A member of the audience who knows the plot of Menander's *Andria* and *Perinthia* – *qui utramuis recte norit ambas nouerit* ('whoever knows one knows both', *An.* 10) – might perhaps appreciate an additional level to the joke here, if the 'shipwreck' plot featured in either or both of them. Such a reader would know something Davos doesn't. But at the moment the implied reader of this play follows Davos in believing that it is *not* the plot of our play. Time and Terence will show, however, that it is.[123]

Not only does Davos read the shipwreck story as fiction, but he also complains that it is not even a very realistic plot: *miquidem hercle non fit ueri simile; atque ipsis commentum placet* ('doesn't seem very realistic to me, but they like it', 225). He thinks the young couple are too easily impressed, not discerning enough about literary realism.[124] He himself, by contrast, knows how to read realism. Simo's plot works at first, and everyone believes the marriage is on, until Davos notices that Simo's production is not very realistic:

[122] Goldberg (1986: 45): 'Davus is probably mimicking the innocent style of fables and children's stories.'

[123] The implied reader is taken in, but the real reader might not be fooled, for, as Brown (2006: 5) says, 'the audience must have been well aware that the playwright was unlikely to make Davos report the story . . . if it was not going to turn out to be true'.

[124] See the next section for discussion of characters as readers of realism in Terence.

> [DA.] redeunti interea ex ipsa re mi incidit suspicio 'hem
> paullulum opsoni; ipsu' tristis; de inprouiso nuptiae:
> non cohaerent.' PA. quorsu' nam istuc? DA. ego me continuo ad Chremem.
> quom illo aduenio, solitudo ante ostium: iam id gaudeo.
> CH. recte dici'. PA. perge. DA. maneo. interea intro ire neminem
> uideo, exire neminem; matronam nullam in aedibus,
> nil ornati, nil tumulti: accessi; intro aspexi. PA. scio:
> magnum signum. DA. num uidentur conuenire haec nuptiis?
>
> (*An.* 359–66)

[DA.] Meanwhile on the way back a suspicion occurred to me: 'Hmm, not much in the way of provisions, himself looking sad, the wedding sudden: it doesn't add up.' PA. Where's this leading? DA. I went straight off to Chremes' house, and when I got there I found no-one outside, which pleased me. CH. Absolutely. PA. Go on. DA. I stuck around. All the time I didn't see anyone go in or go out; no ladies in the house, no decorations, no fuss. I went closer and looked inside. PA. I know. That's a big sign. DA. Does that look like a wedding?

From Davos' point of view, Simo has committed the serious theatrical error of failing to convince the audience, and so he is able to take back the initiative. Davos sets in motion his plan, with Pamphilus as actor, pretending to be happy with the wedding. He hopes to undermine Simo's play by contributing a little more realism to it, in the form of a willing groom. The result will be a play watched by two separate internal audiences, Davos and Byrria (Charinus' slave), giving different readings of the play:

> [BY.] ipsum adeo praesto uideo cum Dauo: hoc agam.
> SI. utrumque adesse uideo. DA. em serua. SI. Pamphile.
> DA. quasi de inprouiso respice ad eum. PA. ehem pater.
> DA. probe. SI. hodie uxorem ducas, ut dixi, uolo.
> BY. nunc nostrae timeo parti quid hic respondeat.
> PA. neque istic neque alibi tibi erit usquam in me mora. BY. hem.
> DA. obmutuit. BY. quid dixit? SI. facis ut te decet,
> quom istuc quod postulo impetro cum gratia.
> DA. sum uerus? BY. eru', quantum audio, uxore excidit.
> SI. i nunciam intro, ne in mora, quom opu' sit, sies.
> PA. eo. (*An.* 415–25)

[BY.] I can see him standing there with Davos. This is what I'll do [i.e. eavesdrop]. SI. I can see them both standing there. DA. Now, be careful. SI. Pamphilus. DA. Look at him as if you're surprised to see him. PA. Ah, father! DA. Well done. SI. As I told you, I want you to marry today. BY. Now I'm afraid for our side as to what he will reply. PA. Neither in this nor in anything else will I ever cause you any obstruction. BY. Oh dear. DA. That's shut him up. BY. What did he say? SI. Your actions become you, that you agree with good grace to my instruction. DA. Am I right or am I right? BY. It sounds to me as though my master has lost his wife. SI. Go inside now, and don't hold things up when you're needed. PA. I'm going.

Both Davos' and Simo's plans are thrown into confusion when they overhear the servant of Glycerium talking to the midwife, about Glycerium's impending delivery. Simo is so tied up in the idea of plotting that he immediately jumps to the conclusion that Davos has invented this plotline, and trained his actors to play it out for Simo's own benefit (or rather, disbenefit), in order to forestall the marriage. Simo, then, thinks that this is Davos' plot, but in fact it will turn out to be Terence's, or rather, 'the truth'. Simo is like a kind of determined and slightly paranoid audience of comedies, seeing plots everywhere, but with no judgement. Like Davos, he is concerned about convention and realism in drama. When Glycerium follows the comic convention for a girl in such circumstances, crying out in the pains of childbirth (473), Simo comments that this is ridiculous, because it is far too soon for her to be in labour. He thinks this is a piece of deceit improvised for his benefit when Glycerium heard that he was there:

> hui tam cito? ridiculum: postquam ante ostium
> me audiuit stare, adproperat. non sat commode
> diuisa sunt temporibu' tibi, Daue, haec.
> (*An.* 474–6)

Huh, so quick? Ridiculous. After she heard me standing in front of the door, she hurried up. You've got your timing wrong here, Davos.

Simo's objection is also a piece of drama criticism (hijacked by the poet), as a comment on the convention that comic births happen remarkably quickly and conveniently timed.[125]

It is quickly followed by another piece of comic convention: as the midwife is leaving, she calls back into the house over her shoulder. Simo scoffs at this standard comic device:

> non imperabat coram quid opu' facto esset puerperae,
> sed postquam egressast, illis quae sunt intu' clamat de uia.
> o Daue, itan contemnor abs te? aut itane tandem idoneus
> tibi uideor esse quem tam aperte fallere incipias dolis?
> (*An.* 490–3)

[125] Kruschwitz (2004: 49–50) notes the metatheatrical aspects of Simo's and Davos' interaction here. Goldberg (1986: 20) comments on the Terentian twist to the convention added by Simo's belief that the pregnancy is a sham. See also Maurach (2005: 103).

She didn't give the orders about what ought to be done for the new mother in her presence, but after she had come outside she shouted from the street to those who were inside. Oh Davos, is this how I'm scorned by you? Do I seem like the kind of person that you can deceive with such obvious tricks?

Since Simo is the audience for this play (for he has deceived himself into the role of audience), he is in fact quite right: Terence's joke on Simo is that he does not know how to be a good audience, does not accept that the audience is part of the play, and so it is perfectly reasonable for the midwife to speak where he can hear.[126] Davos, however, is cleverer at turning the event to his advantage. He snatches Simo's idea that what they are watching is a charade, and changes its meaning by telling Simo that the child is supposititious: Simo will believe this new plot since a supposititious birth is a motif of New Comedy. Davos warns him that the women will try to put the child on Simo's doorstep. This is indeed what will happen, but Davos hereby sets Simo up to interpret it as a trick.

Before that development can happen, however, Simo takes back the initiative and invents a story for Chremes' benefit, saying that Pamphilus and Glycerium have quarrelled. His invention is remarkably successful, and the first part of the play comes to crisis, with the false wedding of Simo's opening pretence and Davos' double-bluffing contribution suddenly becoming horribly real.

That round is definitely awarded to Simo, who celebrates his success by admitting his earlier deceit to Davos. The slave acknowledges it with a metatheatrical comment: *uah consilium callidum!* (589). His own plotting and his ability to read theatrical realism having been undermined, Davos has to work hard to regain his position with Pamphilus when the young master finds out that the marriage is real after all. Like Epidicus, under pressure Davos promises to think up another plot (621–4).[127] In order to ensure his mastery over the performance, Davos refuses to tell either us or his masters what the plot is:

[126] The audience of Roman comedy not only hears the action, but metaphorically watches itself hearing: interplay with the audience such as soliloquy, asides and other types of audience-address are used in Roman comedy far more than any expository requirements would dictate, to enable us to play the role 'audience'. See Bain (1977) and Frost (1988: 7–8) for an 'entry talking back' in Menander. The naturalist device in Greek comedy has clearly become metatheatrical in Terence's use of it.

[127] The scene in which Pamphilus makes demands of Davos (606–24), and the subsequent scene where Charinus joins in and wants help also, have affinities with the scenes between Epidicus and his master and master's friend, mentioned above, pp. 122–3 and 133. The allusion marks out Davos' claim to be a Plautine *architectus*.

dies [hic] mi ut sati' sit uereor
ad agendum: ne uacuom esse me nunc ad narrandum credas:
proinde hinc uos amolimini; nam mi inpedimento estis.
(*An.* 705–7)

I'm afraid the day isn't going to be long enough to act it, so do you think I've got time to narrate it as well? Now clear off out of here. You're in my way.

So spoke his models in the *architectus* tradition: Epidicus said he did not have time to stand around talking about the plot (*Epid.* 376, 665); Pseudolus said he would tell Calidorus the plot later, but did not want to repeat it because these plays are long enough as it is (*Ps.* 388), and in any case the play is being put on for the benefit of the audience (720); and Palaestrio tells his master that certain information about the plot is only available on a need-to-know basis (*Mil.* 810).

Davos takes his cue from Simo's suspicion that the baby was his idea: he decides he will indeed make a plot out of it. He instructs Mysis, Glycerium's maid, to put the baby on Simo's doorstep (725), with some plan in mind that we never learn, although he gives us the impression of knowing what he is doing when he tells Mysis, whether honestly or deceitfully, that he wants her to put the baby there so that he can swear with good conscience that he has not done so. (Mysis, not surprisingly, is not impressed by his sudden scruples, 730.) But then Chremes arrives. Davos throws that plot away (733), whatever it was, and uses the baby to scare Chremes off, by pretending the women are deceptively bringing in a supposititious child and are trying to palm it off on Pamphilus in order to stop the planned marriage. The piece of artistic genius in this (or is it an opportunistic scrabble out of a hole?) is that Davos the actor-manager has left his underling Mysis not knowing that this is a work of fiction. Her confusion is therefore all the more natural and convincing when he suddenly starts abusing her, as he explains to her after Chremes has gone, congratulating himself on making Mysis' performance really lifelike and naturalistic (794–5). Davos here enters into the extreme end of the spectrum of naturalism in ancient art theory, where it tips over the edge of naturalism into nature.[128]

A brilliant intertextualist (or plagiariser), Davos also uses a version of Glycerium's 'citizen' plot, although without believing it himself either in reality (that is, in the play), or within his play within a play: he says accusingly to Mysis, but really for Chremes' benefit, that he has heard

[128] See Morales (1996) for an account of the painful consequences of slipping over that boundary; Carey (2003: 106–7).

some nonsense about Glycerium being a citizen (779). It looks as though Davos will have achieved his aim, but just at that moment enter Crito ('Judgy'), the coup from the playwright that blows all Davos' plotting – and Simo's – out of the water.

Chremes now thinks the baby is real; Simo thinks it is supposititious and a plot (*ficta atque incepta*, 836). Davos comes out (842) apparently unaware of the fathers' presence and apparently celebrating the success indoors, as if he were completely convinced by the new turn of events brought about by the arrival of Crito,[129] but for all his posturing the plot has been snatched from him. First he pretends to continue the plotline in which Pamphilus marries the daughter of Chremes (847–8: or is he already playing out the final marriage?); then he has another go, presumably ironically, at the one in which Pamphilus and Glycerium have argued (853); then he tries to tell the story of the arrival of the stranger, but does so in such a way as to imply that Crito is an imposter (854–7). Whatever he might be trying to do at this point, however, he does not have the opportunity, because he is manhandled away by Simo's slaves to be tied up, since the resolution is not in fact going to include him. Now Terence's plot, the 'citizen-shipwreck' plot that has been hovering around throughout the play, but which no-one has believed, is brought into action.[130] Simo, however, still refuses to believe it: he thinks it is another plot out to get him. His response to the beginning of Crito's case is *fabulam inceptat* – he's saying the prologue (925). Only the recognition scene between Chremes and Crito convinces him. Is that realistic? Are recognitions realistic?[131] How can we tell?

Terence's second play (or third, if we count the first performance of *Hecyra*), *Heauton timorumenos*, shows a similar structure as regards control of the plot: again, one slave is pitted against one *senex*, with the aim of settling the affairs of two boys, two girls, and – although the slave is not really interested in this one – two old men.[132] Plotting in this play is dominated by the slave Syrus, who plays a classic *architectus* role, manipulating

[129] His reference to *hospiti'* (843) must indeed be to Crito, as Donatus (Wessner 1962–3 I: 235) says, but it is not at all clear either what Davos believes to be the case or what he intends to achieve at this point. At best, Crito has only confirmed that Glycerium is a citizen, but that is not much use until she finds her parents.

[130] Nicely put by Gowers (2004: 153): 'the lost story-line is at large all through the play, looking for a home'.

[131] Cave (1988) opens with an appreciation of the artificiality of recognition: 'such scenes are somehow too neat to be real, like the mechanism of a cuckoo clock, and so draw attention to themselves – and to the literary form as a whole – as an artifice' (2).

[132] In the next section, I discuss the plot of this play in more detail with regard to its manipulation of realism, whereas here my interest is in the metatheatrical roles of slave and *senex* as drivers of the plot.

truth and falsehood, tricking enemies and even friends (for the sake of greater realism), let down by his actors but ultimately triumphant. The only other character (apart from Terence) who really tries to get in on the act as regards plotting is the *senex* Chremes, whose attempts to stage-manage his neighbour's treatment of his (the neighbour's) son in fact play right into Syrus' hands. He actually instructs his slave to perform the role of *architectus*, and when challenged as to whether *laudas qui eros fallunt* ('you approve of people cheating their masters', 537), he affirms that he does indeed, *in loco*. While trying to manipulate and so control the play as a comedy in which his neighbour is the (deliberate) dupe, he actually offers on a plate to Syrus the material for a rather different plot – a plot in which Chremes himself is the victim. In this, he is very like the Simo of *Andria*.

His one moment of almost-successful plot-control is doomed to failure – because it is not comic. After the typical Terentian bolt from the blue (which really we should have expected) has caused the girl Antiphila to be recognised as Chremes' daughter, and Syrus' trick on his master has allowed the prostitute-couple to consummate their part of the story, Chremes tries to take control by disinheriting his son: he proposes to give everything he owns to his daughter as dowry. This is the moment for Syrus to beat his Andrian rival Davos in the plotting stakes. Both *architecti* are thrown off-course at the crisis of the play, but it is Syrus, rather than the more colourful Davos, who manages to recover enough to play another trick. His trick is the deceptive but helpful suggestion that Clitipho (the victim of Chremes' attempts to force the play away from comic resolution) should confront his parents with the claim that he cannot truly be their son. Clitipho thus answers his father's anti-comic move with a tragic pose, alluding to the fatal interview between Oedipus and his adoptive parents in Corinth. Chremes cannot do other than answer with down-to-earth comic abuse:

> si scire uis, ego dicam: gerro iners fraus helluo
> ganeo's damnosu': crede, et nostrum te esse credito.
> (*HT* 1033–4)

If you want to know, I'll tell you. You're a buffoon, a useless, deceitful, squandering, debauched waster. Believe that, and believe that you're our son.

This charming comment follows on from another piece of comic stereotyping, when Chremes makes the same point to his anxious wife just before Clitipho comes out:

So. quod filia est inuenta? Ch. non: sed, quo mage credundum siet,
 id quod consimilest moribus
conuinces facile ex te natum; nam tui similest probe;
nam illi nil uitist relictum quin siet itidem tibi;
tum praeterea talem nisi tu nulla pareret filium.

(*HT* 1018–22)

So. Because our daughter has been found? Ch. No, rather, something on account of which this would be more credible: that which is very similar to you in character you'll easily prove was born from you. For he's the spitting image of you. There is no vice in him which isn't the same in you; moreover no-one except you could have borne such a son.

In the end, all the other characters work on Chremes to relent, and the play ends as it should, with Syrus also forgiven. I would suggest that the reason why this play is not generally associated with the tradition of the Plautine manipulative-slave plot is that Terence has developed the art of multiples.[133] This is a typical tricksy deceit plot, but the *architectus* is not allowed to get away with hogging the limelight: instead, along with the complexities of plotting we have a character play, a comedy of manners, in which a great deal of interest (from moderns, perhaps too much interest) is focused on the interactions of the two old men, and in particular the character of Chremes the busybody, whose famous line *homo sum: humani nil a me alienum puto* ('I am a man: I consider no human affair not my business', 77) has been so often quoted out of context.[134]

Syrus' response to Chremes' behaviour in *Heauton timorumenos* injects a sudden shock of tragedy into the comic plot. I will argue in chapter 4 that there is a similar but more significant tragic injection into the *Eunuchus*, but for now I indicate some further developments in Terence's manipulation of the manipulative plot. As in *Andria*, several characters are allowed to contribute to the plotting of *Eunuchus* and to make things happen (most notably Parmeno, Chaerea, Thais and Pythias), but the slave-*architectus* sees his position in the plot undermined as never before. As regards his relationship with the audience, his knowing, cynical commentary on the play, and his superior attitude to other stock characters, Parmeno appears to be written in the tradition of Pseudolus and to act as the eyes and mouth of the poet – until Terence kicks him beneath the belt.

The play opens in classic mode (like *Pseudolus*) with the lover Phaedria being supported and teasingly abused by his knowing slave Parmeno. The slave dominates the scene, offering us an ironic and amusing commentary

[133] It is rightly seen in these terms by Brown (2006: 96–7). [134] See Henderson (2004).

on his master's amatory state, in language which appears at first to be moralistic and didactic. His considered judgement, teasing over, is that Phaedria should get what he can at as little cost as possible.[135] Parmeno is thus established as *architectus* in his control of the audience's view of the play. The first bit of plotting, however, is not his. His rival in this play's plot is not a *senex* but the courtesan Thais, whose actions probably represent a new development in ancient comedy, a courtesan devising a plot on her own initiative and for her own purposes, in order to aid another but incidentally also to improve her own position (as is often the case with the clever slave). Prostitutes before her have made up plots in order to manipulate their lovers into paying, although extant comedy offers rather less of this than is conventionally supposed, with Plautus' *Truculentus* being almost the only developed example; *Bacchides* involves a little plotting by the sisters, but only the minor deceit in which Pistoclerus pretends to be the lover of one sister in order to scare off the rival soldier (thus setting up the misunderstanding with Mnesilochus), whereas the plotting-role is clearly the domain of the slave Chrysalus; others have played along with the roles developed for them by slave-*architecti*, like Acroteleutium in *Miles gloriosus*. The nearest parallel to Thais' behaviour is probably that of her prototype as *meretrix bona*, Habrotonon in Menander's *Epitrepontes*; Habrotonon's closer cousin, Bacchis in *Hecyra*, shows no sign of a propensity to plot. A difference between Habrotonon and Thais is that the Greek prostitute sets up some play-acting for herself but not for anyone else, has no personal interest in what is happening, and is not playing one person off against another nor collaborating with the playwright. In Terence's play, the courtesan creates a plot which looks at first like a deceitful trick to play one man off against another, but it turns out to be the play's plot. Thais claims that she had only shut out Phaedria last night because she is trying to work on his rival, the soldier Thraso, in order to secure the gift of a slave-girl who, Thais says, is probably an Athenian citizen. The girl had been given to Thais' mother as a young child, and was brought up as her own, on Rhodes. After Thais left Rhodes for Athens with her lover of the moment, her mother died, and the girl was sold – by chance, to Thraso, who was now Thais' lover (her Rhodian escort having died). Thraso is about to give her the girl as a servant, but he is hesitating because he sees that Thais is also involved with Phaedria. Thais wants Phaedria to let Thraso have free access to her for a few days, while she ensures the safety of the girl. Alongside all this, Thais has hunted

[135] It is worth noting that both the didactic and the cynical responses are very 'Roman'.

out someone whom she believes to be the brother of the girl, with whom she hopes to achieve a reconciliation during this period. Her actions are realistically motivated, both by the desire to do good to a girl who is like a sister to her, and in the hope of gaining the protection of a citizen in this hostile environment of 'Athens'.

It transpires later that Thais is sharing Terence's plot – she is telling the 'truth': but at the point where she tells this story it is Parmeno who appears to share the playwright's viewpoint. Certainly he shares (and manipulates) the audience's viewpoint. While Thais relates the story to Phaedria (and so to the audience), Parmeno acts as an ironic commentator, using the metaphor of a leaky vessel: if what Thais says seems to Parmeno to be true, he keeps it inside (secret), but if it does not, he will let it flow out. The game is not only with truth but also with confidentiality: an *architectus* on stage says 'I'll keep it secret' only with a big implied wink at the audience. Not surprisingly, he proposes to let flow all over the place all that nonsense about a girl being sold into slavery and turning out to be a citizen – that is a typical New Comic plot, a typical ruse to deceive the innocent. Even Phaedria sees through it.

In the first part of the play, Parmeno is controlling our view of the world, but he is not doing very much for the plot. The same thing happens when the parasite Gnatho appears, boasting of his success as a parasite, watched by the detached, ironic Parmeno, who mediates the scene for the audience. Gnatho has come to deliver the girl, just as Parmeno will deliver the eunuch. It is not much of a contest, between the super-beautiful girl and the decrepit old eunuch, until Terence throws Parmeno a lifeline which lets him do something with the plot. In comes Phaedria's younger brother Chaerea, driven by an outrageously unrealistic desire to get the girl, whom he has happened to see in the street as she was being taken to Thais' house. Here is some decent material for Parmeno's talents. He sets in motion the crux of the plot – to dress Chaerea up as the eunuch, and offer him to Thais in that guise, an idea which Chaerea enthusiastically embraces.[136] But now Parmeno does something no *architectus* has ever done before: he tries to retract. He says he was only joking, and it would be terribly dangerous, and really not a good idea, but he has not reckoned with the dynamism and daring of his pupil. Perhaps Terence has transferred those qualities from the *architectus* to the last person we would normally associate with them, the *adulescens*. Chaerea himself is not so much a plotter as an opportunist – but that feature itself aligns him clearly with the *architectus* tradition.

[136] The scene is discussed in more detail in ch. 4, pp. 221–6.

Parmeno is a clever slave, but Terence will not let him dominate that role.[137]

The final twist in Terence's treatment of Parmeno comes after Thais has arranged for the recognition of Pamphila by her brother, has discovered and forgiven the rape, and has set in motion the comic happy ending in marriage. Thais' slave Pythias, an older slave-woman (therefore near the bottom of the comic hierarchy of characters), decides to pay Parmeno back for the trouble he has caused. She tricks him into believing that Chaerea is about to be castrated, in retribution for the rape.[138] The trickster is tricked, and, worse than that, he is driven to go and confess (quite unnecessarily) to the father, so that he, anti-comic authority figure that he is (though in this particular instance rather a friendly one), can sort out the comic mess. This is Terence's triumph over the *architectus* – not failure, not punishment, but a trick of the plot. Perhaps we might even see this as Terence's triumph over Plautus. Parmeno has been the prime candidate for identification with the playwright: he has been the mediator of other scenes, the audience's friend, the contriver of the crucial element of the plot. He has suffered a setback just as Davos and Syrus did, but although he recovers enough to join in the general celebrations at the end, it is without any active role in the solution, and crucially with an explicit inversion of the normal architectonic triumph over the *senex*.

Terence's triumph is complete in *Hecyra*, where he keeps a vice-like grip on the plot and all knowledge about it. Many characters attempt to influence the action, but fail horrendously because they are stumbling around in the dark. The eponymous mother-in-law, Sostrata, tries first to make friends with her estranged daughter-in-law (who is hiding a pregnancy which is the result of rape), then plans to give the young couple space 'to live together without interference from her', by going off to live in the country. Pamphilus, the husband and unknown rapist, makes feeble attempts to deceive others about his true intentions, posing as intending to leave his wife out of duty to his mother. The victim's own mother also makes an attempt (opportunistic) at deceit, when she picks up and runs with her husband's accusation that the reason she is trying to break up her daughter's marriage is that she is angry over the young man's continued

[137] In a sense, Parmeno here has an ancestor in Palinurus in Pl. *Cur.*, who also acts as an ironic commentator, directing the viewpoint of the audience, but leaves the role of plotter to Curculio the parasite. The difference for Terence is that Parmeno comes much closer to the *architectus* role (the rape is, after all, his invention, and it is one involving disguise), so that Terence can abuse him in it. Palinurus just watches from the sidelines.

[138] See Barsby (1999a: 262) for the legal position here.

affair with a prostitute. None of these has the least direct effect on the plot, or rather, if there is any effect (indirect causation towards the entry of Bacchis), it is wholly unintentional. It is, quite accidentally, the old men whom Terence allows to nudge the play towards resolution, when they ask the courtesan Bacchis to go in and speak to Myrrhine about her relationship with Pamphilus. The recognition of the stolen ring which solves the problem is the most outrageous of Terentian plotting bolts. There is a refusal in this play to allow any other kind of deceit, any clever trick, any change of heart. This aspect of Terence's determination to control the plot is manifested in his manipulation of the slave-helper Parmeno (sharing a name with the *architectus* of *Eunuchus*, who was himself worsted at the end): he ought to be a *seruus callidus* but he is never allowed to play that role. In the opening scenes, we are deceived into thinking that Parmeno is a typical clever slave, because it is he who tells us the plot and instructs us on how to interpret the characters. It is only he who knows about his master's sexual irregularity in the early part of his marriage. But in fact, although Parmeno knows too much for Pamphilus' comfort, he does not know as much as he pretends to, and neither Pamphilus nor Terence will allow him any significant role in the play. He is sent off on various wild-goose chases, simply to get him out of the way. The one useful action he performs is to take the message to Pamphilus that Myrrhine has recognised Bacchis' ring. As Parmeno says at the ending: *equidem plus hodie boni / feci inprudens quam sciens ante hunc diem umquam* ('indeed I've done more good today without realising it than I've ever done previously with full knowledge', 879–80).[139] These, apart from the final *plaudite*, are the last words of the play. They may, I suggest, stand as Terence's comment on the way he has used and abused the comic *architectus*.

VERI SIMILE

> ἴδμεν ψεύδεα πολλὰ λέγειν ἐτύμοισιν ὁμοῖα
>
> (Hesiod, *Theogony* 27)
>
> We know how to make many lies like truth.

The heavy plotting and metatheatricality which I have been considering, and which I have suggested can be found in both these comic corpora, may be seen as aspects of farce. Farce is artificial, anti-realist, anti-rationalist, self-conscious about its literariness and its stereotypes, and about the theatre

[139] This ending is discussed also in ch. 5, pp. 271–3.

(or other medium), inclined to debunk itself as well as everything else, and silly, often with slightly dark undertones. The farcical mode could be figured as in some sense opposed to realism, especially if by 'realism' we mean something closer to 'reality' or 'naturalism'.[140] Much of the history of reading (and not reading) Terence would associate him more closely with a naturalistic than with a farcical mode, driven perhaps partially by the desire to differentiate Terence from Plautus, and also by the ghost of Menander, famed (perhaps saddled with the fame) as the consummate realist. It may be more helpful for reading Terence to distance oneself from the realist trap. The interest Terence has in realism is not a straightforward reflection of reality but a theatrical signification of it, part of which involves gaps and fudging around the interplays of different levels of fictionality and representation.[141]

One end of theatrical realism, especially when it is self-consciously highlighted, is itself an aspect of farce, for in some cases it is the artificiality of theatre which bridges the gap between the naturalistic and the farcical modes. I stressed above how, particularly in *Andria*, Terence has been interested in questions of realism, credibility and theatricality. For all their pose of theatrical sophistication, however, the characters who are looking for a pedestrian biosynthetic realism usually come unstuck. Both Davos and Simo scoff at the unrealistic nature of their opponents' plots – but they are wrong. Theatrical mimesis is much more artful than a simple one-to-one correspondence between art and life, fiction and truth. This is the case even when, as in conventional modern realism, it is the mimetic world rather than the process of mimesis which is foregrounded, but in the case of much ancient literature, where the process of mimesis is far less occluded, our awareness of the representative gap makes aesthetic value out of a heightened sense of creative artificiality.

We may be tempted to counter modern readers who respond as Simo does, by claiming that Roman comedians, especially Plautus, were 'not aiming to be realistic'. The primary value, rather, is theatricality. If by 'realistic' we imply a stress on the *imitation* of reality rather than on

140 Such a configuration of the farcical and naturalistic 'modes' is fundamental to McCarthy's (2000) book, for example.

141 Terence would have had sympathy with the modern playwrights and producers who discovered that the most effective theatrical realism came not from using real drawing-room furniture, apples and books, but theatrical props. Audiences read theatrical signifiers of realism, not real things. But apparently the 'inventor' of fourth-wall naturalism, André Antoine, did in fact use real things instead of theatrical plots, and did various other things to move to a naturalist theatre. The director Peter Hall would say that theatre doesn't work like that.

the imitation of *reality*, then the games of realism become central to the concerns of Roman comedy.

As usual, it is Pseudolus who shows us this comic value most clearly, in his improvisation speech:

> sed quasi poeta, tabulas quom cepit sibi,
> quaerit quod nusquam gentiumst, reperit tamen,
> facit illud ueri simile quod mendacium est,
> nunc ego poeta fiam: uiginti minas,
> quae nunc nusquam sunt gentium, inueniam tamen.
> (*Ps.* 401–5)

But just like a poet, when he picks up his writing tablets, seeks something which exists nowhere in the world – and finds it, and makes what is false seem like truth, so now I shall become a poet: those twenty *minae*, which exist nowhere in the world, I shall nevertheless invent.

Here we can see Pseudolus playing around with invention and creative fiction. He shows how to make literary realism (often what *ueri simile* means) out of something which the epistemological purists would call a lie. His aim is to make the *minae* 'real', in that they really will spring the girl from the pimp, and to make the plot 'real', in that it really will entertain us with its theatrical posturing. He also aims to make both *minae* and plot 'realistic', in that although convincing and satisfying they are also fictional, untrue and – at the time of speaking – non-existent.[142] Two particular kinds of 'realism' which interest the Roman comedians are the production of 'lies like truth' and the provision of a convincing performance (which is what we often mean with the rather loose term 'realistic').

The cleverest, most effective sort of lie is one which sits very close to the truth. The comment holds also metaphorically for theatrical representation: art becomes more mimetic (obviously) as it gets closer to reality, but it is mimetic art only *as long as it remains a 'lie'*. When we, as audience, know that the trickster's lies are close to truth, we get a particular frisson from his close brush with honesty, from his clever manipulation of reality (his ability to make a lie out of material which is largely in fact true is as clever and manipulative as his ability to conjure realistic 'truth' out of lies) and from our own sense of our superior knowledge of how things 'really are'. These feelings can be lumped together under the loose heading of 'irony':

[142] The plot is of course only *pretending* to be non-existent at this point, because at another level the drama is not improvised but scripted – but that's another matter. From Plautus' point of view, in any case, the plot is still improvisational – at the time of writing.

statements which are true but misleading, true but distorted, sort-of true, nearly true – all these categories of utterance have a special status in artistic performance.[143]

We have seen how the *architecti* of (Plautus') *Epidicus* and (Terence's) *Andria* weave multifaceted webs of deceit and fictional truth in order to stage their performance. They offer extreme cases of a common feature of artistic tricks, which is that they are lifelike. Likewise, Syrus in Terence's *Heauton timorumenos* takes great pleasure in the fact that he can deceive by means of the 'truth'. His trick starts with the old Corinthian woman, whose status in the reality of the play extends at first only to a report that she was initially thought to be, but on her death discovered not to be, the mother of Antiphila, beloved of Clinia. Clinia is staying with his friend (and Syrus' master *minor*) Clitipho, the son of Chremes. The prostitute-girlfriend of Clitipho has been brought to the house, disguised (as far as Chremes is concerned) as the girlfriend of Clinia, and has brought with her (at the instigation of Syrus) the real beloved of Clinia, who has been introduced to Clitipho's mother (who will recognise her as her own long-lost daughter . . .). Clinia's father Menedemus, regretting his earlier *pater durus* image, wants to pay through the nose for his son's amorous adventures, but Chremes persuades him only to do so by allowing himself to be tricked. Chremes then tells Syrus to help Clinia's own slave trick his master (in fact Syrus simply takes over). Next, Syrus rehearses his plan with Chremes: he tells him, as if 'true', that once upon a time there was an old Corinthian woman, who was in debt to the prostitute Bacchis, and pledged her daughter ('the girl who has just now been taken in to your wife', 604) as surety. The woman died, and Bacchis is now badgering Clinia (who, in Syrus' story, is Bacchis' lover, but is really the lover of the girl, Antiphila) to pay the debt. As far as Chremes is concerned, that is the true part (we know from the first scene between Antiphila and Bacchis that they have no prior connection). Syrus then proposes to get the money out of Menedemus (on his master's orders), by telling him that the girl is a rich Carian captive, and that if he redeems her he will easily get his money back through ransom. This might sound plausible as a deceit plot: it will be dashed in the next scene by the discovery that Antiphila is in fact the daughter of Chremes (which is itself a 'typical comic plot'), but what matters now is that Syrus

[143] It goes without saying that this kind of irony has huge significance in tragedy. The pleasure we get from comic irony, when characters say something which is true but misleading, and almost seems to challenge the dupe to understand the truth, cannot be very far from the pleasure we get from watching Aeschylus' Clytemnestra wipe the floor with Agamemnon on his return.

has sown the seed of the debt-story in Chremes' mind, as if it were true. It is that lifelike lie which will eventually get the money out of Chremes himself, since Antiphila is his daughter.

In the meantime, however, Syrus' plan (whatever status it 'really' had) is thrown off-course by the Recognition. He has a nice improvisorial debate with himself about what to do (674–8a), at which point he cryptically says that he will pull in that runaway money, though he does not immediately tell us how. It transpires that the plan will be to deceive both old men – by telling the truth (711). And so he does. He tells Chremes that Clinia has told his father that Bacchis is the girlfriend of Clitipho, and that they have moved her to Menedemus' house in order to avoid Chremes' suspicion. Moreover, Syrus claims, Clinia is pretending that he wants to marry Chremes' newly found daughter (771), so that Menedemus will pay for wedding clothes, presents, etc., all of which, he says, will go to Bacchis. So: Syrus tells Chremes that Bacchis is the beloved of Clitipho and Antiphila is the beloved of Clinia, both of which are true, but in such a way as to make Chremes disbelieve both claims. While Chremes is admiring his slave's brilliance, Syrus pops in the point about the Corinthian woman and her debt, which now of course ought to be paid by Chremes, since it is for his daughter. Not that he has to, of course, but a man in his position . . . Chremes falls for it, and even agrees that it would be best for his son Clitipho to hand over the money. That, Syrus claims, would be more *ueri simile* (802): more realistic. It certainly would, since in fact Clitipho will thus be able to put into Bacchis' hands the money which really will grant him entry to the back room with her. Chremes is completely taken in.

A little later, Chremes' susceptibility to theatrical realism comes back to haunt him. Menedemus reports to Chremes how Clinia behaved when told that he could marry Antiphila. Instead of the claims for additional expenses predicted by the deceived Chremes, Clinia expressed only a wish that the marriage should be this very day. Chremes laughs at the *Syri / calliditates* (886–7), so clever that he can control a man's facial expression. He thinks Clinia's behaviour is Syrus' realistic trick on Menedemus. For Menedemus, however, the penny has dropped. He plays along with the idea that this is all Syrus' clever realism, saying it goes so far as to have Clitipho perform as the lover of Bacchis, all 'in order to deceive me' (897–9). *Quid agit?* (900), asks Chremes. Well, not to mention kissing and embracing – he sent Clitipho and Bacchis off into a backroom where a bed has been made up . . . Hang on a minute, says Chremes, this isn't realistic pretence – this is reality (915–19)!

Although the crisis brought about by Chremes' realisation of the truth threatens to upset the comic order of things (Chremes will disinherit his son by giving his daughter everything as her dowry – instead of giving her an appropriate dowry to keep society stable), Syrus is up to the moment. In response to Clitipho's plea for a new plot (*neque me consilio quicquam adiuuas?*, 982), Syrus offers him the tragic trick which I mentioned above. Clitipho should question whether he is really the son of people who are ready to cast him off now that their daughter has been found. That is *ueri simile*, Clitipho agrees (990) – and does as he was told, thus provoking the final resolution. In his first acting scene, Clitipho had let the side down by being unable to resist fondling Bacchis, even though she was meant to be the mistress of his friend. This time, therefore, Syrus tricks him as well, so that he will really think that it is realistic that he should doubt his parentage – and so give a more realistic performance. As Syrus says:

> . . . nam quam maxume huic uisa haec suspicio
> erit uera, quamque adulescens maxume quam in minima spe situs [997a][144]
> erit, tam facillume patri' pacem in leges conficiet suas.
>
> (*HT* 997–8)

. . . for the more this suspicion seems true to him, and the more the young man is placed in the least possible hope, the more easily he'll make peace with his father on his own terms.

As Davos did with Mysis (*Andria*), so Syrus exploits the ultimate realism that comes from deception.

A similar pattern of 'lies like truth' drives part of the action in Plautus' *Poenulus*, a deceit play which seems almost Terentian in its tricking of the trickster by the playwright. In this case, the *architectus* Milphio (who, like the Terentian clever slaves, is not always in control of the *role*, not to mention the plot) plans a disguise trick which will involve the newly arrived Carthaginian Hanno in pretending that he has come looking for his long-lost daughters (*festiuom facinus uenit mihi in mentem modo*, 'a merry crime has just come into my mind', *Poen.* 1086). In fact, Hanno really is there to look for his long-lost daughters. Having got Hanno to agree to the principle of playing a trick on the pimp, Milphio starts telling him the plot:

[144] Lindsay in the OCT prints as above, commenting that *duos uersus in unum a librariis fusos sic fere refingendos putamus*. Barsby in his 2001 Loeb edition does not include 997a. Without the notion that the genuine suspicion causes a more realistic performance, neither version, with 997a or without, makes particularly good sense.

nunc hoc consilium capio et hanc fabricam paro,
ut te adlegemus, filias dicas tuas
surruptasque esse paruolas Carthagine,
manu liberali caussa | ambas adseras
quasi filiae tuae sint ambae. intellegis?
(*Poen.* 1099–103)

Now, let me tell you the plot and fashion the fiction. Here's your commission: you say that they are your daughters and that they were stolen when they were little from Carthage, and you demand that they should both be free, as if they were both your daughters. You understand?

Hanno replies *intellego hercle* ('I certainly understand') – for his daughters were stolen in childhood with their nurse. He is actually telling the truth, but Milphio thinks it is just great acting – *lepide hercle adsimulas* ('you pretend beautifully', 1106). He even celebrates Hanno's ability to cry to order (Hanno is in fact really crying for his really lost daughters), and proclaims that *me quoque dolis iam superat architectonem* ('he's even outdoing me, the master craftsman, in tricks', 1110). A few lines later, the recognition scene will show that Milphio's plot was so realistic that it actually turned out to be real. 'Reality' is not normally what is required for drama, where only the 'realistic' will do. But in this case, by happy chance and authorial fiat, the truth will do just as well. From the audience's point of view, it matters little whether this is fiction within fiction or just fiction. Both are 'lies like truth' that keep us entertained, precisely because they are not real.

CHAPTER 4

Repeat performance

A situation is invariably comic when it belongs simultaneously to two altogether independent series of events and is capable of being interpreted in two entirely different meanings at the same time.

(Bergson 1913: 96)

We're in the stickiest situation since Sticky the Stick Insect got stuck on a sticky bun.

(Blackadder Goes Forth: 'Major Star' (BBC))

Ps. io!
io te, te, turanne, te, te ego, qui imperitas Pseudolo,
quaero quoi ter trina triplicia, tribu' modis tria gaudia,
artibus tribu' tris demeritas dem laetitias, de tribus
fraude partas per malitiam, per dolum et fallacias; [705a]
in libello hoc opsignato ad te attuli pauxillulo.

(Plautus, *Pseudolus* 702–6)

REPETITION COMEDY

Oh no, not that one again!
I always fall for that one!
You can say that again!

Comedians of many times and places know that their success depends on the artful manipulation of repetition. Comic genius delights to walk along the tightrope which separates by a fine margin the brilliant from the banal, the sensational from the simply silly. In the juggling-act of comic performance, the old can be as fresh as the new, the familiar as effective as the incongruous. It is sometimes said that a child's lack of understanding of humour means that she does not realise that it is not funny to retell a joke at which everyone laughed a moment ago when her sister told it – but how many of us have nonetheless laughed at such an event, and not just to humour the child? Indeed, the joke about the 'tired old joke' is itself a – tired old joke.

Aristophanes opened his amphibian masterpiece with it,[1] while Terence served up a soldier (with the added bonus for posterity of a quotation from Livius Andronicus) in *Eunuchus* in the same manner: performing to his parasite Gnatho about his past triumphs in wit, and unaware of the wider audience, the soldier Thraso repeats as if it were new the tired old proverb *lepu' tute's, pulpamentum quaeris* ('a hare yourself, you're hunting game', 426).[2] This, according to the ancient scholar Vopiscus, is a saying from one of Livius' comedies, probably in similar circumstances.[3] Thraso is quoting himself, Terence making fun out of him being made fun of (trying to make fun of someone else – since that was the context of his account). Gnatho replies with hysterical laughter and says: 'Wonderful! Is that yours? I thought it was an old one', thus insulting Thraso and drawing attention to the hackneyed quotation while pretending to applaud him.[4] Not just any old repetition will do, of course, since without the magic of comic genius the 'same old jokes' are just that, while catchphrases get boring, and alliteration becomes the verbal version of the Chinese water torture.[5] As Pseudolus says in one of the best lines in the whole of Plautus: *temperi ego faxo scies. / nolo bis iterari, sat sic longae fiunt fabulae* ('I'll let you know in good time. I don't want to repeat it twice: these plays are long enough as it is', *Ps.* 387–8). But so pervasive is the comedy of repetition that it is even active in denial: the BBC radio show 'Just a Minute' famously

1 Ar. *Ra.* 1–2: Εἴπω τι τῶν εἰωθότων, ὦ δέσποτα, / ἐφ' οἷς ἀεὶ γελῶσιν οἱ θεώμενοι; ('shall I tell one of the old jokes, master, the sort that always makes the spectators laugh?'), to which Dionysus replies by making-and-negating several jokes that Xanthias absolutely must not use because they are too hackneyed for words. Fraenkel (1960: 227) appreciates the comic value of trumpeting – and trumping – 'the stuff that gets the audience laughing'.

2 Translations are provided for substantial passages of Latin in this chapter with a powerful sense of their inadequacy in that they make no attempt to capture the genius of the original, the sound of which is crucial to the discussion here.

3 Although it is not certain that the speaker was a soldier in Livius' play, the manner of its quotation by Vopiscus makes it likely, since the context is a praetorian quoting Virgil. See Wright (1974: 24–7); Fraenkel (1960: 41); Brothers (2000: 180). For the proverbial nature of this joke, see Otto (1890: 190–1). See also Karakasis (2005: 199 and n. 134). Frangoulidis (1994a) argues that the stories Thraso tells here are not simple entertainment but programmatic precursors of events later in the play. That, however, does not stop them from being 'tired old jokes'. Something about tired old jokes, although not necessarily a joke about them, probably occurred in Menander's *Kolax*, from where Terence says the soldier and parasite are taken, as is suggested by the fragment preserved at Plu. *Mor.* 57a, easily available in Barsby (1999a: 306). For the connection between this fragment and our passage, see Brown (1992: 94).

4 See Damon (1997: 84–5).

5 In his psychoanalytical reading of comedy ancient and modern, Mauron (1964: 105) uses the example of a stuck record as something which is funny at first, but quickly palls.

(repeatedly) requires its participants to talk on a given subject for one minute 'without hesitation, repetition or deviation'. That, surely, is a joke on repetition.

This chapter attempts to capture a range of repeating devices used by Plautus and Terence, from sound-plays and pop-ups to stock characters and intertexts to restaging as a comic act. It seeks, moreover, to offer a holistic interpretation of them, by suggesting that they all partake in different ways in the same underlying phenomenon – the comedy of repetition. I do not claim that everything that repeats itself is straightforwardly funny, and funny in the same way: indeed, the 'artful manipulation of repetition' itself walks along a tightrope, since artistic failure in this area pays the ultimate price – boring the audience.[6] The fun is in dicing with the danger. Rather, I suggest that the very notion of repetition is so deeply ingrained in the comic project that it has some status as a generic marker, and is available as a device to be exploited for significatory purposes even in situations somewhat remote from the pure form of repetition.[7]

Nor does comedy have a monopoly on repetition: it is impossible to escape the brooding presence of a not particularly humorous 'strong father' to the discussion, in the form of Freud and his famous work on the role of repetition in the suppression and the processing of the unconscious and its desires. His little grandson's repeated game of back and forth (*fort-da*)

[6] As Quintilian says with regard to repetitive figures in oratory: *nam per se frigida et inanis adfectatio, cum in acris incidit sensus innatam <gratiam> uidetur habere, non arcessitam.* (Inst. 9.3.74). Ancient rhetorical theorists are keen to encourage an artistic use of repetitive features in all discourses, though they stress the need for moderation and attention to context and purpose – something which is exactly in keeping with the activity of repetition in comedy, although the context-sensitive appropriate degree of 'moderation' here might be limited. I am extremely grateful for many valuable conversations on these matters to Joanne McNamara. On poetic repetition and its varied effects, see esp. Guggenheimer (1972); Frédéric (1985); Wills (1996).

[7] The 'holistic theory' aspect to this chapter is something offered to the reader to take or leave. If the reader decides to leave it, then the idea of repetition can function merely as a convenient tag on which to hang some points about Roman comedy. There are some affinities to the effects considered in this chapter in the list of the causes of laughter in the *Tractatus Coislinianus*, both in diction and in substance (which includes deception). See Cooper (1922: esp. 224–6). The idea that repetition is indeed a holistic essential of comedy is by no means unknown among the modern theorists, see e.g. Charney (1987: xi): 'repetition in all its forms is crucial to the structure – and also the metaphysics – of comedy, since comedy revels in overemphasis and exaggeration'. While I would certainly not wish to offer 'repetition' as any sort of universal theory of comedy, I would suggest that repetition and my reading of repetition partake in the common drive towards (and resistance to) universalising in comic theory: see Purdie (1993) as both an example of and reflection on the universalising phenomenon. She makes an incidental contribution to the inherent comedy of doubling as part of a discussion of the ab-use of language: 'the most obvious improper linguistic excess is probably the simple doubling of a verbal signified: a pun' (38).

has gained iconic status in the history of psychoanalysis.[8] Modern critical thought, particularly in the traditions of Derrida and Lacan, Nietzsche and Heidegger, has (we might say) reified repetition to quasi-sacral status in literary as well as philosophical discourses.[9]

Still more important, and predating much of Freud's work, is the essay by the French philosopher Henri Bergson *Laughter: An Essay in the Meaning of the Comic* (1913), originally published in French in 1900 (and serially earlier in *La Revue de Paris*). Bergson ties repetition into his scheme of things, according to which something is comic insofar as it displays a certain inelasticity and a kind of automatism, as if it were a puppet or clockwork. He places together the comedy of twins, of people doing things in unison, and of the imitation of actions (including for example the miming of chopping wood, etc.):

> We instinctively feel that the usual devices of comedy, the periodical repetition of a word or a scene, the systematic inversion of the parts, the geometrical development of a farcical understanding, and many other stage contrivances, must derive their comic force from the same source, – the art of the playwright probably consisting in setting before us an obvious clockwork arrangement of human events, while carefully preserving an outward aspect of probability and thereby retaining something of the suppleness of life. (Bergson 1913: 36)

For Bergson, then, repetition is of the essence of comedy precisely because it is artificial.[10] The comedy of repetition is integral to the artificiality of comedy, which is itself a parodic version of the mimesis in all literature; it

[8] Rogers (1987) gives a clear account of Freudian repetition. Although I have, perhaps flippantly, described Freud as 'not particularly humorous', his role in the history of comic theory is very considerable, and his *Jokes and their Relation to the Unconscious* is actually quite funny. For a summary of the joke techniques which relate to the features at issue in this chapter, see Freud (1960: 41–2). For useful bibliography on psychoanalysis and humour, especially during the first half of the twentieth century when it was particularly active, see Mauron (1964: 155–64). Brief but useful is Orr (1996). Useful also is Mary Douglas' anthropological response to jokes and the theory of joking in the Freudian mode (1999: ch. 10, an essay first published in 1970). She argues that we do not have to give up the attempt to interpret the jokes of other cultures, hiding behind cultural relativism, but rather that we need to read humour according to the social context of its manifestation, something which, admittedly, we may not always be able to reconstruct. Her working definition of joke structure is worth quoting, even though, like all such definitions, it provokes attempts at refutation: 'any recognisable joke falls into this joke pattern which needs two elements, the juxtaposition of a control against that which is controlled, this juxtaposition being such that the latter triumphs' (150). See also Hokenson (2006: esp. ch. 2).

[9] My own first book (1994) was a widow's-mite witness to this discursive strategy. In keeping with the comic spirit of affirmation, see Bearn (2000), who compares the role of repetition in Derrida and Deleuze, arguing that the former is negative and the latter positive.

[10] This is not the place, nor am I qualified for it, to examine Bergsonian philosophy, but I would mention that Bergson's particular interest in machines and automation as central to his understanding of comedy, and as central metaphors for thinking about life and creativity, must be seen

also has to do with the unnecessariness of comedy – its delight in redundancy and irrelevance. Here is Charney (1987: 84): 'Literal repetition may involve certain tag lines or catch phrases that keep cropping up regardless of context. The line has a life of its own apart from the character.' On comic repetition as redundant, here is Frye (1957: 168): 'The principle of the humour is the principle that unincremental repetition, the literary imitation of ritual bondage, is funny . . . repetition overdone or not going anywhere belongs to comedy, for laughter is partly a reflex, and like other reflexes it can be conditioned by a simple repeated pattern.'

PITTER-PATTER PLAUTUS

Repetition pervades the Plautine experience at all levels. The most basic is that contained in the magnificent and irrelevant piling up of language which is the hallmark of his style. Critics, bounded though they are by the pedestrian requirements of their discourse, have been attracted to words like 'exuberance' in attempts to express Plautine verbal excess.[11] A whole host of iterative devices contribute to this exuberance: alliteration, anaphora, assonance, *geminatio*, homoeoteleuton, polyptoton,[12] and any other form of homophony and pointed heterophony one might care to mention.[13] Alliteration, as is well known, is a feature of archaic Roman style, being associated particularly with sacral, legal, official, magical and similar

against the background of the late nineteenth- and early twentieth-century technological revolution and the social response to it. I would stress other things comic as well, such as incongruity (which Bergson thinks only draws our attention to the comic, rather than in any way constituting it) and admiring laughter, and what Baudelaire (orig. 1855) calls absolute humour as opposed to reductive. Baudelaire's account is anthologised in Enck, Forter and Whitley (1960: 24–8). For an interesting response to Bergson on the comedy of machines, see Bermel (1990: 30–1), where he describes the earlier work as 'an annunciation of the film farce that would be unleashed a decade or so later, in which machines behaved humanly and took over the operative parts in incident after incident'. See also Douglas (1999: 148), where Bergson's theory is described as a 'general protest against the threatened mechanisation of humanity'. Useful also for the particular connection of automatism with the comedy of twins (although also showing its limitations) is Ferroni (1981b), who suggests that the twins of comedy are paradigmatic of the essence of comic theatre. He refers this in particular to the role of twins in offering us both distance and identification at the same time; I would add that the twin plays out the nature of imitation, sameness and difference, which makes theatre happen.

11 On these matters, I am grateful to David Langslow for many illuminating conversations. See Traina (1977: 99–170) on Plautine phonic iteration, and for earlier bibliography on the subject, see esp. 100–1.

12 Hofmann and Szantyr (2002: 41–3, and n. 67): 'il poliptoto trimembre e plutimembre si trova spesso nel latino arcaico, per esempio in Pl. *Am.* 34 . . . *Cas.* 826 . . . Enn. *scen.* 298V'.

13 Interestingly, however, according to Traina (1977: 163–5), not often onomatopoeia, since Plautine language aims at magnificence rather than mimesis. This judgement would be in keeping with my sense of the comic value of purposelessness. On whether alliteration is about initial-sound homophony or is extended to any phonic iteration, see Traina (1977: 11, 75).

discourses.[14] It would be impossible to claim a comic function for alliteration per se, given its widespread uses through Latin literature and subliterary writing, but there can, I hope, be little doubt that, in the context of intensity of iterative features and of outrageous excess, it is simply funny.

According to Mahoney's study of alliteration in Saturnians and other early Latin verse (2001: 81), 'from the available evidence, we cannot correlate alliteration with either seriousness or levity', but it should be noted that the evidence consists of a very small sample. Moreover, Mahoney is concerned only with the presence of some alliteration, not with its intensity, and intensity is what marks out comic iteration as funny (and generically comic). De Meo (1983), in his account of work on technical Latin, notes that a lot of Saturnian epigraphic material shows this kind of alliteration, being dedicatory and sacral.[15] Very many alliterative examples in legal, magical, ritual and similar discourses come in groups of only two (to take the examples from De Meo 1983: 114: *fides fiducia, manu mancipio, palam publice, reddere restituere, uinctus uerberatus*, or his 145: *dabo dedicaboque, oro obsecro, do dico dedico* (cf. *ueni uidi uici*), *scio sentio*, etc.), as indeed do vast numbers of Plautine alliterative acts.[16] But the funniest and most effective examples are where the performance is taken to excess. Alliteration in excess does exist outside comedy, but to a much lesser extent. Hofmann and Szantyr (2002: 34) say that multiple alliteration is limited outside the archaic poets (excluding Terence, who makes little use of it).[17] They, like De Meo,

[14] De Meo (1983: 113–14, 144). On alliteration and other aspects of '*carmen*-style' in Ennius, see Erasmo (2004: 20–4). On the use of such devices in archaic prose, see von Albrecht (1989: ch. 1, esp. 4–7, 14–15). On the ritual aspects of alliteration etc., see Langslow (2005: 290–1). Wilkinson (1963: 25–31) treats alliteration and assonance as part of 'verbal music'. For his project in analysing golden Latin artistry, not surprisingly, the excesses of Plautine playfulness are by and large delicately ignored (mentioned on 27 and 28). Palmer (1954: 86–9) discusses Plautine alliteration as initially 'a feature of the most ancient latinity as we can see from proverbial phrases' (86), and as contributing to the 'elaborate stylisation' of Plautus' language. In the late nineteenth and early twentieth centuries, there was great interest in early Latin alliteration, which included efforts to find systematic patterns and to connect its effects with that of early Celtic alliteration. See Ebrard (1882); Baske (1884); Evans (1921); Marouzeau (1946: 47–8). The most systematic modern analysis of Plautine sound-play is that of Traina (1977): he identifies Plautine hapax usages (of various sorts), and then calculates the percentage of those that occur in iterative situations. The results are 35.3 per cent for Plautus (151) and 18.77 per cent for Terence (157). On alliteration, he limits his discussion to initial phonemes (128–9). For alliteration as belonging to the language of proverbs, religion, law and official pronouncements, see Hofmann and Szantyr (2002: 30–1); Courtney (1999: 3); McCarthy (2000: 140), who notes how close are the repetitious styles of serious ritual and farce. Habinek's case (2005) for Roman song as a unified cultural phenomenon is relevant here also.

[15] He goes on to say: 'nei poeti arcaici l'allitterazione diventa un artificio stilistico del quale si usa ad abusa' (145), which puts it in a nutshell.

[16] See Palmer (1954: 122–3) on archaic alliteration in pairs.

[17] Cf. Karakasis (2005).

quote the magnificent comic line of Naevius *libera lingua loquemur ludis Liberalibus* ('we shall speak with free tongue at the Liberalia', *com.* 113R). They are perhaps unusual among the linguists in overtly associating alliteration with comic effect in Plautus (30). It may be a sign of the possibility that excessive alliteration is inherently comic that critics have wondered whether the (in)famous alliterative line of Ennius might in fact be parody.[18] It is true that Ennius, across the range of genres in which he was active, does make extensive use of the kinds of wordplays and iterative devices that I am examining here, which would tell against their inherent, context-less, connection with comedy: the point about repetition in comedy is that it makes a joke of something that it repeats from the straight version, one time too many.[19] As an example of the fine line between tragic and comic use of such devices (in this case, the 'surfeit', which I describe in more detail below, pp. 172–5), compare Pl. *Am.* 1062: *strepitus, crepitus, sonitus, tonitrus*, with Pacuvius *trag.* 336: *strepitus fremitus clamor tonitruum.* Only one of these is over the top.

These devices, I suggest, pertain to the bread-and-butter of comedy: so much so, indeed, that it seems somehow invidious to pick out any instance for particular consideration.[20] Here is Mercury praising the night for being extra-long, so that Jupiter Optimus Maximus can enjoy his adultery – *optumo optume optumam operam das, datam pulchre locas* (*Am.* 278).

Not surprisingly, the arrivals of grand comic characters are particularly fertile with comic repetition. The first entrances of both Ballio and Pseudolus himself are marked in such a way in *Pseudolus*, as indeed is Pseudolus' speech throughout. Curculio's entry, at 280 in his play, is a magnificent parody of a running-slave scene which is full of such devices.[21]

[18] See Wilkinson (1963: 26). Erasmo (2004: 30) alludes to the possibility that *Ps.* 702, quoted at the head of this chapter, is a parody of Ennius' notorious line *o Tite, tute, Tati, tibi tanta, tyranne, tulisti* (*Ann.* 104 Skutsch). Such a case is in fact already well made by Sedgwick (1927: 88). Contra: Sheets (1983: 19), coincidental connection; Skutsch (1985: 254–5), who plays down the oddity of Ennius' tongue twister, and rightly points to the chronological difficulty that the play predates the *Annals* by at least ten years. The latter point would not stop the Ennian line being a self-parody, or a self-allusion to some lost line which Pseudolus parodies, a suggestion regarded as possible also by Zwierlein (1991b: 148 n. 359). *Ps.* 702 escapes Zwierlein's knife, although 705 and 705a are excised in order to slim down the triplication.

[19] Boyle (2006) argues for considerable generic crossover and mixture in early Roman theatre; see esp. 62–6 for wordplay and sound play in Ennius. Various iterative devices are indeed prevalent in Ennius' tragedies; see e.g. the discussion of *figura etymologica* at Jocelyn (1967: 228, 339).

[20] Palmer (1954: 87) comments that almost any page of Plautus will produce a good example.

[21] See Duncan (2006: 113–14); Petrone (1983): 170–5 on Curculio's (rude) parodic scene, and 175–81 on comic parody of comic roles. Moore (1998a: 14, 128–9) suggests that Curculio could even be running through the audience at this point.

After a pun on *uentum* as accusative masculine past participle of *uenire* (to come) and as accusative of *uentus* (wind), Curculio pretends to be dying of hunger:

> perii, prospicio parum,
> gramarum habeo dentes plenos, lippiunt fauces fame,
> ita cibi uaciuitate uenio lassis lactibus.
>
> (*Cur.* 317–19)

I'm done for, I can hardly see, my teeth are rheum-y, my jaws are conjunctivised with hunger, such absence of sustenance I've come to with tired intestines.

It is not surprising that this piece of absurdity is obsessed with food. What is remarkable is that it is also obsessed with vision, in that not only does one-eyed Curculio pretend not to be able to see properly, but also his organs of eating are suffering from illnesses of the eyes.

At *Epid.* 331–6, simple humour of repetitive language is enhanced by the fact that the foolish speaker does not realise what he is doing. The interlocutor picks it up and twists it for all it's worth:

> CH. si hercle habeam pollicear lubens, uerum aliquid aliqua aliquo modo
> alicunde ab aliqui aliqua tibi spes est fore mecum fortunam.
> ST. uae tibi, muricide homo! CH. qui tibi lubet mihi male loqui?
> ST. quipp' tu mi aliquid aliquo modo alicunde ab aliquibus blatis
> quod nusquamst, neque ego id immitto in auris meas,
> nec mihi plus adiumenti ades quam ille qui numquam etiam natust.
>
> (*Epid.* 331–6)

CH. If I had any I'd certainly promise it gladly, but something somehow in some way from somewhere by someone I have some hope of better luck for you together with me. ST. Gerroff, you wimp! CH. Why are you being nasty to me? ST. Because you blab away in some way from somewhere by someone something that is nowhere. I won't let it into my ears. You're no more help to me than someone who was never born.

Calidorus has a similar tendency to allow language to carry him away. His opening scene with the eponymous Pseudolus has the slave calling the alliterative shots. Throughout the scene, there is a play on *miser*, which Pseudolus sets in motion and Calidorus copies. At 23, Pseudolus throws a bit of *l*-alliteration into his anthropomorphising joke (*quaerunt litterae hae sibi liberos*, 'these letters are trying to make babies'), into which Calidorus falls with the (possibly programmatic) polyptoton *ludis iam ludo tuo?* Pseudolus expresses his disregard for the communicative power of the letters without his interpretation, with the help of the anaphoric *nisi Sibulla legerit* (25), which causes Calidorus to go off into *l*-ish paroxysms:

qur inclementer dicis lepidis litteris
lepidis tabellis lepida conscriptis manu?
(*Ps.* 27–8)

Why do you speak so harshly to the lovely letters, written on lovely little tablets by a lovely hand?

It should not be thought, however, that these devices are associated only with the grand comic extravaganzas such as *Pseudolus*, *Curculio* or *Epidicus*. The following example comes from the better-behaved *Cistellaria*, although not surprisingly it is in the mouth of the slave Lampadio, who is getting exasperated at the failures of his interlocutors to understand the background to the plot:

prius hanc compressit quam uxorem duxit domum,
priu' grauida facta est priu'que peperit filiam;
eam postquam peperit, iussit paruam proici:
ego eam proieci. alia mulier sustulit.
ego inspectaui. erus hanc duxit postibi.
eam nunc puellam filiam eiius quaerimus.
quid nunc supina susum caelum conspicis?
(*Cist.* 616–22)

He seduced her before he took her home as his wife: before that she got pregnant, and before that she bore a daughter; after she bore her, she ordered her to be cast out when she was little. I cast her out. Another woman took her up. I watched. Later my master married her. Now we are looking for that girl who is her daughter. Why are you now leaning backwards and looking up into heaven?

A form of verbal repetition which suits comedy particularly well is polyptoton. Although certainly not unknown in other alliterative discourses, it is perhaps particularly effective in comedy, precisely because it is slightly silly, because it is often communicatively redundant. Take for example the exclamation of Alcesimarchus at *Cist.* 644: *o Salute mea salus salubrior* ('oh my salvation more saving than Salvation'); or Mnesilochus' bombastic self-apostrophe in the angry monologue when he thinks his friend has betrayed him (*Bac.* 385–404), at 399: *nunc, Mnesiloche, specimen specitur, nunc certamen cernitur* ('now, Mnesilochus, your species is being inspected, now the contest is contested'); or Ergasilus' nonsensical banter with Hegio at *Capt.* 150: *tibi ille unicust, mi etiam unico magis unicus* ('he's your only son, but to me he is more only than only').

Comic repetition can be of grammatical forms, where there is humour going beyond the near-inevitable assonance of Latin words in the same form.[22] Among the best examples is the string of impersonal passives in the meeting scene between Pseudolus and the two old men, Simo and Callipho, who will seek to stop (or to enjoy) his performance. Pseudolus has been eavesdropping on their conversation (a position of power),[23] and then judges the moment right to interact with them. *itur ad te, Pseudole*, he says ('going to you is being done', 453), addressing himself as the great Plautine *architecti* do.[24] He greets his master and their neighbour. Simo responds with a greeting containing a conventional passive: *salue. quid agitur?* ('Hello. What is being done?', 457), to which Pseudolus replies that *statur hic ad hunc modum* – 'standing around here is being done in this way'. With the third, and unconventional (although by no means of itself odd) passive, the sequence becomes a joke, spiced by the cheekiness of Pseudolus' refusal actually to give any but the blatantly obvious and logical (non-)answer. Simo picks it up in the next line, with a complaint that is very close to admiration: *statum uide hominis, Callipho, quam basilicum!* ('Look at the standing of the man, Callipho, how kingly!', 458).[25]

Well-behaved Latin uses only sparingly long strings of nouns (or other homogeneous grammatical constituents). When Plautus (over)does it, it's funny, and funny for the same reason as the repetition of sounds, words, images, etc. under consideration in this chapter. I call this feature the 'surfeit of nouns', although in fact the surfeit[26] may be of any form.[27]

[22] On rhyme in such cases, see Hofmann and Szantyr (2002: 36), and for the role of rhyme as an instance of homophony, again associated with sacral and archaic language, 36–9. Homophonic endings, whether or not they are precisely homoeoteleuton, make ancient and modern critics uncomfortable, but an artful comic whose purpose involves a calculated element of offence can get away with it. See Hofmann and Szantyr (2002: 40–1) on the Plautine preference for particular forms of words in order to create homoeoteleuton; see Traina (1977: 114), where he discusses Plautus' use of *celere* (in preference to his more common *celeriter*) in order to match *propere* at *Cur.* 283.

[23] See Franko (2004: 30–1), though not specifically about Pseudolus; Slater (2000: 133–6); Fraenkel (1960: 203).

[24] Cf. Jocelyn (1967: 166 n. 5), apropos *Poen.* 4, who says: 'cf. the way those personages of comedy who are given to paratragic pomposity sometimes issue greetings in the third person'.

[25] Simo will re-echo this line in his final showdown with the drunken trickster: *sed uide statum* (1288). Joking sequences which come from the same stable include the string of versions of *quidam* ('a certain man') at *Cist.* 735–40, where the 'certain' people are the speakers themselves; also the string of parts of *hic haec hoc* at *Cur.* 716–17, which sounds like a modern parody of a traditional grammar lesson.

[26] The reference, in case it is not obvious, is to Sellar and Yeatman's *1066 and All That*, where various people and places suffer from surfeits of various kinds.

[27] Karakasis (2005: 122–3) describes Plautus as 'very keen on accumulating long lists of synonyms or other parallel items'. The 'asyndeton bimembre', as Jocelyn describes the formulation *pugnant*

Collateral support for regarding the phenomenon as funny (if it is needed) comes from a rare occurrence in more conventional Latin literature. Ovid's Cyclops, Polyphemus, a ridiculous lover if ever there was one, suffers from a surfeit of comparatives in his attempts to woo Galatea at *Met.* 13.789–807. Despite (or enhanced by) the respectable allusion in 791, *splendidior uitro*, to Horace's decorous Bandusia ode (*Carm.* 3.13.1), the sequence is farcically funny. There are many examples of surfeits of language in the comic corpus, often enhanced by other features of repetition, usually associated with excitement, and often with food or sex.

I start with a couple of well-known examples. The newly converted Pistoclerus is accosted by his *paedagogus* Lydus (*Bac.* 109), who wants to know where the young man is going with all that nefarious party stuff; the reply is *huc* (standard hyperlogical non-reply to a figure of authority). The tutor falls into the usual trap: 'What d'you mean, *huc*?' So Pistoclerus goes from the laconic extreme to its expansive opposite:

> Amor, Voluptas, Venu', Venustas, Gaudium,
> Iocu', Ludus, Sermo, Suauisauiatio.
> (*Bac.* 115–16)

Love, Desire, Sex, Sexiness, Joy, Jokes, Play, Speech, Kissifications.

Despite his disapproval, Lydus cannot entirely resist the comic force of Pistoclerus' performance, and responds with an alliterative echo demanding to know what the young man has to do with *dis damnosissumis*, which Pistoclerus turns into a mock-theological discussion about the existence of the god *Suauisauiatio*.[28] Be that as it may, the pile-up of personifications is just funny.

Similar, and again in an erotic context, is the letter from the prostitute Phoenicium to her soppy lover Calidorus in *Pseudolus*. It might perhaps be noted that the letter is being read aloud to us by Pseudolus (and indeed

proeliant at Ennius *trag. fr.* VIII, is common in Ennius (Jocelyn 1967: 175). He says that 'comic asyndeta either consist of old-fashioned proverbs or formulae of the official language or occur in the company of other stylistic devices aping the style of tragedy'. This is no doubt correct, although the additional multiplicity of this type of repetition belongs especially to the excess of comedy. Further on archaic asyndeton, including bimembre, see Courtney (1999: 6).

[28] Barsby (1986: 107): '[t]he comic effect of the invented compound *Suauisauiatio* depends on the assonance of *suauis* ('sweet') and *sauium* ('kiss') and on the formality of the abstract-noun ending *-atio*'. See Feeney (1998: 88) for the divinity of abstracts taken to comic extremes. For deverbal nominalisation as a feature of technical language (which is being parodied here and in similar Plautine contexts), see Langslow (2005: 300). It perhaps goes without saying that the contingency of meaning contributes also to the absurd humour. On Plautus' playfully repetitious use of superlatives, see Traina (1977: 113–14).

Phoenicium never speaks), so one might suspect that he has played around a little with his script:[29]

> Ps. 'nunc nostri amores, mores, consuetudines,
> iocu', ludus, sermo, suauisauiatio,
> compressiones artae amantum corporum,
> teneris labellis molles morsiunculae,
> nostr[or]um orgiorum * -iunculae, [67a]
> papillarum horridularum oppressiunculae,
> harunc uoluptatum mi omnium atque ibidem tibi
> distractio, discidium, uastities uenit,
> nisi quae mihi in test aut tibist in me salus . . .
> (*Ps.* 64–71)

Ps. 'Now our loves, habits, customs, jokes, games, speech, kissifications, close pressing of loving bodies, soft little bites with tender lips [67a . . .], caressing of quivering breasts, of all these pleasures for you and me there comes ripping, tearing and destruction. My only hope is in you and yours in me . . .

The passage presents not just a line of nouns, but also a sparkling display of fantastic phonological features, and a magnificent redundancy which amuses and titillates the audience, excites Calidorus and plays into Pseudolus' hands. When he finishes reading, Calidorus calls on him to praise the pitiful expression of the piece: *est misere scriptum, Pseudole* (74), to which Pseudolus replies, picking up the dysgraphic joke from 23, with a mocking echo – *oh! miserrume.*

Later in the play, Charinus, the helpful friend (whose role is dramaturgically small),[30] himself has a go at a surfeit of language:

> murrinam, passum, defrutum, mellam, mel quoiuismodi;
> quin in corde instruere quondam coepit pantopolium.
> (*Ps.* 741–2)

Myrrh wine, raisin wine, grape-juice syrup, honey-water, honey of any kind, indeed, he once began to set up a general store in his heart.

It might not be the most extreme example, but it is quite neat, and is enhanced by alliteration, assonance, a kind of polyptoton (*mellam*, a honey-drink, and *mel*, honey), all summed up with a Greek word for a

[29] Pseudolus may not be the only culprit here. Something has clearly gone wrong with the text at 67a, where a line is transmitted in the Ambrosian palimpsest which is not in the Palatine family of manuscripts. See Willcock (1987: *ad loc.*), who also reports the suspicion that has been applied to line 65, as a possible interpolation from the *Bacchides* passage above. Zwierlien (1991: 80) cuts both 65 and the first 67.

[30] See Lefèvre (1997: 37–8).

general store.[31] But it is Pseudolus' reaction that interests me here. He acknowledges Charinus' efforts as an attempt at comedy: *eugepae! lepide, Charine, meo me ludo lamberas* ('Hurrah! Nicely done, Charinus, you lick[32] me at my own game', 743).[33] Not just any comedy, but Pseudolus' comedy.

There are many examples of this phenomenon in Plautus. Particularly worthy of note is the daft speech of Alcesimarchus (*adulescens*) when he first enters *Cist.* at 203. Amongst other farcical phonological features, he expresses his erotic torment by a series of first-person passive present verbs: *iactor, crucior, agitor*, etc. (206–9) and a string of third-person active (finished off with a deponent) presents for the action of Amor (*ludificat, / fugat, agit, appetit, raptat, retinet, / lactat, largitur*, 215–17), together with a host of other tongue-twisters and paradoxical parallels.[34]

> What I tell you three times is funny.
> Lewis Carroll, *The Hunting of the Snark*, misquoted

Once is just a word; twice is *geminatio*; three times gets a laugh: how far can you go? It's all in the timing.

The simplest piece of daft farcical repetition in Roman comedy is what I call the '*licet*-type', after its prime exemplar. At Pl. *Rud.* 1212, the *senex* Daemones starts giving a series of instructions to the slave Trachalio, who replies *licet* each time. Since this word means something like 'okay', it is not of itself funny. What makes it funny is the repetition, and Trachalio's control in contrast with the old man's eagerness and excitement. One might imagine this scene staged with Trachalio about to leave with each piece of Daemones' story, and then being pulled back by the fussy old man. The audience are mentally saying *licet* with Trachalio (might they actually shout it out?), while laughing at the old man who can't see the joke. (Not that this is in any sense an abusive scene or a trick on Daemones, nor is there any ill feeling, just fun.)

31 Gowers (1993: 65, 95). Karakasis (2005: 83) reviews the discussion of the use of Greek words in Roman comedy, where it is particularly associated with slaves and lower-class characters. See also Palmer (1954: 81–4).

32 The verb exists only here and in the attempted explanation of it by Festus, who suggests that it means *scindit ac laniat*. Some connection with *lambere* (to lick) seems likely, as is suggested also by *TLL* VII.2.897.79.

33 Proverbial: Otto (1890: 197).

34 On the comic absurdity of the word *cruciabilitatibus* in 205, see Kümmel (2004: 353–4), and on the improvisatory nature of parts of the play, see Lefèvre (2004) in the same volume. For further examples of grammatical surfeit, see *As.* 666–8, 693–5, *Cist.* 405, *Cur.* 285, 442, *Epid.* 230, *Ps.* 814–15, *St.* 226–31, 657, 690. The surfeit of ablative absolutes at *Per.* 753–4 is a particularly nice example, coming in the context of a parody of Ennius: see Scafoglio (2005: 636).

DA. eloquere ut haec res optigit de filia;
eum roga ut relinquat alias res et huc ueniat. TR. licet.
DA. dicito daturum meam illi filiam uxorem. TR. licet.
DA. et patrem eiius me nouisse et mihi esse cognatum. TR. licet.
DA. sed propera. TR. licet. DA. iam hic fac sit, cena ut curetur. TR. licet.
DA. omnian licet? TR. licet . . .

(*Rud.* 1211–16)

DA. Tell him how things have turned out about my daughter; ask him to drop everything else and come here. TR. Okay. DA. Tell him that I'm going to give him my daughter as his wife. TR. Okay. DA. And that I know his father and he's a relative of mine. TR. Okay. DA. But hurry. TR. Okay. DA. Make sure he's here straightaway, so the dinner can be sorted out. TR. Okay. DA. Is that all okay? TR. Okay . . .

This is Trachalio's cue to turn the interaction round, and he tricks Daemones into saying *licet* to a series of delights for Trachalio:

. . . sed scin quid est quod te uolo?
quod promisisti ut memineris, hodie ut liber sim. DA. licet.
TR. fac ut exores Plesidippum ut me <manu> emittat. DA. licet.
TR. et tua filia facito oret: facile exorabit. DA. licet.
TR. atque ut mi Ampelisca nubat, ubi ego sim liber. DA. licet.
TR. atque ut gratum mi beneficium factis experiar. DA. licet.
TR. omnian licet? DA. licet: tibi rusum refero gratiam.
sed propera ire in urbem actutum et recipe te huc rusum. TR. licet.
iam hic ero. tu interibi adorna ceterum quod opust. – DA. licet.

(*Rud.* 1216–24)

. . . But you know what I want you to do? Make sure you remember what you promised, that I should be free today. DA. Okay. TR. Make sure you beg Plesidippus to free me. DA. Okay. TR. And make sure your daughter begs him: she'll easily succeed. DA. Okay. TR. And that Ampelisca should marry me, once I am free. DA. Okay. TR. And that I get the appropriate reward for my efforts. DA. Okay. TR. Is that all okay? DA. Okay. A taste of your own medicine. But hurry off as fast as possible to the city and get yourself back here. TR. Okay. I'll be back in a mo. You meanwhile get everything ready as needed. DA. Okay.

Daemones realises he has been verbally tricked, and half-knowingly half-accidentally doubles up the joke by a punning exclamation: *Hercules istum infelicet cum sua licentia!* ('Hercules! May Hercules bring him bad luck with his cheek!', 1225). The joke in this line is enhanced by the fact that the word which repeats the letters of *licet* is not the cognate word, *licentia*, but the unconnected *infelicet.*[35] And then, to cap it all, in comes the unknowing

[35] The Romans certainly did make puns which involve a change of metrical quantity. See Ahl (1985: 35–40).

Gripus and asks: *Quam mox licet te compellare, Daemones?* ('How soon will it be okay to talk to you, Daemones?', 1227).[36]

The device clearly worked, because there is a repeat performance forty lines later, again involving Trachalio.[37] Plesidippus is asking Trachalio's advice as to how he should approach his beloved and her newly found parents (Daemones and his wife). Trachalio starts off with a series of one-word answers, which turns into a repetition of *censeo* ('I think so'), as Plesidippus plays through in words the scene of emotional meeting. When he gets too familiar, however, proposing to hug the father, Trachalio turns it round with a quick *non censeo* (1277). The joke is in the gap between the calm and controlled judgement of the detached and ironic slave, and the silly excitement of the *adulescens*, who does not notice the irony of repetition, only that it is stopping him hug his beloved. As ever, it is clever slaves and other controlling characters who use repetition knowingly, or push others into using it ignorantly.

Similar in style and situation to the classic *licet* in an exchange between Lesbonicus (*adulescens*) and Stasimus (*seruus*) at *Trin.* 583–90, where the operative phrase is *i modo*. The slave ends it with an exasperated repeat of his repetition: *i modo, i modo, i modo. / tandem impetraui abiret*[38] (590–1). We see the same basic idea, but with both sides involved in a verbal tug-of-war, in the altercation between Lysidamus and his neighbour Alcesimus over whether the latter will help the former in his attempts on the eponymous Casina, where the operative word is *quin* (*Cas.* 602–9). It will be noted that this device works best with 'filler' words rather than those with strong significatory force. The weak filler *immo* is used effectively, along with other iterative devices, at *Bac.* 6–12, as is *quippini* at *Poen.* 730–45, in the context of a passage of extraordinary intensity of iteration. The *aduocati* who have been brought in supposedly to help settle the legal dispute seem unable to speak without anaphora, alliteration, homoeoteleuton, or some such nonsense, which are no doubt intended to mock legal language as well as raise a laugh of themselves:[39]

36 This is an example of the 'comic echo' which will be discussed below, pp. 178–90.

37 The repetition of the joke is enhanced by metre, since both passages are in trochaic septenarii: Marshall (2006: 243).

38 As in *Rud.* 1225, here also the operative word (*i*) is repeated within the closural *abiret*, although of course in this case it is also the same root word.

39 See Rawson (1993: 216–18) for the *aduocati* as freedmen with a strong sense of their personal dignity and civic role. Duncan (2006: 100–1) reads them as frauds in the tradition of the *alazones* whom she sees as metaphors for the actor.

AG. quid nunc mi auctores estis? ADV. ut frugi sies.
AG. quid si animus esse non sinit? ADV. esto ut sinit.
AG. uidistis leno quom aurum accepit? ADV. uidimus.
AG. eum uos meum esse seruom scitis? ADV. sciuimus.
AG. rem aduorsus populi saepe leges? ADV. sciuimus.
AG. em istaec uolo ergo uos commeminisse omnia,
mox ad praetorem quom usus ueniet. ADV. meminimus.
AG. quid si recenti re aedis pultem? ADV. censeo.
AG. si pultem, non recludet? ADV. panem frangito.
(*Poen.* 721–9)

AG. Now what do you advise me? ADV. That you should be moderate. AG. What if my mind won't allow it? ADV. Be as it allows. AG. Did you see when the pimp received the money? ADV. We saw. AG. Did you know that he was my slave? ADV. We knew. AG. Something which is against the laws of the people? ADV. We knew. AG. So then, I want you to remember all these things when the opportunity arises in front of the praetor. ADV. We remember. AG. What if I were to knock at the door, while the matter's fresh? ADV. Good idea. AG. If I knock, and he doesn't open? ADV. Break the bread.[40]

COMIC ECHO

Roman comedy is artificial. There is one kind of repetition to be found here which is offensive to narrowly realist aesthetics of reading: I call it 'comic echo'. It occurs when one character's lines pick up something said by another character either aside or before the second or subsequent speaker came out, as in the case of Gripus' final *licet* above. Modern realist readers would explain this phenomenon as the result of the second speaker half overhearing the first. That is possible, but in addition I suggest that there is something more comic and artificial at work.[41] The play, after all, is 'being acted for the benefit of the audience', as Pseudolus points out (720) – and the audience's appreciation of the echo, and sense of superiority over the actors, is more important than realism. Indeed, these echoes are not a failure of realism but a refusal of realism.

[40] A 'silly pun', according to Skutsch (1937). *panis* and *puls* are both staple foods, while *pultem* could be accusative of *puls* as well as subjunctive of *pulto*. When the immediate whole-word repetition is of a more significant word, the humour depends less on multiple repetition than on other iterative devices, such as alliteration and puns. As case in point is the possibly programmatic *palla* which has been stolen by the Epidamnian Menaechmus, when he is confronted by his wife (*Men.* 609–10: MA. *pallam* – MEN. *pallam?* MA. *quidam pallam* – PE. *quid paues?* MEN. *nil equidem paueo.* PE. *nisi unum: palla pallorem incutit*).

[41] See Slater (2000: 133–6).

In *Mercator*, the lecherous old man narrates to us a dream he has had about a lovely young she-goat, an old she-goat, a kid and a monkey (225–71). We might be able to guess what it means: that the young she-goat is the girl who has inspired inappropriately youthful passion in the old man, the kid is his son, her lover, the old she-goat is his wife and the monkey is his old neighbour whom he asks to take in the girl so that his (the lecher's) wife does not know about his lechery (the dream is prophetic at this point, because we have not yet heard that part of the plot). The old man's monologue telling us the dream is followed by someone, who has not heard him, talking back into the house about castrating that he-goat if he gives any trouble (272–3). The joke, of course, is on the *senex*. The one character in the dream whose animal-mask had not been mentioned is obviously a he-goat, and he is certainly causing trouble.[42] Neat, fun, self-contained and irrelevant, the *Mercator* echo is the ur-case, but there are others which play with the same device.

For a simple example of a piece of non-overhearing which is appreciated by the audience, we might cite the meeting scene between Mnesilochus and Pistoclerus at *Bac.* 534:

> PI. estne hic meu' sodalis? MN. estne hic hostis quem aspicio meus?
> (*Bac.* 534)

PI. Is that my friend? MN. Is that my enemy I see there?

According to convention, neither hears the other at this point.[43]

In Ter. *Eu.* 431, the slave Parmeno, who is overhearing the soldier Thraso and the parasite Gnatho, says, aside, *at te di perdant!*, which Thraso's next speech (Gnatho says a few words in between) picks up with *perditus*. But of course Thraso does not know that Parmeno is there, does not know that he is in a play, and that he is being exposed. It is for the benefit of the audience that he picks up *perditus* and damns himself. In Plautus' *Stichus*, the girls are about to meet their father, both sides knowing there is likely to be some altercation, but pretending they don't and there won't. Panegyris says: *noui*

[42] Connors (2004) analyses monkey imagery in Greek and Roman literature, particularly Plautus, and shows how the monkey acts as a programmatic image for Plautine comedy, as a symbol of deceptive imitation, a 'distorted imitation of human form and action' (184). She draws out a whole range of puns and plays on words, esp. the interaction between *simia* and *similis*/*simulare*. See esp. 194–5, on *Mercator*.

[43] See Anderson (1993: 13). His aim in discussing this passage with its (unusually – known) Greek original is to show Plautus at work in the deconstruction of Menander. Although his purpose is different from mine here, his comment on the line seems to me just right: 'Plautus inserts a line that varies the usual stage direction of his plays – there's so-and-so – and has Mnesilochus deny (without having heard Pistoclerus' line) that Pistoclerus is his buddy: no, he's an enemy (line 534).'

ego nostros: exorabilest[44] ('I know our [people, i.e. my father]: it will be easy to persuade him', 74). The father Antipho enters and starts speaking before he meets the girls (as is conventional), wondering how to approach them, for *scio litis fore (ego meas noui optume)* ('Of course there'll be a squabble (I know my [daughters] well)', 79). The visual and performative joke here is an old one, much repeated: it involves two people or groups coming towards each other at the same time with the same purpose in mind, and perhaps the same prop in hand, only to crash into their doppelganger while the audience laugh from outside. The point here, additionally, is that both sides are also wrong: yes, they do know each other, they do know what the problem is, but in fact neither side behaves initially as the other expected.[45] The young man Stratippocles has a somewhat similar interaction (or rather, non-interaction) with his father in *Epidicus*. At 381, Stratippocles goes into the house celebrating (so he thinks) his and Epidicus' triumph:

uirtute atque auspicio Epidici <u>cum praeda</u> in castra redeo. –
(*Epid.* 381)

By the valour and the auspices of Epidicus I return to the camp with the spoils.

Enter Periphanes (father). He too celebrates (so he thinks) his victory, also contrived by Epidicus, and says:

sed meu' sodalis it <u>cum praeda</u> Apoecides.
(*Epid.* 394)

But my friend Apoecides is coming with the spoils.

They are both wrong.[46]

A rather more delicate scene of echoing occurs later in the same play, in the extended meeting scene between Periphanes and Philippa, the woman he raped years ago and whose daughter is the object of his, Epidicus', and (unknowingly) Stratippocles' plans. Philippa opens with a laughably typical piece of miserable misery:[47]

[44] On the spelling of *exorabilest*, see Petersmann (1973: *ad loc.*).

[45] Arnott (1972) is an insightful account of the contribution of verbal repetition to the meaning of this play. He argues that Plautus here (and only here) uses the Menandrian technique of linguistic characterisation by repetition of key words or stylistic devices which then become typecast and thus available for humorous repetition by other characters. On the scene between the daughters and the father, see 56–7, and on comic echoing, esp. 66.

[46] Similar is the balance of scenes featuring the two fathers in *Bacchides*. Philoxenus enters at 1076 with *quam magis in pectore meo foueo quas meu' filiu' turbas turbet*. This is echoed at 1091 by Nicobulus (after a magnificent surfeit of self-insults at 1088), with *magi' quam id reputo, tam magis uror quae meu' filiu' turbauit*. He, presumably, has not heard Philoxenus' previous speech.

[47] Slater (2000: 25) described the scene as 'an elaborate, choreographed sequence'.

Si quid est homini miseriarum quod miserescat, miser ex animost.
id ego experior, quoi multa in unum locum confluont quae
meum pectu' pulsant
simul. (*Epid.* 526–9)

If someone is in a state of misery which might be commiserated, he is miserable indeed. That's what I experience, with many things flowing into one place which beat on my heart at once.

After some more lines of the same, Periphanes notices her, but does not accost her, and the two spend several lines repeating but not addressing each other. The text unfortunately suffers from corruptions, but there are some clear echoes:

PE. certo east * *
quam in Epidauro
pauperculam memini comprimere.
PH. plane hicine est
qui mi in Epidauro uirgini primu' pudicitiam perpulit.
PE. quae meo compressu peperit filiam quam domi nunc habeo.
quid si adeam – PH. hau scio an congredias – PE. si haec east. PH. sin is est
homo,
sicut anni multi dubia dant. PE. longa dies meum incertat animum.
(*Epid.* 540–4)

PE. Surely that's her, whom I remember seducing as a poor little woman in Epidaurus. PH. That's clearly him, who first struck out my modesty when I was a virgin in Epidaurus. PE. From my embrace she bore the daughter whom I now have at home. What if I were to go up to her . . . PH. I don't know whether one should go up to him. PE. If it's her . . . PH. If it's the man himself, such doubts arise from many years. PE. The long time renders my mind uncertain.

And it goes on. Theoretically, they cannot hear each other until 548:

PE. salua sies. PH. salutem accipio . . .
(*Epid.* 548)

PE. Greetings. PH. I accept your greetings . . .

But the audience, of course, can hear both. Even when they break through the comic requirement not to recognise each other immediately, they still dance delicately around their sordid comic history, echoing each other in such a way as to present them as a couple with a shared secret – to which the audience is party. During the interplay over greeting, Philippa says: *quod credidisti reddo* ('I give you back what you have entrusted to me', 549), which on the surface refers to the greeting which Periphanes has just offered and requested. The audience may also hear it as a reference to the daughter who is the talisman of this play.

More playful, and less meaningful, is the echoing ring-composition which surrounds the *puer* scene in the dramaturgically outrageous *Pseudolus*.[48] Pseudolus, whose control of repetition, as of everything else, is consummate, ends his previous speech (now alone) with lines of typical alliterative and homoeoteleutive force:

> nunc ibo ad forum atque onerabo meis praeceptis Simiam,
> quid agat, ne quid titubet, docte ut hanc ferat fallaciam.
> iam ego hoc ipsum oppidum expugnatum faxo erit lenonium.
> (*Ps.* 764–6)

Now I'll go to the forum and pile up Simia with my instructions, what he should do so as not to falter and to carry off the trick cleverly. Now I'll make sure that that pimpish town is properly beseiged.

The boy then comes out for his bit of stage-stuffing, with the line *quoi seruitutem di danunt lenoniam* ('the one to whom the gods give pimpish servitude', 767), clearly echoing the last of Pseudolus'. The boy's speech ends *erus eccum recipit se domum et ducit coquom* ('there's my master coming home and bringing a cook', 789). Ballio enters, and echoes the boy's speech closely, with an indirect glance also at Pseudolus' most recent words:

> Forum coquinum qui uocant stulte uocant,
> nam non coquinum est, uerum furinum est forum.
> (*Ps.* 790–1)

Those who call the forum a place of cooks are speaking nonsense. It isn't a place of cooks but a place of crooks.

The echo is enhanced by *geminatio* of *coquinum* and *uocant*, then a pun on *fur* and *forum*, aided by the two (possibly invented) adjectives relating to professional roles.[49] Ballio and Pseudolus are in parallel, though there is no doubt who has the upper hand.[50]

Sometimes the echo is more visual than verbal. At line 609 in his play, Curculio is trying to ward off Planesium's determined efforts to find out more about the ring: *elusi militem, inquam, in alea* ('I cheated the

[48] See Sharrock (1996); Barsby (1995); Lefèvre (1997: esp. 67). For an account (and a table) of the metrical structure of *Ps.*, see Moore (1998b: 265).

[49] Both adjectives are attested only here: see *TLL ad loc.*, where *furinus* is described as an adjective deriving from *fur* '*per iocum*'. See Fraenkel (1960: 64).

[50] It should be noted also that Pseudolus said he was just off to instruct Simia, and Ballio comes in with the cook. Simia and the cook are both foils to the play's heroes (Pseudolus and Ballio).

soldier, I say, at dice'). Enter soldier (Therapontigonus), right on cue. Something similar happens, again with a soldier, in *Epidicus*, where the father Periphanes has just been reminiscing to himself about his own days as a young man ('and therefore he should not be so harsh on his son'), with the surprise characterisation of himself not only as a lover but also as a *miles gloriosus* (431–4). Cue entry of the *miles*, that character whose reality or fictionality within the scope of the play has been in some doubt up to this point.

In some cases, one partner in the cycle of repetition is in a position of power, working with the audience. That is clearly what is happening in Plautus' *Amphitruo*, in the scenes between Mercury and the confused slave Sosia, where Mercury leads Sosia into saying ridiculous things, because the god has control over the dialogue, whether he is initiating or reacting. In amongst the intense display of reciprocal duplicity which characterises this play,[51] there are two clear cases of 'pure' comic echo. In the first scene after the extended prologue, Mercury is observing the approaching Sosia and commenting on his entrance monologue for the sake of the audience. He picks up the joke he had used earlier, about who is really a slave, when he says:

> satiust me queri illo modo seruitutem:
> hodie qui fuerim liber, eum nunc
> potiuit pater seruitutis;
> hic qui uerna natust queritur.
>
> (*Am.* 176–9)

It would be more appropriate for me to complain like that about my slavery: I who today was free have now been placed in slavery by my own father. He who was born a slave is complaining.

Sosia, who at this point can neither see nor hear Mercury, is nudged into reflecting the god's words to his own disadvantage (with a piece of alliteration that might hint at a punning false etymology between *uerna* and *uerbero*): *sum <u>uero</u> <u>uerna</u> <u>uer</u>bero* ('I am truly a rascally slave', 180).[52]

[51] Christenson (2000: esp. 14–17). As he says (15), '[m]otifs of doubling pervade *Am.* to an absurd degree'. The meeting scene between Sosia and Mercury is described by Bertini (1981: 309) as 'uno dei capolavori del teatro comico di tutti i tempi e . . . un modello ineguaglioato ed ineguagliabile per gli autori che hanno voluto riproporla come "pezzo forte" nei loro rifacimenti', a situation which he ascribes to its masterly management of the inherent comedy of doubles. Lefèvre (1998: 20–4) argues for the particularly Plautine and particularly Italian role of the comedy of doubles. Petrone (1983: 188–91) also sees the double as comic.

[52] See Christenson (2000: 171), who comments on the 'multiple ironies' present here; also Traina (1977: 120).

After another hundred or so lines of this, Mercury causes Sosia to pick up his words again, and to push the play into movement (immediately after this interchange, Sosia notices Mercury, although the two do not actually interact directly for some time further). Mercury comments on Sosia's comments about the long night as good for one hiring an expensive prostitute:

> meu' pater nunc pro huius uerbis recte et sapienter facit,
> qui complexus cum Alcumena cubat amans, animo opsequens.
> (*Am.* 289–90)

My father now acts wisely and correctly according to his words, since he is sleeping with Alcumena as a lover, to his heart's desire.

The comment, still unheard, causes Sosia to remember what he is supposed to be doing:

> ibo ut erus quod imperauit Alcumenae nuntiem.
> (*Am.* 291)

I'll go and announce to Alcumena what my master ordered.

On 180, Slater (2000: 188) says that 'the action does not take place within a plane of illusion, but appeals directly to the spectator for approval'. This is quite right. In addition, the anti-realist action combines with other devices to give the echo a programmatic function. As Christenson (2000: 14) shows for the repetitious aspects of this prologue as a whole, such duplication is self-referential in this play of twins, since the whole structure of the play depends on the duplicity of twinning, with Mercury and Jupiter theatrically contriving a mocking echo of Sosia and Amphitruo.

Other echoes are overtly ironic and mocking, usually (although surprisingly not always) under the control of powerful characters. Such is the case in the opening scene of *Curculio*, where the supersoppy young lover Phaedromus is mocked by his ironic slave Palinurus:

> PH. huic proxumum illud ostiumst oculissumum.
> salue, ualuistin? PA. ostium occlusissumum,
> caruitne febris te heri uel nudiustertius
> et heri cenauistine?
> (*Cur.* 15–18)

PH. Next to it is the dearest little door. Hello, how are you? PA. Shuttest little door, were you free of fever yesterday and the day before and did you eat well yesterday?

Anaphora, homoeoteleuton, a pun created by the rearrangement of letters and an ironic echo, not to mention the image of the door eating, which is programmatic for the food imagery (Phaedromus as breakfast for Venus) and the anthropomorphic physicality of Things in the play: it is all followed up with an unaware echo by Phaedromus, who celebrates the door in more superlatives (*bellissumum . . . taciturnissumum*, 20) which again reflect images in the play.[53]

If the repeater knows that he or she is repeating (as in the case above), then the power is considerable. It is used to good effect in *Bacchides*, another play (like *Am.*) which is full of verbal reflections of duality that mimic its meaning.[54] When Pistoclerus is trying to resist the charms of the Bacchis sisters and thus his initiation (presumably) into sex, he calls Bacchis a *rapidus fluuius* ('swift river', 85) which he does not dare to cross. She responds by saying that there is no risk to him in *hunc fluuium*. His resistance does not last long (about another six lines), and his seduction is complete when Bacchis sets him up for dinner. She asks him to go to the market – 'with her money': *tu facito opsonatum nobis sit opulentum opsonium* ('you make sure our sustenance is suitably sustained', 96: alliteration, assonance and *figura etymologica*). The young man is caught, and replies: *ego opsonabo* – he, of course, will pay.

A parallel piece of playful duality comes right at the end of that play, when the old men are charmed into joining the party (1120-finis). The Bacchises initially abuse them, calling them 'sheep for shearing', a metaphor which the old men pick up – *haec oues uolunt uos* ('these sheep want you', 1140a) – and try to turn to their advantage, presenting their complaint that the Bacchises have taken their lambs, and threatening: *arietes truces nos erimus, iam in uos incursabimus* ('we'll turn into fierce rams and butt you', 1148).[55] Nice try at asserting their masculinity, but the trouble is the Bacchises are ahead of them, and decide to play to the inherent ambiguity in that

53 This kind of mocking echo is, not surprisingly, moderately common. Cf. Lampadio's parodic play on priority at *Cist.* 616–22, which drums out Melaenis' attempt to make a joke about first and last (615); *Cur.* 577, *Epid.* 624–7 (bis); Labrax and Daemones' slanging match with *tangedum* at *Rud.* 784–97; and many others, not least the mocking mirror which Terence's Syrus holds up to Demea at *Ad.* 423–9.

54 One might expect the other doubles comedy, *Men.*, also to exhibit an intensity of comic repetition and duplication. Christenson (2000: 16 n. 49), indicates that the features which he identifies in *Am.* are present but much less marked in the 'early and less-sophisticated' *Men.* Not everyone agrees with that assessment of the play's merits: see Bertini (1983: 308). In that article, Bertini treats the three twin plays (*Men.*, *Am.*, *Bac.*) together, but he is not particularly concerned with the kinds of 'creeping duality' which interest Christenson and the present discussion, but rather in the basic presence of twinning and its effect on the comedy and psychology of identity, considering the twinning in the *Bac.* as simply a matter of the sisters' names being homonyms. One might add that *Mil.* also partakes in a type of twinning, although, in this case, one twin sister is imaginary. On theatrical doubling, see also Bertini (1981); Dupont (1976).

55 The metaphor is completed by the characterisation of the *paedagogus* Lydus as the sheepdog (*mordax canis*, 1146), and the apportionment of tasks (i.e. the seduction of the respective fathers) among the sisters as a *pensum* (1152), i.e. an allotted task or 'weight of wool', each. Fraenkel (1960: 68).

masculinity – it might be what makes them tough and fierce, but it is also what makes them susceptible to the power of sex.

Such inequality of power in the management of repetition plays into the hands of the eponymous *architectus* of *Pseudolus*. In this play, things exist because Pseudolus creates them, and the audience is privileged to view the ramifications of his power even when he is not present.[56] His lines are unknowingly reused by his enemies, to their loss. As the first act in the movement of the plot, Pseudolus demands that his young master Calidorus should *ask* Pseudolus to get the money for him (thus enforcing the desirable relation of power between the two):

> roga me uiginti minas,
> ut me ecfecturum tibi quod promisi scias.
> roga, opsecro hercle. gestio promittere.
> (*Ps.* 114–16)

Ask me for twenty *minae*, so that you may know that I will do what I promised you. Ask me, I beg you. I'm dying to promise it.

Calidorus, naturally, complies. The interchange is echoed at the other end of the play, unknowingly, by the pimp Ballio, who engages in an almost identical interaction with the old man Simo, when he thinks he has Pseudolus beaten:

> roga me uiginti minas,
> si ille hodie illa sit potitus muliere
> siue eam tuo gnato hodie, ut promisit, dabit.
> roga, opsecro hercle; gestio promittere.
> (*Ps.* 1070–3)

Ask me for twenty *minae*, if he today ever manages to get possession of the woman or gives her to your son today, as he promised. Ask me, I beg you. I'm dying to promise it.

Not only is it Ballio who will lose out on this, in terms both of finance and of power relations, but also his foolish request here actually contributes to the final showdown in the movement of money. The twenty *minae* function as a pop-up repetition throughout the play. It can be hard to keep track of where they all are, especially since they are nowhere except in Pseudolus' creative imagination (404–5). The collocation *uiginti minas* occurs nine times in the play, always at the end of the line and with

[56] I have considered this play in some detail in Sharrock (1996), and it has been well treated by Slater (2000), but these points deserve rehearsing here specifically in the context of the comedy of repetition.

noticeable clustering (113, 114, 117, 404, 412, 484, 1070, 1077, 1241). The other order (*minas uiginti*) occurs once, at 280. In the nominative, the phrase doubles up at 1223:

> HA. hercle te hau sinam emoriri, nisi mi argentum redditur,
> uiginti minae. SIMO. atque etiam mihi aliae uiginti minae.[57]
> (*Ps.* 1222–3)

HA. By Hercules, I certainly won't let you die, unless I get my money back, twenty *minae*. SIMO. And also another twenty *minae* for me.

A moment of intensity shows the talismanic force of the phrase and what it signifies:

> CALI. meam tu amicam uendidisti? BA. ualide, uiginti minis.
> CALI. uiginti minis? BA. utrum uis, uel quater quinis minis.
> (*Ps.* 344–5)

CALI. You've sold my girlfriend? BA. Indeed, for twenty *minae*. CALI. Twenty *minae*? BA. Or, if you prefer, four times five *minae*.

But when Pseudolus is the repeater, he is in control. In his crucial scene with the old men Simo and Callipho, which sets up the trick, Pseudolus makes Simo promise him twenty *minae* if he succeeds in getting the girl from the pimp, Callipho aiding and abetting his extortion of the promise. Simo replies: *non demutabo* ('I won't change', 555). When the old men leave at 560 and 561, Pseudolus addresses the audience.[58] So, they think he won't pull it off, eh? Well, *non demutabo* (566). The echo is an aural wink at the audience. The non-changing will turn out to Pseudolus' benefit and Simo's discomfiture when he has to pay Pseudolus for tricking him.

The consummate repetition of the play, however, is that which is also operative to it: the variations on *caue* – 'watch out!' This play constitutes a trick in which you are constantly being warned to watch out for trickery, exactly while it is happening.[59] Again, Pseudolus makes his double and rival, Ballio, copy his words. (In addition to the *cauere* motif throughout the play, there is also an *edicere* motif, which Ballio likewise copies, unknowingly, from Pseudolus.) This is how Pseudolus sets the ball rolling:

[57] *minae uiginti* occurs at the beginning of the line at 1068, while variants in other cases occur at 52, 344–5, 1228.

[58] There is a nice bit of conspiratorial polyptoton here: *suspicio est mi nunc uos suspicarier*... (562), and the rest of the speech is full of such devices.

[59] Sharrock (1996). I am discussing here a series of repetitions that *are* operative and central to the meanings of their texts, despite my claim that repetition is delightfully irrelevant. Sometimes it only poses as being irrelevant, but *Ps.* is also thick with irrelevant repetitions.

nunc, ne quis dictum sibi neget, dico omnibus,
pube praesenti in contione, omni poplo,
omnibus amicis notisque edico meis
in hunc diem a me ut caueant, ne credant mihi.
(*Ps.* 125–8)

Now, in case anyone should deny that he had been warned, I announce to all, to the people present in this assembly and all the population, to all my friends and acquaintances I proclaim that on this very day they should watch out for me and not trust me.

Moments later, Ballio bursts onto the stage with his spectacular entrance monologue in which he demands that all his household serve his every whim, including giving him birthday presents. Not only his goal of control but also his very language present him as the double of Pseudolus.[60] I quote only the magnificent opening, though the whole speech is thick with comic constructions:

Exite, agite exite, ignaui, male habiti et male conciliati,
quorum numquam quicquam quoiquam uenit in mentem ut recte faciant,
quibu', nisi ad hoc exemplum experior, non potest usura usurpari.
(*Ps.* 133–5)

Out, come on, out, you lazy lot, bad to keep and bad to obtain, none of whom ever let it occur to them to behave rightly, for whom no possible use can be found unless I try you out in this way.

Ballio is marked out as unknowingly echoing Pseudolus' previous speech. The slave warned everyone to watch out, using the language of an edict to the people; now the pimp proclaims his edicts to his people (*edictionem*, 143 and *edixeram omnibus*, 148).

Still more closely are Ballio's words tied to those of Pseudolus when he repeats (unknowingly) the language of both *cauere* and *edicere* in his account of how Simo warned him against Pseudolus, a warning which plays into the trickster's hands:

nam mi hic uicinus apud forum paullo prius
pater Calidori | opere edixit maxumo
ut mihi cauerem a Pseudolo seruo suo
(*Ps.* 896–8)

For my neighbour, Calidorus' father, impressed upon me a little while ago in the forum that I should watch out for his slave Pseudolus.

[60] It may be a sign of the high profile of the part that the late republican actor Roscius played the role of Ballio (Cic. *Q. Rosc.* 20): Brown (2002: 234).

In case we missed it, he ends his speech with another edict about not trusting Pseudolus:

> nunc ibo intro atque edicam familiaribus
> profecto ne quis quicquam credat Pseudolo.
> (*Ps.* 903–4)

Now I'll go inside and tell my household that on no account must anyone trust Pseudolus.

When the truth comes out, Simo has a moment of glory over Ballio, and is in a position to effect the repetition himself, with an 'I told you so' (*dixin ab eo tibi ut caueres centiens?*, 1227) – ironic, because his warning actually helped the trick, not hindered it. There is a coda to the *cauere* motif in Pseudolus' drunken finale. After burping bibulously in his face, the slave tells his master to hold him softly to stop him falling – *caue ne cadam* (1296). The final bit of 'watching out' that Simo has to do for Pseudolus is that which shows the roles well and truly reversed.

'Watch out' is a watchword for comic dupes, which (naturally) most of them do not heed. The most unusual old man, Hegio in *Captiui*, is in a position to make comic capital out of the need for caution:

> qui cauet ne decipiatur uix cauet quom etiam cauet;
> etiam quom cauisse ratus est saepe is cautor captus est.
> (*Capt.* 255–6)

He who takes care not to be deceived is hardly taking care even when he's taking care; even when he thinks he has taken care often this caretaker is caught.

For all his caution, he will be deceived, but will ultimately be the beneficiary of his own deception. Other great trickster plays also warn their dupes and audiences to watch out for the trick. Chrysalus' manipulation of the old man in *Bacchides* depends on the letter that warns Nicobulus to beware of him. Dictated by Chrysalus to his young master Mnesilochus, it reads:

> 'atque id pollicetur se daturum aurum mihi
> quod dem scortis quodque in lustris comedim, congraecem, pater.
> sed, pater, uide ne tibi hodie uerba det: quaeso caue.'
> (*Bac.* 742–4)

'And he promises that he's going to give that money to me to give to the prostitutes and to spend in brothels and to Greek-it-up, father. But, father, see to it that he doesn't deceive you today: please take care.'

Without a clear chronology for the plays,[61] and with so many other plays missing, it is as ever dangerous to argue for specific allusion in either direction, but it seems likely that the *caue topos* would be recognised and appreciated as such by the audience in all the plays mentioned here. Whether *Pseudolus* is the chronological original of the motif (unlikely), or its pinnacle, the audience would enjoy recognising it as an intensified version of a wider phenomenon. That is another kind of repetition.

POP-UPS

Three useful contributors to the comic project are iteration, incongruity and irrelevance. They are combined in a technique which I call the 'pop-up figure', taking the lead from Bergson's analysis of the Jack-in-a-box. Bergson develops the basic Jack-in-a-box to a more complex reading of comic scenes:

> Many a comic scene may indeed be referred to this simple type. For instance, in the scene of the *Mariage forcé* between Sganarelle and Pancrace, the entire vis comica lies in the conflict set up between the idea of Sganarelle, who wishes to make the philosopher listen to him, and the obstinacy of the philosopher, a regular talking-machine working automatically. As the scene progresses, the image of the Jack-in-the-box becomes more apparent, so that at last the characters themselves adopt its movements, – Sganarelle pushing Pancrace, each time he shows himself, back into the wings, Pancrace returning to the stage after each repulse to continue his patter. And when Sganarelle finally drives Pancrace back and shuts him up inside the house – inside the box, one is tempted to say – a window suddenly flies open, and the head of the philosopher again appears as though it had burst open the lid of a box. (Bergson 1913: 71–2)

Bergson then states what he calls a 'law': '[i]n a comic repetition of words we generally find two terms: a repressed feeling which goes off like a spring, and an idea that delights in repressing the feeling anew' (Bergson 1913: 73).

There is an obvious connection with Freudian analyses such as that of the famous cotton reel. It is likely that the particular expression of the point about repeated suppression and explosion relates to the late nineteenth-/early twentieth-century zeitgeist, but the effect seems to apply well to comedy across a wider historical range. A nice modern example of the comic cotton reel, so to speak, which I imagine that few readers will recognise, comes from the Welsh television channel Sianel Pedwar

[61] Duckworth (1994: 55). *Ps.* is one of the more datable, with only a doubt between 194 and 191 BC. *Bac.* has been dated to approximately 189 (e.g. Lefèvre 1978a), which would suggest that Chrysalus is referring to Pseudolus rather than the other way around.

Cymraeg. There was in my teen years in Wales a comedy programme in Welsh, which I appreciated for its comedy despite my limited command of the language. About three times in each episode, a scuba-diver would appear out of nowhere, push back his snorkel and ask: 'Ych chi'n gwybod y ffordd i Nefyn?' – 'Do you know the way to Nefyn?' Nefyn is a village in North Wales, and is completely irrelevant to the programme.

It has long been noticed that many of Plautus' jokes have this kind of plot-stopping irrelevance and tendency to pop up again at random moments.[62] While running-slave scenes and sequences like the one about the swift-footed arms of Stratippocles at *Epid.* 29–35, or the absurd series about the anal-retentive Euclio at *Aul.* 298–320, are obvious cases of irrelevant humour[63] for its own sake, I suggest that the sign of the 'pop-up' might be a fruitful way to consider them, rather than simply as examples of how Plautus works. What makes them funny is not just that they work, but that tried and tested formulae work because we don't always see them coming, even when we think we are waiting out for them, but then we enjoy recognising them when they do.

The character whose repeated attempts to get in on the act are repeatedly suppressed has a Graeco-Roman history at least as far back as Aristophanes, where it contributes to the basic structure of what are sometimes called the 'impostor scenes'. Another classic Aristophanic manifestation is Philocleon in *Wasps*, whose attempts to leave the house get increasingly more absurd (and intertextual) each time his son tries to push the lid back down. At a quieter level are the efforts of Xanthias to get himself noticed during the interaction between Dionysus and Herakles (*Ra.* 87–8, 108, 115, 159–60).

The best example of attempted self-intrusion into the plot in Roman comedy comes from an unlikely source, Terence's *Hecyra*. Here we have a slave, Parmeno, who is never allowed to know what is going on, never allowed to play the role of knowing *architectus* that he tries to set up for himself at the beginning and is sent on wild-goose chases out of the play. The repeated intrusions of Parmeno and the rebuffing of his efforts to turn this painful piece into a more conventional comedy constitute one of the few comic touches of this difficult play, on which see pp. 233–49.

The intruder's role is often a matter of things failing to happen. Such, perhaps, is a saving comic grace of the play where nothing

[62] E.g. Duckworth (1994: 196). The point relates also to the underlying principles of Fraenkel's Plautine methodology (1960).

[63] That is, if anything in literature could ever be ultimately irrelevant. On the inherent humour of irrelevance, see Charney (1987: 25–36).

happens – Plautus' *Stichus*.[64] Two sisters are married to two brothers, who have been away for over two years, attempting to revive their flagging fortunes. The sisters' father at first wants to get them to marry again, but then the husbands come home rich and all is well. The rest is just a party, or rather two parties, one free, one enslaved. Most of the humour in the play comes from the efforts of Gelasimus to play the role of parasite, which has been lost to him while the brothers have been away, and which they finally deny him on their return.[65] He pops up first at 155, with a tour de force of parasitism, overseen and commented on by the slave Crocotium. A hundred or more lines of fooling serve only to produce the false apparent plot movement that Crocotium's mistress wants Gelasimus to do a job for her – go down to the harbour to see whether there is any news of her husband. Even this hopeful sign is dashed, however, when the slave Pinacium, who has apparently also been sent on that errand, turns up to perform the classic scene of announcing the arrival of the ship at the harbour (274). All Gelasimus' attempts to do anything – join in with the housework, oversee a sacrifice, get involved in the kitchens or whatever it might be – are rebuffed; then when the brothers finally arrive, one after another, he has a scene with each and with both in which he attempts to get in on the act – to get an invitation to dinner. Each time, he is repressed, like a child's rocking toy which bounces back however hard you hit it.[66] That is his comic role. Ergasilus in *Captivi* plays a similar pop-up role, though he is not repressed to the same extent. The parasite, as neither enemy nor

[64] The view that nothing happens in this play seems to be shared by most commentators, even Petersmann (1973). Arnott (1972: 54) sums up the attitude of the critics by calling the play 'Plautus' problem pupil', before setting out to offer it a rehabilitation. Others have also sought to find purpose in the play, e.g. Leigh (2004b), who relates it to the celebrations at return after the Punic Wars, likewise Owens (2000). Owens also reads the role of Gelasimus as serious social comment on the situation of the Roman poor, presenting Gelasimus as a dependent Roman *cliens* to whom the brothers and their families owe a duty of care. In the light of the discussion below about Plautus and Ennius (esp. pp. 204–5), it might be worth noting Ennius *trag fr.* LIII Jocelyn, (*Cresphontes*) in which a daughter argues against her father's attempts to separate her from her husband, as do the women here: *iniuria abs te adficior indigna pater. / nam si inprobum esse Cresphontem existimas, / cur me huic locabas nuptiis? sin est probus, / cur talem inuitam inuitum cogis linquere?*; cf. *St.* 130–1: *nam aut olim, nisi tibi placebant, non datas oportuit / aut nunc non aequomst abduci, pater, illisce apsentibus.*

[65] Flaucher (2003) shows how Gelasimus is always an outsider to the rest of the play, Crocotium being the only person who even thinks he's funny. In his view, the audience would not be greatly troubled by the potentially tragic figure of Gelasimus' failures, because they know that underneath it all is only the stereotype of the hungry parasite. See Arnott (1972: 64) for Gelasimus' role as one of linking the various parts of the play together.

[66] Damon (1997: 65–74) describes Gelasimus as 'more thoroughly abused than any other Roman parasite'. My reading of Gelasimus as a 'pop-up' character has some affinity with that of Bettini (2002), whose analysis of the joke sequence about Gelasimus being pregnant with his mother Hunger shows well the power of a recurrent image.

member of the family, is perhaps particularly well suited to this kind of treatment.

Gelasimus and Parmeno function within single plays, but perhaps we can see the same phenomenon occurring when items, scenes and characters pop up from one play to the next.[67] When a ring or other token acts as the mechanism for recognition, for example, our pleasure comes from our only pretending to be surprised, really recognising our old friend the plot device for what it is.[68] The same could be said of repeated scenes, usually called 'stock': door scenes, meeting scenes, cook scenes, etc., repeated within a play and from play to play. In an important essay on innovation, repetition and modern aesthetics, Umberto Eco shows how much of the pleasure of art resides in the expectation and enjoyment of iteration, rather than in the supposed innovation. He hypothesises that if we had access to all the plays of classical Greek tragedy, for example, we would appreciate that 'perhaps where we see absolute invention, the Greeks would have seen only the "correct" variation on a single scheme, and sublime appeared to them, not a single work, but precisely the scheme' (2005: 206).[69] Translated into comic language, with 'sublime' replaced by 'funny', this insight better expresses the workings of Plautus and Terence than does the conventional language of stock scenes and stock characters.

This explains (if the non-comic language of explanation is appropriate) the gratuitous cook scene in *Pseudolus*. Yes, Ballio is having a party because it is his birthday, but there is really no logical justification for the extravagant scene of gourmet grotesquerie starting at 790. What the scene does here is to cause the audience to groan in recognition of yet another act of conventional comic excess. Oh no, not a cook scene again! Gratuitous though he is, however, the cook has an additional comic function as a double to Ballio, just as Simia is a double to Pseudolus, and Ballio and Pseudolus, Simia and the cook are doubles to each other.[70]

[67] Parmeno himself pops up in other plays, or at least his name does, since the slave of *Eu.* shares the same name. The repeated names of which Menander and Terence are fond might be considered to be part of the same phenomenon.

[68] Recognitions use non-human tokens in Pl. *Cist.*, *Cur.*, *Rud.*, Ter. *HT*, *Hec.*, a list which adds up to less than one might expect: see Duckworth (1994: 412 n. 58) for the claim that recognition in Roman comedy is 'almost always a token or ring'. Telò (1998: 909) points out that in Greek tragic *anagnorisis* a physical *tekmerion* is always required. Rings occur as somewhat talismanic plot devices also in *Bac.*, *Cur.* (most extreme case), *Mil.*, *Ps.* and *Trin.*

[69] On the metatheatricality of stock characters drawing attention to themselves, see Moore (1998a: 14 and n. 26).

[70] Everyone doubles everyone else here: the cook, along with Pseudolus and Simia, also has a role as image of the playwright himself. See Gowers (1993: 52–6, 78–9 and esp. 93–107); also Lowe (1985b); Danese (1997). For Simia and Pseudolus as doubles of each other, see Slater (2000: 110–14). For the

SWEEPING THE SPIDERS: *AULULARIA*

I mentioned above that comic repetition is not limited to the great masterpieces of Plautine humour. It would not be too much of an exaggeration, I hope, to claim that iterative devices are the comic saving grace of that almost-painful study in paranoia, *Aulularia*.[71] It is conventional to say that *Aulularia* and its hero Euclio are comic because they are ridiculous (perhaps a tautology) and totally over the top: the play, on this reading, is a satire on the stock figure of the miser.[72] But this is painful, and for anything painful to be funny, like the children's television cartoon 'Tom and Jerry', it has to build up a relationship with its audience which makes it very clear, somehow, that this is comic.[73] Personally, I was only able to make friends with *Aulularia* when I saw the duality in Euclio: a paranoid miser to laugh at, and a comic genius to laugh with. It is the comic repetition in his language and performance that makes this work. The central duality of the play is, as Konstan (1983) has shown, the essential connection between the pot of gold, and the pot-bellied girl, a connection which comes to a head in the superlative scene of the play, that interaction between Euclio and Lyconides where they talk at cross-purposes about the two crimes against Euclio. But the play is structured around many other dualities, including Euclio and Staphyla, Euclio and Megadorus, Euclio and Lyconides.

A remarkable feature of the play is that the best comic language belongs to Euclio, not to one of the slaves and cooks that flock around him (to his annoyance). His violent opening interaction with Staphyla could be held to be programmatic for the tone of the play as a whole – a mixture of comedy and serious problems, saved by the style. After the sedate prologue

monkey-ish implications of that connection, and a further link with Simo, see Connors (2004: 190 and n. 27).

71 See Konstan (1983: 33–46) for a reading of the play in relation to the requirements of civic life; Kruschwitz (2002) for the history of reading the play as a character study. Kruschwitz's argument is that the play is neither simply about character nor simply a morality tale about money as the 'root of all evils', but rather that it is only so in the wrong hands – i.e. any hands other than those of Lyconides. Good brief account in Stockert (1983: 18–20).

72 Euclio is not really so much miserly as paranoid, but much of the farce of the play depends on his miser-like hoarding of the gold. See Lefèvre (2001: 33–8) for readings of the character as φιλάργυρος or ἄπιστος: his summary view is that the character in the original was more the former, and that Plautus has developed 'δύσκολος-like aspects in the original into a comic study in paranoia.

73 Glasgow (1995) is an interesting and entertaining study in comedy and cruelty, which is not afraid to run the two uncomfortably closely together. Comedy's salvation, although it is by no means guaranteed, comes from the workings of humour, as in the example on his p. 248 from the absurd theatre of Alfred Jarry, where 'statistically fantastic tortures' are described thus: 'twisting of the nose, tearing out of their hair, insertion of the little wooden stick into the nearoles, extraction of the brain via the heels, laceration of the posterior' (*Ubu Roi* 5.1). On Roman comedy and pain, see also Dutsch (2008: ch. 3); Parker (1989).

from the Lar Familiaris, Euclio rushes on-stage, pushing Staphyla before him:

> Exi, inquam, age exi: exeundum hercle tibi hinc est foras,
> circumspectatrix cum oculis emissiciis.
>
> (*Aul.* 40–1)

Out, I say, come on out: you must get the hell out of here, you looker-rounder with spying eyes.

The first (ten-word) line falls over itself in its eagerness to repeat, pushing out its point – *ex- ex- ex-*. The second (four-word) line slows right down, with that highly self-expressive word *circumspectatrix* (five long syllables in one word): one could imagine Euclio playing out what he says, unconsciously, as he looks suspiciously around the audience, thus turning himself into what he accuses Staphyla of being.[74] The on-going assonance of *c* and *s* sounds in the line adds to the point. Staphyla's response to the play's outburst is a meekly murmuring *me miseram* (42), which is immediately picked up by the aggressively alliterative Euclio:

> . . . ut misera sis
> atque ut te dignam mala malam aetatem exigas.
>
> (*Aul.* 42–3)

. . . so that you can be miserable and, being bad, live a bad life that suits you.

But the mocking echo is not all on one side, for, as I suggested, Staphyla is one of the doubles of Euclio. She now picks up his determined OUT:

> nam qua me nunc caussa extrusisti ex aedibus?
>
> (*Aul.* 44)

For what reason do you push me out of the house now?

Not to be outdone, Euclio turns the alliteration in a new direction:

> tibi ego rationem reddam, stimulorum seges?
> illuc regredere ab ostio. illuc sis uide,
> ut incedit. at scin quo modo tibi res se habet?
> si hercle hodie fustem cepero aut stimulum in manum,
> testudineum istum tibi ego grandibo gradum.
>
> (*Aul.* 45–9)

[74] See also Lefèvre (2001: 118). Stockert (1983: 44) discusses the possibility that the second *exi* should be deleted, as mentioned by Lindsay in his apparatus, but it is not necessary. As he says, 'vielleicht soll die ärgerliche, sich überschlagende Stimme Euclios untermalt werden!' His next note brings out the comic military metaphor in *oculis emissiciis*. For the tone of excited extrusion from the house, cf. *Cur.* 276: *exi, exi, exi, inquam*. See also Stockert (1982: 5–6), where attention is drawn to Euclio's clipped, asyndetic style and his earthy language.

I give you reason, field of rods? Go over there away from the door. Well, look at that, how she walks! But do you know how things stand with you? If by Hercules today I take a stick or a rod in my hand I'll increase that tortoise step for you.

And so it goes on. We will soon learn, however, that this very scene is a repeat of something which happens ad nauseam, ten times a day (70). The action of throwing Staphyla out of the house is symbolic of Euclio's problem and a core issue of the play – denial of domestic norms and of appropriate societal behaviour.[75] It also marks the beginning of the joking interaction of problems and playfulness which characterises the play. While Staphyla is alone, during one of Euclio's periodic sudden absences, she repeats his linguistic behaviour with a mixture of real problems and a joking expression of them:

> neque iam quo pacto celem erilis filiae
> probrum, propinqua partitudo quoi appetit,
> queo comminisci; neque quicquam meliust mihi,
> ut opinor, quam ex me ut unam faciam litteram
> †longum, laqueo† collum quando opstrinxero.
> (*Aul.* 74–8)

Now I cannot devise how I can hide my young mistress's shame, when she is about to give birth; I think there's nothing better for me than to make myself into one letter . . . by drawing a rope around my neck.

Throughout the play, Euclio's language is thick with repetitions of various sorts. He has a small surfeit of nouns, with homoeoteleuton, at 95, and another with an appropriate repetition of 'expensive' at 374–6; examples of redundant polyptoton, as at 181; proverbial expressions, for example at 195, 229, 555; mocking repetition of phrases, such as at 426 and 432; and many examples of alliteration and assonance, of which 181, 184–5, 220–2, 465–74 and 623–7 are just a few instances.

Euclio is indeed a madly, idiotically, obsessionally, satirically miserly type. But there is a second level of character here, just barely winking out at the audience from behind the mask of the Character. We can see the winks most clearly, I suggest, in those places where Euclio is most absurd: not the violent outbursts of pot-rage, but the moments where logic is thrown to the winds. After Euclio has assured himself of the safety of his secret inside, he rather more calmly tells Staphyla to go back in and perform her proper role as *serua*. She responds with a typical 'poverty' joke about there being

[75] As critics have noted, the most extreme example of this point is Euclio's instruction to Staphyla to put the fire out (91–2): Konstan (1983: 36).

nothing inside for her to serve (a play is intended perhaps between *seruare* and *seruire*), because the place is full of spiders (81–4). Euclio replies that he may be poor, but she can jolly well just look after the spiders:

> mirum quin tua me caussa faciat Iuppiter
> Philippum regem aut Dareum, triuenefica.
> araneas mi ego illas seruari uolo.
>
> (*Aul.* 85–7)

It's a wonder that, for your sake, Jupiter doesn't make me King Philip or Dareus, triple poisoner. I want those spiders looked after.

Instead of the spiders' webs being what she would be expected to clear away, they are now to be the object of her tender care.[76] Similar paralogical anthropomorphic jokes about animals occur at 465, 562 and 669.[77] The first of these features in Euclio's monologue complaining about Megadorus having sent a cook in to prepare for the expected festivities. Euclio is convinced that the cook has been sent along by his neighbour in order to spy on the pot of gold, but it is his own household that is accused of conniving with the enemy. Euclio's own cockerel had the temerity to peck around in the region of the pot's hiding place, because 'obviously he is in league with the old woman' (Staphyla, 466) and was 'probably bribed by the cook' (470). But Euclio was too quick for him, and the daylight thief (the cock) paid the penalty – that is, Euclio killed his own rooster for doing what roosters do. The story is daft and farcical of itself, but notice also the comic force of the language in which it is expressed, full of iterative and playful devices:

> condigne etiam meu' med intus gallus gallinacius,
> qui erat anui peculiaris, perdidit paenissume.
> ubi erat haec defossa, occepit ibi scalpurrire ungulis
> circumcirca. quid opust uerbis? ita mi pectus peracuit:
> capio fustem, optrunco gallum, furem manufestarium.
> credo edepol ego illi mercedem gallo pollicitos coquos,
> si id palam fecisset. exemi ex manu † manubrium.
> quid opust uerbis? facta est pugna in gallo gallinacio.[78]
>
> (*Aul.* 465–72)

Fittingly then that cocky cock of mine inside, who was matey with the old woman, almost ruined me. Where this was buried, he began scratching all around with

[76] Cf. Gelasimus' joking concern that the poor little spiders will get cold if he sweeps away their webs (*St.* 349).

[77] See Stockert (1982: 9–11).

[78] Note that the phrase *gallo gallinacio*, itself polyptoton, echoes the opening line of the cockerel story and is unconsciously echoed by Megadorus' *Gallicis cantheriis* at 495.

his talons. Why say more? It pierced me to the heart: I snatch up a club and slay the cock, a thief caught red-handed. By Hercules, I reckon the cooks promised a reward to that cock if he showed them where it is. I got the handle out of the hand. Why say more? The battle with the cocky cock was over.

This dastardly chicken is followed up by a curious sheep (which enables Euclio to be in control of a poverty joke with Megadorus, 561–6)[79] and a helpful raven, who receives the extraordinary distinction of being promised a good word from Euclio (671–2).

Normal logic takes its hardest knock, however, in a scene the absurdity of which is matched only by its predictability, at least to modern audiences. Euclio confronts the slave of Lyconides (rightly, although prematurely) with his theft of the gold, and demands that the miscreant show his hands, one after the other – and then the third (641). And then again (650). The slave does not actually have the pot at this point, nor would it be likely that he could hold it in one hand in any case, but part of the humour depends on our knowledge that he has every intention of getting his hands on the dosh. In this scene, that invisible pot almost – metaphorically – pops in and out of our vision.[80]

Such jokes, visual and aural, depend in part on duality of levels of experience. One place where we can see particularly clearly the multiple layers in Euclio's character is at the climax of his obsessive suffering, when the event that he has feared for so long, and which has been constantly deferred throughout the play, finally takes place – the gold is stolen:

> Perii, interii, occidi. quo curram? quo non curram? tene, tene. quem? quis?
> nescio, nil uideo, caecus eo atque equidem quo eam aut ubi sim aut qui sim
> nequeo cum animo certum inuestigare.
>
> (*Aul.* 713–15)

I've perished, died, deceased. Where shall I run? Where shall I not run? Hold, hold. Whom? Who? I know nothing, I see nothing, I go blindly and I cannot ascertain where I am going or where I am or who I am.

Assonance, alliteration, homoeoteleuton, *geminatio*, polyptoton and all the rest of it are here. We must surely suspect not only self-parody, but also tragic parody, whether general or specific. The aporetic cry sounds tragic,

[79] On which see Fontaine (2004).

[80] The scene itself is also involved in a multiple series of repetitions. It matches Euclio's scene with Congrio, when he accuses the cook of stealing the pot, a scene which itself echoes the opening scene, when Staphyla is thrown out of the house. The scene between Euclio and the slave of Lyconides is also matched with Euclio's confrontation with Lyconides himself, and also with the young man's own confrontation with his slave.

perhaps even evocative of the famous tragic cry of Medea at Enn. *trag. fr.* CIV Jocelyn (*quo nunc me uortam?* followed by more rhetorical questions), while the reference to blindness could create a link to the famously blind such as Oedipus or Tiresias, or to the trauma-induced loss of sight (real or metaphorical) of any suffering hero. Euclio's language will be picked up immediately after his song, by Lyconides, at 727–30. At the moment of tragic climax, however, Euclio does something which probably no tragic actor ever did: he addresses the audience directly, like a modern pantomime actor, and pulls no punches in smashing the dramatic illusion, in order to ask for the audience's help to find the thief.

> opsecro ego uos, mi auxilio,
> oro, optestor, sitis et hominem demonstretis, quis eam apstulerit.
> quid ais tu? tibi credere certum est, nam esse bonum ex uoltu cognosco.
> quid est? quid ridetis? noui omnis, scio fures esse hic compluris,
> qui uestitu et creta occultant sese atque sedent quasi sint frugi.
> hem, nemo habet horum? occidisti. dic igitur, quis habet? nescis?
> (*Aul.* 715–20)

I beg you, I pray, I call you to witness, help me and show me the man who took it away. What do you say? I'm inclined to trust you, for I can see that you are honest from your face. What is it? Why do you laugh? I recognise you all, I know that there are lots of thieves here, who hide themselves in clothes and chalk and sit as if they were honest. Hmm, does none of them have it? You've killed me. So tell me, who has it? You don't know?

And then he goes into a daft and highly alliterative song about his sorrows. More than anyone else in the play, Euclio speaks aside. The Euclio who is the butt of our farcical laughter is speaking to himself at these points, cut off as he is from normal societal interaction, but Euclio the comic hero is in constant dialogue with us. All asides are at some level directed at the audience:[81] Euclio thus encourages us to laugh, not at some other butt, as would the likes of Pseudolus, but at the speaker himself.

Euclio makes a fine Jack-in-a-box, bouncing in and out of the stage like a spring that might go off at any moment. His are some of the most sudden entrances and exits in the whole of Roman comedy, the latter leaving his interlocutors wondering where on earth he has gone. Four times during the play itself, he suddenly breaks off from the conversation in which he is involved in order to plunge back into the house and check on his gold: at 66 with Staphyla, at 203 and 242 with Megadorus, and at 444 with Congrio. Likewise, the presence of two hiding scenes in close proximity (in

[81] Bain (1977), but see Marshall (2006: 166) for further nuancing of this phenomenon.

the temple of Fides and the rural shrine of Silvanus) has a similar spring-like effect.[82]

The best comic moment of the play is the scene (731–807) in which all the strands and layers come together, and the truth necessary to the play's resolution comes out. Euclio and Lyconides are talking at cross-purposes about the crime of the younger man against the older, thus placing the audience in a position of delightful superiority to the blind confusions of both, and of enjoyment of the double entendres which are created by the language of touching *illa* (the *aula* or the *puella*), which reach their height when Lyconides outrageously suggests that having touched once he feels it is his right to hold for ever (755–6). Despite their great difficulties in mutual communication, Euclio and Lyconides are linked as doubles not only by their common interest in *illa* but also, comically, by the echoes and dualities which surround their interaction. Here is the opening of the scene, after the separate linked monologues of tragic parody referred to above:

> EVC. Quis homo hic loquitur? LY. ego sum miser. EVC.
> immo ego sum, et misere perditus,
> quoi tanta mala maestitudoque optigit. LY. animo bono es.
> EVC. quo, opsecro, pacto esse possum? LY. quia istuc facinus quod tuom
> sollicitat animum, id ego feci et fateor.
>
> (*Aul.* 731–4)

EVC. What man is speaking here? LY. I am miserable. EVC. No, I'm miserable and miserably lost, the victim of such terrible misery. LY. Cheer up. EVC. How on earth can I do that? LY. Because that crime which troubles your mind, I did it and I confess.

The two men are contending for the position of most miserable. The ensuing scene will not only (eventually) put them both to rights, but also enhance the link between them by bringing both of them back into the proper roles in society which they ought, but have been failing, to play. A verbal echo reinforces this movement. At the opening of the interaction, after the passage quoted above, Euclio confronts Lyconides with *quid ego ex te audio?* ('What's this I hear from you?', 734). The rhetorical question will be repeated near the end of the scene, when Euclio finally realises what Lyconides was talking about: *ei mihi, quod ego facinus ex te audio?* ('Oh no, what crime do I hear from you?', 796). It may be a terrible deed,

[82] So much so, in fact, that the repetition has been subject to censure. See Hunter (1981) on this point, and esp. 41 for the suggestion that the scene with the temple of Fides is a Plautine addition to the Greek original. See also Lefèvre (2001: 21). Raffaelli (2000) notes the popping effect of Euclio's movements and his surreal (il)logic.

but it is ultimately what brings Lyconides into his right social role. In the next scene, Lyconides is no longer the snivelling youth, but is now the authoritative master. When his slave tells him about the theft of the pot of gold, he responds in unconscious echo of his prospective father-in-law: *quod ego facinus audio ex te?* (822), and demands the pot's return in a way that would make Euclio proud.[83] The parallelism between Lyconides and Euclio is both comic and socially meaningful.[84]

PARODY AND INTERTEXTUALITY: THE ARTIFICIAL REPETITION OF LIFE AND LITERATURE

> But I find that a certain movement of head or arm, a movement always the same, seems to return at regular intervals. If I notice it and it succeeds in diverting my attention, if I wait for it to occur and it occurs when I expect it, then involuntarily I laugh. Why? Because I now have before me a machine that works automatically. This is no longer life, it is automatism established in life and imitating it. It belongs to the comic. This is also the reason why gestures, at which we never dreamt of laughing, become laughable when imitated by another individual. The most elaborate explanations have been offered for this extremely simple fact. A little reflection, however, will show that our mental state is ever changing, and that if our gestures faithfully followed these inner movements, if they were as fully alive as we, they would never repeat themselves, and so would keep imitation at bay. We begin, then, to become imitable only when we cease to be ourselves. I mean our gestures can only be imitated in their mechanical uniformity, and therefore exactly in what is alien to our living personality. To imitate anyone is to bring out the element of automatism he has allowed to creep into his person. And as this is the very essence of the ludicrous, it is no wonder that imitation gives rise to laughter. (Bergson 1913: 32–3)

> ille referre aliter saepe solebat idem
>
> (Ovid, *Ars amatoria* 2.128)
>
> He often used to relate the same thing in different ways.

Repetition has a lively comic function of its own. There is simple pleasure in recognition, and in this regard comedy epitomises and makes a joke of something rich and strange about drama generally, which is the aesthetic pleasure that comes from an artificial repetition of life in literature. Apropos the powerful case made by Bergson for the inherent comedy of repetition,

[83] See Lefèvre (2001) and the bibliography cited there for the belief that the return of the money was instrumental in granting the marriage to Lyconides.

[84] Megadorus is also a kind of double for Euclio. Although his opposite as rich man to poor man, Megadorus shows himself also a man after Euclio's own heart, in his diatribe against luxury at 475.

Mauron claims that many modern critics, particularly scholars of Plautus and of Molière, make a mistake which he attributes also to Bergson, which is being too willing to mix up the comedy of life and the comedy of theatre as simply the same thing.[85] The point is valid, but I would like nonetheless to draw attention to the comic power that comes not so much from treating literature as 'the same thing' as life, but from seeing how literature is parasitic on life, other literature and everything else. This kind of repetition is not perhaps so immediately obvious as the verbal iterative types that I have been considering so far, but it is crucial to drama because it has to do with mimesis.[86] In its simplest form, we call it parody. Very frequently in comedy, the words and actions which are the constructive signifiers of the work (the things that make the representation happen) point not only to the mimetic world – what the play is *about* – but also to some external thing, which may be real or fictional. The act of pointing may itself be directly relevant and informative or delightfully irrelevant and nonsensical. This is true of all literature: the special contribution of comedy is to make a joke about it.

If mimesis, then also intertextuality, the ultimate repetition: as Kristeva famously said (paraphrasing Bakhtin), 'any text is constructed as a mosaic of quotations; any text is the absorption and transformation of another'.[87] All literature points to other literature: not only is Roman comedy no exception, but rather it might be deemed to be the epitome of this doctrine. This universal claim about literature is especially pertinent in a genre which *presents* itself as repetition with a difference: the *fabula palliata* is a comedy dressed up as a Greek, a Greek play translated (in some sense) into Latin. Part of the self-conscious pose of humility in which Roman comedy partakes involves presenting itself as just a barbaric copy of the real thing. As Plautus says himself, with joking self-deprecation, at *As.* 11, *Demophilus scripsit, Maccus uortit barbare* ('Demophilus wrote it, Maccus turned it barbarian'), and at *Trin.* 19 *Philemo scripsit, Plautus uortit barbare* ('Philemon wrote it, Plautus turned it barbarian'). This is a dramatic

85 Mauron (1964: esp. 10). He agrees that the primary purpose of Plautus and Molière is to make us laugh – but that is not the same as everyday-life laughter. His psychoanalytical approach to comedy makes interesting reading alongside that of the near-contemporaneous study by Segal (1987: 1st edn 1968). Both are Freudian-style psychoanalytical readings of comedy, with Segal concentrating on the pleasure principle versus the reality principle, and Mauron concentrating on father–son conflict as the cause of humour.

86 See Orr (1996: 206): '[m]imesis itself is, of course, a matter of repetition'.

87 Moi (1986: 37); Kristeva's essay 'Word, Dialogue and Novel' was first published in *Séméiotiké* (1969). For the theoretical underpinning of intertextuality as repetition, encompassing also parody and stock elements, see Orr (1996: 210).

illusion there to be broken, as it is most obviously when Plautus parades his triumph over Greek plays in such moments as Chrysalus' disparaging comment about *isti . . . Parmenones, Syri, / qui duas aut tris minas auferunt eris* ('those Parmenoes and Syruses who cheat their masters of two or three *minae*', *Bac.* 649–50),[88] or Tranio's ironic offer to any friend of Diphilus or Philemon to provide some better material for comedies.[89]

Intertextuality, especially intertextuality as a form of repetition, is, then, a model for the relationship between Roman comedy and its Greek 'originals', as well as between Roman comedy and other literatures. The general truth that all texts grow out of a nexus of other texts is enhanced, reduplicated even, in the case of this genre, by a kind of 'special relationship' between Roman comedy and Greek New Comedy. 'The original' thus becomes a 'strong intertext', while a range of other intertexts may also be seen to be at work. The major obstacle in the way of investigating ancient comedy in this manner is that so much material is missing.[90] The only actual texts of more than a few words that we can put side-by-side are the famous parallel passages of Plautus' *Bacchides* and Menander's *Dis exapaton*.[91] Although we know a great deal more about both Roman and Greek comedy and their possible interactions than the bald statement above would suggest, it is worth remembering how shifting are the sands on which our readings in this area are built. With that caution, I recommend the vocabulary of intertextuality in order to consider the relationship between, for example, Menander's *Dyskolos* and Plautus' *Aulularia*, or Menander's *Epitrepontes* and Terence's *Hecyra*. It might not be entirely unreasonable to consider these plays as more important for our understanding of the Roman plays than the 'true originals' of Plautus and Terence, at least if our aim is to appreciate the play texts rather than to identify 'elementi Plautini'.

Repetition is also, I suggest, a better way of understanding the 'stock plot', which we are taught is the basis of most new comedies, and the 'stock characters' which go along with it. The audience's fun in the stock

88 See Damen (1995) for a reading of this line and of the 'duplex' trickery at *Bac.* 641 as a joke (active and passive trickery counting as two – same trick), in which it is Plautus' joke with Menander that is most important and amusing. Fraenkel (1960: 57) argued that the third deception is a Plautine invention.

89 See Anderson (1993), esp. 30, 48, 58, and indeed his entire ch. 2, which is written under the aegis of that offer at *Mos.* 1149.

90 See Eco (2005) for a similar argument with regard to Greek tragedy.

91 The seminal article of Handley (1968) has gone a long way towards getting out of these parallel passages what they are willing to give. See also Damen (1992) and (1995), where he argues, rightly I think, that 'likenesses can be misleading'; the interpretative potential of the parallel passages is limited. See Halporn (1993), who suggests that we ask 'How did Plautus read?' (sc. Menander), in preference to Fraenkel's question 'How did Plautus translate?'

elements of comedy comes from the humorous pleasure of recognition and in spotting the sameness and difference – what one might perhaps call the gaps in iterability.[92]

PLAUTUS – ENNIUS – EURIPIDES: *UT PARATRAGOEDAT CARNUFEX!*[93]

Parody is a comic mixture of intertextual allusion, repetition and the Bergsonian 'automative' Jack-in-the-box. Comic parody repeats another work's lines a little bit askew, out of context, inappropriately. It often, though not always, involves an element of self-parody of the comic work's own pretensions. Often the parodic repetition has a kind of life of its own, beyond anything directly relevant to the ends of the play. Plautus was an early master of this kind of parodic repetition, as we can see even from the few snippets we can identify. Even from the meagre scraps of republican tragedy that have come down to us, it is abundantly clear that Plautus and his audience, like Aristophanes and his audience, enjoyed playing around with tragedy and tragic parody. Classic examples are the tragicomic masterpiece *Amphitruo*, the great Troy metaphor in *Bacchides* and a mad scene in *Menaechmi*.[94] What follows here is not a general assessment or a complete account of what is known about tragic allusion in Plautus, but a consideration of how the interplay with tragedy might work, taking *Rudens*

[92] On stock characters in Roman comedy, see esp. Hunter (1985: ch. 3); Duckworth (1994: esp. 236). On the contribution of stock characters to the theory of humour, see Charney (1987: esp. 69–74).

[93] *Ps.* 707, the old man commenting on the performance of Pseudolus: my suggestion, by means of the poetological role of Pseudolus, is that the *carnufex* who *paratragoedat* in this case is actually Plautus – or could it be also Euripides or Ennius? Silk (2000b) writes movingly of Aristophanes' love affair with tragedy and its role in the creation of his poetic genius.

[94] The major discussion of Fraenkel (1960: 60–8) links Pl. *Bac.* 932 (*o Troia . . .*) specifically with Ennius' *trag. fr.* XXVII Jocelyn, *o pater, o patria, o Priami domus*, as do Jocelyn (1967: 87) and Erasmo (2004: 29–30). Scafoglio (2005) argues for reading Pl. *Bac.* 962–5 as a parody of Ennius' *Hecuba*. Zwierlein (1992: 13–19) excises most of Chrysalus' song, but even what is left is a much slimmed-down Trojan parody. Knapp (1919) is a seminal work for the role of intertextual reference (although he could not call it that) in Roman comedy, which he found to include 'especially in Plautus, a surprising amount of material bearing on Latin literature rather than Greek' (231). Tragic intertexts are most clearly at work in *Am.*: Stewart (1958); Lefèvre (1999b); Slater (2000). Lefèvre (1998) reaffirms his case that *Am.* derives from a tragedy of the same myth, refining it also with contributions from native Italian improvisatory drama. Oniga (2002), who opposes (205) the view of Stewart and Slater that there is a particular relationship with *Bacchae*, presents the construction of this play as a kind of 'bricolage' (208) of many different genres, including epic (Naevius) as well as tragedy (Ennius). Petrone (1983: 62–3) connects the swapping of places of Philocrates and Tyndarus in Pl. *Capt.* with that of Orestes and Pylades in Euripides' *Iphigenia Taurica*. Sheets (1983) argues against seeing direct parody in most cases, but rather takes the view that Plautus 'appears to be participating in the creation of a new Roman comedy, one which combines the formal structure of Roman tragedy with much of the style and humour of the country farce' (206), a parallel tradition, perhaps, to the Lefèvre school. I stick with parody. Andrews (2004) reads Pardalisca's big scene in *Cas.* 621–719 as a tragic parody.

as an example. I present these generic games as a form of repetition, in which much of the humour depends on how both the specific intertext and the generic framework pop up and are recognised in the comic text.

The issue of allusions being recognised touches on a problem at the heart of the Plautine question: to put it simply, when is the allusion 'in Plautus' and when is it 'in the Greek original'? Answer: when it is recognised by the audience, since allusion is in the eye of the beholder. My concern here is with an audience (be it original, revival or modern, reading or viewing) of the Plautine play; therefore, even if the Plautine allusion or parody can be shown to have a parallel allusion or parody in the Greek comedy on which the Roman is in any sense modelled, that does not of itself undermine the role of the allusion in the reception of the Plautine play by its audience (for some audiences and situations, indeed, it may even enhance it). One of the ways in which Plautus' audience will know the plays of Euripides is through adaptations of them by recent and contemporary tragedians, including Livius Andronicus, Naevius and Ennius. Moreover, the kinds of interactions at work here may have a number of different routes into the consciousness of those involved, even if we restrict ourselves only to ancient audiences: direct knowledge of Euripides (in particular) through texts and through performances, albeit not necessarily of complete plays; indirect knowledge of Euripides through Diphilus (presumably only as text, which we have to assume is the way that Plautus and a select few others knew the Greek comic writers); direct knowledge of Ennius, together with other republican playwrights, through performance and later texts; indirect knowledge of Euripides through performance (and later texts) of Ennius.[95] Add in the possibilities of some epic texts, both Greek and early Roman, and we have a very complicated mix.

Plautus' *Rudens* is an unusual play, with its wild coastal setting,[96] its opening shipwreck and the extent of its flirtations with tragedy.[97] It rivals

[95] See Skutsch (1968: 179), apropos the *Rud.* prologue: '[w]e may certainly rule out the possibility that an accident could have brought a Plautine mention of the Euripidean play as translated by Ennius into this close contact with a Diphilean prologue line imitating and varying Euripides'. See Gentili (1979: 16–34) on the dissemination of Greek theatre in southern Italy, including (19–30) on the life of excerpts, esp. from Euripides.

[96] See Konstan (1983: 86) on the significance of the setting, and Leach (1974) for the point that Plautus is concerned more with theatrical effect than with geographical accuracy.

[97] The play's major modern commentator, Marx (1928), provides a useful summary of scenes with tragic connections in *Rud.* (274–5). He assumes that much or all of the tragic allusions in the play are to be attributed to Diphilus rather than Plautus, a view which will not stand up to the identification of Plautine allusions to Ennius, although of course those connections by no means undermine the possibility that Diphilus also wrote a play containing allusions to Euripides and others. Telò (1998) argues convincingly for a close connection, including at the verbal level, between the recognition scenes of *Rud.* and of Euripides' *Ion*.

even its likely near-chronological neighbour *Amphitruo* in interweaving farce and high drama. The setting, a wild, uncivilised, African coast away from the town of Cyrene, itself an exotic location, would evoke a Euripidean tone through such plays as *Helen* and *Iphigenia among the Taurians*, in contrast with the urban propriety which is the norm of comedy.[98] More significant still is the shifting generic framework of the play, which moves through four model play-types, from 'escape' and 'suppliant' (broadly and generically tragic) to 'arbitration' and 'recognition' (broadly and generically comic).[99] The play also offers extremes of verbal repetition, a farcical 'in-and-out' structure where the characters constantly keep missing each other and a massively reconciliatory ending, in which even the baddies join the party. Piled up on the (quasi-)tragic side are Arcturus, the shipwreck, the priestess, suppliants at the altar, various gods and divine forces, and moralising notions about vengeance; on the other side are Sceparnio, the love story, bickering slaves and a happy ending.

The action opens with a divine prologue spoken by the star Arcturus, who has an inflated sense of his own and the play's importance. It will be thirty lines before he gets around to telling us anything about the play, so he uses his warm-up act not to ingratiate himself with the audience but to threaten and impress us. Arcturus is the policeman for a vengeful Jupiter, who seeks out the pious and the perjured and deals with them according to their deserts (10–21). We should be reminded of that other divine helper of the king of the gods in his interactions with mortals – Mercury in *Amphitruo*;[100] the disreputable behaviour of the gods in *that* tragicomedy throws into sharp relief the generic claims of *this* prologue for a far more morally serious interaction with high drama. But Plautus is winking at us behind Arcturus' back, for this opening is likely to be a parody of Ennius:

98 Handley (2002: 109–10) compares this setting with that of Menander's *Leukadia*, a play set 'on a cliff-top on the island of Leukas' (from which the fictional Sappho makes her legendary leap). That play also featured a friendly (female) temple custodian. Handley is surely right to see significant intertextual activity between the two plays.

99 One might wish to see a connection here with Euripides' *Alcestis*, which moves from a tragic paradigm in its first half to a comic paradigm in the second. See Wohl (1998: 144–51), and the references in her n. 65, for the debate about the generic interplays of *Alcestis*. Wohl herself sees the most interesting interplay as being between 'not tragedy and satyr, but rather tragedy and sympotic literature' (149). Recognition is, of course, by no means wholly comic, since it has a crucial tragic role as *anagnorisis*. This favourite device of the New Comedy of Greece and Rome descends mainly from Euripides.

100 The impossibility of being sure about the relative chronology of the two plays means that we cannot make any strong claims about the direction in which the allusions work here for the original audiences, but some degree of interaction seems inevitable. See Lefèvre (1998: 13).

> Qui gentis omnis mariaque et terras mouet,
> eiius sum ciuis ciuitate caelitum.
> ita sum ut uidetis splendens stella candida
> (*Rud.* 1–3)

He who moves all nations, seas and lands, of his city of sky-dwellers I am a citizen. And so I am, as you see, a shining bright star.

He who moves all nations, seas and lands: the tone is elevated, the language formulaic and almost ritual. Skutsch has argued for seeing an allusion in *Rud.* 1 to the opening line of Ennius' *Alcumena*,[101] which itself probably derives from Euripides' lost *Alkmene* (and must, given its subject matter, have some intertextual connection with Plautus' *Amphitruo*). The likely Ennian identity of this opening is enhanced by further Ennian hints in the second and third lines. Formulations like *splendens stella* have parallels in the fragments, for example at *trag. fr.* LXXXIII Jocelyn: *o magna templa caelitum commixta stellis splendidis* ('oh great temples of the sky-dwellers mixed with shining stars').[102] Especially with the presence of *caelitum* in our line 2, there may well be a direct allusion here again, reinforced if Skutsch is right to think that we should have *trag. fr.* CLXIa Jocelyn (*incerta*)[103] in mind here, *qui templa caeli summa sonitu concutit*, since the *templa caeli* there would link with *templa caelitum* in *trag. fr.* LXXXIII and *ciuis ciuitate caelitum* in *Rud.* 2.[104] According to our source, Varro *L.* 7.6, *fr.* LXXXIII Jocelyn comes from Ennius' *Hecuba*, and is likely to be early in the play.[105] A few lines later (and even fewer if any version existed without 6–8), comes another similar formulation to describe Jupiter: *qui est imperator diuom atque hominum Iuppiter* ('Jupiter who is emperor of gods and men', 9). Just in case we had not got the message.

So Arcturus says: 'I am a citizen of his city of sky-dwellers. And so I am, as you see, a shining bright star.' Do we see any such thing? Can we tell what he is meant to be before he tells us? In a modern performance

[101] See Skutsch (1968: 177–81). The identification comes by way of the possible Ennian allusion in Ter. *Eu.* 590, on which see pp. 222–3 below, an identification not accepted by Jocelyn (1967: 63). Fraenkel (1942: 13) suggests a connection (of Diphilus' underlying prologue) with a fragment of Philemon.

[102] Possibly to be compared also is Enn. *trag. fr.* XXXIII Jocelyn (Andromacha): *quae caua caeli / signitenentibus conficis bigis*, which our source (Varro *L.* 5.19) says is addressed to Night.

[103] Skutsch (1968: 179) refers to the fragment as '*scen.* 380' because he is using Vahlen's numbering. For consistency, I have continued to use Jocelyn's numbering, where it is counted among the *incerta*: see Jocelyn (1967: 137).

[104] See Jocelyn (1967: 307) for more on the tone of *templa caeli/caelitum*.

[105] See Skutsch (1968: 177–9). Since Varro says it is spoken by Hecuba, it may not be the prologue, which was probably spoken by the ghost of Polydorus.

perhaps he might have a shiny badge shaped like a star.[106] I'm a star I am, can't you see? And moreover, can't you see I'm an Ennian star? Even if the extent and precision of the Ennian references must remain uncertain, for Plautus' purposes what matters is that Arcturus draws attention to his heroic status, with the overblown language and overdetermined allusions to the heroic world. If Arcturus starts out somehow standing on the stage house, as in Aeschylus' *Agamemnon* and parodies like *Amphitruo*,[107] then his divine and tragic status is further enhanced. It might even be possible that he starts up on the house, and comes down to stage level at line 7,[108] when he mentions walking among mortals in the day.[109]

Arcturus has a strong sense that the wicked (that is, the perjured) will come to no good, while the good will be saved. Hindsight gives us a clear programmatic reading to this threat, since perjury will be personified in the pimp Labrax, and indeed even a first-time reader might be able to guess where things are going; there is also a generic game going on here, with tragic notions of revenge and the evil which necessarily comes of evil. Arcturus' world-view belongs to high drama and serious poetry, but the seeds of comic comeuppance are already sown.[110] Not only will no-one finally suffer in this play, but also Arcturus lets his tragic mask slip for a moment when his threat is formulated in comic slave terms: *quis hic quaerat malum* ('who is looking for trouble around here', 16).

Arcturus' account of the plot is something suitably comic: a recluse who lives next door to a temple;[111] a citizen girl (his daughter) lost in childhood and brought up as a slave, then seen and courted by a rich young Athenian

106 Beare (1964: 194) describes Arcturus 'who apparently wears a "bright star"'.

107 *Am.* 1008 makes reference to the roof, from which Mercury proposes to empty pots of water on the unsuspecting mortals. Stewart (1958: 371) is among those who say that the passage in *Am.* is the only one in Roman comedy to make use of two levels on stage; see also Moore (1998a: 122). Beare (1964: 180) says that in our scene the roof 'would seem to be mentioned'. Frost (1988: 23) mentions the possibility that Tyche, who delivers the delayed prologue in Menander's *Aspis*, could use 'an upper level such as that used for divine epiphanies in fifth century tragedy'. That play is perhaps the most obviously paratragic of the works of Menander: see Hunter, in Fantuzzi and Hunter (2004: 427).

108 It should be noted that lines 6, 7 and 8 are bracketed by Marx (1928) as later interpolations.

109 Fraenkel (1942) analyses this policing behaviour of Arcturus as a lively allusion to Greek philosophical ideas about the stars as divine beings. He attributes the entire ploy to Diphilus, like Anderson (1993) constructing the Greek play directly out of the Roman one. Although his purpose is different, it is worth noting Konstan's presentation of the opening lines of the prologue as self-consciously Roman in their vocabulary and civic thought-patterns (1983: 86).

110 See Moore (1998a: 77–80) on the comic morality of this play: '[i]n *Rudens*, a similar seduction of the audience [i.e. a situation in which "the audience realises by the end that it has been seduced into a play that is anything but edifying"] is accompanied by explicit scepticism about the value of comic moralising' (77).

111 My hint at a connection here with Menander's *Dyskolos* is meant to be nothing more than suggestive of a possible intertextual touch, but a stronger case is made for interaction between the two plays by Lloyd (1963). His particular interest is with the divine prologues.

who seeks to buy her; a perjured pimp who is ready to cheat the young man for extra cash. The pimp was persuaded by a friend to uproot and move to Sicily, where he could expect greater returns on his girls, but Arcturus is having none of it, and as the pimp, friend, girls and treasure sail away he whips up a storm:

> increpui hibernum et fluctus moui maritumos.
> nam Arcturus signum sum omnium <unum> acerrumum:
> uehemens sum exoriens, quom occido uehementior.
>
> (*Rud.* 69–71)

I whipped up a storm and set in motion the waves of the sea. For I, Arcturus, am of all stars the most fierce: violent when I rise, still more violent when I set.

So begins the storm that dominates much of this play, and links it not only with such tragedies as Sophocles' *Nauplios,*[112] and perhaps Euripides' *Alkmene,*[113] but still more with the world of epic, where storms have a programmatic force.[114]

Be that as it may, at the end of the prologue the slave Sceparnio comes in – by the immortal gods what a mess!:

> Pro di inmortales, tempestatem quoiusmodi
> Neptunus nobis nocte hac misit proxuma!
> detexit uentus uillam – quid uerbis opust?
> non uentus fuit, uerum Alcumena Euripidi,
> ita omnis de tecto deturbauit tegulas;
> inlustriores fecit fenstrasque indidit.
>
> (*Rud.* 83–8)

By the immortal gods, what a storm Neptune sent us last night! The wind took the roof off – why say more? It wasn't a wind, but the Alcumena of Euripides, such that it messed up all the tiles on our roof; it made them brighter and gave us some extra windows.

Sceparnio pushes aside Arcturus' epic and tragic pomposity and simplistic moralising with an Aristophanic joke about windy words. It wasn't a wind, but the tragic hot air which did the damage.[115] That overblown tragic

[112] See Marx (1928: 84, 275).

[113] In the argument over line 86 of this play, scholars have seen a reference to a storm sent by Jupiter in order to put out the fires burning Alcumena.

[114] As Fraenkel (1942) says, whipping up a storm is just what we would expect Arcturus to do.

[115] Jocelyn (1966) suggests that the comparison in line 86 is between the wind and Alcumena as the heroine of Euripides' play, who (he suggests) 'may have received her husband's accusation of infidelity with a display of outraged temper that . . . could be compared by contrast with a wind-storm'. Skutsch (1967) replies: '*uentus* and *Alcumena Euripidi* is a contrast not only, in form, of a storm and a play, but also, in essence, a natural storm and a theatrical one. The incidental ambiguity of *Alcumena* as the person and as the play adds to the humour of the passage.' If Skutsch is right about the connection between the Ennian allusions in this prologue and in Ter. *Eu.*, where

prologue has almost blown this comedy inside out. It all comes down to the level of a literalised metaphor – the wind has kindly given us a lighter house and some extra windows. Now the play can start.[116]

Sceparnio's main role is as a programmatic embodiment of comedy. After he has pulled the wind out of Arcturus' sails, he plays a solidly comic opening scene alongside his master (with whom his first interaction is an ironic pretence of liberty: *quasi me tuom esse seruom dicas, Daemones*, 'why, you speak as if I were your slave, Daemones', 99), and the young lover, who tries to get a more respectable romantic comedy off the ground. Plesidippus has to suffer having his conventional greeting (103) mocked, and his masculinity questioned (104), in order to establish the comic tone of the scene, as well as to provide the audience with a programmatic wink about the plot. The slave then keeps on interrupting and insulting the young man as he tries to engage in reasonable conversation with the *senex*, and it is unsurprisingly the slave who holds the upper hand:

> Pl. peculiosum esse addecet seruom et probum,
> quem ero praesente †praetereat† oratio
> aut qui inclementer dicat homini libero.
> Sc. et inpudicum et inpudentem hominem addecet
> molestum ultro aduenire ad alienam domum,
> quoi debeatur nihil.
>
> (*Rud.* 112–17)

Pl. A slave must be excellent and well-off [whom the speech passes by or] who speaks rudely to a free man in his master's presence. Sc. And a man must be lawless and shameless who comes here making a nuisance of himself in someone else's house, where he is owed nothing.

Later in the scene, Sceparnio reduces Plesidippus' attempts to explain all about the pimp's perjury to a joke about that most comic commodity, food:

> Sc. heus tu qui fana uentris caussa circumis,
> iubere meliust prandium ornari domi.
> Da. fortasse tu huc uocatus es ad prandium,
> ill' qui uocauit nullus uenit? Pl. admodum.
> Sc. nullumst periclum te hinc ire inpransum domum:
> Cererem te melius<t> quam Venerem sectarier:
> amori haec curat; tritico curat Ceres.
>
> (*Rud.* 140–6)

the context is a young man comparing himself with Jupiter who entered through the roof in order to have his way with Danae, then there could be an additional connection in the removal of the roof tiles here.

116 See Moore (1998a: 80), where he reads a similar tragic-moralising and comic-debunking interaction between Daemones and Gripus.

SC. Hey you, who go around temples for the sake of your stomach, it would be better for you to order dinner to be prepared at home. DA. Perhaps you have been invited to dinner here, and he who invited you has not turned up? PL. Indeed. SC. It wouldn't do you any harm to go home unfed. It would be better for you to follow Ceres than Venus. The latter has a care for love, but Ceres looks after wheat.

Sceparnio's other scene also plays him as a piece of comic relief, among the heavy stuff about shipwrecks, suppliants and priestesses. It is a classic 'borrowing' scene, where Ampelisca has been sent to get water from next door; this time, Sceparnio's comic mind is not on food but on sex. He will only give Ampelisca the water (that which even enemy gives to enemy, 434) if she will give him *operam . . . quam ciuis ciui commodat* ('the service which citizen grants to citizen', 435). Being a programmatic character who can openly refer to plays of Euripides (and Ennius), he can also make good use of comic costume for an almost Aristophanic innuendo:[117]

> SC. quid nunc uis? AM. sapienti ornatus quid uelim indicium facit.
> SC. meu' quoque hic sapienti ornatus quid uelim indicium facit.
> (*Rud.* 428–9)

SC. What do you want now? AM. A sensible person would be able to see what I want from my equipment. SC. A sensible person would be able to see what I want from my equipment too.

Along with Sceparnio, it is the girls, Palaestra and Ampelisca, who carry the main force of generic play in this comedy. Although as *meretrices* (in the case of Palaestra, uninitiated and therefore to be recognised as a marriageable citizen) the girls clearly belong to the world of comedy, several of the scenes in which they are involved have strong tragic interplays. They ought to be playing comedy, but they keep trying to play tragedy. Our first sight of the girls is not in fact a sight at all, but is mediated through Sceparnio's voyeuristic narrative of their escape from the sea, parallel to Daemones' similar description of the escape of the pimp and his ally, and commented on with ironic unconcern by the unknown father, Daemones himself. This unusually vivid messenger speech sets things up for the paratragic appearance of Palaestra in the next scene. She enters at 185 with a *canticum* (the first of the play) bewailing her sufferings, which she attributes not just to the immediate situation, but to something rather close to the 'slings and arrows of outrageous fortune'. Her world-view as expressed here is similar to that of Arcturus, in that she feels the wrongness

[117] Marshall (2006: 62–3) is surely right to consider it likely that the slave's costume included a visible phallus, here at any rate. There is a nice (illustrated) account of the verbal and visual jokes in this scene by Fontaine (2007: 214–20).

and injustice of someone of her good family and pure morals suffering like this. Her downfall was clearly the result of being in a boat with the wicked.[118] She has lost even her one friend and is now alone (201), like any number of abandoned heroines. She does not know where to turn:

> nunc quam spem aut opem aut consili quid capessam?
> (*Rud.* 204)

Now what hope or help or bit of a plan can I take?

This expression, the content of which is repeated in the scene of her second disaster at 664, resonates with the paradigmatically tragic rhetorical question *quo nunc me uortam?*[119] But there is also a non-tragic element here: Palaestra is not Medea, her predicament is not the result of her own actions, and her situation touches also on the world of epic, at least in its Odyssean adventure-story manifestation. Palaestra is washed up on what looks to her like a barbaric, inhuman shore, where one might expect to meet one-eyed monsters or cannibalistic giants:

> saltem | aliquem uelim qui mihi ex his locis
> aut uiam aut semitam monstret, ita nunc
> hac an illac eam incerta sum consili;
> nec prope usquam hic quidem cultum agrum conspicor.
> (*Rud.* 211–14)

I should like at least someone who could show me a way or a path out of these places. I am so uncertain at the moment whether I should go this way or that way. I don't see any signs of cultivation around here.

But at this point, in case the excitement is too much for the comic audience, we have a comforting piece of dramatic irony for the audience in the know:

> haec parentes mei hau sciti' miseri
> me nunc miseram esse ita uti sum.
> (*Rud.* 216–16a)

My poor parents, you don't know what's going on, how miserable I am now.

After Palaestra's little bit of unnecessary comic exposition, her friend enters for a repeat of her tragic lament, and the two girls go into a visual game which makes a joke of conventions of meeting in comedy, that neither party sees the other until the introductions have been made well and truly clear to the audience. In this case, they skip around each other with echoes

[118] A proverbial view, on which see Otto (1890: 239). [119] See Jocelyn (1967: 118).

and repetitions, finally using a pretence of 'follow my voice' in order to meet up:

PA. quoianam uox mihi
prope hic sonat?
AM. pertimui, quis hic loquitur prope?
PA. Spes bona, opsecro,
subuenta mihi,
AM. eximes ex hoc miseram metu?
PA. certo uox muliebris auris tetigit meas.
AM. mulier est, muliebris uox mi ad auris uenit.
PA. num Ampelisca opsecrost ? AM. ten, Palaestra, audio?
PA. quin uoco ut me audiat nomine illam suo?
Ampelisca! AM. hem quis est? PA. ego Palaestra.
AM. dic ubi es? PA. pol ego nunc in malis plurumis.
AM. socia sum nec minor pars meast quam tua.
sed uidere expeto te. PA. mihi es aemula.
AM. consequamur gradu uocem. ubi es? PA. ecce me.
(*Rud.* 229–41)

PA. What voice is that which near me sounds? AM. I am afraid, who speaks nearby? PA. Good Hope, I beg, help me. AM. Will you release poor me from this fear? PA. Assuredly a woman's voice has touched my ears. AM. It is a woman, a woman's voice comes to my ears. PA. Surely that is not Ampelisca, please? AM. Palaestra, is that you I hear? PA. Why don't I call so that she can hear me speak her own name? Ampelisca! AM. Who is it? PA. It's me, Palaestra. AM. Say, where are you? PA. By heaven I am in terrible trouble at this moment. AM. I am your companion and no lesser part is mine than yours. And I'm dying to see you. PA. You contend with me in that. AM. Let us follow voice with step. Where are you? PA. Here I am.

The scene is delightfully ridiculous, playing knowingly with the conventions of comedy and with the absurdities of realism, while also offering a piece of comic relief which laughs in the face of tragedy. When the girls finally get together, however, there is a return to a paratragic tone, with the acceptance of the need to suffer whatever happens (252), followed by prayers to the gods for deliverance (257–8).

Those prayers are answered immediately by the next scene, with the entrance of the priestess of the shrine of Venus, Ptolemocratia. Here is a character who has stepped straight out of tragedy: almost the only older comic woman not to suffer abuse, clearly named for grandeur, and modelled on such characters as the priestesses in Aeschylus' *Eumenides* and Euripides' *Ion*.[120] Just in case the tragic tone were too much, however, Ptolemocratia

120 See Marx (1928: 98–9): 'es folgt eine neue Szene, einzig in ihrer Art durch das tragische Pathos in Inhalt und Ausdrucksweise'.

responds to the news that the girls have come by ship with the elevated excess that marks a particular kind of tragic parody as quintessentially comic:

> PT. nempe equo ligneo per uias caerulas
> estis uectae? PA. admodum.
>
> (*Rud.* 268–9)

PT. Have you then been borne on wooden horse across the sea-green paths? PA. Yes.

Ut paratragoedat carnufex! Marx (1928: 99) says that the line displays a high pathos of tragedy, although his two quoted examples are Hom. *Od.* 4.708 and Cat. 64.9. A wooden horse, joking metalepsis for 'ship', cannot avoid also epic connotations. Marx mentions (100), without comment on the implications, that *caerulus* occurs only here in Plautus, and elsewhere in preclassical Latin only in Ennius.[121] This is the kind of line where hardly any members of the audience could miss the pop-up from higher genres.

Ampelisca has two comic scenes before the next major tragic moment: the one with Sceparnio discussed above (p. 211), and one with Trachalio (351–413), which constitutes the first meeting of the plot elements whose union is the final goal of the play (the lovers Plesidippus and Palaestra, represented and reflected in their side-kicks Trachalio and Ampelisca). The scene makes interesting contributions to the generic games of this play, not only in the account of Palaestra's high-flown grief over the epic-induced loss of her quintessentially comic tokens of recognition, but also in the third replay of the foundational idea of the plot, the shipwreck. Ampelisca recounts in dynamic terms, with a fair admixture of self-admiration, the girls' escape from the shipwreck (365–71), which had previously been presented through the moralistic blindness of Arcturus and the voyeuristic interest of Sceparnio:

[121] See *TLL* on *caeruleus, caerulus* (the form *caerulus* is preferred by *uetustiores et qui eos imitabantur*), which suggests also the possibility of an early occurrence of *caerulus* in Naevius (reported by Varro *L.* 7.7). According to *TLL*, Ennius has *caerulus* six times and *caeruleus* three, and Plautus one of each. The word, with the form *caeruleus* taking over, becomes more common in classical Latin, being popular with Virgil (sixteen *caeruleus* plus seven of the plural *caerula*) and Ovid (thirty-two *caeruleus* plus nineteen *caerulus*). The other instance in Plautus (none in Terence) is a case of *caeruleus* in *Trin.* 834, *caeruleos per campos*, in another mock-elevated hymn to Neptune, which opens: *salsipotenti et multipotenti Ioui' fratris et Neri Neptuno / laetu' lubens laudis ago*... (820–1). The use of the word *caerulus* to refer to the sky at Enn. *Ann.* 48 Skutsch *caeli caerula templa* may suggest that we should see a hint at Ennius in the use of the word here, given the Ennian sky-allusions in the prologue to this play. I am not suggesting an allusion here to the later *Annals*, but to the likely Ennian usage. It seems reasonable to suppose that Plautus' use of the word here would hit people in the eyes as Ennian and paratragic.

AM. scibis faxo.
<de> naui timidae ambae in scapham insiluimus, quia uidemus
ad saxa nauem ferrier; properans exsolui restim,
dum illi timent; nos cum scapha tempestas dextrouorsum
differt ab illis. itaque nos uentisque fluctibusque
iactatae exemplis plurumis miserae perpetuam noctem;
uix hodie ad litus pertulit nos uentus exanimatas.

(*Rud.* 365–71)

AM. I'll tell you. We both in fear jump from the ship into a little boat, since we saw the ship being carried towards the rocks; quickly I undid the rope, while they were all afraid; the storm took us with the little boat far away from them, over to the right. And so we were tossed by winds and waves in all ways miserable through the whole night; when day came the wind just about brought us to shore half dead.

A little later, while Ampelisca is awaiting the outcome of the comic scene of water-borrowing, the plot takes a sudden turn by means of a repeat of the device whereby a character on stage sees and reports in real time events down at the shore (442–50). Ampelisca sees the arrival of Labrax and Charmides, and suddenly the paradigm shifts to that of a suppliant play:

sed quid ego cesso fugere in fanum ac dicere haec
Palaestrae, in aram ut confugiamus priu' quam huc
scelestus leno ueniat nosque hic opprimat?

(*Rud.* 454–6)

But why don't I hurry up and run into the temple and tell Palaestra all about it, so that we can take refuge on the altar before the wicked pimp arrives to overpower us?

The suppliant scene is doubled up: first presented within the temple of Venus, where the sacrilegious Labrax attempts to drag the girls from the altar to which they are clinging (reported by Trachalio to Daemones at 48–9), and then again on-stage when at Trachalio's suggestion they sit on the altar that is standing there as part of the stage conventions (688).[122] (In the meantime they have paratragically prayed for death.) Such suppliancy, particularly with women as victims, has plenty of tragic intertexts.[123] Of particular interest is a possible connection with the scene in Euripides' *Herakles* when the tyrant and all-round baddie Lycus threatens to burn the family of the absent hero, who have taken refuge at an altar.[124] Now,

[122] Duckworth (1994: 83). In this case it is an altar to Venus. [123] See Marx (1928: 148).

[124] See Marx (1928: 155): he mentions the *Herakles* passage amongst several other examples of burning suppliants, including the disputed Euripides' *Alkmene* and the possibility that the storm alluded to in *Rud.* 86 was sent by Zeus in order to put out the fires that Amphitruo had set against the

the *labrax lupus* is 'a ravenous sea-fish', according to LSJ S.V. λάβραξ, used 'proverbially of greedy persons', and *lupus* is the Latin equivalent of the Greek λύκος, a wolf.[125] In Euripides' play, Lykos gets as far as sending men to fetch wood (*HF* 240–5). In *Rudens*, Labrax introduces the idea through a comic-sounding personification – *Volcanum adducam, is Venerist aduorsarius* ('I'll bring Vulcan; he's the adversary of Venus', 761), and tries to enter into a comic door-knocking routine to borrow wood from next door (i.e. the house of Daemones). But Labrax is on the wrong side, and the slaves refuse to play along: *nullum habemus ignem, ficis uictitamus aridis* ('we haven't got any fire; we live on dry figs', 764).[126] Labrax plans to go and find some wood from somewhere else in order to burn the girls out, and it is at this point that Daemones wakes up to the situation and realises that this tragic tyrant is really just the monkey from the dream.[127]

High poetry does not have a monopoly on the gods and religion, but they do take a significant role in the generic games of this play. Not only does Arcturus open with his mandate from Jupiter, but also the action seems to take place under the guardianship of Neptune. On the surface, this consists simply in a series of jokes, but at another level it links the action with the epic journeys and marine trials of the *Odyssey* story. There may be, in addition, a third tutelary 'god' of this play, the old man Daemones, whose name marks him out for divinity and whose role in the action is as guardian and saviour of all concerned, as much as it is beneficiary of the recognition plot. Daemones unusually is not tricked by anyone, and succeeds not only in controlling his slaves but even in commanding their respect.

Repetitions contribute to the creation of this divine ambience, jokingly so in their immediate contexts, but with an underlying sense of a bigger picture. Even the clichéd exclamation *pro di inmortales!* has a role to play here. It is with these words that Sceparnio interrupts Arcturus' pompous prologue and sets the play in motion (83); with the same words Daemones suddenly notices the shipwreck (148) for the first time and moves the

suppliant Alcumena. Potentially interesting is the Oxyrhyncus fragment of Menander's *Perinthia* (*P.Oxy.* 855), printed in Arnott's Loeb edition (1996) at 480–4, where an old man threatens to burn/smoke out a slave who has taken refuge at an altar, but that scene – old man threatening slave – belongs more obviously to comedy.

125 The connection of the names, and their association with the sea, is noted by Marx (1928: 64). As he notes, the *leno* in *Poen.* is called Lycus. See also Ahl (1985: 93).

126 A rude joke is likely here. Cf. Mart. 1.65: *Cum dixi ficus, rides quasi barbara uerba / et dici ficos, Laetiliane, iubes. / dicemus ficus, quas scimus in arbore nasci, / dicemus ficos, Caeciliane, tuos*; 4.52.2, 6.49.11, 14.86.

127 Connors (2004: 195–6).

play on. The phrase occurs six times in the play, twice from Daemones and three times from Sceparnio, with the final example being, remarkably, from Labrax (1293) when he overhears the words that indicate his 'salvation'.[128]

Another pop-up with serious undertones and comic overtones is the complex of references and jokes about Neptune, washing, drinking and dining.[129] Of the ten direct references to Neptune in *Rudens*,[130] several are typical prayers or personifications (e.g. 84, 486, 906), including one case where the powerful comic Sceparnio heralds the sight of the girls' shipwreck with a moment of paratragedy:

> sed, o Palaemo[n], sancte Neptuni comes,
> qui | Herculei socius esse diceris,
> quod facinus uideo!
>
> (*Rud.* 160–2)

But, o Palaemon, sacred companion of Neptune, you who are called the ally of Hercules, what a crime I see!

Marx (1928: 56) quotes Euripides' *Iphigenia in Tauris* 270–1 here. On one occasion Neptune is hailed by Trachalio as a clever dice-player who has managed to get one over on the cheat;[131] later the same character jokingly likens the sea god to a scrupulous aedile, who has tossed the girls out (of the boat) as *inprobae . . . merces* ('bad merchandise', 372–3). Neptune is associated by both the good and the bad victims of shipwreck with bathing: Labrax calls him *balineator frigidus* ('cold bath-attendant', 527); Palaestra bolsters her suppliant prayer to Venus by pointing out that both girls have been well washed by Neptune (699) and therefore they are ritually pure. It is perhaps worth noting that the two examples just given both serve to link together the two parties from the shipwreck. The final group of references to Neptune links the god to the imagery of drinking which is woven into this play: Ampelisca, expressing to Trachalio the (mistaken)

[128] There are a total of twenty-eight instances of this phrase in Plautus, with the largest number occurring in *Rud.*, and three instances the highest in any other play, in (for the record) *Men.* and *Mos.*

[129] One of the times Sceparnio uses the exclamation *pro di inmortales!*, it introduces a nice commentary on the watery imagery of the play. This is at 458, when he returns with the full water jar to give to Ampelisca (who has unfortunately taken refuge in the shrine on having seen Labrax), and remarks on the pleasure he has got from water, since never before has he found it so easy to draw water from the well: *in aqua numquam credidi / uoluptatem inesse tantam.*

[130] Perhaps unsurprisingly, out of nineteen occurrences of the name Neptune in Plautus, ten are in this play.

[131] Trachalio (358–60): *oh, Neptune lepide, salue! / nec te aleator nullus est sapientior; profecto / nimi' lepide iecisti bolum: periurum perdidisti.* I presume that the sound play in the final two words is intended to suggest that Neptune the dice-player has beaten Labrax at his own game.

view that Labrax and his friend have already perished, says that the pimp was invited by Neptune for a serious drinking bout (362); later, when Labrax has gone off to attempt to get his girls back, Charmides decides to go and sleep off the drunkenness that he has suffered through the excess of Greek wine offered at Neptune's party (586–9).

These repeated Neptune jokes form part of the comic structure of this most repetitious of plays, constructed out of the farce of entrances and exits in which characters keep just failing to meet each other, and epitomised in the scenes of absurd repetition discussed above. There is a serious undertone, however, in that drinking with Neptune really is a matter of life and death, and these repeated scenes of non-meeting are finally guided to their *telos*.

I have been suggesting that *Rudens* is a comedy shot through with tragic moments and generic games. There is one particular kind of tragic moment which belongs quintessentially to comedy – that is parodic direct reference. The 'wind from Euripides' Alcumena' (86) is such a case. There may be another in the reference to Philomela and Progne at 604, in Daemones' dream where the little birds descended from these child-killers are the old man's fellow citizens (Philomela and Procne, as she is more commonly spelt, being also Athenian) and therefore to be protected by him.[132] The same story has already been referred to, along with its kindred spirit in teknophagy, as part of the dinner jokes which are another take on the shipwrecking storm:

> CH. scelestiorem cenam cenaui tuam
> quam quae Thyestae quondam aut posita est Tereo.
> LA. perii! animo male fit. contine quaeso caput.
> (*Rud.* 508–10)

CH. I had a more wicked dinner with you yesterday than the one that was served up to Thyestes or Tereus. LA. Oh no! I feel ill. Please hold my head.

Labrax reacts to Charmides' tragic reference by being sick. As Highet (1942) has convincingly argued, he must be continuing the tragic reference, acting out the reactions of Thyestes and Tereus to their cannibalistic meals.

It is Labrax who gets one of the last tragic laughs. I suggest that many audiences would see a reference to the notorious line in Euripides' *Hippolytus* about the lying tongue when the pimp reneges on his promise to pay

[132] On the difficulties of line 604, see Fraenkel (1960: 78–9), where he attributes the amplification of the story to slightly hazy Plautine mythic knowledge.

Gripus for helping him get the trunk back: *meus arbitratust lingua quod iuret mea* ('I'll decide, what(ever) my tongue swears', 1355).[133]

All these generic games in *Rudens* add up to a programmatic statement of comicness: one which repeats askew the scenes, values, language and characters of tragedy – and trumps them.

BACCHIC REVELS: INTERTEXTUALITY IN TERENCE'S *EUNUCHUS*

In the discussion of *Rudens*, I have taken the intertextual allusions to other plays as parody, as deriving their humour and much of their point from the recognition of the repetition, and the deflating of tragic pomposity which it entails. Terence takes the hint from Plautus, and, as usual, does something different. Like Plautus, but in his own understated way, Terence plays around with the gap between the character/construct you see and the stereotype/stock character you expect: this too is a game between the playwright, audience, character and stereotype.[134]

I begin with an easy and moderately well-known example. As promised in its programmatic prologue, *Eunuchus* introduces a typical comic double act featuring a *miles gloriosus* and a parasite.[135] We are meant to be looking out for them, and to recognise them in advance from what the prologue says, what the parasite Gnatho says about the soldier Thraso, and most of all from our knowledge of earlier plays: the *Kolax* of Menander, those of Naevius and of Plautus, and no doubt also the eponymous *Miles gloriosus*, among others. We have been told to read the play and the pair as repeats of earlier versions. The very notion of repeating with a difference is pushed to centre stage by Terence with this dubious duo. Thraso is the perpetrator and unknowing butt of the 'tired old joke' joke,[136] while Gnatho is the 'knowing character' who does not know that he is not in fact a very good example of the 'knowing character'. He contends with Parmeno the slave

[133] Marx (1928: 231) makes no suggestion of an allusion to Euripides here, but rather refers to his own note on 558 (p. 135), which gives parallels for the notorious perjury of *lenones*, who intend their tongues to serve them, not destroy them.

[134] Gratwick (1987) has an excellent paragraph on Plautine theatricality and the play of persons, which he follows with the claim that 'Terence entirely rejects this complex "play" between audience, representers and represented'. I deny the charge.

[135] See Duncan (2006: ch. 3) for this pairing as meta-characters figuring the actor. She argues that whereas in the Greek comedy it is most of all the *alazon*, or fraudster (from whom the braggard warrior derives), who embodies the Greek world's perceptions about actors, in the Roman world that role is taken by the parasite. See also Muecke (1986).

[136] See above, pp. 163–4.

for the position of *architectus* in this play, a competition which Parmeno just about wins on points.[137]

Gnatho is not a really good example of the stock character, but more like someone *playing the part* of the parasite.[138] His long entrance speech, beginning at 231, is watched by Parmeno, unnoticed and directing the audience's response to the new arrival. Gnatho makes a spectacle of himself, as he recounts his great deeds. On the way, he met an old friend who was in dire straits. When he takes the man to task for not doing better for himself, the poor unfortunate explains that he can't play the fool. Gnatho scathingly points out that parasites are not like that any more. He himself has found a new way of being a parasite: don't try to make your master/victim laugh at you, but rather laugh at him, and admire and agree with him. Parmeno interjects, for the audience's sake: *scitum hercle hominem!* ('a clever man, by Hercules!', 254). The ironic interjection is a statement of Gnatho's stock role, as when Pseudolus comments aside on Callipho as the *lepidum senem!* ('a nice old man!', *Ps.* 435); it is undercut, however, by the fact that Gnatho is not aware of the metatheatrical aside, and so is not really very clever after all. Nor is Gnatho aware that his account of his own cleverness exposes him to the very ridicule to which he imagines he exposes the soldier, who also recounts his own past conquests in wit. Gnatho is no better than Thraso. As Duckworth (1994) and others have noted, Gnatho's programme is not in fact new, for his technique is really very similar to that of Artotrogus with the eponymous *miles* (Pyrgopolynices). This is Terence's joke with the stock character – someone who thinks he is clever, original and good at exposing others, who turns out to be exposed himself. Could there be any self-irony in such a practice?

Self-conscious repetitions of character in the roles of soldier and parasite form part of a complex range of intertextual interactions with earlier comedy which are always at work in Terence; but there is in addition a substantial body of allusions to other literature which find their starting place, perhaps, in parody, but also go beyond such a designation. These allusions seem to be most intense in *Eunuchus*.

[137] Each acts for his master, and is much more effective than him; each serves up the presents which constitute one of the plotlines of the play (Chaerea-Pamphila); each interacts with the audience and tells us how to view the other characters. It is a competition which Parmeno wins, right up until the end, when Parmeno is tricked into confessing to the father, whereas Gnatho gets to set up the final accommodation.

[138] On Duncan's reading (2006), this would make him the perfect example of the parasite, a role which she understands, rightly, precisely as someone 'playing the part'. The difference, however, is that Gnatho does not seem to be self-aware.

The most remarkable feature of *Eunuchus* is that it presents a rape not in the background but part-way through the play.[139] This is one of Terence's most adventurous pieces of writing, not just because it offends against comic convention, but more particularly because it does so by half-jokingly, half-seriously entangling the play with tragedy.[140] In brief, my case is that the young man's disguised intrusion into Thais' house and the off-stage rape together constitute an allusion to the off-stage events of tragedy which drive the action and the tragedy of the play. Specifically, the scene in which the slave Parmeno suggests to his excitable younger young master Chaerea that he might enter the house in disguise finds a powerful intertext in the scene in Euripides' *Bacchae*, where Dionysus tempts Pentheus into dressing up as a woman in order to spy on the maddened Theban women (including his own mother) out on the hillside.[141]

Let us compare the two scenes. In the tragedy, the young king Pentheus has been fulminating against the women who have followed (by force) the new god Dionysus and have been led by him into all sorts of wild and immoral practices. Pentheus is arguing with the disguised Dionysus (disguised, that is, as his own devotee), when suddenly the god calls him to halt, and casts a spell over him with the temptation that he could watch those immoral practices. In order to avoid being seen and torn to pieces by the women (as eventually happens), Pentheus must dress up as a woman.

139 Olson (1968: 82–3) calls it a 'mistake of art'; Goldberg (1986: 115) calls it 'sordid'; see Smith (1994) and Barsby (1999a: 185–6) for other scholars' reactions. Most scholars assume that Terence follows the outlines of Menander's plot, unless there is evidence to the contrary, and that therefore the lapse of taste, if so it is, should be attributed to Menander (although they are rarely explicit about that part of the argument: Whitehorne (1993: 123) is unusual in explicitly ascribing this 'dubious honour' to Menander). See further Barsby (1993: esp. 173–4), where he discusses the likelihood that Menander's *Kolax* contained a siege or an abduction scene, or both, which might (although Barsby does not suggest this) be reflected in the real-time rape. Donatus' choices about when to mention Menander are apparently so random that nothing can be made of his silence on this matter. It would not be impossible for the real-time action to be something more like the violent theft of the prostitute in *Ad.*: this will be unusual for someone who turns out to be freeborn, but a rape within the time of the drama is currently unique in our knowledge of ancient comedy, and therefore the unusual cannot be the enemy of the possible. See Barsby (2000) and (2002) on Donatus as a source of information about Terence's use of his Greek models: as he points out, it is likely that much of the information was already second-hand in the work of Donatus himself, whose work as we have it is only a version cobbled together by some later scholar. In listing the many questions left unaddressed by Donatus with regard to the relationship with Menander, Barsby (2002: 259) makes no mention of the rape.

140 The metatheatrical possibilities of this scene have been noted by Frangoulidis (1993), although not with reference to any play external to that of Terence.

141 The *Bacchae* is possibly the most powerful tragic intertext in the mid republic. See Stewart (1958) 352 for a close reading of parallel scenes in Pl. *Am.* and Euripides' *Bacchae*, again focusing on the interaction between Pentheus and Dionysus, and 356–8 for the popularity of the *Bacchae* in Hellenistic and Roman times.

With some reluctance, Pentheus agrees, and submits to being adorned and led by Dionysus.

The setting for Chaerea's temptation is quite different: he has been enthusing about a young girl, the chance sight of whom in the street has driven him to such a frenzy of desire that he has left his guard duty, temporarily forgotten the friends for whom he was meant to be arranging a party, and chased after her to the place where she is to stay – by chance right next door to his own home. As he fantasises to Parmeno about the good fortune of the slaves in the house with this wonder-girl, Parmeno suddenly says: 'What if you yourself were to become so fortunate?' All he has to do is dress up as – not as a woman, but as the eunuch whom Chaerea's brother Phaedria is just about to send over to Thais. The trap snaps shut. Chaerea picks up the idea. As Parmeno says, he can play the part easily because he looks rather like a eunuch anyway. This barbed comment is really the nub of the matter: Chaerea, like Pentheus, is a very young man, struggling to achieve adult sexuality and unambiguous manhood, but still caught in ephebic ambiguity. Chaerea *is* the eunuch, just as Pentheus is a Dionysiac by nature.[142] But just as the trap shuts, in the comic version the tempter tries to break the spell with laughter – I was only joking, says Parmeno, and tries to dissolve the tension of the scene. But Chaerea is caught, and will not give up on the plan. He will not admit it is all a joke, all a comedy, but instead wants to play the tragic roles that have been suggested to him.

Moreover, it is clear that this young man is rather inclined to notions of tragic grandeur. He wants to play out the roles of heroes, suggested to him by the great intertexts of his text. Inside the courtesan's house, when the girl has been entrusted to him, Chaerea is encouraged in his plan of rape by a picture on the wall, of the rape of Danae by Jupiter, in a shower of gold. The girl herself is looking at it (584–5), presumably uncomprehendingly; Chaerea looks too, but he knows, or thinks he knows, how to read it.[143] Since the god took any opportunity he could, Chaerea would be at fault if he did not do likewise, and 'what a god!', he exclaims, in a parody of Ennius, '*qui templa caeli summa sonitu concutit*' ('who shakes the high temples of heaven with his noise', 590). Donatus tells us that *sonitu concutit* is from Ennius, unfortunately omitting to say which work, although it is clear that it is a tragedy, while *templa caeli* he describes as said *tragice*, but

142 See Dessen (1995).

143 See Barsby (1999a: 195–8); Hunter, in Fantuzzi and Hunter (2004: 430), on the paratragic paradigm of Danae in Menander's *Samia*.

de industria, non errore (Wessner 1962–3 I: 397).[144] Both Livius Andronicus and Naevius, as well as Sophocles and Euripides, wrote a *Danae* tragedy.[145] Although it is by no means a quotation, there is some affinity in Terence's tragic line with a fragment of Naevius' *Danae*:

suo sonitu claro fulgoriuit Iuppiter

Jupiter flashed with his own loud thunder.[146]

The picture is for Chaerea a window into tragedy, and into a divine and heroic role for this confident young man.

There are several verbal and thematic parallels between the *Bacchae* and *Eunuchus* scenes. If there ever was a knowing character in a play, with special access to the poet's voice, it would have to be Dionysus, god of dramatic poetry himself. In Terence's comic version, his role is appropriately taken by the slave Parmeno. Although Parmeno does not play the role of *architectus* in a straightforward way, he is clearly, at least at this point, the 'controlling character', and especially the knowing character, of the play. We must remember the special status of the clever slave in comedy, and in particular the ironic force it has – the clever slave is someone pretending to be less than he is, just like the disguised Dionysus: the *architectus* is well cast as the god of theatre.[147]

Disguised entry into the house leads in the direction of tragedy: in Aeschylus' *Oresteia*, for example, the deaths first of Agamemnon then of Clytemnestra are preceded and prefigured by contests for control over the door, to the extent that entry to the house becomes a metaphor or a sign of the murder itself. It is not hard to translate that observation into the erotic context; the elegiac *paraclausithyron* (song before the closed door) is such a translation, where entry into the house becomes a metaphor for entry into the beloved. But disguised and deceptive entries into houses are surprisingly few in comedy: indeed, although there is a lot of off-stage action in all, including many revelations, there is very little which has the proactive force of this rape.[148] The most important surviving intertext in

144 See Karakasis (2005: 96), in his discussion of markers of elevated language in comedy. Elsewhere (115) Karakasis notes that Chaerea has 'a particular propensity for rhetorical questions . . . , and very frequently uses alliteration and assonance, often linked to the verbal repetition'. The young man is clearly marked out as both comic and paratragic in his language.

145 For the *Danae* of Naevius, see Erasmo (2004: 16–18). That subject is not recorded for Ennius, but it would not be necessary for the quotation to be from a *Danae* play.

146 Text and translation from Erasmo (2004: 18).

147 Frangoulidis (1994b) presents Chaerea as an actor playing a role and Parmeno as his stage director.

148 Off-stage action: many recognition scenes are off-stage; sometimes a character will come out and tell us about the merriment within; babies are born, of course, and sometimes babies are discovered

this regard is probably the entry of the old relative into an all-female festival, in Aristophanes' *Thesmophoriazousae*. Given the intertextual relationship between that play and Euripides' *Bacchae*, a play which I am suggesting is active in Chaerea's scenes, it is not impossible that the most astute members of Terence's audience could pick up some kind of a hint at *Thesmophoriazousae* here, or at least the paradigm.[149] That incident, as in the *Bacchae*, involves a man dressing up as a woman. The other clear example from Roman comedy is in the final scenes of Plautus' *Casina*, where a male slave dresses up as the eponymous girl, and plays the part of bride to his rival slave and the lecherous old man. His purpose is exposure of the lechers. As in *Thesmophoriazousae*, the cross-dressing in *Casina* works like rugby-club drag, to enhance masculinity.[150] Our scene involves a man dressing up as a eunuch, a not-really-man (at whom, incidentally, the *miles* nearly makes a pass, 479). What links *Eunuchus* and *Bacchae* is the way in which it is precisely the demasculinisation of the young man that is crucial to the disguise, and to the entry to the site of erotic desire. It is, moreover, a demasculinisation which draws attention to the less-than-complete manhood of the young man even before the disguise.[151]

After the rape, Chaerea still has not had enough tragedy. His effusive account of the events indoors, to Antipho, is as much like a tragic messenger scene as a New Comic monologue.[152] Indeed, Terence makes a joke of the monologue convention by not having Chaerea address the audience, as we

by fathers; there is the case of Knemon falling down the well in Menander's *Dyskolos*, but that too has tragic overtones, on which see Hunter, in Fantuzzi and Hunter (2004: 427–9), in the context of a valuable discussion of the relationship between New Comedy (esp. Menander) and tragedy which combines elements of parody, role-play and serious appropriation. For the tragic messenger scene as an ancestor of off-stage action in comedy, see Del Corno (2002: esp. 124). Johnston (1933: 143–9) gives a full account of comic off-stage action taking place in a stage house. The rape in *Eu.* is demurely hidden in a list of 'scandalous or exciting scene[s]' (146). See Lowe (2000: 196–7) on the 'typology of comic houses' and their symbolic role in plots.

149 The escape scene in Pl. *Mil.*, although it is not an entry, may also have some affinities with what is going on here. It probably relates to the escape plays of Euripides, such as *Helen* and others that feature in Ar. *Th.* The travelling Menaechmus in Pl. *Men.* does also gain illicit entry into the courtesan's house, but by mistaken identity rather than deliberate disguise.

150 On the cross-dressing in *Eu.* and others, see Whitehorne (1993); Gold (1998), mostly concerned with *Cas.*; Muecke (1982) on Aristophanes and (1986) on Plautus; James (1998c) on this play; and the classic articles of Zeitlin (1981) and (1985). On transvestism in Euripides' *Bacchae*, see Seaford (1996: 222–28); Segal (1997: 170).

151 For the sexual and gender liminality of Chaerea, see Dessen (1995: 132–3).

152 Donatus' comment on this scene is: *bene inuenta persona est, cui narret Chaerea, ne unus diu loquatur, ut apud Menandrum* (Wessner 1962–3 I: 387). Scholars have taken this to mean that Menander had a monologue at this particular place in his corresponding play, but the comment is far too vague to bear that specific meaning, rather than the generally acknowledged point that the Roman poet tends to replace Menander's monologues with dialogue. Many of Donatus' parallels are fairly distant from his *comparandum*.

might expect, but covertly wish someone would come along for him to show off to. His concern to check that there is no-one around is conventional for the telling of secrets and intimate tales on stage, but it is developed by Chaerea in a characteristically lively manner when he imagines someone pestering him with questions about why he is so happy (549–56). As if by magic, Antipho appears. It is only after Chaerea has got it out of his system that he can turn to the lighter comic matters of the evening's party for the young men.

The parallels between Chaerea's and Pentheus' temptations are close on the more detailed level also. There is the fact that the victim asks questions about how the plan will be done; the tempter dresses and adorns the victim himself; tempter and victim must go inside to carry out the adornment; the tempter leads the victim; the victim must go by quiet streets to avoid the notice of the citizens (this is what Chaerea does after the rape when he is trying to get first to the party and then home without being seen in his eunuch costume); Pentheus is worried about the Bacchants laughing at him, while Chaerea actually suffers (or enjoys) that from Antipho. Pentheus' death, for being a man in a woman's world, involves an implication of castration:[153] that is the punishment that the slave-woman Pythias tricks Parmeno, later, into thinking Chaerea is about to suffer.[154] In some cases, the verbal connections are quite close. When asking questions about the plan, each says something like 'what next?' (*Ba.* 832 and *Eu.* 370). Each remarks a version of 'well said: that was clever'. At *Ba.* 824 Pentheus says: εὖ γ' εἶπας αὖ τόδ'· ὥς τις εἶ πάλαι σοφός ('you speak well here; how wise you are from of old'); at *Eu.* 376, Chaerea says: *dixti*[155] *pulchre: numquam uidi meliu' consilium dari* ('you have spoken well: I have never seen a better plan'). There is a secondary link also with Pentheus' final acceptance (846): ἢ τοῖσι σοῖσι πείσομαι βουλεύμασιν ('or I will obey by your counsels'), the final word of which is also picked up by *consilium*. The injunction to go into the house is of course extremely common in drama, but I note that both victims insistently make the suggestion before they actually go. Exactly what is happening depends on an insecure text at *Ba.* 843,[156] but certainly

[153] See Segal (1997: 204–6) for the argument that the cutting down of the pine tree is a symbolic castration.

[154] Barsby (1999a: 262) speculates on the various punishments available for adulterers in different ancient societies, but agrees that castration is probably what is at stake here.

[155] Lindsay prints *dixti* at 376, in keeping with the manuscript, but Barsby (1999a: 154) prints *dixisti* as required by the metre.

[156] Pentheus says (843): ἐλθόντ' ἐς οἴκους . . . ἂν δοκῇ βουλεύσομαι, according to older editions. In Diggle's 1994 OCT, that is said by Dionysus. But note that Pentheus has talked previously about resenting the delay.

at 845–6 Pentheus says: στείχοιμ' ἄν· ἢ γὰρ ὅπλ' ἔχων πορεύσομαι / ἢ τοῖσι σοῖσι πείσομαι βουλεύμασιν ('I'll go in. For either I will take arms and go forth, or I will be persuaded by your counsels'), and earlier resents any delay. Chaerea says (377): *age eamus intro nunciam* ('come on, let's go inside right now', which he follows with the very Pentheusesque *orna me abduc duc quantum potest*, 'costume me and lead me off and on as quickly as possible'), and then repeats the point insistently three lines later – *eamu'*.

By dressing up, Chaerea becomes a sign for Drama as a whole; by cross-dressing, the fact of his disguise is a self-referential sign for the play: he is, quite spectacularly, not what he seems.[157] What this allusion offers us is a comic version of the glimpse of a young man going through the stormy passage to adulthood, until the atmosphere dissolves from passionate tragic emotion into light-hearted comic carelessness. Chaerea does indeed, paradoxically, fail to achieve adulthood through the rape itself. Like Pamphilus' rape of his future wife Philumena, Chaerea's rape can only be a parody of marriage, not the real thing.[158] Pentheus eventually dies, a baby in his mother's arms; while Chaerea, despite everything, is able to slip comfortably into the adult world of marriage, once it has been discovered that his victim is a citizen. That's comedy.

Despite the ludic title of this section and the comic conclusion to my discussion of *Eunuchus* in relation to Euripides, I have been suggesting an intertextual practice for Terence which is rather different from the way in which the *carnufex* Plautus *paratragoedat*. As a coda to that discussion, I present a similar possible Terentian connection with Sappho. Two lines of arguments contribute to an intertextual relationship between Terence and Sappho, one going forwards from the Hellenistic reception of Sappho, and one backwards from Catullus and the later Roman elegiac lover.

It is generally known that an element in the persona of the elegiac lover comes from the *adulescens amans et egens* of comedy, grown up and tidied up somewhat.[159] Although by the time the character reaches his

157 Dessen (1995) reads the eunuch as the organising metaphor of the play, encompassing its ambiguities, dualities and tensions.

158 See Philippides (1995) for the argument that the rape is a symbolic marriage; James (1998c) for this play as an account of boys becoming (Roman) men; McCarthy (2004: 112): 'the *Eunuch*'s main plot-line revolves around a citizen who uses the conventions of stage naturalism to take on the characteristics of a slave, and out of this amalgam emerges an authorised future *paterfamilias*'.

159 See James (1998b: 3 and n. 1); Barsby (1999a: 4). In the past, scholars have been inclined to attribute the connection to a common source in Greek New Comedy. Goldberg (2000) makes a strong case for reading Terence as an important predecessor for Catullus, while Fedeli (2000) in the same volume connects Roman comedy with Propertian elegy in particular in the *topos* of love as a sickness requiring *remedium*.

Ovidian climax he has at least in part returned to his self-centred Plautine origins,[160] there is nonetheless a developing tradition which gives expression to something that relates to later notions of romantic love. Barsby argues that Terence develops a new kind of subjective love or way of expressing love, which is beyond anything in Menander and which constitutes an important precursor to Catullus (and through him also to the elegists).[161] There seems to me to be a good case for this argument, which I do not think is undermined by an earlier presence in this intertextual web, whose work has also been argued to be an important voice in the development of western subjectivity, Sappho.[162] If we can see connections between Terence and Catullus, in places where there are also clear connections between Catullus and Sappho, the question is whether there might be an active connection between Terence and Sappho even before Catullus interacted with either (or both).

A stepping-stone towards seeing allusions to the poet Sappho in the text of Terence is the lively role of the fictional Sappho in Greek comedy.[163] A second step takes us to the convincing case made by Traill (2005) for reading Pyrgopolynices in Plautus' *Miles gloriosus* as a sustained parody of Phaon, with the cleverly deceitful actress Acroteleutium posing in the role of Sappho. The origins of such a parody would be in the biographical/mythic tradition, much used in comedy, of Sappho's love for the beautiful young man Phaon (once an elderly ferryman), who had been rewarded by Aphrodite with irresistible charm, which had gone to his head. Traill takes the argument further, however, by showing how Acroteleutium's expressions of desire also relate directly to the famous Sapphic poem 31, φαίνεταί μοι.[164] My argument is that where Plautus parodies the lyric tradition in its comic form, Terence has his suffering young lover draw subtly and intertextually

[160] Indeed, the ideal Ovidian elegiac lover, as trained by the *praeceptor* of the *Ars amatoria*, also has important affinities with the Plautine tricky slave.

[161] Barsby (1999b): his interest is not so much in the question of literary history as in coming to an understanding of the nature of love as presented by Terence, which he rightly sees as significantly different from both Plautus and Menander. Konstan (1986) is an important precursor to Barsby's paper: he sees 'in Terence's *Eunuchus* an anticipation of elegiac subjectivity' (391). Brown (1993), arguing for the connection between love and marriage in Greek New Comedy, admits that there is little space for reciprocity in even the romantic relationships of Menander, although he does identify it in some cases of already married couples.

[162] See DuBois (1995: esp. 6–7, and ch. 7) on Sappho and subjectivity.

[163] See Most (1996). Most argues that the two 'Sapphos' (the lyric poetess and the nymphomaniac of comedy) must have seemed far less contradictory to classical and Hellenistic audiences than they do to us, against the view that the 'obscene comic invention rushed to fill in the vacuum of accurate historical knowledge' (14).

[164] Traill (2005: 524–5), where she describes Acroteleutium's feigned reaction to seeing Pyrgopolynices as mimicking Sappho's 'panic attack' at the sight of her beloved.

on a famous early expression of love as part of his attempts to develop a new way of talking about emotion.[165]

The action opens with a scene between lovesick young master and helpful, if somewhat cynical, slave, such as we are familiar with from plays like Plautus' *Pseudolus* and *Curculio*. We expect to laugh at the pathetic uselessness of the young man, who does not entirely disappoint, with his rhetorical questions, his self-address,[166] and his slave's parody of his broken, barely coherent language:[167]

> 'egon illam, quae illum, quae me, quae non . . ! sine modo,
> mori me malim: sentiet qui uir siem'
>
> (*Eu.* 65–6)

'I her, who him, who me, who not . . . ! Only let me, I would choose to die: then she'll feel what a man I am.'

His opening words come from the grey area between tragic parody and genuine pathos: *quid igitur faciam?* Donatus (Wessner 1962–3 I: 278) quotes a parallel from Menander – ἀλλὰ τί ποιήσω; ('But what shall I do?') – which scholars have assumed is indeed the opening line of the Greek playwright's own *Eunouchos* on which this one is modelled,[168] but the ancient commentator does not actually say so, and interestingly the other parallel he offers is a misquotation of Dido, at Verg. *A.* 4.534. This is a text which Donatus knows extremely well, but which he now makes to sound as if it is a comedy: *hem quid agam* (Wessner 1962–3 I: 278) instead of the correct *en, quid ago*.[169] Be that as it may, it is possible to see why Donatus should have thought of this particular passage from the *Aeneid*: Dido's despair takes the form of asking rhetorically where she can turn now that Aeneas has betrayed her. It is the moment of *aporia*, epitomised, for example, by Orestes' despairing τί δράσω (Aeschylus' *Choephori* 899). We might laugh at silly Phaedria, but we might also not be quite sure that we are meant to laugh.

165 Traill ends (2005: 532–3) by attributing the whole Sapphic connection to Plautus' Greek original, claiming that although the Roman audience could be expected to appreciate parodies of tragedy and the odd Greek word they could hardly manage an interaction with Sappho. It is not unreasonable to suppose, however, that playwrights, like the writers of children's books, might put in something just for the best-read members of their audience. In any case the situation with Terence is generally accepted to be different.

166 See Barsby (1999a: 94) for the textual problem over the attribution of lines 50–5.

167 It would, perhaps, be going too far to suggest an allusion to Sappho's famous 'broken tongue' here.

168 See e.g. Lowe (1983: 432), in a major discussion of the relationship between the *Eunuchs* of Terence and Menander; Konstan (1995: 132). As Lowe and others (e.g. Brown 1990) have indicated, this opening scene was particularly famous in later antiquity.

169 It is of course possible that the problem lies with the copyist rather than Donatus' memory, esp. for the offending *hem*.

In this play where his overenthusiastic younger brother will perform an absurd 'love at first sight', Phaedria has a much more subtle emotional response to the sight of the beloved. When Thais comes out to meet him, she speaks in monologue, observed by lover and slave, about her concern for the young man. Phaedria's reaction is explicitly to the sight of Thais, but it may reasonably be understood also to be affected by her conciliatory words, supposedly reflecting private thoughts.[170] Phaedria describes the effect she has on him in terms highly reminiscent of Sappho:[171]

totus, Parmeno,
tremo horreoque, postquam aspexi hanc.
(*Eu.* 83–4)

I'm trembling all over, Parmeno, and quivering, as soon as I saw her.

Phaedria's account is a close match to Sappho's:

ὡς γὰρ ἔς σ' ἴδω βρόχε'
(31: 7)

When I see you even a little . . .

and:

τρόμος δὲ
παῖσαν ἄγρει
(31: 13–14)

Trembling overtakes me all over.

As with Sappho, this is a matter not of the dart of Cupid through the eyes causing someone to fall in love (as for Chaerea), but rather an expression of the effect aroused by an existing relationship that has become painful for the speaker because of the involvement of a rival.[172]

Parmeno recognises the allusion, at least to 'symptoms of love' if not directly to Sappho, when he responds pseudo-pragmatically with the rather

[170] Barsby (1999a: 101) refutes the suggestion of Donatus that Thais 'has already seen Phaedria and is saying this for his benefit': being addicted to theatrical deception, I'm with Donatus. The ancient commentator actually attributes the suggestion to others, whom he describes as thinking *non imperite* (Wessner 1962–3 I: 285), since this would fit with the character of the courtesan elsewhere.

[171] Barsby (1999a: 102), commenting on the lemma *tremo horreoque*, says rather non-committally: 'this kind of description of the physical symptoms of love belongs to the lyric and elegiac tradition, best exemplified by Catul. 51 and its Greek model Sappho *fr.* 31'.

[172] Most (1996: 30–1) dwells on the textual and grammatical difficulties of Sappho's sight. There is a strand in the extensive literature on this poem which argues for seeing Sappho's response as one not of jealousy towards the rival, but rather purely of love for the beloved. Be that as it may, the involvement of a rival is clearly not wholly without relevance and is available to Terence to exploit, as Catullus will do later. See Greene (1999).

more common fire metaphor (cf. the λέπτον . . . πῦρ of Sappho 31. 9–10), convenient since he is also warning his master of the dangers of getting too close, while ostensibly inviting him to warm himself up (from his chill, *horreo*) by this embodiment of fire.[173]

Terence's *totus* . . . / *tremo* echoes Sappho's τρόμος . . . / παῖσαν, enhanced by the sound of the cognates *tremo* and τρόμος, a collocation not shared by Catullus' close imitation of Sappho's poem. Catullus shares many of Sappho's symptoms, but not trembling (unless it is missing in the lacuna), and does not describe himself as a 'whole' (Sappho παῖσαν, Terence *totus*) which undergoes these effects.[174] What Catullus does share closely with Terence, however, is the language for describing sight:

> nam simul te,
> Lesbia, aspexi,
> (Catullus 51.6–7)

> postquam aspexi hanc.
> (*Eu.* 84)

Depending on exactly how one understands Catullus' *simul*, it could be said that, despite using some of Terence's vocabulary for his translation of Sappho, Catullus has actually moved away from Sappho's description of the effect of sight towards the more conventional 'love at first sight'.

There are, however, instances of clearer connections between Terence and Catullus.[175] After Thais has secured Phaedria's agreement to keep out of the way for a few days while she makes sure of the soldier's gift, Parmeno is teasing him about his likely inability to hold to his plan of firmness, to which Phaedria responds in 'Catullan' terms with:

> eiciunda hercle haec est mollities animi; nimi' me indulgeo.
> (*Eu.* 222)

This softness of mind must be cast out, by Hercules; I'm indulging myself too much.

[173] Donatus on these lines gets distracted by interest in the paradoxical burning effect of cold, shivering of fire (Wessner 1962–3 I: 284). For the connection between Terence and Sappho we might also note the thought of Ter. *An.* 959–61, where Charinus talks in possibly Sapphic terms about the divinity conferred by proximity to the loved one. It is possible that this is a matter of erotic koine rather than any specific interaction, but there is a potential additional link in Donatus' comment on *An.* 959, that the sentiment has been transferred from Menander's *Eunouchos* (Wessner 1962–3 I: 258). See Fraenkel (1960: 208).

[174] He does talk about all his senses being snatched from him (5–6), but that is not precisely the same.

[175] See Barsby (1999b: 7–10) for the connections between *Eu.* and Catul. 85 and 109.

The language and thought are not dissimilar to those of the final stanza of Catullus' version of Sappho's poem, where he appears to mark a turn away from his model:[176]

> otium, Catulle, tibi molestum est:
> otio exsultas nimiumque gestis:
> otium et reges prius et beatas
> perdidit urbes.
>
> (Catullus 51.13–16)

Leisure is harmful to you, Catullus. You exult in leisure and desire it too much. Leisure has previously destroyed both kings and blessed cities.

The very Catullan idea about the need to strengthen one's spirit against the power of love manifests itself here in the self-accusation that dwelling on Sapphic poetry encourages erotic weakness. It is most familiar from Catul. 8.11, *sed obstinata mente perfer, obdura* ('but with determined mind hold fast, be firm'), language and thought reflected in Phaedria's expressions such as the need to cast out *mollities*, and his enquiry (217–18) about whether Parmeno thinks he can *obfirmare et perpeti* in order not to return earlier than the prescribed three days (not a chance!).

Catullan also, as is pointed out by Barsby (1999a: 96), is Phaedria's expression of his torn emotions:

> o indignum facinu'! nunc ego
> et illam scelestam esse et me miserum sentio:
> et taedet et amore ardeo, et prudens sciens,
> uiuos uidensque pereo, nec quid agam scio.
>
> (*Eu.* 70–3)

Oh unworthy wrong! Now indeed I understand that she is wicked and I am miserable; I'm both sick of it and burning with love, and, although thoughtful and aware, alive and seeing, I perish, nor do I know what I am to do.

The thought here is indeed a 'less pointed and epigrammatic'[177] ancestor of *odi et amo*, but the paradoxical expressions are perhaps more marked than the modern commentator allows. His ancient colleague is more struck by the paradox, which he calls *mire et noue* (Wessner 1962–3 I: 282). Now that we are attuned to it, perhaps we might see the beginning of the allusion to Sappho here, since she too talks about dying as a result of sight (τεθνάκην, 15).

[176] D'Angour (2006) offers a nice reading of this stanza (and alternatives) and its possible interaction with Sappho's fragmentary equivalent.

[177] Barsby (1999a: 96). His discussion at Barsby (1999b: 8) develops the connection.

If I am right to read Terence's use of Sapphic motifs as a way to explore the romantic subjectivity of Phaedria in a sympathetic way, this fits uncomfortably with the notoriously problematic ending of *Eunuchus*, in which Phaedria is easily persuaded to share Thais with the soldier.[178] There may be all sorts of reasons for the odd ending, but the tolerance of a rival is not unknown even in the possessive Catullus:

quae tamen etsi uno non est contenta Catullo,
  rara uerecundae furta feremus erae,
ne nimium simus stultorum more molesti.
  saepe etiam Iuno, maxima caelicolum,
coniugis in culpa flagrantem concoquit iram,
  noscens omniuoli plurima furta Iouis.
(Catullus 68.135–40)

Even if she is not content with Catullus alone, I will bear the occasional 'thefts' of my modest mistress, lest like a fool I should be too much of a nuisance. Often even Juno, greatest of the heaven dwellers, stomachs her burning anger against the fault of her husband, knowing the many thefts of all-desiring Jove.

Sappho, likewise, has to tolerate rivals of various natures. What we have here, I suggest, is something of an intertextual love triangle between Catullus, Terence and Sappho.

INSTAURATIO

There remains one kind of repetition to consider: the literal repeat performance. A mid-republican Roman drama was produced for one particular occasion, although there is clear evidence that revivals did happen, and made an important contribution to later literary culture.[179] One reason why a play might be repeated almost immediately, however, was if the religious ritual of which it was part were in some way flawed. Roman religion

[178] See below, pp. 274–5. Konstan (1986) reads the situation as being in tension between a personal and a commercial love. On Catullus and Terence and sharing the beloved, see also Konstan (1986: 391).

[179] Goldberg (1998: esp. 15–16) argues that the *ludi* may have involved several performances of the same play over the period of the festival, in order to make the play available to more people than could be accommodated in the cramped conditions on the Palatine. The evidence for this is scanty: the only direct piece is the well-known statement in the ancient *Vita Terenti* that the *Eu.* was staged twice in one day (Wessner 1962–3 1: 5), but the idea of 'multiple or even continuous' performance is not implausible, nor would it greatly affect my case, since those repeats would be within the same festival and the same event. On initial and revival performances, see Beare (1964: 164–5); Goldberg (2005b: 64–5). It is possible that performances went on the road outside Rome and outside the festival for which they were commissioned: Goldberg (2004: 394); Marshall (2006: 19–20). The myth of the single performance, as we might perhaps term it, nonetheless retains some currency.

required the correct performance of its rituals: if something went wrong, the ritual had to be started again or the gods would be angry. This practice, *instauratio*, seems to have been extremely prevalent during the mid republic.[180] A number of scholars over the years have suggested that the high prevalence of *instaurati* games during this period might reflect some convenient or devious contrivance in order to ensure repeat performances of popular plays.[181] This would not be to deny that there are political implications in the repetition of rituals which were also public spectacles; indeed, it would reinforce the point.

A classic account of *instauratio* comes in a story told by Livy (2.35.8), and in slightly different form by Cicero (*Div.* 1.55). In Cicero's version, the *ludi* were under way, when a call to arms meant they had to be interrupted; when the crisis was over, the people returned and the ceremony was started again. But just before the events began, a slave wearing a yoke was driven through the forum, being beaten. The games went ahead, but a man suffered terrifying dreams of pollution, until he told the authorities about the harm done to the *ludi*. As a result, they were *instaurati* again, and the gods were appeased.[182] Correct observance applies to the entertainments as well as the more obviously liturgical elements of the *ludi*. There is a proverbial saying: *salua res est, senex saltat* ('It's okay: the old man is dancing').[183] The origin of this, as reported by Servius commenting on Verg. *A.* 8.108, is that once during a mime-performance which was part of the Ludi Apollinares, it was announced that Hannibal was attacking. (This looks like a *topos*.) Everyone rushed to arms. When they returned, they expected that the *ludi* would have to be started again, but they found an old man still dancing, and so the ritual had not been interrupted. Hence the saying.[184]

A READING OF *HECYRA* THROUGH REPETITION

There is one play of Terence which presents itself as having been performed three times, the first two incorrectly. It is the *Hecyra*, a difficult and dense play in which comic convention is examined and found wanting, a play which marks an important theatrical development in fourth-wall realism,

[180] See Scullard (1981: 24). For the specific case of the involvement of *ludi scaenici* in *instauratio*, see Green (1932–3); see also Gruen (1992: 187); Marshall (2006: 18, 21); Duncan (2006: 121).

[181] Duckworth (1994: 78). The arguments, together with previous scholarship going back especially to Taylor (1937), are rehearsed by Cohee (1994) and found wanting. He argues that genuine religious sentiment was the primary reason for the practice of *instauratio*.

[182] Variations of the story are regularly told in Latin literature and historiography: see Cohee (1994: 451–2 and n. 6).

[183] See Otto (1890: 317).

[184] See Beard, North and Price (1998).

the position of the audience, knowledge and silence. Although there is no evidence that the *ludi* at which it was performed, on any of the three occasions, were in any formal sense *instaurati*,[185] it is my suggestion that the practice of *instauratio* provides a useful image for coming to terms with this play, and that the principles behind the practice might well have been in the back of the mind of the playwright and audience. Two rituals have gone wrong in the story of this play: the marriage, and the theatrical performance. Both, I suggest, are tacitly informed by the ideology and practice of *instauratio*, and each reflects on the other. Terence makes an issue of the repeated attempts to perform the play properly, because the play itself makes an issue of the repeated attempts to perform the marriage properly. Both repetitions expose one of the painful truths of Roman culture: women have to be blamed; the Mother-in-Law has to be hated.[186] Both offer the chance of finally getting it right, but not without a sense that other voices are oppressed by that final rightness.

Of all plays of Greek and Roman drama, *Hecyra* is the one which shows the widest gulf between the play-plot as the audience perceives it, and the story which underlies the play and is gradually uncovered.[187] The one aspect of Roman comedy which even the most philomenandrist critic is likely to allow to the barbarians is the development of dramatic suspense and audience misunderstanding through the abandonment of expository prologues.[188] The elements in italics below are those which neither the audience nor the characters know in their right chronological order.

Two prostitutes discuss a young man's marriage, which at least one of them perceives as an act of infidelity to his former lover, also a prostitute. The young man's slave comes out and is enticed to tell the story of his master's marriage. The young man, Pamphilus, was having an affair with a courtesan, Bacchis; his father put pressure on him to marry the daughter of the man next door, and eventually Pamphilus capitulated (*but not before he had raped a girl in passing in the street, and stolen a ring from her, which he gave to Bacchis. The girl was in fact his future wife.*) After the marriage,

[185] See Morgan (1990: 20 and n. 31). She argues that *instauratio* was rare by the time of Terence.

[186] The point is well made by Henderson (1999: 47). See Slater (1988), who reads the play as the story of how male ideological fictions are imposed on inner 'female' truth, which can only slip out for a moment before being suppressed by the decision of Pamphilus to sign up to the oppressive male ideology. Important also is Konstan (1983: 130–41), who designates the play 'ironic comedy', in which the major interest is in 'the operations and tensions of the traditional moral code' (141).

[187] The nearest parallel is the detective story in Sophocles' *Oedipus Tyrannus*, a play which has several affinities with *Hec.*, in that the investigator and in some sense the indirect victim of the crime which stands at the heart of the plot is also the perpetrator. The crucial difference there is that the audience would have external knowledge of the plot.

[188] See esp. on this play Gilula (1979–80); Lefèvre (1999a).

however, he still could not give up his courtesan affair, and did not sleep with his wife for the first few months. (*This point is known by the audience, because Parmeno knows it and tells the prostitutes, but it is not known by the other principals, Pamphilus' parents and Philumena's father. Whether the claim about the continuation of the courtesan affair is true or not is never finally known.*) After Bacchis became increasingly distant (*at least, so we are told by the not-very-reliable Parmeno, but she herself denies that there was any relationship after the marriage*) and the wife, Philumena, showed herself modest and devoted, Pamphilus transferred his affections in the proper direction, and did then consummate his marriage. But then he was sent away by his father on a business trip, leaving his wife with his parents. In his absence, a quarrel has arisen between the wife and her mother-in-law, which has caused her to return to her own parents, an act which undermines her marriage. (*In fact, she has returned because she is about to give birth, and believes that the child cannot be fathered by her husband, being the result of the earlier rape – which in fact was performed by the husband.*) So ends the narrative by the slave. After various arguments between both sets of parents, Pamphilus returns, longing for his wife. When he enters the girl's family home, however, he discovers that the true reason for Philumena's return to her mother is that she is about to give birth. Pamphilus 'knows', as do Philumena and her mother Myrrine, that the child cannot be his, because he did not sleep with her for the first few months. Although he generously (?!) agrees to help cover Philumena's shame, he cannot possibly take her back, despite the fact that the baby is the result of a rape (*and without remembering the fact that he himself had been the perpetrator of such a rape just before his marriage, while he was also involved in another affair*).

Various complications ensue. Sostrata, Pamphilus' mother, generously offers to vacate the house, so that the young couple can live without offence from her. The fathers find out about the birth, believing it to be a normal marital conception. They think that Myrrine is trying to get rid of the baby (which she is) because she is angry (which she is not) that Pamphilus is continuing his affair with Bacchis (which he is no longer, although possibly he was at first). If she were doing so, she would be undermining the marriage. The fathers decide to ask Bacchis to assure Myrrine and Philumena that she no longer has dealings with Pamphilus. When Bacchis goes in to talk to the respectable women, Myrrine notices the ring which belonged to Philumena and was stolen the night she was raped. This part of the story we are told by Bacchis, who knows that this was the ring stolen from the girl raped by Pamphilus. It becomes clear that Pamphilus is the father of his wife's child. All can therefore end happily. Only Myrrine,

Philumena (who does not appear), Bacchis and Pamphilus are allowed to know the truth, in this odd play where no-one knows what is going on most of the time – audience included.[189] It would be nightmarish if it did not – somehow – manage to hold to its comic tone. All is forgiven in Pamphilus' closing metatheatrical coup:[190]

> placet non fieri hoc itidem ut in comoediis
> omnia omnes ubi resciscunt. hic quos par fuerat resciscere
> sciunt; quos non autem aequomst scire neque resciscent neque scient.
> (*Hec.* 866–8)

I don't want it to be here like it is in the comedies, when everyone ends up knowing everything. Here those who need to know do know, but those who rightly should not know do not know and won't find out.

When the play opens, the marriage, which should be the *telos* of the plot, has already taken place,[191] but it is deeply flawed. We can see more clearly its flaws, its repeated failures and its attempts to start again if we place the linear progression of the story in tension with the – different – linear development of the plot.[192] The plots of comedy have an overwhelming generic drive towards marriage, or quasi-marriage. *Hecyra* is firmly placed in that tradition, and indeed is painfully aware of its generic requirements and its own repeated 'failure' to live up to them. The plot of the play interacts significantly in this regard with a whole range of what we might call normative comic plots, and it is in this interaction that we can see the compulsive repetition of *Hecyra*'s plot.

[189] As Slater (1988: 255) rightly points out, since the premarital rape is kept secret, blame for the apparent estrangement would remain with Philumena and Sostrata. But, in true comic style, this point is glossed over.

[190] Donatus marks this moment with his favourite term of approbation *mire*, saying: *mire, quasi haec comoedia non sit sed ueritas* (Wessner 1962–3 II: 340). On this ending, see also Anderson (2002); Lefèvre (1999a: 54–60), who suggests that Terence may have drastically cut the ending in order to avoid comic conventionality.

[191] As is noticed by critics, including Slater (1988: 251). Penwill (2004: 130–1), noting that the original chronology of the plays makes *Hec.* the near neighbour to *An.*, suggests that we should see the young married couple in *Hec.* as a kind of continuation of the marrying couple in *An.*, asking what would happen if the first Pamphilus bowed to parental pressure and married Philumena instead of Glycerium/Pasibula. He reads the play as 'the comic love-hero stripped bare', which is 'not a pretty sight' (141). The point would add to my suggestion that the marriage in this place requires and is subject to repetition.

[192] It is perhaps inevitable that, driven by the play's agenda, we construct the story from the vantage point of Pamphilus, rather than Philumena. The nearest she gets to impinging directly on our notice is reference by other characters to her cries of labour pain, which we do not ourselves hear (314–18). If the story were told from her point of view, it would again be structured around a series of attempts at marriage which go wrong, but which culminate in a final achievement of marriage, however uncomfortable it might be for moderns (and, perhaps, for her), but it would be a story in which she is the passive victim, rather than any sort of agent.

Premarital rape usually leads to marriage, but the rape is acknowledged before the beginning of the play, and the problem is one of courage or of some social barrier to marriage (e.g. Pl. *Aul.*, Ter. *Ad.*, *Eu.*), unless the rape is in the distant past, in which case its purpose is the production of citizen status for one of the young lovers (e.g. Pl. *Epid.*). Courtesan affairs fall broadly, for this purpose, into two types: a first relationship of someone believed to be a courtesan or otherwise unmarriageable, which will turn into marriage by recognition; or a 'genuine' courtesan relationship which is, for the woman, neither first nor last. Examples of the first type include Pl. *Cist.*, *Rud.*, Ter. *An.*, *HT*; of the second, Ter. *HT*, *Ad.* and many in Plautus. The courtesan affair is presented as a common, even 'natural' precursor of marriage for citizen men, but it is something which a man must give up if he is to become a proper adult. Although this idea is lodged in the bedrock of comic plays, it is actually manifested more often in the complaints of fathers ('I tolerated your affairs, but it's time for you to grow out of it and marry': elements of the idea are found, for example, in Pl. *Cist.*, *Mos.*, *Trin.*, Ter. *HT*, *An.*) than in the realities of the plot. In practice, the courtesan affair is something which usually belongs to the *other* plot in a Terentian double play. In *Hecyra*, the double plot has only one protagonist, lover of citizen girl and of courtesan at the same time. The courtesan affair, the rape, the marriage, the remarriage (consummation) are all there, but have all happened before the play began.

Another remarkable feature of *Hecyra* is that we see here the amicable but no longer romantic relationship of recent former lovers. This is unparalleled in Greek and Roman comedy, and provides a scene of extraordinary delicacy, humanity and realism. This really is comedy growing up:

> PAM. o Bacchis, o mea Bacchi', seruatrix mea!
> BA. bene factum et uolup est. PAM. factis ut credam facis;
> antiquamque adeo tuam uenustatem obtines
> ut uoluptati obitu' sermo aduentu' tuo', quoquomque adueneris,
> semper siet. BA. at tu ecastor morem antiquom atque ingenium obtines
> ut unus hominum homo te uiuat numquam quisquam blandior.
> PAM. hahahae, tun mihi istuc? BA. recte amasti, Pamphile, uxorem tuam;
> nam numquam ante hunc diem meis oculis eam, quod nossem, uideram:
> perliberali' uisast. PAM. dic uerum. BA. ita me di ament, Pamphile.
> (*Hec.* 856–64)

PAM. Oh Bacchis, oh my Bacchis, my saviour! BA. You're welcome; it's a pleasure. PAM. You make me believe you by your deeds. And even now you still have your old charm, such that it will always be a pleasure to meet you, talk to you, be visited by you, whenever you arrive. BA. And you indeed still maintain your old ways and character, such that there is no man living more charming than you. PAM. Ha, ha. Can you say that to me? BA. You are right to have fallen in love with your wife, Pamphilus. I have never set eyes on her before today, as far as I know. She seems very well bred. PAM. Tell me the truth. BA. It is the truth, so may the gods love me, Pamphilus.

One of the challenges of the play, especially for modern readers, is the character of Pamphilus himself. We would like him to be nicer, more just, more modern in his attitudes to sex, love, responsibility; we would like him to come to a better understanding of himself and what he has done; we would like to be able to explain his actions. Donatus (Wessner 1962–3 II: 190) mentions, as one of the *res nouae* of the play from a comic perspective, which *nec tamen abhorreant a consuetudine* ('novelties which nonetheless are not out of keeping with custom'), alongside the *beniuolae socrus* ('good-natured mothers-in-law') and the *uerecunda nurus* ('modest bride'), a *lenissimus in uxorem maritus et item deditus matri suae* ('a husband who is most gentle with his wife and at the same time devoted to his mother'; and a *meretrix bona*, incidentally). Most modern readers would find it difficult to designate Pamphilus in this way, however much they might acknowledge that Donatus is right to mark out as unusual in comedy the presentation of a husband in love with his wife (which Pamphilus certainly is).

We could explain Pamphilus in psychological terms, as a study in self-delusion, weakness and uncertainty, in someone who is nonetheless attractive and creates in the viewer a desire to like him, albeit constantly frustrated by his own behaviour. That is all too realistic. On the other hand, we have to confront a character whose actions are sometimes so outrageous that they are inexplicable when read realistically. What do we make of someone who, when supposedly suffering romantic grief at being forced into a marriage despite his love for a courtesan, on the way to visiting that courtesan casually and drunkenly rapes a girl in the street, stealing a ring from her in the process?[193] This is the really *non ueri simile* action on Pamphilus' part (this is what Philotis says at 140, about the non-consummation). We might, perhaps, psychoanalyse it as an effect of the strains caused by the situation, a cry for help or a rejection of authority, but none of this will really help us towards a straightforward realist reading. Moreover, although rapes of citizen girls are a *topos* of comedy, they usually take place at festivals, not in the street. What was Philumena doing alone in the street?

[193] See Penwill (2004: 138): 'one can only come to the conclusion that Pamphilus' rape of Philumena is the worst example of its kind'.

Maybe our information is wrong – we have it only from Bacchis' report of Pamphilus' incoherent confession. Or maybe Pamphilus' actions need to be read primarily in symbolic terms. The question, then, should not be how or even why the rape happened, but how it symbolises one failed, inadequate, improper version of the marriage.

These various plot elements are fitted together by Terence in such a way as to present the story of Pamphilus and Philumena as a series of failed attempts at marriage, as a ritual which is constantly going wrong, constantly being interrupted. Schematised:

Rape (*interrupted by continuation of affair, and by marriage*); marriage (*interrupted again by continuation of affair, either actually or in desire and suspicion*); love/consummation (*interrupted by (a) death of relative and by (b) false quarrel with in-laws leading to (c) return home = divorce*); (*illegitimate*) birth (*interrupted/saved by false accusation of continuation of affair*); overt rejection of affair = recognition = reconciliation.

The story begins with the rape. This act is a metaphorical parody of citizen marriage, a close but false imitation, which serves not to enact the adulthood of the lover (as does true marriage) but to emphasise his immaturity.[194] In normal comic plotting, however, from this act would come personal growth: it would be the first stage on the way to marriage. But in this play, the rape plot (normally precursor to marriage) is itself interrupted by the courtesan affair (which the rape itself interrupts). In the midst of the affair, the next attempt at getting the ritual right is the marriage proper – or rather improper, because it is a ritual left seriously incomplete by the non-consummation. This stage also is interrupted by the continuation of the courtesan affair, or, if we believe Bacchis that the affair did not continue (which we may or may not believe, as we choose),[195] then at least a desire on Pamphilus' part. There is some movement, as Pamphilus gradually transfers his affections (and, symbolically, grows up), during which a further attempt is made to complete the ritual, with the sexual consummation of the marriage; but this too is (*coitus interruptus*) interrupted, by the death of the distant relative which requires Pamphilus to leave his unfinished business. This bolt from the blue may be seen as similar to those stories of *instauratio* where the ritual is interrupted by a

[194] James (1998c) makes a strong case for reading the rape of this play and of *Eu.* as stories of how Roman boys become men. Fantham (2004) makes a case for interpreting Terence's particular interest in young men growing up as arising from him being a teacher. Given his own early death, it seems unlikely that he could have gone very far in developing such a role.

[195] Gilula (1980: 154–61) argues for assigning the lie to Bacchis, in keeping with her reading of all Terentian prostitutes as liars.

call to arms. Sociality and religion (cultural life) are interrupted by business and war (political life).

The beginning of the play also intrudes at this point. Before Pamphilus can return to pick up the pieces, Philumena's situation causes her to send the path to marriage right back to the beginning when she returns to her parents' house. For a handful of lines, Pamphilus' return constitutes a fourth attempt at the marriage. He might have hoped that he would find a situation like that in the story about 'the old man still dancing', which would mean that he would not have to start the ritual again from the beginning, but instead he finds Philumena back at her parents' house, thus symbolising the non-existence of the marriage. In this we can see the damaging effect of improperly performed ritual. Pamphilus is ready to try again, but his next attempt is almost immediately interrupted by the supposedly illegitimate birth. The courtesan affair makes its last appearance now, and causes the act of recognition which changes the baby's birth from being an interruption into becoming the most powerful symbol and enactment of the proper completion of the marriage. The baby now brings retrospective 'redemption' to all the previous failed attempts: it is the completion and justification of the rape, the marriage, the consummation, the return home and the reconciliation. Everything is thus put right. The marriage of Pamphilus and Philumena, we might say, is a *coniugium vies instauratum*. The marriage can start again, and the play can end, its ritual having been properly performed, and social and religious society restored to its proper order. Comedy, for Pamphilus, is getting away with all that.[196]

But does he get away with it? Has the ritual been performed properly this time? According to comic norms and male ideology, all wrongs have been righted. At the level of ritual, this is all that is required. But we might be left wishing that Pamphilus had taken some responsibility for what has happened, rather than just rejoicing in the legitimacy of his son and the – accidental – physical fidelity of his wife (whose personal fidelity was never in doubt). Terence requires us to see a pointed contrast here with this play's strongest surviving intertext, Menander's *Epitrepontes*, in which the rapist-husband Charisios recognises his guilt and is reconciled with his wife in advance of the realisation that his act of rape and the one suffered by his wife

[196] Anderson (2002: 7) suggests that Pamphilus is an 'anti-comic' character, because of his selfish refusal to allow everyone into the secret, but while I am quite taken with Anderson's claim that 'there are no truly happy endings . . . in Terence's comedies' (3), I take this as a sign of Terentian ironic genius, which allows an outrageous comic happy ending in spite of the traces of irony.

were one and the same event. The connection between these two plays was noted already in late antiquity by Sidonius Apollinaris (*Letters* 4.12) when he describes a happy scene of education in which his and the addressees' *filius communis* is reading Terence's *Hecyra*, while the writer himself sits alongside with a copy, so he says, of Menander's *Epitrepontes* in his hands, which he describes as being a *fabula[m] similis argumenti*. The two of them were reading, praising and making jokes together (*legebamus pariter laudabamus iocabamur*) when they were interrupted by (but that's another story . . .). Interestingly, he does not say that they were comparing the two plays directly.[197] The point, however, is the long history of reading *Epitrepontes* as the major intertext for *Hecyra*. Terence may have expected some of his audience also to have that intertext in mind, and to note the distressing violence that the Roman playwright does to the more comfortable solution of increased self-awareness.[198] We know very little about Apollodorus' *Hekyra*, but it must be assumed that some (perhaps very few) members of the audience would have had at least reading access to the play, and might also have noticed Terence's treatment of comic convention there also.[199] Taliercio (1988) reads the small differences which Terence appears, from the briefest of references in Donatus, to have introduced to the text of Apollodorus (*hominem* added to the speech of Laches at 214 (Wessner 1962–3 II: 229), *fidelis* instead of *firmus* for βέβαιος and, depending on the textual reading, the transposition of Apollodorus' ὀλίγαις applying to prostitutes to *paucos . . . amatores* at 58–9 (Wessner 1962–3 II: 203–4)) as holding the key not only to this play but also to Terence's dramatic world. The paucity of our knowledge makes the argument problematic to pursue, but at the very least we can clearly see Terence refusing to behave according to the demands of convention.[200] Terence thus exposes the prejudicial nature of (conventional comic) attitudes to women, and he maintains

[197] It would seem likely that there is some family resemblance between this tale and the famous account in Aulus Gellius (2.23) comparing Menander's *Plokion* and Caecilius' *Plocium*.

[198] See Fantham (1984) for a rather pessimistic account of the extent of Roman readers' first-hand familiarity with Menander. See Konstan (1995: ch. 1) on the gender equality and justice (or otherwise) of *Epitrepontes*.

[199] Lefèvre (1999a) argues for considerable independence in Terence's treatment of Apollodorus. While much of what he says is valuable to the study of the play, and while I would personally be pleased to think in terms of Terentian originality, it does seem to me that the arguments are somewhat circular.

[200] It might be argued that what we can see is Apollodorus refusing to behave like Menander, but the evidence is simply not there. See Hunter (1981: 42), who discusses the interesting relationship as being that between Menander's play and Apollodorus', rather than Menander's and Terence's. Lefèvre (1999a: 160–3) also compares the structures of the two plays.

to – and beyond – the end the uncomfortable innovation of this play, in that we *do not know*.[201]

This question of uncertainty is another aspect of the play which can be explored under the sign of *instauratio*. In this most extreme case of the manipulation of knowledge in any ancient play, readers and viewers are, crucially, not gods: they know nothing more than the characters themselves know. We might even say that viewers are not recipients of the ritual of this play, but partakers in it, only guessing at what the truth might be, what the gods might want, how to get things right.[202] The opening scene provides a good example of the interactions between repeated beginnings and certainty of knowledge.

The play opens with a dialogue between two courtesans, who are soon joined by Pamphilus' slave. They introduce the marriage plot to us through their own vision, which is skewed, according to the standards of citizen (male) ideology (Philotis regrets the marriage, seeing it as an act of infidelity towards Bacchis), but which conveys precisely the uncertainty and instability which characterises the situation. Philotis has just come home from an unhappy sojourn with a Corinthian soldier. Her return enacts a miniature, and more effective, version of Pamphilus' homecoming: it is an act of renewal, a resuming of interrupted relationships which can be happily continued from the point at which they were interrupted. For Philotis, *res salua est, senex saltat*. For Pamphilus, however, the resumption is not so easy, because it is not clear that the relationship was ever properly forged in the first place. The first indication we have that there is a marriage in this play is performed in denial: it is Philotis' indirect quotation (60–2) of Pamphilus' oath that he would never marry while Bacchis lived (a *topos* which erotic language borrows from the marital context which it, in some ways, imitates), followed by the stark comment *em duxit* (63). The next attempt to talk about the marriage directly repeats the same uncertainty. Philotis says to Parmeno *quod ego numquam credidi / fore, ut ille hac uiua posset animum inducere / uxorem habere* ('I never believed it would happen, that he would be able to bring himself to take a wife while she was alive', 98–100). It is answered by Parmeno's rhetorical question which doubts the

201 In Menander's play a slightly delayed prologue gives it all away and so fundamentally changes the meaning of the story for the audience. It seems to me that the absence of reliable information about the major Greek intertexts is a convenient accident of history which makes a programmatic comment on the nature of Terence's play.

202 The realities of ancient dramatic performance would, literally, place the audience as partakers in ritual rather than receivers of it. Conventional metaphorical reading of the audience of drama, however, uses the image of divine power to trope the audience's sense of superiority to the events on stage. The physical layout of both ancient and modern theatres encourages this notion.

substance of the marriage: *habere autem?* (100). He goes on to explain that, although Pamphilus is indeed married, he fears that the marriage may not be secure. This is the cue for exposition of the story, which is then duly produced.

It is Parmeno's task to give us the necessary background information, which, in the normal way of things comic, we would expect to be accurate. But at the end of the play, the last act of which is the explicit denial of knowledge to Parmeno,[203] we would have to look back and question whether he really knows as much as he claims. Parmeno tells us that Pamphilus continued his affair with Bacchis after his marriage; Bacchis later denies this. The answer to the question of which of them is lying or mistaken matters less than the fact that we, the audience, never come to know the truth. Likewise, Parmeno is unclear about exactly when the marriage was consummated (and the question has provoked a great deal of critical interest, since it affects what might or might not be expected of the timing of the birth): all Parmeno says is: *paullatim elapsust Bacchidi atque huc transtulit / amorem* ('gradually he slipped away from Bacchis and transferred his love in this direction', 169–70). We can see in this not just the fact that Parmeno is perhaps less intimate with his master than he would like to suggest (realist reading) but also the implication that even this, rather crucial, moment in the development of the marriage was somehow vague, inadequate, not quite right (unlike normal consummation). This is a play in which nothing is done quite right; it is no wonder that it has to be started again.

The most extraordinary story of failure, repetition and eventual success in Roman comedy comes not in some plot but in the bizarre account of the repeated failures of *Hecyra*. Before we examine the evidence in more detail, we might note that the idea of an 'ill-fated play' is not unique in theatre history. The famous modern example is *Macbeth*, or 'the Scottish play' as the superstitious call it to avoid ill luck. There, as in our case, there is a neat link between the content of the play and the context of its performance. A full-blown tradition of the 'jinxed play' would be unlikely in antiquity, with its strong emphasis on single and first performances, such that under normal (or at least normative) circumstances there would be little opportunity for repeated failures, or, indeed, successes. There is, however, one originary seed in the aetiological account of the word *komoidein*: that troupes whose performance had not been well received in the city tried the countryside

[203] *Hec.* 879–80 (finis): *equidem plus hodie boni / feci inprudens quam sciens ante hunc diem umquam.* The slave-*architectus* bows out.

instead.[204] There is also a small but self-consciously literary tradition of re-presenting poetic collections in 'second editions' for aesthetic purposes, as proclaimed in the pre-opening two couplets of Ovid's *Amores*, which playfully problematise the collection as already a repeat, already a reduction, and an imitation of Callimachus' 'second edition' of the *Aetia*. Perhaps the nearest direct parallel in an ancient dramatic text to such authorial revision, and to the 'failure' of a first version, is the text we have of Aristophanes' *Clouds*, a revision (probably not originally performed) of an unsuccessfully performed play, which the author claimed – within the play itself – was not sufficiently appreciated by the original audience. Aristophanes gives a somewhat ambiguous account of the play's original poor reception in the parabasis of the text we have; if Aristophanic parabases are active intertexts for Terentian prologues, then an oblique allusion to that play might be discernible here.[205]

The story of *Hecyra*, as derived from the text itself, and from the ancient *didascaliae* and *Vita Terenti* which are likely to be highly dependent on Terence's text,[206] goes that on the occasion of its first performance, *Hecyra* had hardly got started when a disturbance of some kind, involving rumours of alternative and less sophisticated entertainments, caused the play to be abandoned. On a second try, at the *ludi funebres* for Lucius Aemilius Paullus, at which Terence' *Adelphi* was also performed, the play managed to get through its opening section, but then pretty much the same thing happened, this time with gladiators. Now, on the third try, later that same year, the play is being presented again. This time, according to the *didascalia*, it was successfully performed.

What, then, is the evidence for *Hecyra*'s troubles? The manuscripts preserve two prologues: one, a mere eight lines long, purporting to belong to the second performance; the other, a more respectable forty-nine lines long, presenting itself as presenting the third performance. Both these prologues are concerned only with the story of failure (repeated, in the case of the second prologue). Also preserved are two ancient *didascaliae*, which belong to different manuscript traditions and report slightly different information, such as that the first performance was at the Ludi Megalenses (*secundum A*) or at the Ludi Romani (*secundum* Σ, although C1 reports *Megalensibus*

[204] Aristotle (*Po.* 1448a) reports the Dorian claim for the origin of drama on linguistic grounds, including the claim that comedy derives from κατὰ κώμας, 'around the villages', from the habit of plays touring the outlying villages when they were dishonoured in the towns.

[205] Rosen (1997: 404) reads Aristophanes' explicit reflection on his rewriting of *Clouds* as 'the actual process of reconceptualizing a performed work as a textual one'.

[206] See note 111 on p. 65 on the reliability of the *didascaliae*; also Sandbach (1982), Parker (1996), Barsby (1999a: 3), Goldberg (1986).

while C2 says *Romanis*). Extant also is the fourth-century commentary by Donatus, who clearly knows much of the same information as the writers of the *didascaliae* (he shares phrasing with the better version in particular), although they disagree even on the question of the authorship of the Greek original (Apollodorus or Menander).[207] All these witnesses add up, by happy accident, to a wonderfully self-referential story of repetition and failure. It is important to remember that Donatus and the writers of the *didascaliae* are probably deriving most of their information directly from the Terentian text. There is no strong reason to suppose that the entire story of failure and re-performance is invented,[208] but there is every reason to ask why we have the evidence we have, and what Somebody (presumably Terence) thought he was doing in consigning this set of evidence to posterity.

If there ever was a first performance, which failed even to get started at the Ludi Megalenses (or, indeed, the Romani) under the curule aedileship of Sex. Iulius Caesar and Cn. Cornelius Dolabella, then it is near-impossible that it was performed *sine prologo*, as is claimed by Donatus and the A *didascalia*. Every other Terentian play opens with a prologue proclaiming, displaying and performing the literary feud between our playwright and his critics. They all open with a concentration on the playwright and what he thinks he is doing right now. If there was a 'first performance', then almost certainly it had such a prologue, which has since been suppressed.

For the second performance, alongside the highly successful *Adelphi* at the *ludi funebres* for Aemilius Paullus, there is a prologue which the author had reason to preserve even after the second failure of the play. It is presented in the manuscripts and by Donatus as being the prologue as delivered in the second performance. I would suggest, however, that this eight-line prologue makes best sense in the context of the more substantial prologue to the third performance, which follows it in the manuscripts. In the second performance itself (assuming there was one), the prologue was probably much longer and more fully developed. A self-deprecatingly brief prologue is not of itself an innovation – several Plautine prologues make this one look prolix – but given the homogeneity of the other Terentian prologues it is unlikely that a play would have been introduced in this way, starkly bringing the play itself up-front immediately (it opens *Hecyra est huic nomen fabulae*), and then mentioning only its previous failure and

[207] It is widely agreed that Apollodorus is the correct attribution.

[208] Segal (2001a: 220) reports the view that the story might be fiction, although at 242 he takes it as fact. Gruen (1992: 213–18) questions the historicity of the Prologue's story. Gelhaus (1972), in his schematic analysis of the rhetorical divisions of Terence's prologues, treats only the third (81–8).

its present newness. If the failure-story were not something out of which Terence is making a big issue, then most likely the Prologue would have used it, if he mentioned it at all, as a springboard for another round with Luscius Lanuvinus (as, for example, he uses that business about the mad young man and the deer in *Phormio*). If the failure-story *is* the big issue, however, then this mini-prologue is perfect, and fits into a neat sequence: no prologue, mini-prologue, complete prologue.

The details preserved are perfect also. Terence says that, in the first performance, an unprecedented disaster struck the play: *nouom interuenit uitium et calamitas* (2). Donatus comments that the vocabulary comes from ritual (specifically, augury): *'uitium' enim est, si tonet tantum, 'uitium et calamitas' uero, si tonet et grandinet simul uel etiam fulminet* ('for it is a "fault" if it only thunders, but a "fault and a disaster" if it thunders and hails at the same time and even clashes with lightning') (Wessner 1962–3 II: 193). (He interprets the twofold trouble as *'uitium' quod non spectata . . . 'calamitas' quod non cognita*, '"fault" because it was not watched . . . "disaster" because it did not become known', which is an interpretation typical of his style and time.) The interruption, then, is presented as an ominous disturbance to the play's ritual, which would need to be expiated by *instauratio*. Next he mentions the prosaic actualities: tightrope-walkers and the *populus . . . stupidus* (this word also has religious connotations).[209] And finally, he offers a cryptic comment which is bait to the historian of the economics of ancient theatre, claiming that Terence is not bringing this play on again in order to be able to sell it again, but rather it is completely new, because 'you can't really be said to have seen it last time'. Whatever the answer to the economics of the case may be, there is an interesting echo of this claim in the first scene of the play: when Parmeno comes out, speaking back into the house, he indicates that if the *senex* is looking for him, then the other slaves should say that he has gone to seek news of Pamphilus' arrival, but that *si non quaeret, nullu' dixeris, / alias ut uti possim causa hac integra* (79–80). If this excuse is not used up now, it can be used again. Like the play.

And then the third prologue, a full-blown Terentian rhetorical performance. Now the *poeta* who usually opens a Terentian prologue is replaced by

[209] Parker (1996), defending the popularity of Terence in his own day, argues that it was not a case of the audience rejecting the play but others rushing in to wait for boxers/tightrope-walkers/gladiators *after* it. Gilula (1978) demonstrates that the audience did not go anywhere but were disrupted by others. Sandbach (1982) is a succinct account of the case for understanding elements in the audience as expecting and demanding a different kind of entertainment. The demands of the uncultured for inferior entertainment have something of the air of a *topos*: cf. Hor. *Ep.* 2.1.182–6.

an *orator... ornatu prologi* (9 = first line of second preserved prologue).[210] As with *Heauton timorumenos*, it is the actor-manager who speaks on behalf of the poet.[211] He comes to defend the poor little play which has suffered so unfairly – just as the other prologues defend Terence from the unfair attacks of jealous critics. Like many other prologues, this one offers a *narratio* of its case (the tale of two failures) and arguments from the persona of the accused, and the persona of the accusers, together with flattery of the audience. Even the jealous-rival *topos* slips in briefly at the end (*ne eum circumuentum inique iniqui inrideant*, 'lest he should be cheated and unjust critics should unjustly laugh at him', 54), just before the final call for attention. This looks like a proper prologue.

My suggestion, then, is that Terence is using the story of re-performance as a way into the understanding of his play: it shows us how precarious, and precious, is the correct performance of comedy, as of social and religious ritual; it shows us how wrongs need to be put right, and how far we are implicated in the wrongs.[212] The series of prologues has been preserved in this form in order to contribute to making precisely these points about failure and repetition. It is possible that we have here a question not of preservation but of invention, but we should remember that the original audience may be presumed to know whether Terence invented the whole story in order to make a point, or opportunistically appropriated the situation that really did arise. I suspect the latter. Although one could imagine a modern production in which the story of interruption and re-start, which the manuscripts play out for us in written form, could actually be performed in the theatre, it would be surprising if so startling an occurrence could have happened in antiquity without leaving any trace in the ancient witnesses.

This play takes to extremes a Terentian norm, which is to deceive the audience into conventional but incorrect ways of viewing. As we watch the opening scenes, we construct the various characters according to stereotype. When Pamphilus' father comes in abusing his wife, we are taken in by it – it is one of the few 'light' scenes in the play – and are encouraged into viewing the mother-in-law like that, into judging by the standards of comic stereotype. This is the story of the play: the *Hecyra* – the Mother-in-Law – has

[210] Donatus says (Wessner 1962–3 II: 196) that Terence uses the term *orator* in place of *poeta* because an orator is sacrosanct and cannot be interrupted without impiety.

[211] It is not sufficiently often remembered that although the speaker is Turpio the author is Terence, exactly as in any other part of his text.

[212] Gowers (2004: 161) also sees the connections between the content of the play and the story of its performance problems.

to be hated. It may be that Terence even offers us a hint, which we can only recognise in retrospect, about this point. The prologue relates how, in the second performance, *primo actu placeo*, 'in the first act of the performance I give pleasure' (39): might this perhaps mean that the first section of the play is the sort of easy comic stuff that audiences expect, and it is only later that we come to realise that we have misinterpreted what we are seeing, that our interpretation has failed?

There is one remaining witness to this sorry tale which we need to consider. Towards the end of the *Phormio* prologue, the speaker asks for the ritual silence and attention: *ne simili utamur fortuna atque usi sumus / quom per tumultum noster grex motus locost* ('lest we meet with the same luck as came about when our troupe was shoved out of its place by an uproar', 31–2). Donatus (Wessner 1962–3 II: 356) makes the obvious interpretation: *apparet Hecyram ante Phormionem actam esse, cui contigit id quod queritur populum subaccusans* ('it appears that *Hecyra* was performed before *Phormio*, since what he complains about, implicitly accusing the people, happened to that play').[213] Assuming that no-one has fiddled with this prologue outside the performance (Prime Suspect: Terence), then this is another performed reference to the first failure of *Hecyra*. The plot of *Phormio*, the one other Terentian play which has Apollodorus, rather than Menander, as its primary model, is also the one which is closest to *Hecyra*'s story of a previously but improperly contracted marriage, which has to be put right for the play to end. Indeed, *Phormio* presents two such marriages: not only the young couple who have married without approval, but also the father who has got himself into a mess by having contracted *two* marriages in the past, in different cities.

Whatever may have happened or not happened earlier, in the final performance Terence manipulated the play's history for his own purposes. It is, after all, a play about misjudgement, about people who jump to conventional comic stereotypes and 'run after tightrope-walkers and gladiators' (metaphorically) rather than seeing true worth. You have been warned – yet you still fall into Terence's trap. (The most sophisticated and self-aware spectator may be allowed to imagine someone else being taken in, rather than himself. There is always a mixture of deception and flattery in the poet's relationship with the audience.) The play is about misjudgements made on the basis of ignorance, something which fits the prologue-story very well. If Turpio's claim that *primo actu placeo* (39) means that people

[213] The ordering of these two plays is confused in the tradition. The natural explanation is that *Ph.* was produced sometime during the on-going saga of *Hec.*

only listened to the scene between Parmeno and the protatic prostitutes, then it is hardly surprising they do not know what is going on.

> You say I am repeating
> Something I have said before. I shall say it again.
> Shall I say it again?
>
> T. S. Eliot, 'East Coker' 3 (No. 2 of *Four Quartets*)

CHAPTER 5

Endings

What begins, must end. From Aristotelian formalists through New Critical aesthetes to post-modern deconstructionists, we all agree that the ending of a work of literature is not just a matter of neutral stopping but is one of the most (perhaps, *the* most) highly charged and semiotically important moments of interpretative activity for readers and audiences.[1] How something ends affects how we finally imagine it to have been all along. Although at the performative level the comic ending is trumpeted by a grand array of signs which signal the end, at the level of plot the comic ending is frequently delayed, repeated and even denied. This playfulness about the possibility of closure is, at the same time, cut across by the Big Bang which almost arbitrarily imposes the end. As Charney says: 'the conclusion of the comic action violates the feeling we have that comedy is dimensionless, nontemporal, infinitely extensible, and not amenable to finite solutions or resolutions.'[2] The comic coup which Plautus and Terence achieve in their different ways is the combination of boundlessness and the transcendence of limits with the powerfully end-stopped consummation, so often signified by the big party.[3]

I begin with exposition of some closural signals which complete a performance, and then consider some of the emplotments and other tricks which cause the play to transcend its own boundaries. In the briefest of summaries, the principal signals which create the end-stop are resolution of the Problem of the play (with or without tying up of loose ends), 'going in' (often to a party), reflection on the play and the final call for applause.

1 'Closure' has been one of the organising principles of the theoretically minded strand in classical scholarship, with major works such as Roberts, Dunn and Fowler (1997). See also Sharrock and Morales (2000). Dunn (1996) is important here, since Euripidean ending, like that of the Roman comedians, represents the triumph of theatre over realism.

2 Charney (1987: 92). In this it is different from the joke, in which the punchline is crucial.

3 I have found useful connections with Shakespearean critics, esp. White (1981), who analyses the interactions of heavily end-stopped comedy and the endlessness of Romance – where there is always another dragon to fight. See also Wilson (1990).

The signs which transcend the end are a whole range of delays, repeats and denials of ending, at the levels both of plot and of performance, together with enticing hints at a fictional continuation beyond the end, again both of the plot and of the mechanics of performance. Tying all this together into one glorious dance (metaphorically, and occasionally literally) is an increasing wildness – farcical, almost surreal – which characterises the comic climax.

HAVING THE LAST WORD

> tu quid ego et populus mecum desideret audi:
> si plosoris eges aulaea manentis et usque
> sessuri donec cantor 'uos plaudite' dicat . . .
>
> (Horace, *Ars poetica* 153–5)

> Listen to what I and the people with me desire. If you want the applauder to wait for the curtain and to stay seated until the *cantor* says 'you lot, applaud' . . .

When a performance finally ends, that fact has to be communicated to the audience quickly and clearly, otherwise the consequences for the whole event are dire because no-one has the confidence to realise that this is the moment to clap. Not all the onus in this regard is on the performers, since the audience also needs to learn to read the signs properly and react accordingly, but the performance itself has a lot of work to do in order to achieve an ending. Applause is not a spontaneous response of pleasure and appreciation: it is a ritualised convention which itself plays a part in the act of performance. Roman comedy, as is well known, had a very simple way of telling the audience '*That's All, Folks!*': an actor says directly to the audience *plaudite*, 'clap now'.[4] All extant Roman comedies end on this note, with some, but not much, variation in the formula. Terence is the more consistent, with three plays ending simply *plaudite* (*An.*, *Hec.* and *Ad.*), while the other three end *uos ualete et plaudite* ('you lot, goodbye, and clap!'). Plautus is much more varied, with only *Cur.*, *Mil.*, *Poen.* and *Trin.* sticking to the basic formulation. Variants are equally easy, however: *plausum date*, *aequom est clare plaudere*, etc., or additions like *exsurgite*,

[4] The modern stage curtain does not always make such issues clear. A lot of modern performance does not use a curtain, and musical performance never has, nor indeed does oratorical performance, including academic seminar papers. The ancient *plaudite* is little different from the conductor's turn towards the audience, the speaker's 'thank you', the singer's bow. They are all ways of saying: 'I've finished, I present this performance to you, it's your turn now.' On the ritualised nature of applause, note the convention that one does not clap between movements in a major orchestral work.

perhaps with the joking familiarity of *lumbos porgite* (e.g. *Epid.* 733), which binds audience and performers in sympathy with each other. In any case, the signs are clear.

What is more interesting and diverse, however, is how we reach that magic moment; how (and if) the signal is integrated into the play, for the *plaudite*, even when it consists of just the single word, does not exist in a vacuum. Occasionally, it might pretend to be unconnected with the play and to be leaping in suddenly (like a *deus ex machina ad absurdum*) to stop the play in its tracks – but it is only kidding.[5] In reality, it has been prepared for in a whole range of conventional but also creative ways through which the coming of the end is signalled. Somehow, the ending has to undo all the work which the prologue began, and move the event, whether smoothly or shockingly, out of the play-world back into ordinary time. This process has been at work from the very beginning, but it is especially the last few lines of plays that stay with the reader or viewer and are most readily available to the audience for questioning over what is going on and what is at stake in the performance.

Conventionally, he who laughs last laughs loudest. In all forms of literature, it is common for the speaker or focaliser of the final lines to gain a power over the procedings which contributes to our interpretation of the work, and I suggest that this is the case in Roman comic plays even where the final speaker is not the protagonist. The reading of last words is made complicated by insecurities of attribution of lines to speakers, but the available evidence is at least suggestive that it might matter who has the final word. In the case of Terence, the manuscripts and Eugraphius on the end of the *Andria* state that a *cantor* speaks the final *plaudite*.[6] It is very likely, however, that the late antique and medieval scholars are being influenced here by a critical history derived from Horace's statement quoted above (p. 251), which probably does not reflect second-century practice. There

[5] In some cases, including all the plays of Terence except *An.* and some Plautine cases including the final (probably non-Plautine) alternative ending of *Poen.*, also *Rud.* and *Trin.*, the closing instruction *plaudite* (or its close relatives) does not grow organically out of any explicit summing up or formal epilogue addressed to the audience. Such an organic growth does happen in most plays of Plautus, including for example *Bac.*, *Capt.*, or even *Men.* It might, therefore, appear to come in almost out of nowhere, but in fact even where it is doing so the end is integrated in other ways. For a more vulnerably tragic version of this point, see Dunn (1996: 13): 'Perhaps because they are so uncertain and so provisional, endings seem anxiously to demand validation; they want gestures to confirm that this is the proper place to end.'

[6] It may in fact not even be Eugraphius himself who says this, still less any trace of Donatus. The comment PLAVDITE, *uerba sunt Calliopii eius recitatoris, qui dum fabulam terminasset, eleuabat auleam scaenae et alloquebatur populum 'uos ualete', 'uos plaudite' siue 'fauete'* is not transmitted by all manuscripts. See Wessner (1962–3 III.i: 85).

is no evidence for a *cantor* who might act in this way in the theatre of Plautus and Terence. I propose, therefore, in common with most modern editors, to understand the farewell formula as spoken by the previous last speaker.[7]

In the case of Plautus, the *plaudite* is usually spoken by one of the characters, continuing from his (or, very occasionally, her) last speech.[8] In some cases, the manuscripts attribute the final lines (including the *plaudite*) to the *grex* or *caterua*.[9] At times, it is dramatically clear that the words cannot be spoken by the previous named speaker, and so the assumption of the manuscripts is almost certainly correct. The *grex*, in these cases, would be playing a role similar to that of the chorus in Greek tragedy, a point to which we will return later.[10] By coming together to address the audience and comment on the play, they signal their own transition out of 'character' and into their role as performers who communally present the play to the audience. This can clearly work well, but there are also cases where the attribution to *grex/caterua* seems less secure, and less dramatically effective. In the cases of *Persa*, *Poenulus* (alternative)[11] and *Trinummus*,

[7] Barsby (1999a: 289) on Ter. *Eu.* also believes that the Horatian passage accounts for the late antique attribution of the final word to a *cantor*. He suggests that the instruction would have been spoken either by all the actors on stage at that moment, or by one, 'here presumably Phaedria'. Unfortunately, the OCT text which I have decided to follow throughout does attribute the final words to a *cantor*. The exits of comedies are almost all in trochaic septenarii, the 'recitative' metre accompanied by music. The designation *cantor* might seem appropriate to this, but it is an anachronism. Beare (1964: 166) takes *cantor* to be simply another word for 'actor'. On the particular issue of who this 'cantor' is to whom Horace attributes the task of speaking the exit-word, Brink (1971: 231) has a firmly agnostic note. In his translation of the plays of Terence, Brown (2006) gives the *plaudite* to the final speaker. See his note on 312, where he also justifies his attribution of the final speech, the *ne expectetis*... lines at 980–1, to Pamphilus rather than Davos.

[8] This is reasonably clearly the case in *Am.*, *Cur.*, *Men.*, *Mer.*, *Mil.*, *Mos.*, *Ps.*, *Rud.*, *St.*, *Truc.* The ending of *Aul.* is missing, and the fragments of *Vid.* do not include the ending.

[9] These terms must mean essentially the same thing. Barsby (1999a: 289) takes both words to indicate those actors who are currently on-stage, which must be right, since there is no evidence for anything like the modern curtain-call involving all members of the troupe.

[10] The plays which seem to me to end unequivocally with a closing speech from *grex* are *As.*, *Bac.*, *Capt.*, *Cist.*, *Epid.* The last of these, for which it would otherwise be nice to argue that the closural formula comes from the mouth of Epidicus, is perhaps however the clearest, since it offers a delightfully absurd *ecce homo* on Epidicus himself.

[11] This assumes the second 'alternative' ending for *Poen.* The ending offered first by the manuscripts has Agorastocles speak the *plaudite* as a continuation of his final speech: *nunc, quod postremum est condimentum* [because he has just been talking about going in to dinner] *fabulae, / si placuit, plausum postulat comoedia* (*Poen.* 1370–1). If that is the correct ending, then it fits the pattern of plays such as *Ps.*, but the metre (iambic senarii) would tell against it, since no other Plautine play ends in that metre (most end in trochaic septenarii). Slater (2000: 160) wonders whether the existence of the two alternative endings might reflect Roman unease about the treatment of Lycus and the law at the ending of that play. For discussion of the ending, see Maurach (1988: 210–13). Lowe (2007: 114) points out that the large number of characters involved shows that Plautus has made major changes to the Greek original, whichever of the endings is the original. On this ending, Henderson (1999: 4):

almost certainly the same phenomenon is occurring as in the Terentian manuscripts, where just the final *plaudite* is attributed to the *caterua.* In these cases also, the endings work better dramatically if the *plaudite* is taken as belonging with the final words spoken immediately before, and probably as spoken by that speaker. This leaves only *Casina*, in which the final speech, including its delightful variation on the *plaudite*, is usually attributed to Chalinus, although there is 'disagreement', as MacCary and Willcock (1976) put it, over the identity of the speaker. I follow them, and Lindsay in the OCT, in leaving the whole speech with Chalinus – who after all has earned it.

A substantial majority of plays are finished off by a pro-comic character. Most of those plays which are finished off by the *grex* also give their penultimate speech to a pro-comic character. By this term, I mean one of the controlling figures of the play, who in 'real life' would be of low social status and little or no power, or a beneficiary of the play who was previously disadvantaged by its problem: that is, it is the powerful underdog whose role affirms comic licence and comic exuberance, and who thus has the opportunity to put the final stamp of his power on the play and on its relationship with the audience. Commonly, although by no means always, this is the *architectus*. Pseudolus' magnificent metatheatrical sleight of hand at the end of his play is, as ever, one of the best examples:

uerum sei uoltis adplaudere atque adprobare hunc gregem
et fabulam in crastinum uos uocabo.
(*Ps.* 1334–5)

But if you want to applaud and approve this company and play, I'll invite you tomorrow.

But he is not exceptional. He is joined not only by other clever, controlling slaves, but also by parasites, prostitutes and badly behaved young men, who get the last laugh in affirmation of their pro-comic status. Here is the roll-call: Chalinus (slave) in *Casina*; Messenio (slave) in *Menaechmi*; Eutychus (*adulescens*) in *Mercator*; Toxilus (slave) in *Persa*;[12] Pseudolus (slave) in *Pseudolus*; Stichus (slave) in *Stichus*; Phronesium (prostitute: the only woman to close a play on her own, which is significant given how unusual it is to have a prostitute dominate a play) in *Truculentus*; Agorastocles

'exit via a sequence of three pick-n-mix finale-scenes, or tattered relics of finale-scenes, each taking a shot at tying up ends that different readings of the play can see as having worked loose'.

[12] Slater (2000) on Toxilus finishing the play, with his own name: 'virtually the Aristophanic hero reborn' (44). Anderson (1993: 78) sees it thus: 'Toxilus the lover has been upstaged by Toxilus the rogue'.

(*adulescens*) in *Poenulus*; Davos (slave) in *Andria*;[13] Phaedria (*adulescens*) in *Eunuchus*; Phormio (parasite) in *Phormio*; Parmeno (slave) in *Hecyra*. And in those cases where the play is closed by the *grex*, the final speakers include Argyrippus (*adulescens*) in *Asinaria* (admittedly, all he says is *ego uero sequor*); Bacchis (prostitute) in *Bacchides*; Epidicus (slave) in *Epidicus*. Perhaps all this is not surprising, since we would probably expect the likes of Pseudolus to take this controlling role, but the prevalence of pro-comic characters speaking the closing lines does show the significance of the ending note as an act of dramatic control.

But what about the other plays? A small but significant minority of plays are closed by a character who might be termed 'anti-comic': that is, someone, usually a *senex*, who in real life would be powerful but who has been defeated in the world of the play, as by comic rules he must be. Given the strength of this closing position (as indicated in the previous paragraph), and given the conciliatory nature of what these characters say, their role and function here can be taken as contributing to the sense of integration, wholeness, completion and jolly good fun with which comedies must end.

A few characters use the final moment to signal their acceptance of what has happened to them during the play, to declare that there are no hard feelings and to affirm the comic spirit. Amphitruo comes into this category, accepting Jupiter's instruction that he should not mind about his wife's unintentional adultery, and giving up on the idea of calling Tiresias and turning all this into a tragedy:[14]

> faciam ita ut iubes et te oro promissa ut serues tua.
> ibo ad uxorem intro, missum facio Teresiam senem.
> nunc, spectatores, Ioui' summi caussa clare plaudite.
> (*Am.* 1144–6)

I'll do as you command and I beg you to observe your promises. I'll go inside to my wife, and give old Tiresias a miss. Now, spectators, for the sake of great Jove, loudly applaud.

Similarly, it is the roundly abused soldier in *Miles gloriosus* who gets to finish off his play, with a 'moral' that signals his acceptance of the ragging he has just received – 'so applaud', because it all ends happily.

[13] With some manuscript support, Brown (2006: 52, 312) assigns the final lines to Pamphilus. It would suit my reading of the play better to assign them to Davos, but it would not matter much here, since Pamphilus is the major beneficiary of the play.

[14] Lowe (2000: 195) notes the closural importance of Amphitruo going inside to his wife, the whole play having been structured around attempts to get through that door.

This is a far cry from the parting shot of such Shakespearean agelasts as Malvolio in *Twelfth Night*, who has to be expelled, threatening revenge, from the finale because he cannot be integrated in the scheme of that kind of comedy's world. In my list I would include also Therapontigonus, the *miles* of *Curculio* who has not only been tricked but also has just 'lost' his bride (though found a sister); Chremes (*senex*) in Terence's *Heauton timorumenos*; and Charmides (*senex*) in *Trinummus*. In all these cases, one effect of it being *this* character who closes the play is to assert or reassert his authority and status, which has been damaged by the process of the play.[15] The last of these cases, however, is an unusual play in that the trickery is stage-managed, albeit somewhat clumsily, by a *senex*, Callicles, on behalf of his friend Charmides and generally for the good of all. It could be said, therefore, that Charmides' role in speaking the play out is an affirmation of the play's inversion of norms.

A contribution to righting the balance may be at work in the ending of Terence's *Adelphi*, a highly complex and problematic exit which also, as it happens, sees Terence bow out of the stage entirely. The fact that it is Micio who closes the performance, after having lost so much ground so quickly in the final scene of a play in which he had appeared to hold the moral upper hand, redresses the balance slightly, but significantly, in his favour. Such a recovery of status and control can sometimes also benefit characters in my first group (pro-comic underdogs), especially when their status in that role has been somewhat dented. Such is the case with Davos in *Andria* and Parmeno in *Hecyra*: Davos had played a full-blown clever slave, but *his* plot has been overturned by Terence's, while Parmeno has had the role of clever slave spectacularly refused him throughout *Hecyra*. Both recover a little, and remind us of their 'proper' role as pro-comic characters, by speaking the play out.

This account just leaves four plays (all Plautine) unassigned: *Captiui*, *Cistellaria*, *Mostellaria* and *Rudens*. I would not accept that it is necessary to 'account' for each of these, in order to bolster my argument about the function of closing words, since four out of twenty-five looks more like *uariatio* than counter-example. In fact, however, there is a story to tell about each of them. In the cases of *Captiui* and *Cistellaria*, there is a *grex* speech which slightly softens the significance of closing speakers, and which is highly metatheatrical, turning attention quickly away from

[15] It is not the case, of course, that all humiliated characters, who are usually *senes*, get to regain status by closing the play. Lysidamus regains a small portion of his severely damaged dignity at the end of *Cas.*, when he receives back his cloak and stick (1009), but he does not get as far as having the last word.

the plot of this particular play into the performative world more widely. In *Captiui*, however, it is significant who does speak last before *Caterua* begins the epilogue. It is Stalagmus, the wicked slave who had kidnapped Tyndarus in childhood, and really set the whole plot in action, though he plays very little role in the play. Responding to Hegio's suggestion that they go inside in order to get a blacksmith to take the chains off Tyndarus and give them to Stalagmus, the slave's reply is ironic: *quoi peculi nihil est, recte feceris* ('that's kind of you, since I haven't a bean', 1028). Not only is this (nearly) the last word, but also it has something of the carefree jokiness in the face of authority and of potential suffering which characterises the clever, controlling slave and pertains to the comic spirit. It is odd that Stalagmus, who has been in no sense a 'clever slave' or a pro-comic character through the play (and indeed has only been brought in, by the magic of comic coincidence, near the end and as part of the resolution), should be given this opportunity to redeem himself. On the other hand, perhaps it does make sense – in a play which has done so much to disrupt normal expectations about freedom and slavery, and which has seen a *senex*, of all people, play something of the controlling comic role. It is perhaps only the ironic unconcern of Stalagmus for his own fate that redeems the play for comedy, allows us to read its end as anaesthetic farce, allows us not to feel – or at least to have a chance of thinking we might not feel – the force of the moral issues raised by the interplays of slavery and freedom.[16]

In the case of *Mostellaria*, the *plaudite* is spoken by the *senex* Theopropides, the object of the play's deception, whose closing words signal the achievement of comic harmony and mutual reconciliation which is necessary for a play to end. He shares the limelight here with the heroic slave Tranio. The final stasis of the play, which delays it from ending, is an argument about whether or not Tranio should be punished for the comic misrule that he has just orchestrated. The master finally gives in only when Tranio points out that there will be other opportunities, other plays, to come in the future:

[16] Leigh (2004b: 89–92) reads Stalagmus as the final piece in the picture of wrongful enslavement and insecurity about status with which the play has been concerned, suggesting that Stalagmus 'did nothing more than what was done to him' (91). In this, he opposes the views of those who see Stalagmus as an Aristotelian 'natural slave', particularly Konstan (1976). See Konstan (1983: 57–72) for an account of the morality of this play, in which he sees Stalagmus as 'the perfect foil for Tyndarus' (70). My reading would support Leigh's interpretation of Stalagmus as showing flashes of a character all too similar to that of Tyndarus, and from there to that to a Plautine *architectus* like Palaestrio, although he uses the point to ram home the moral message of the play, rather than to lighten it. The closural doubling of this play is considered below, p. 286.

> quid grauaris? quasi non cras iam commeream aliam noxiam:
> ibi utrumque, et hoc et illud, poteris ulcisci probe.
> (*Mos.* 1178–9)

What are you making a fuss about? As if tomorrow I won't be committing some other crime: then you can take as much revenge as you like, for this and that.

Theopropides implicitly acknowledges that the issue is metatheatrical when he elaborates the closing formula thus:

> spectatores, fabula *haec* est acta, uos plausum date.
> (*my emphasis, of course*) (*Mos.* 1181)

Spectators, this comedy is finished: applaud.

In *Rudens* likewise, the last words signal not the recovering of status but the celebration of comic integration, most intensely expressed in this play, which ends with everyone, including the pimp and the grumpy slave, invited in to dinner:

> [DA.] uos hic hodie cenatote ambo. LA. GR. fiat. DA. plausum date.
> (*Rud.* 1423)

[DA.] You two both dine with me today. LA. and GR. Okay. DA. Applaud.

On that dinner party, more later.

A PLAY WITH A MORAL

There is a strand in the history of comedy which claims for it a moral function, justifying its excesses by pointing to the cathartic and didactic effect of publicly displaying the downside of human life. There is also a counter-tradition of resistance to this idea of the moralising force of comedy, according to which comedy needs to be saved from the utilitarian agenda and celebrated in its purity.[17] The Roman comic playwrights, in common with some other practitioners through the ages (Aristophanes

[17] Segal's 1987 book (1st edn 1968) is a good example of this pro-comic strand, as is his later book (2001a), although here his thought takes a more serious turn and moves the carnivalesque celebration rather nearer to the tragedy which is never far away. Whitman's celebration of the Aristophanic hero (1964) also partakes of this tradition, which is not unconnected to the major twentieth-century movement around the work of Bakhtin. Kern (1980), whose interest is mostly in Molière, offers a full-scale celebration of what she calls the 'absolute comic'. The best reading of Roman comic drama as a morally serious endeavour is Konstan (1983). Recent critics of Aristophanes (especially) have seen the moralising position as always already self-undermining. The first chapter of Hokenson's study of comic theory through the ages (2006) shows some of the gaps opening and closing between theory and practice in classical and mediaeval attitudes to the moralising force of comedy.

and Molière, to mention only two of the most obvious), tease around the edges of the moral agenda, offering their shows 'for the edification of society', while at the same time undercutting and ironising their position with regard to moral and cultural norms, by offering morals that sound respectable at first sight, but are just a bit askew, just a bit (or more than a bit) wicked. However much a comedian professes to 'teach the city' (Aristophanes), his teaching is always already ironised by the comic context, and most comedians make a virtue of this necessity. Plautus, in particular, exploited the moralising force of tragedy in the endings of some of his plays, by borrowing tragedy's (particularly, Euripides') sententious exit, in which the chorus make some comment on the play's 'lesson', in order to draw a line under and curtain over the proceedings, and to facilitate the transition between the world of play and the world of audience. These tragic 'morals' are often quite banal, and deliberately so, for they represent an ordinary person's attempt to come to terms with the extraordinariness of tragedy. These 'morals' are sometimes themselves also ironised as a deeply inadequate response to the tragic situation, but they are all that the chorus can manage by way of closure for the events of the play.[18] Plautus appropriates both the main features of the Euripidean sphragis *sententia*, if I may so term it: the moralising comment on the tragic situation, and the metatheatrical comment on the performance, usually couched in tragedy as a prayer for victory (which Dunn 1996 also sees as related to the comic *plaudite*). It may seem that there is a harsh disjunction here between the 'inside' of the tragedy and its 'outside', when the chorus suddenly stop talking 'in character' and speak for themselves as actors and the poet as playwright, but this is just one way of marking a crucial moment in the ending of performance: somehow, you have to 'wake up', and find your way back into the real world. And for comedy, where the notion of performance is foregrounded and the distinctions of 'worlds' are always more fuzzy and playful, the slippage is easier still.

If republican Roman comedy does indeed fulfil the function of 'instructing with a smile',[19] and supporting the norms of society, the ending of a play would be just the place for the job: 'You've enjoyed laughing at these fools, but now you've got to come out of the comic world and remember that they *are* fools, and that you've got to behave better.' Undoubtedly there is an element of this potential moralising in all public performance, but we would do well to consider also that one of the first duties of comedy is to

[18] Dunn (1996) has made an excellent study of this phenomenon. See esp. 14–20.

[19] Cf. Horace's famous claim to be writing *lectorem delectando pariterque monendo* (*Ars* 344).

laugh at pomposity. I shall begin with those closing morals which purport to take their sententious job most seriously, then move on to those where the 'moral' seems more like an affirmation of a disruptive comic spirit, and finally consider briefly the use of closing *sententiae* for metatheatrical purposes (although this will always have been in the background to the discussion).

Miles gloriosus ends with the *miles* himself acknowledging 'point' to the *architectus* Palaestrio, when the messenger (in a parody of the tragic messenger, especially of Euripidean escape plays) relates how the 'sailor' and the girl behaved once they were out of sight. Pyrgopolynices has already been abused for his attempted adultery with the pretended wife of his neighbour, and now he has lost the prostitute as well. 'Ah, well,' he says, 'I got what I deserved.' He ends the play:

> si sic aliis moechis fiat, minus hic moechorum siet,
> magi' metuant, minus has res studeant. eamus ad me. plaudite.
> (*Mil.* 1436–7)

If other adulterers were treated thus, there would be less adultery around. They would be more fearful, and less inclined to these affairs. Let's go in to my house. Applaud.

This sententious moral plays into the tradition of the satirists, who see comedy's role as correcting morals by exposing them, and is in keeping with the ultimately conservative strand in some comic theory. On this reading, we 'hear' the 'voice of the playwright' here, proclaiming the moral of this story and upholding the norms of society, and neatly guiding us back into our everyday world, in which adulterers are to be punished. We could just leave it there. But we could also note a hint of irony in the moral: if we really took Pyrgopolynices' advice seriously, where would that leave comedy? *minus has res studeant* (which could be translated 'they would be less interested in these matters') does not sound good for business. If everyone behaved properly there would be nothing to make into a play. But we need not worry too much about comedy's prospects, because the purported 'lesson for society' here is somewhat undermined by the fact that the *miles* does not generally get the girl in comedy anyway, not for reasons of societal morality, but because the comic spirit says so.[20]

A play more consistently po-faced about its own morality is *Captiui*, which has been set up from the beginning as a 'different sort of play',

[20] Konstan (1983) sees the soldier's unlucky role as deriving from his position as a rich outsider to the *polis*, fighting for money and not contributing to the good ordering of society. Whether Plautus' plots and characterisations are quite so well behaved as that I rather doubt.

containing none of the usual comic outrages.[21] The play ends with the grandfather of all closural morals from the *caterua*,[22] whose members must step rather abruptly out of their character-roles in order to deliver the epilogue. They could indicate the transition by removing their masks, perhaps, but it would be naïve to think that even this action takes them outside the world of the play. Rather, it returns them to the beginning, to the moment when the prologue-speaker drew us into the world of the play, frozen for the moment until he kicked it into action.[23] He claimed the moral high ground, as now does the *caterua*:

> Spectatores, ad pudicos mores facta haec fabula est,
> neque in hac subigitationes sunt neque ulla amatio
> nec pueri suppositio nec argenti circumductio
> (*Capt.* 1029–31)

Spectators, this play has been made for modest morals. It has no titillations or love-makings, no substitution of babies nor financial scams.

This is a delightful piece of pomposity, which leaves us in absolutely no doubt about the *pudicitia* of the play, and by implication of ourselves. We, it implies, crave not such things as comedy usually offers – of which, by way of compensation, we then get a list, made absurd by linguistic excesses, like the series of unusual nouns enlisted to describe comedy's norms. *subigitationes* is a hapax legomenon, with a sexiness about its sound which seems almost onomatopoeic, thus belying its high moral pose;[24]

[21] See Franko (1995) for a good analysis of the interactions between comic playfulness and serious morality in this play. He argues (157 n. 2), rightly, that the 'apparent gravity of the circumstances' does not make this play wholly *sui generis* and therefore irrelevant to general discussion of Plautus, since 'the action of the play is in fact standard Plautine fare'. The play has a long tradition of being read as the prologue and epilogue say it should be (although I am suggesting that Plautus is speaking tongue-in-cheek). See Konstan (1983: 58) and Leach (1969a). Konstan (1976) is a sensitive reading of the ethics and politico-moral ideology at issue in the play. As he says, the effect of the comically coincidental ending is that 'the moral issue is deflected or sidestepped, after the fashion of comedy, where a general contradiction in values tends to be resolved by an arbitrary or contingent circumstance which serves for the given instance but fails to meet the problem as such' (85).

[22] If the *caterua* is everyone present on stage, then the moral is spoken by the actors of Stalagmus, Hegio, Tyndarus and Philocrates – which is quite remarkable.

[23] A possible production technique could be to freeze the characters on stage just in the act of walking off, and to have someone else deliver the epilogue, in exact matching of the prologue. As far as I am aware, however, there is no evidence of such a technique being used. Indeed, we have no real evidence about the tableaux at the end of plays at all. The characters go on about 'going in', and we generally assume that they do indeed 'go in', but do they come out again to receive the applause? Or do they simply hear it from inside? Applause is clearly an important part of the performance, but what is happening while it takes place? We do not know.

[24] The word probably sounds like pedantic crudity, the pseudo-technical invented abstract noun playing against the underlying earthy metaphor. Palmer (1954: 70): '[t]he interests of the herdsmen are evident in the term *subigere* "to submit the female to male" or "to bring the ox beneath the yoke"'.

amatio occurs five times in extant Latin literature, all of them in Plautus, and some of the others in similarly verbally playful contexts; *suppositio* occurs four times in Plautus, and otherwise only three times in extant Latin literature (Servius on *A.* 6.317, and Columella twice in the same passage, about the substitution of eggs, Col. 8.5.9 and 8.5.11); *circumductio* has a whole fourteen occurrences in Latin literature, nine of which are in the astronomical writings of Hyginus, and the other four (apart from ours) shared two each by Quintilian and Vitruvius. In authors other than Plautus, then, the diction of these forms is technical. The joke comes not only from the unusual forms and repetitive sound-pattern, but also from the use of rather pedantically prosaic formulations more suited to technical prose than to verse drama.

The play is quite determined that it has nothing to do with the usual sorts of amatory-deceit plots – and yet, as we remember from the prologue, it is not quite so consistently well-behaved as it pretends. While it might be true that *neque . . . amans adulescens scortum liberet clam suom patrem* ('no young lover freed his whore without his father's knowledge, 1032), nonetheless deceit of the father does take place, and an odd sort of *scortum* does also have a role. Still, the epilogue insists on its originality in matters moral: *huius modi paucas poetae reperiunt comoedias* ('the poets invent few comedies of this type', 1033), it claims, with suitably comic alliteration. If we take the epilogue at the substance (rather than the vehicle) of its word, we should not be surprised that not many playwrights produce comedies like this, because the language used here is dangerously close to making us think of tragedy, still more so in the next line: *ubi boni meliores fiant* ('where the good become better', 1034). It is hard not to hear here a reference to the famous Aristotelian definition of tragedy as showing men 'better than they are' and comedy as showing them 'worse than they are' (*Po.* 1448a). We should remember that, in the prologue also, the play flirted with tragedy. So, this pompous epilogue which is so keen to proclaim its good behaviour and by implication to denigrate other comedies ends up by 'accidentally' almost moralising itself right out of comedy altogether! The closural *plaudite* is equally edifying, inviting us to clap if we want to see virtue rewarded. (We should remember this when looking at the endings of *Casina*, *Asinaria* and *Epidicus*, to name but a few.) But underneath the pompous exterior, the signals are still there which tell us that this is all a joke, that we are to take the moralising with a pinch of irony (even if our serious selves, in another context, would actually agree with its values). The classically comic *p*-alliteration of the final three lines performs the same comicising function as the monstrous noun-series a few lines earlier.

The two plays we have considered so far could be read as ending with a 'straight' moral. The next play also poses as offering an edifying reflection on society, but the comic spirit's smile is a little more obvious. The ending of *Bacchides* is overdetermined with closural signals: the young men are inside enjoying the party, the old men have in effect capitulated and are being half-ragged, half-seduced by the prostitutes into joining their sons inside; it is going dark (*it dies*, 1203; *uesper hic est*, 1205) and dinner and bed are waiting inside.[25] When the old men finally agree to be led off (*ducite*, 1205) in order to complete their subjugation and the play, Bacchis comments: *lepide ipsi hi sunt capti, suis qui filiis fecere insidias* ('these men, who laid traps for their sons, have been nicely caught', 1206). Comic justice, the hunter caught. The *grex* picks up her words, to deliver a moral judgement in the manner of a Euripidean chorus – and then slips into the metatheatrical mode which helps to wake us up from the entrancing image of that warm space inside the stage house:

GREX
Hi senes nisi fuissent nihili iam inde ab adulescentia,
non hodie hoc tantum flagitium facerent canis capitibus;
neque adeo haec faceremus, ni antehac uidissemus fieri
ut apud lenones riuales filiis fierent patres.
spectatores, uos ualere uolumus, [et] clare adplaudere.
(*Bac.* 1207–11)

GREX If these old men had not been worthless from youth, they would not today when their hair is white have committed such a crime; nor would we have played the play like this, if we had not seen before now fathers becoming the rivals of their sons in brothels. Spectators, we bid you farewell and invite you to clap.

The tone parodies that of closural comments by Greek tragic choruses, perhaps applying the old moral to 'call no man happy till he dies', or otherwise banally reflecting on the enormity of what we have witnessed.[26] The basic moral is clear: the old men are behaving badly, as they did in their youth, and their opposition to the young men's comic activities throughout the play was therefore just hypocrisy (which, alongside pomposity, is another great comic butt). After that, however, a neat twist: just as the old

[25] The prostitutes' house, more than ever, works in this play as a kind of black hole or warm dark space of decadence or delight, depending on your position with regard to the comic spirit. There may also be a closural hint in the semi-ironic comment of Nicobulus about death: *quam quidem actutum emoriamur* (1204).

[26] Dunn (1996) opens his study of Euripidean ending with the fable about Croesus and Solon, and comments that Euripides subverts this kind of tragic end-story: 'for the rhetorically and morally persuasive end of a hero, Euripides substitutes a flourish of formally persuasive closing gestures' (7).

men would not have acted like this if they had not been bad from youth, so we (the company) would not have put on a play like this if we had not seen such behaviour before.[27] On one level, this means 'we are just telling it how it is; we are exposing the vices of society with a laugh'. Inevitably also, however, the comment must make us think not only primarily of life, but also of other plays (*ut apud lenones riuales filiis fierent patres*) such as, for example, *Asinaria*, *Mercator* and *Casina*.[28] The *sententia* has subtly metamorphosed from a claim for the moral value of comedy in exposing vices into an intertextual celebration of the comic spirit. If Anderson is right in his conjecture that Plautus (in *Bac.*) has substantially rewritten Menander's ending (in *Dis exapaton*), in humiliating the old men rather than engineering a reinstatement of societal and familial values, then the claim that we have seen all this before, and know how to read plays, gains a delightful additional spice.[29]

This comic spirit is affirmed in two similar closural 'morals' which do not even pretend to be respectable: those of *Asinaria* and *Casina*. In both plays, the old man is a rival to his son for the favours of a prostitute[30] (which indicates that *Bacchides* was right about its intertexts), and is exposed at the end in front of his formidable wife. *Asinaria* first:

GREX

Hic senex si quid clam uxorem suo animo fecit uolup,
neque nouom neque mirum fecit nec secus quam alii solent;
nec quisquam est tam ingenio duro nec tam firmo pectore
quin ubi quidque occasionis sit sibi faciat bene.
nunc si uoltis deprecari huic seni ne uapulet,
remur impetrari posse, plausum si clarum datis.

(*As.* 942–7)

GREX If this old man has indulged his pleasure without his wife's knowledge, he has done nothing new or surprising, or different from what others do. There is no-one of such harsh mind and firm heart that he would not do the same thing given half a chance. Now if you want the old man to be let off and not be beaten, we think you'll gain what you want, if you applaud loudly.

The *grex* makes the same kind of claim for the ubiquity of the situation as it does in *Bacchides*, but this time the effect is not to say 'and

[27] *fuissent – uidissemus*; *facerent – faceremus*.

[28] I do not intend to imply that the epilogue of *Bac.* is alluding specifically to those plays, since it is likely that at least *Cas.* is later than *Bac.*, but the motif is not uncommon.

[29] See Anderson (1993: 27–8).

[30] In *Cas.* the girl in question turns out to be freeborn, so the son marries her, while in *As.* she clearly has no chance of that kind of ending, but/so the son gets her anyway, once mother and comedy have conspired to fight off father.

we are exposing this behaviour in order to teach you not to do it', but 'and you would do the same if you got the chance'. The audience is not expected to learn from the experience, but rather is invited to enjoy the vicarious idea of indulging in such comic licence 'ourselves'. And then into the *plaudite*: but this is presented not as 'clap for the triumph over the old man', but 'clap if you want him to get away with it'. The *senex* is necessarily to some extent the 'enemy' of the comic characters, but here, when he is a badly behaved *senex*, even he ends up as a comic character who must be celebrated, not punished. Possibly there is a double meaning in the phrase *deprecari huic seni ne uapulet*, playing on the inversions of power and status endemic to comedy in order to slide the *senex* out of his internal role as Roman gentleman and into his external role as (possibly slave) actor: i.e., if you want the person playing this old man not to be punished for a bad performance, then clap. Such a hint would not, however, destroy the outrageous comic 'moral' in which we are invited to participate.[31]

The slave Chalinus (probably, see above, p. 254) does the same job for *Casina*:

spectatores, quod futurumst intus, id memorabimus.
haec Casina huiius reperietur filia esse ex proxumo
eaque nubet Euthynico nostro erili filio.
nunc uos aequomst manibus meritis meritam mercedem dare:
qui faxit, clam uxorem ducet semper scortum quod uolet;
uerum qui non manibus clare quantum poterit plauserit,
ei pro scorto supponetur hircus unctus nautea.

(*Cas.* 1012–18)

Spectators, we'll tell you what's going to happen inside. This Casina will be found to be the daughter of the man next door, and she will marry Euthynicus our young master. Now it is right for you to give the warranted reward with your deserving hands: whoever does so, may he always get away with a whore when he wants to, without his wife's knowledge; but whoever doesn't clap as loud as he can, may he get off with a goat scented with bilge-water instead of a whore.

Chalinus begins in character, jokingly claiming that he should be the one to complain at his treatment, because he has been 'married' twice in the play, but neither groom has succeeded in his proper role. (He was

[31] Konstan (1983: esp. 51), reading Plautine comedy through the lens of serious social issues in the ancient city state, sees the ending as an affirmation of a moral that Demaenetus must learn his lesson and behave better in future, though he acknowledges (51 n. 5) that the play does not 'conclude in a tone of moral severity'. Henderson (2006: 214–15) reads the end – for the audience – as '[w]alking the line between *uolup* | and *uapulet* | – "kicks" and "a kicking"'. The play celebrates 'the old'uns' – *senes* and old jokes – but it is the audience who have the last word.

disguised as the bride Casina, who was married to the old man's slave so that the old man himself could exercise *droit de seigneur* with her – but Chalinus turned the tables on master and slave.) After that, Chalinus moves a small step further out of the play, to remind us that there is also a recognition plot hiding in the background of this bawdy farce, and that Casina will turn out to be the daughter of the man next door and will marry the son. This wonderfully off-hand piece of plot-completion, which takes only two lines, is (among other things) a parody of the tragic, particularly Euripidean, closural device of continuing a story beyond the confines of the play, usually by means of prophecy.[32] At the level of plot, a recognition and a citizen marriage is the ending we expect, since Casina is a virgin, but at the level of performance the love plot is not much more than a red herring. Chalinus returns to the real business of the play for his well-developed *plaudite*. It is an even naughtier affirmation of the comic spirit than that in *Asinaria*. 'Clap if you want to enjoy a prostitute without your wife knowing; if you don't clap, may you be cursed with a smelly goat instead of a *scortum*.' This would be a suitably comic retribution for anyone not appreciating the play.[33] The *hircus* may implicitly reflect on the wife herself, while the embarrassing substitution of a goat for a girl neatly repeats the high point of the play – the substitution of Chalinus for Casina.

A variation on the celebration of comic licence is offered by an *adulescens* (Eutychus, not the play's 'hero' but his friend) as epilogue to *Mercator*. The play's issues have been solved, more or less, and just as the remaining characters are about to go inside to finish it off (*eadem breuior fabula / erit*, 'to make the play shorter', 1007–8, as is pointed out, interestingly by the *senex* Demipho), Eutychus stops the action for a moment, in order to lay down a law about the appropriate comic behaviour of the generations. The 'law', expressed in a parody of legal language,[34] provides that old men, especially fathers who try to be amatory rivals to their sons, will not be allowed to get the girl, and that if anyone tries to get in the way of his

[32] See Dunn (1996), on the Euripidean practice in pointing outside the confines of the play: see esp. ch. 5. Dunn (1996: 64): 'Greek tragedy, unlike many other forms of drama, presumes a historical and cultural continuum that embraces both the events enacted onstage and the viewers themselves, and the Euripidean aition overtly complicates this thread. Yet the drama implies (or seems to imply) another more essential continuum: the thread of events that constitute the plot.' The interesting thing about Roman comedy is the way it manages likewise to imply continua both of plot and of cultural and (fictional) historical worlds, without the context of received myth.

[33] Moore (1998a: 179) reminds us that the audience's natural identification is in some sense with Lysidamus.

[34] Note, for example, the repeated conditional clauses. See McCarthy (2000: 67–8, 134–5) for the comic use of legal proposals.

son's affairs, he will be punished by greater financial losses than if he had simply supported him.[35] In other words, Eutychus' 'law' amounts to a comic programme. 'So, *adulescentes*, clap if you want more comedies.' No doubt anyone might, at least vicariously, identify as an *adulescens* for the purposes of comic appreciation.

So far, then, actors are not to be blamed for putting on naughty shows, because they are only copying life (and other plays); old men are not to be punished for their adulterous behaviour; and young men are entitled to expect parental support in their affairs. The most extreme pro-comic *sententia*, however, relates (perhaps not surprisingly) to a slave. *Epidicus* ends when the eponymous hero finally, after repeated delays, agrees to forgive his master and graciously allow him to free him. Someone then plays the tragic-chorus role of commenting on the fortunes of the hero:

> Hic is homo est qui libertatem malitia inuenit sua.
> plaudite et ualete. lumbos porgite atque exsurgite.
> (*Epid.* 732–3)

Here is the man who found freedom for himself by his own badness. Applaud and farewell. Stretch your legs and get up.

The penultimate line looks for a moment like a kind of 'ecce homo' moral that we might expect from a hero-centred tragedy,[36] with the series of monosyllabic words and the redundant *is* adding to the archaic solemnity of the tone – until it dissolves into carefree familiarity in the final words. But even the *sententia* is askew: Epidicus has won freedom through his *malitia*, 'so applaud'. The moral says that the clever slave not only has the status of the hero, but also that he deserves to win. The point of making this obvious programmatic statement here is not to tell us something we did not already know, but, first, to tease us with a pretence at the moral high ground and, second, to signal the end by making a (pretended) solemn pronouncement on what has gone before.

35 It might be possible to see a moralising qualification in Eutychus' provision for young men: *quod bono fiat modo* (1022), meaning that fathers are only required to support their sons' affairs if they are pursuing them in an appropriately moderate manner. That sounds rather Horatian to me! I would be inclined to think that *bono* here is a simple term of approbation – the young men are expected to do their affairs 'well', in comic terms.

36 The most obvious case is the choral epilogue to Sophocles' *Oedipus tyrannus*, which begins (1524–5): ὦ πάτρας Θήβης ἔνοικοι, λεύσσετ', Οἰδίπους ὅδε, / ὅς τὰ κλείν' αἰνίγματ' ᾔδει καὶ κράτιστος ἦν ἀνήρ . . . The fact that it is generally held to be spurious is no obstacle to it acting as an exemplar of the kind of ending at which Epidicus is playing. Dawe (2006: 202) makes a comment on the tailpiece which prepares it beautifully for Plautus: 'behind this demented balbutience we can at least discern what the moral of *Oedipus Rex* was to one aspiring if ill-starred versifier'.

All these morals stand liminally on the edges of the play, and help to bring it to a close by holding up a mirror to it. Some plays end even more artificially, with explicitly metatheatrical comments which might seem to have as their primary justification simply the fun of talking to the audience. Such an ending comes to *Cistellaria*. The mystery of this recognition play has been solved, and the father comes on stage having heard a rumour that his long-lost daughter has been found. After a piece of horseplay about Lampadio (the slave) having 'increased' his master's family,[37] the father is sent indoors to have his own bit of recognition and finish off the play. According to the manuscripts, the *caterua* then speaks the epilogue. It could perhaps better be spoken by Lampadio, but if we are to imagine *caterua* to mean 'whoever is left on stage', then that would indeed be Lampadio, or at most Lampadio and Demipho:[38]

> Ne exspectetis, spectatores, dum illi huc ad uos exeant:
> nemo exibit, omnes intus conficient negotium.
> ubi id erit factum, ornamenta ponent; postidea loci
> qui deliquit uapulabit, qui non deliquit bibet.
> nunc quod ad uos, spectatores, relicuom relinquitur,
> more maiorum date plausum postrema in comoedia.
> (*Cist.* 782–7)

Don't wait around, spectators, for them to come out again to you. No-one will come out; they'll all finish off the business inside. When that's done, they'll put aside their costumes; then whoever has gone wrong will be beaten, and whoever hasn't gone wrong will have a drink. Now all that remains for you, spectators, is in the manner of your ancestors to send this comedy off with your applause.

This is a particularly clever piece of closure, which slips imperceptibly between worlds: first the characters are to 'finish off the business' – i.e., the recognition and its fall-out, which constitute the 'end' of the plot; then when they have done that, they will take off their costumes and reflect for themselves on how the performance went. 'All that remains, for completion, is that you should play your proper comic role, and clap.' (Note the typical alliteration in the *plaudite* formula.) If we notice the slippage, we might try to resist it, and point out to ourselves that, on the level at which the

[37] Anderson (1993: 72) appreciates the 'mild ribaldry' with which Plautus ends this play, but for me undermines the joke by presenting it as (simply) a mockery of 'Menander's delicate love situation' in which lovers are ignored in the interests of comedy.

[38] If anything could be relied on in the attribution to *caterua*, the fact that only Lampadio is present before this moment might be of considerable significance. It seems plausible, as printed in Lindsay's OCT, to assume that Demipho goes into the house at 781, as Lampadio tells him to, especially given the comment of *caterua* in the next line about people not coming out again. I think the actor of Lampadio would be the best candidate for speaking these lines.

characters are going to take off their costumes, they will not in fact finish off the business of the plot, because everyone knows that, on a realistic level, the whole play-world falls apart the second the actors get behind the scenes. But the temptation is the very point. We are being invited to think beyond the edges of the performance, both into the continuation of the characters' lives and the great party which they will have, and into the continuation of the *actors*' lives and the great party *they* will have. Here, for the first time (in our reading – this is not a comment on the chronology of the plays) we are tempted with the prospect of the post-performance party.[39]

Terence, who is generally more restrained in his closural dynamics than Plautus, picks up this motif to finish off his first play, *Andria*. The clever slave[40] speaks the last bit of dialogue to his master, and then addresses the audience:

> ne exspecteti' dum exeant huc: intu' despondebitur;
> intu' transigetur siquid est quod restet. [CANTOR.][41] plaudite!
> (*An.* 980–1)

Don't wait around for them to come out here: the engagement will happen inside, and everything that remains will be done inside. Applaud.

It seems not unlikely that we are meant to hear an echo of the *Cistellaria* ending here.[42] There is direct quotation in *ne exspectetis dum exeant* (in *Cist.* 782 the words are not contiguous); the stress on the internal activities is repeated with *intus*; both Plautus' description of the events inside and his invitation to the audience to complete the proceedings are reduced to a mere *quod restet*. It is the perfect, understated, metatheatrical ending to this highly self-conscious play. Some later reader was so taken by the temptation which such an ending evokes to imagine what is going on under that *intu' transigetur* that he just had to write it up. Several manuscripts of *Andria* offer us an *alter exitus suppositicius* ('spurious alternative ending').[43] Pamphilus'

[39] These lines are often taken as evidence that actors were slaves, because of the implication of punishment for those who have not performed well: Brown (2002: 234–5); Marshall (2006: 87–8, 214). This would seem to me to be a dangerous implication if it came only from such passages, because the language here is so slippery between the metaphorical and the literal, and we are still in the comic world, where even upstanding members of the senate might be threatened with a beating. This is not to deny the likelihood that some actors were slaves.

[40] Brown (2006: 312) gives the lines to Pamphilus.

[41] As discussed above, pp. 252–3, it is extremely unlikely to be the case that Terence's performance involved a *cantor*, hence my use of square brackets around 'CANTOR.' as printed by Lindsay.

[42] Inevitably, it is hard to be sure how clear this would be to an audience who knew so many more plays than we do. On the motif, see p. 32.

[43] Skutsch (1957) shows how the scene could follow on from Pamphilus' *memini* in 977, and amends the text of the alternative to improve it in a number of ways. His discussion of the date of the forgery

and Glycerium's lives are sorted out, Davos has been released from being tied up, and let out to finish the play off, Charinus has overheard the news that Pamphilus is to marry Glycerium (and therefore not his own beloved Philumena), the young men have been reconciled – so why do we need to make sure of the happy ending for Charinus? Terence's metatheatrical 'let's go in and finish it off – it will take too long to wait for Chremes to come out here' creates a better sense of ending than the pedantic tying up of all possible ends. If Chremes were dragged out to make absolutely sure the plot is going the right way, that would resolve the plot, but not the play. On the metatheatrical level, Davos' last speech is a joke about endings, but on the fictional/theatrical level it also works to create a sense of things going on, and as an enticement for us to want to know more, to write our own ending, however much we may also feel that the play has ended satisfactorily. Some sorts of plays are only satisfactorily ended when they have not really ended, when there is a feeling of more happening.[44] This is what the alternative ending fails to deliver. But the false extra ending offers us *readers* a neat joke on the play: the *alter exitus suppositicius* is appropriate to a play in which the theme of a supposititious child is brought on – falsely.[45]

'Inside' is the place of the party, but it is also the never-never land which we desire but know we cannot attain, for if we peeked, the spell would be broken. Pseudolus, consummate Plautine magician, is almost surreal in tempting us to think we might join the party. All matters of finance and power relations having been satisfactorily settled, Pseudolus invites his master to come in with him to the party. As they leave, Simo finally notices the audience (there is a slight question of attribution here, but it does not greatly affect the point), and says: *quin uocas / spectatores simul?* ('Won't you invite the spectators as well?', *Ps.* 1331–2). This enquiry provokes a rude reply which turns into an enticing promise and a novel *plaudite*:

(64–8) shows that the question must remain open. Victor (1989) strongly favours, on metrical grounds, a date between the second century AD and the time of Donatus in the fourth century. Brown (2006: 7) says that the scene was 'probably written some 300–500 years after the time of Terence'. See also Zwierlein (1990: 49); Reeve (1983: 418–19). Victor (1989) offers a full edition, translation and discussion of the alternative ending, together with the prose third alternative (his p. 68).

44 See White (1981).

45 It is amusing to note that Skutsch (1957: 67) attributes one of the allusions in the alternative ending to an earlier line in the play precisely to the action of a reader rather than a stage worker. The motif of the alternative ending has a small but lively future in Western literature, but I suspect that this (non-)Terentian example is just a distraction from the business of understanding Roman comic stage practice. Terence's character did not come out again. Manuscripts offer an alternative ending also for *Poen.*

hercle me isti hau solent
uocare, neque ergo ego istos;
uerum sei uoltis adplaudere atque adprobare hunc gregem
et fabulam in crastinum uos uocabo.
(*Ps.* 1332–5)

By Hercules, they don't invite me, so I won't invite them. But if you would be so good as to applaud and approve this company and play, I'll invite you tomorrow.

The 'dinner' we are promised for 'tomorrow' must surely be another play. 'That's another story . . . '

Not such an act of metatheatrical genius, but generically important nonetheless, is the closing party of *Rudens*.[46] This ending is the embodiment of the comic spirit, since everyone gets to party, even the spectators – or nearly. Daemones turns to us and assures us that he would invite us in as well, if he were not sure we already had invitations. Like Pseudolus, he turns the *plaudite* into a promise of another dinner invitation, though the metaphorical implication of the dinner as 'another performance' is somewhat undercut by the fact that we cannot expect it for sixteen years! This means, effectively, 'never'.

Terence does not want his plays to end 'like the other comedies' (to misquote one of his characters only slightly), so he tends to avoid closural jokes about the 'moral of this story', and only subtly and somewhat coyly does he loosen the theatrical spell by (literally or metaphorically) stepping forward towards the audience. The first play, *Andria*, is the most Plautine in this regard, as discussed above. I would suggest, however, that it is worthwhile seeing many Terentian endings against the background of the kind of closing comment which has been considered in this section. Terence achieves closure with the help of metatheatrical jokes precisely because his audience is aware of the simpler, more obvious tradition he has inherited from Plautus; we should be ready for plays to be more self-aware as they draw to a close, as they prompt the audience to wake up from their dream. Such is what happens in *Hecyra*. In the closing scene, when the necessary recognition has taken place off-stage, and the 'hero' is celebrating his good fortune in discovering the rapist who fathered his wife's child is none other than himself, he meets the courtesan who has facilitated the unravelling of the plot's mystery, and asks her to keep it all as confidential as possible:

[46] Konstan's chapter on the play programmatically ends 'to serve and guarantee the civic constitution' (1983: 95). See also Moore (1998a: 77–80).

placet non fieri hoc itidem ut in comoediis
omnia omnes ubi resciscunt. hic quos par fuerat resciscere
sciunt; quos non autem aequomst scire neque resciscent neque scient.
(*Hec.* 866–8)

I don't want this to end up as in the comedies, where everyone knows everything. Here those who ought to know do know, but those who ought not to know will neither find out nor know.

The obvious irony of saying this in a comedy is not the only metatheatrical point here. There is also the fact that this conversation about confidentiality is taking place in the presence of the audience, who, for once in this play, are thereby allowed into the company of those *quos par fuerat resciscere*. This comforting situation achieves a great sense of closure to a play in which, more than ever before in the history of Graeco-Roman theatre, the audience has been asked to appreciate a play where they do not understand, do not know what is going on, for most of the time. However much Terence may have challenged the audience, the play cannot end without them knowing the solution: the fictional ending where the reader is left *not* knowing some crucial element in the plot is still many centuries in the future.[47] Not everyone is so lucky, however. The slave, Parmeno, who has been constantly refused his proper role in this play, enters for the final lines, and asks: *ere, licetne scire* . . . ('Master, could I know . . . ?', 873), to which his master simply says, 'no'. The two then engage in a brief exchange of repartee about knowledge and the lack of it:

PAM. nescis . . . ('You don't know')
(*Hec.* 875)

PAR. immo uero scio . . . ('Indeed I do know')
(*Hec.* 877)

PAM. ego istuc sati' scio. ('That I know well enough' – where the formula for polite agreement takes on an ironic sense)
(*Hec.* 877)

When Parmeno is left alone to close the play, he finally admits that he does not in fact know:

[47] So much modern literature (in the broad sense) ends with hooks for sequels that it is difficult to define clearly an incomplete end in this sense, but my impression is that it is not something which has ever found great popular favour, especially outside the readership of literary types who like thinking about the deconstruction of the sense of ending. On this Terentian passage, there is a nice comment from the ancient commentator Eugraphius (Wessner 1962–3 III.i: 291): *VT IN COMOEDIIS* OMNES OMNIA VBI RESCISCVNT*: quasi haec comoedia non sit: constat enim in comoediis in postrema parte personas plurimas poni omnes quae agunt, sic errorem solui et ab omnibus cuncta cognosci.*

equidem plus hodie boni
feci inprudens quam sciens ante hunc diem umquam. plaudite!
(*Hec.* 879–80)

Well, today I've done more good unwittingly than I've ever previously done knowingly. Applaud.

The clever slave in comedy 'should' be the controlling character, the one who *knows*. Parmeno acknowledges his own rather unusual position with regard to this tradition, and claims for the play a startling novelty. The things which he has 'knowingly done in the past' must, I submit, be other, traditional, Plautine plays.

ENDING IN FARCE

We have seen from these metatheatrical jokes how a play gets more artful, artificial and self-conscious as it nears its edges. Such jokes are miniaturised versions of a general tendency of ancient play-endings, which is a movement away from fictional realism and into something wilder, and nearer to farce. This is apparent in many plays of Euripides, as Dunn (1996) has brilliantly shown. A classic example is *Orestes*, in which Apollo's *deus ex machina* scene wrests the play from its tragic disorder – which comes scarily close to being a comic mess – and sends it back onto the proper Aeschylean path. This, surely, is near to dark farce. Dunn (1996: 172) remarks that Menelaus' judgement on the story that Helen has been spirited away as πολὺς γέλως ('a big joke', 1560) 'might as well be commenting on the play itself, which proceeds to unravel at the seams'.

Plautus combines this kind of Euripidean self-consciousness with Aristophanic terminal celebration.[48] Many of his plays have great examples of intensified farcical ending, like the auction of everything, including the wife, at the close of *Menaechmi*. We are not meant to ask what this could possibly mean, for it means nothing – except perhaps that the comic spirit

[48] I am commenting here on the effect of the plays and the traditions in their background, rather than making a claim for direct allusion. Plautus seems to me in some ways close to the spirit of Aristophanes, even if it turns out that he never actually knew his work directly. See Slater (2000: 146). On the farcical, anti-realistic nature of Plautine comedy, and its connection with the spirit of Aristophanes, see Chiarini (1983: 232); for the particularly Plautine, and farcical, nature of the plays' endings, see esp. 234: 'nel "lieto fine" delle commedie di Plauto l'applauso non va all'immagine gratificante ma improbabile di una communità di buoni [as in Menander], bensì a una compagnia di attori di farse, i quali, terminate la giocosa celebrazione dei ludi, tornano, serenamente, ad essere qual che sono: degli uomini'. For Chiarini, the definitive contrast is with Menander's *Aspis*, where the trick is directed towards the highly moral *telos* of stopping the bad guy and getting the right people married, which is totally unplautine (208); for Plautus, on his reading, the realistic *telos* is not the important part, but the trick itself.

shows a callous disregard for the feelings of others.[49] Closural farce, together with closural delay, also explains why the two Menaechmi take so long to recognise each other, and have to be forced into it by the slave Messenio. Then there are the spectacular triumphs of Epidicus and Pseudolus (with afterglow as well), who end their plays rubbing their masters' noses in their own plotting success. In *Casina* there is the public performance, explicitly a play-within-the-play, of Olympio's and Lysidamus' disgrace at the hands of Chalinus-in-drag, while a similar piece of nonsense at the expense of the *senex* ends *Asinaria*. In *Miles gloriosus*, Palaestrio's Euripidean escape-ending keeps nearly falling apart as it hurtles the play to its climax, while Epidicus' plans go through a similar series of increasingly sillier near-disasters as the play approaches its end. Almost all plays get wilder as they race towards the finishing line – even if some of them are running backwards.

It is not usual to associate Terence with farce, but I suggest that doing so may help us make sense (or, perhaps, nonsense) of some of his odder moments, including endings. Take, for example, *Eunuchus*, a play which is remarkable for its congruence of neat plotting and outrageous plot. The ending is certainly neat: Chaerea gets to marry his citizen girl; Chremes gets to acknowledge and marry off his sister; Demea gets a role as indulgent father, when it is past the time for that to be a problem; Parmeno is tricked, for not playing the role of clever slave properly, but is reintegrated into the group; even Thais gets Demea as protector, and Phaedria as lover. There remain only Gnatho and Thraso, those two characters which Terence claimed do not really belong in this play. Gnatho engineers an ending for them, which involves dinners for him, the promise of future entertainment, and keeping the soldier in the dark, but also with enough nights with Thais to keep him paying. The ends are tied, the sense of ending complete and the actors all go in. Why, then, does this play leave so many viewers and readers feeling dissatisfied? As Barsby says (1999a: 280): 'the final scene provides a surprise conclusion to the play, for which there has been no real preparation . . . the conclusion seems to go against the characterisation developed in the rest of the play'. Terence has achieved an extraordinary piece of comic messing here, combining highly sophisticated and allusive construction of character and situation with some of the most licentious

49 Bergson (1913: 5) describes this comic phenomenon as 'a momentary anaesthesia of the heart'. Olson (1968: 78) says that 'the extreme comic is produced by making the observer so indifferent to the fortunes of the persons he is observing that he can concentrate on the absurdities of action and fortune as such, without emotional commitment'. Comedy and morality do not have a single point of interaction, however. Sutton (1994: 59): '[i]t is not that morality is foreign to the world of comedy, but rather that comedy has a peculiar way of switching our faculties of moral evaluation on or off as it chooses'.

comedy of the second century. Not only that, it is a play which above all depends on the artful artificiality of its characters and plot. Thais herself is an ambivalent character: her motives are amusingly but harshly questioned by Parmeno in the early exposition scene, while throughout the play we see her largely through the lens of her male viewers.[50] However much the dramatic structure revolves around her, the narrative does not focalise through her. And so in the ending. Aesthetically, this is a farcical ending set up through an anti-realist (or is it, in a sense, realist?), anti-sentimental collusion between playwright and parasite. At one level, because plays have crazy endings, because they can pretend that actions do not really have consequences and nothing really matters, *Eunuchus* can play itself out in one big farcical party. But underneath that, there is the seed of social comment, which comedy allows us to take or leave. It is a social reality for lovers of prostitutes to share their women: stripped of its playful pretences, this ending takes a stark look at that reality.[51] In doing so, it again throws a spotlight on another convention that is central to this play – that of rape leading to legitimate marriage. Terence uses his uncomfortable mixture of sensitive characterisation and farcical plotting to push the conventions of comedy and of society as far as they will go.

In comedy, nothing is sacred. No character, however realistically and sympathetically drawn, can achieve ultimate immunity from comic chaos. The moment, for example, that Chremes in *Heauton timorumenos* started pontificating about the right way to bring up children, we knew that Comedy would contrive his comeuppance. In this world, no-one can get away with keeping the audience's sympathy entirely, least of all a *senex*. The

[50] When Thais attempts to tell her story and explain why she has given preference to the soldier over Phaedria, Parmeno promises to keep quiet about what is 'true' but to allow 'lies' to flow out all over the place (103–5). His ironic intrusions into her story may well characterise him, but they are also very close to the comic norm. Phaedria, for his part, rather more *wants* to believe in her affection than actually does so. Thais' brief monologue which closes the scene (197–206) appeals to the audience to believe her, something in which the modern reader might be more inclined to oblige than the ancient one.

[51] Although I do not entirely agree with the argument of Gilula (1980) on the universal badness of Terentian prostitutes, her comment on critics' reading of the end of this play seems entirely apt: critics are uncomfortable with the sharing of Thais because '[i]t runs counter to the modern convention that a loved heroine should be won by one man only and rewarded either by marriage or by the devotion of one lover' (164). That can never be the reality for a courtesan in Roman comedy, and except in the case of marriage (in which case the girl is magically not really a prostitute) there was never any pretence that the arrangement is anything other than temporary and potentially inclusive. Brown (1990) gives a useful account of the main objections to the sharing arrangement and possible solutions to them, and says (49) that there is 'no solid reason' why the sharing arrangement could not have occurred in Menander's play, but there is also no evidence that it did. See also Konstan (1995: 135–41). Pl. *As.*, however, does hint at a possible sharing arrangement between two rivals for a beloved prostitute (915–19), which is neither affirmed nor denied.

farcical tendency of ending may also help us to come to terms with the hopelessly problematic and much-discussed ending of Terence's *Adelphi*, in which the angry brother Demea apparently has a change of heart, and forces Micio into some uncomfortable concessions which, Demea claims, show that his generosity was just laziness.[52] Can it really be that Micio, who seemed to be on the side of the comic angels, is actually to become the agelast, the comic butt who has to be badgered and browbeaten into accepting the beneficent conclusion? Can it really be that the *senex lepidus* and the *senex iratus* are swapping places?[53] A further spanner is thrown into the already messy works of this ending by Donatus' enigmatic comment (Wessner 1962–3 II: 176) that *apud Menandrum senex de nuptiis non grauatur: ergo Terentius* εὑρετικῶς, 'in Menander the old man does not complain about the marriage: therefore Terence is being original'. This comment is a very flimsy basis for intertextual analysis of Menander's and Terence's plays. If it does reflect something genuine in a Menandrian play, however, it perhaps hints towards another sign of the farcical exuberance of which Terence was capable, and of his refusal to accept the easy comforts of the Menandrian world.[54]

This ending has to be approached on several levels: one is, quite simply, that it is farce. Comedies end with a Big Bang, and if reason, order and justice are somewhat mangled in the process then that hardly matters. But this kind of farcical free-for-all at the end does not necessitate denial of more serious undercurrents, since part of the licence that society gives comedy (and comedy gives society) is to allow the audience/reader to take or leave the message at will. So: on another level, the meaning of the play and its ending is that there *is* no answer to the problem of how to bring up children, and of managing the adopted relationship, particularly in a society where adoption is done for financial and political reasons as well as for the reasons of orphanage, and in a play produced at *ludi funebres*

[52] See Gratwick (1987: 68) for this ending and the wide-ranging discussion of it.

[53] Gratwick (1987: 28) has a brief but excellent assessment of the way in which Terence manipulates and undermines our expectations: 'In real life we Romans respect the old-fashioned gravity of the strict father-figure. But at the theatre we are not watching "real life"; it is a holiday, we leave that behind. We are "for" the *senex lepidus* and it will be thanks to him that young love triumphs in spite of old Grumpy. Or so we think for more than four-fifths of *Brothers*.'

[54] Gratwick (1987) takes the line that the original audience would have had no thought or knowledge of Menander's play. He says of the ending (17): 'This is certainly not how Menander ended his play; how he did, what Terence's changes amount to, and whether in Menander Micio was shown to be "wrong" (which is one thing) and Demea "right" (which is another) are the central problems of the play. But we, as members of Terence's audience, will be unaware that Menander said anything different and will assume that what Terence vindicates in Demea, namely respect for what happen to be very Roman ideas about fatherhood, and what he condemns in Micio, that is a denial of those ideas and parasitism, were both likewise dealt with by Menander.'

by sons for their famous father, sons who had both been adopted into other famous families.[55] Perhaps also there is a sense in which *both senes* are reintegrated into society by this ending, in that Demea, whether 'sincere' or not, is accepted by the younger generation, and it is probably Micio who calls for applause, and even if he doesn't say *plaudite*, his *istuc recte* is an integrating action. Possibly Demea's speech in the closing lines, claiming that his actions are designed to expose Micio's generosity as laxity and laziness, and offering himself as a guide to the boys, might be seen in the tradition of the moralising *sententia* which finishes several Plautine plays. On the other hand, it might just sound like a continuation of his narrow-minded self-importance. Only a reading which incorporates the irrational and the artificial in its aesthetic can really allow these various 'meanings' to coexist. Only an aesthetic of farce would allow Terence to talk about fathers and sons in this way in such a context.

ENDING IN PARTIES

Drinking, eating, dancing and sex: these are the goals of comedy, and they signify the End (both finish and purpose) more simplistically and straightforwardly than anything else. No-one, perhaps, has ever matched the great orgies of comic exuberance which characterise the climax of an Aristophanic play, but the inheritance of Dicaeopolis and Trygaeus lives on throughout ancient (and later) comedy in more muted form.[56] The marriage (either actual or mirrored in the enjoyment of a prostitute) towards which most New Comic plots and plays are directed is only its marginally more realistic direct heir. So much is well known. Critics from

[55] Hunter (1985: 108–9) stresses the farcical nature of the ending, but reads it as a rather straightforward 'preference' for traditional farce over meaning, or 'humour over dramatic coherence', as he puts it. Henderson (1999: ch. 2) answers the problems of this play's ending and its relationship with Roman socio-politics in such a way as to encourage me to say that it ends the debate – except that to do so would be to enter into the same farcical solution that the play, and Henderson's reading, send up. Leigh (2004b: ch. 5) argues extensively for the importance of the funeral games as context for the play, seeing in Demea many features of Aemilius Paullus, including generalship as fatherhood, and thus explaining the ending as a vindication of Paullus and Roman discipline. While his argument is at many points convincing, I do not consider that it can wholly solve the tensions of the ending, nor need it undermine the aesthetic of closural farce. Lape (2004) centres the father–son relationship in this play, as in *An.* and *HT,* in the context of Roman social kinship, by contrast with the civic ideology which dominates Menadrian family plots. See also Gowers (2004: 162–3). Hunter, in Fantuzzi and Hunter (2004: 419–25), usefully analyses the play and its ending in terms of role playing and the complicated relationship between drama and 'real life'.

[56] Franko (2004) notes that Menander prefers to report rather than display parties. He shows (32–3) that ensembles (i.e. with four or more characters) have a marked concentration in final scenes in Plautus, and therefore contribute significantly to the ending with a bang of which Plautus was fond.

Aristotle on have responded to comedy's final flourish by identifying it with the very definition of comedy (the hero's triumph, a move from bad fortune to good) and with its supposed origins in fertility ritual. The playwrights themselves are most concerned with the theatrical effects of the climax. Aristophanes, indeed, was explicit about the closural force of his grand celebration, for example, when the dance of Philocleon and the 'sons of Carcinus' at the end of *Wasps* is presented not only as an opportunity of parodic rivalry of other dramatists, but also as a clever way of ending a play.

Structurally, it is convenient for comedies to end with a party inside, as motivation for the actors to leave the stage. Symbolically, the party encapsulates the vital energy of even the most muted comedy, and enables integration of the characters (often including those who had been antagonists) which reflects the integration of society that is also at the heart of comedy. Metatheatrically, the party papers over the gaps between the world of the play and the world outside. As Frye says (1957: 170): 'The watcher of death and tragedy has nothing to do but sit and wait for the inevitable end; but something gets born at the end of comedy, and the watcher of birth is a member of a busy society.'[57]

As the play dances its way to a climax, the forces of reason lose ground against the forces of fun. The overriding pressure is to get everyone dancing, and some plays end with agelast characters being badgered, bullied, enticed and cajoled into joining in. (Here, the 'dance' is a metaphor for comic celebration, not a comment on choreography.) The party thus contains a fair admixture of closural farce. Almost the only farcical scene in extant Menander is such a closure – the ragging of Knemon which forces him to take part in the celebrations at the end of *Dyskolos*.[58] Several Plautine

[57] Nelson (1990: ch. 4) considers the question of whether comedy is inherently connected with procreation, a common assumption that he finds to be problematic, in that very many references to babies and children in comedy are negative (he is concerned with comedy through the ages). He comes to what must surely be the right conclusion, that procreation, as likewise marriage, in the form of serious responsibility is not entirely comfortable for the comic world, but – or perhaps rather because – that world is itself childish. Marriage and procreation contribute to the comic spirit, it seems to me, more in metaphor than in harsh reality.

[58] In common with many readers, I find this ending a particularly cruel piece of comic cajoling, perhaps because it does so much violence to the rationality of the play and of what we know of Menander's work generally. O'Bryhim (2001: 96–109) attempts a justification of this ending by suggesting that the violent integration of Knemon into society through the wedding party should be seen against the background of a play in which all characters have worked through stereotypical roles which they find to be prejudiced and inadequate, only the grumpy old man holding to his (false) stereotype. His analysis of the cook and slave's dance which Knemon is forced to join as a parody of the women's dance at a wedding celebration is persuasive, but it does not reduce the sense of disjunction caused by the scene. See also Lowe (1987) on the uncomfortable critical response to this ending and its importance for social integration; Hunter, in Fantuzzi and Hunter (2004: 416),

plays end with a *forced* integration of antagonists into the final celebration. *Rudens* ends with the pimp invited in to dinner, along with the slave with whom he has just been in conflict over ownership of the chest. In *Bacchides*, the play follows a rather drawn-out movement towards its ending as the angry old men Nicobulus and Philoxenus are gradually insulted, pressed, and enticed into joining the party and forgiving their sons and Chrysalus. In *Persa*, comic justice has been done – as Toxilus' off-hand closural formula puts it (*leno periit. plaudite*, 858)[59] – in a final scene made up almost entirely of abuse against the pimp, who at the same time is being forced and cajoled into coming in to the party. We could take this at a purely metatheatrical level, and say that these forced reintegrations are directed purely towards ending the play. 'You've got to come in, because otherwise the play will never end.' But they are also designed, if we may so put it, to honour the comic spirit.[60]

Some plays, after all, actually show us their parties. In doing so, they not only create the opportunity for a great deal of entertaining horseplay, but also work on us (as the Bacchises work on the *senes*), enticing us – vicariously allowing us – to join in. By bringing the backstage to the front, the playwright not only ends with a bang, but also transcends the end. In a sense, we are watching something beyond the end, pretending that the stage world does *not* all evaporate the moment it leaves our sight.

If one effect of the visible party is to let us see beyond the end, it also pushes the 'proper' end of the play further back. After the early resolution of the problem in *Stichus*, the family go in to dine, and the parasite, who entertainingly fails to get in on the act and the dinner, finally goes 'in' himself, to indulge in an orgy of poison, so that no-one can say he died of hunger.[61] Not that we believe him, of course. All this signals the end, by line 640. Nice for them, but not really enough for a comedy – so we are treated to a full-blown party courtesy of the slave Stichus, his rival-friend who was with the travelling husbands, and their shared beloved. It is these characters who finish off the play, with 130 lines of carousing.[62] Naturally,

on the farcical nature of this scene 'marked by the use of nearly unparalleled iambic tetrameters to the accompaniment of the *aulos*'.

59 The last word is attributed to *caterua* in the OCT.

60 Accessible discussion of the role of ending in the definition of comedy in postclassical theory can be found in Purdie (1993: 116–21).

61 Arnott (1972: 74) hints at reading Gelasimus the professional comedian as a cipher for Plautus (or even Menander).

62 There is a nice metatheatrical game with the musician near the end, on which see Marshall (2006: 214), who also reminds us that *St.* is one of only three plays, the other two being *Per.* and *Ps.*, to end in a mixed-metre *canticum* rather than in trochaic septenarii.

they cannot at the end 'go in to the party', so instead they go in to recover, when Stichus finally decides that that's enough of that nonsense, and sends the audience away for their own party:

> intro hinc abeamus nunciam: saltatum sati' pro uinost.
> uos, spectatores, plaudite atque ite ad uos comissatum.
> (*St.* 774–5)

Let's go in now: that's enough dancing for the wine. You, spectators, applaud and go off for your own party.

A more sophisticated version of the same idea concludes the action-packed *Pseudolus*. The play almost 'ends' at the end of 'Act 4',[63] when Ballio realises that he has indeed been tricked by Pseudolus, that the girl is with her lover and that he owes money not only to the soldier but also to Simo, in fulfilment of the bet between them. Ballio and Harpax, the soldier's representative, go off to the banker's, giving out several closural signals:

> BA. . . . sequere sis me ergo hac ad forum ut soluam. HA. sequor.
> SIMO. quid ego? BA. peregrinos apsoluam, cras agam cum ciuibus.
> (*Ps.* 1230–1)

BA. So please follow me to the forum so that I can pay the debt. HA. I'm following. SIMO. What about me? BA. I'll pay the foreigners; tomorrow I'll deal with the citizens.

'I'll follow you in' is common in endings, as is the reference to something that will be done 'tomorrow', that is, beyond the end of the play. Then Ballio reflects on the plot of *hodie* (1233) and acknowledges Pseudolus' triumph, both of which are also closural hints. After another injunction to Harpax to follow him, he addresses the audience:

> nunc ne exspectetis dum hac domum redeam uia;
> ita res gestast: angiporta haec certum est consectarier.
> (*Ps.* 1234–5)

Now don't wait around for me to come back home by this road. This is how it is: I'm resolved to go along the alleyways.

While just barely remaining formally within the world of the dramatic illusion, Ballio clearly tells the audience about the end of the play (*exspectetis* must be addressed to the audience, not Simo, being plural, and is a closural

[63] Act-divisions do not, of course, belong in the Roman comic world. See Moore (1998b) and Marshall (2006: ch. 5).

formula we know from elsewhere), making joking reference to semantic conventions about which directions lead on and off the stage, and about the possibility of confusing the audience by sneaking around by back routes in the non-existent *angiporta* of the stage world.[64] The *res* which has been done is, of course, the plot. After an ironic comment by Harpax on Ballio's prolixity, the pimp has another try at getting the last word, creating a ring-compositional echo of his first scene:

> certumst mihi hunc emortualem facere ex natali die.
> (*Ps.* 1237)

This is obviously my death-day, not my birthday.

After Ballio's attempt to impose the end on the play, Simo has a turn at trying to be the controlling character of this performance. 'Good riddance to Ballio,' he says, 'but this is not in fact the end of this play. I shall finish it off, by doing the opposite of what a *senex* should usually do – I'll go up to Pseudolus in the street and give him the money.' That phrase *quam in aliis comoediis fit* (1240) is another metatheatrical hint that the end is nigh.[65] Simo leaves, celebrating Pseudolus' epic performance. This is line 1245. The remaining ninety lines of this play (which, indeed, the prologue warned us was long) offer an extraordinary piece of triumphant afterglow. Most unusually, the entirety of 'Act 5' is sung – and no doubt also danced, in what must have been a virtuoso piece of drunken acting. Whereas the vast majority of plays end in trochaic septenarii, *Pseudolus* plays around with *cantica* right up to the end. (The previous scene, with Ballio, Harpax and Simo, is indeed in trochaic septenarii.) This metrical exuberance is signalled straightaway by Pseudolus himself, when he comes out for this final section to share the party with us:

> Quid hoc? sicine hoc fit, pedes? statin an non?
> (*Ps.* 1246)

What's this? Now then, feet, what's going on? Will you stand or not?

Of course, he is having trouble walking straight, because he is drunk, but also his feet just can't stop dancing. ('Foot' jokes about metre are a speciality of the Augustan poets, but Pseudolus, it seems, got there first.) We do not actually witness the party, as in *Stichus*, but rather we allow Pseudolus, who has controlled the play throughout, to present it to us in

64 Marshall (2006: 55): '[t]he *angiportum* is most often used in Roman comedy to explain why a given character does not return to the stage by the same means that he had left it'.

65 Cf. Ter. *Hec.* 866.

word and, presumably, action, with all the magnificent creativity of which only he is capable. The party, and his telling of it, are enough to make us feel close to the divine:

> . . . deis proxumum esse arbitror.
> (*Ps.* 1258)

. . . I think he is next to the gods.

It may not be insignificant that this spectacular celebration ends a play performed as part of the ritual dedication of the temple of the Magna Mater of the gods.

Pseudolus makes it clear that this is a post-play party, which is happening *postquam opus meum ut uolui omne perpetraui hostibus fugatis* ('after I had completed my work as I intended, the enemy put to flight', *Ps.* 1269/70). As they are all drinking (etc.), his companions press him to dance (as he is doing for us now), and when he has finished, they applaud and beg him to return for an encore (as also he is doing for us now). But Pseudolus instead makes a comic mess with his cloak (*pallium*), to the further delight of the (internal) audience. This too, surely, must have been mimed on stage for the (external) audience.[66] And now, to bring the narrative into real time, he has come out on stage, to take a break from the pressures of performance and sober up a little bit. He must also enjoy a final triumph over Simo.

At this point, the play starts again:

> aperite, aperite, heus, Simoni me adesse aliquis nuntiate.
> (*Ps.* 1284)

Open up, open up, hey, someone tell Simo I'm here

'Open up, we are having another door scene – we are starting again!' When Simo comes out in response to this demand, he too repeats the beginning, as they play again the nonchalant joking which characterised the first meeting of Simo and Pseudolus:

> SIMO. salue. quid agitur? PS. statur hic ad hunc modum.
> SIMO. statum uide hominis, Callipho, quam basilicum!
> CALL. bene confidenterque astitisse intellego.
> (*Ps.* 457–9)

SIMO. Hello, what's going on? PS. Standing around in this way. SIMO. Look at the kingly stance of the man, Callipho! CALL. I understand him to be standing well and confidently.

[66] I have discussed the metatheatrical implications of this passage in Sharrock (1996). The interplay of stage and off-stage, on which see Del Corno (2002), is here particularly creative.

SIMO. Vox uiri pessumi me exciet foras.
sed quid hoc? quo modo? quid uideo ego?
PS. cum corona ebrium Pseudolum tuom.
SIMO. libere hercle hoc quidem. sed uide statum.
(*Ps.* 1285–8)

SIMO. The voice of the worst of men will summon me outside. But what's this? How? What do I see? PS. Your Pseudolus drunk with a garland. SIMO. Indeed, very freely. But look at your stance.

In among the delightful delaying tactics of drunken horseplay, this final scene plays out in miniature the substance of the play – the power struggle in which Pseudolus overcomes the world. For his victory to be complete, the final crucial ingredient is that Simo should be forced into joining the party. If he will come in and drink in accordance with Pseudolus' orders (1327–8), then Simo might even get some of his money back. The money, after all, is merely a symbol, not the true victory.

This coda to the most metatheatrical (as well as the funniest) of Roman comedies elides the difference between the inside and the outside of the play, putting performance on show and behind-the-scenes *en-scène*. Since the endings of comedies are so irreducibly artificial, it is not surprising that plays-within-plays should proliferate in this position. In *Asinaria*, never the most serious of plays, the big party which 'should' be the comic end (father, son and prostitute together) becomes a play within its own play, instead of the ending which it might have been. The party-goers – or at least one of them – have made the mistake of reckoning without the other half of the plot. Parasite, working for the rival to the son's affair, sets the rich wife onto the scene, with the result that we actually see the party through the eyes of the watching wife and parasite, as – with the encouragement of son and prostitute – the *senex* digs himself deeper into his hole. When Artemona confronts her husband, the parasite slips away, in satisfaction at having produced this result. He hopes/suggests that the young rivals Diabolus and Argyrippus will share the prostitute, thus giving also a kind of careless comic closure to that entanglement. Since the party is in progress before our eyes, the actors can hardly 'go in for the party', so Artemona drags Demaenetus off home, making a parody of a wedding hymn with the refrain *surge, amator, i domum* ('get up, lover, go home', 925). Young lovers go back in to prostitute's house, the generations having righted themselves. Jokingly, ironically, this play manages thus to finish with a 'marriage' (or two), as a good comedy should.

This is clearly a farcical ending at the expense of the *senex*. Similar is the play-within-a-play in *Casina*, constructed by the wife and her slave Chalinus, in which the *senex* of that play is abused and humiliated while the wife and her neighbour sit comfortably and watch. In that case, the internal audience-members are fully conscious about their position of voyeuristic power. I suggest that, in *Asinaria* also, there may be an element of anti-realist collusion between the playwright and the son and prostitute, who seem to be a little more aware of the situation and their role in it than rationally they should be. It could be that they might actually realise that the wife and parasite are there, and are deliberately encouraging the old man to behave outrageously, abuse his wife and promise further crimes. Argyrippus' relaxed greeting to his mother (*mater, salue*, 911) would be in keeping with the suggestion of collusion, as would the continued tempting by Philaenium even after the game is up, right up almost to the last words of the play (*de palla memento, amabo*, 939). Argyrippus and Philaenium, then, constitute a third level in this play's audience: first us, then Artemona and the parasite watching from their hiding places, and finally the son and prostitute watching from within. Such anti-realistic, farcical artificiality is what takes the play towards its end. Terence's *Phormio* ends in a markedly similar way.

ENDINGS DENIED, REPEATED AND FORECLOSED

This discussion has so far concentrated more closely on performance than on plot. And yet the closure of the plot – or even, occasionally, the denial of closure – is arguably the prerequisite for the closure of performance. This is not to deny, though it might be to nuance, what Charney says: 'Since comedy is so highly plot-orientated – so highly artful or artificial, as we might say – there is no chance of devising an ending that will seem natural and fitting.'[67] A comic ending is not likely to be 'natural and fitting' in the ordinary realist sense (but is any literary end really 'natural and fitting', or does it just make a good imitation of being so?), but rather it will achieve narrative closure by a range of means which may fly directly in the face of Aristotelian propriety.

[67] Charney (1987: 92). He makes a good point in this paragraph: '[a] normative, moralistic theory of comedy is bound to have difficulties with endings, where the restoration of the social equilibrium is very imperfectly and very partially carried out'. That is true, but the comic response is that we allow the playwright to get away with such imperfections, and in doing so somehow allow his nonsense to achieve the social cohesion that on a rationalistic level spectacularly fails.

We saw how, in *Casina*, the play has run ahead of the plot, achieving its climax with the worsting of the *senex* rather than with the recognition and marriage, which have to be hurried through in a carefree coda. Marshall's account of Plautine metre in terms of 'arcs' is effective in exposing the exhausting musical and dramatic intensity of the later parts of the play, in which 'the audience becomes increasingly certain it [the play] is about to end, which makes its prolongation all the more impressive'.[68] Sometimes, it is the plot which seems to get ahead of the play, and tricks us with premature ending. In *Curculio*, it looks like the end after only about 500 lines: the girl is settled with her lover, having been released by means of a letter signed with the ring which Curculio stole from a soldier in Caria. The pimp Cappadox goes in to offer apparently terminal sacrifice for his successful business transaction. But then his offhand mention that he bought the girl as a *paruola*[*m*] (528), for ten *minae*, makes this too-early end into a new beginning, by giving out a fairly broad hint at a recognition. We have had no prologue to this play, but we might – if we are at all attuned to reading plays – guess that the ring was a clue to a future recognition plot, as well as being operative in a deceit plot. Enter soldier, angry, telling the banker Lyco that the plot with the letter was all rot. To cut a long story short, when the recognition scene has been forestalled by the angry posturing of the soldier, and of the lover, and it looks like the plot has got stuck in the mire of chaos, the ring does its magic, and we discover – what perhaps we should have guessed – that Planesium is the soldier's sister. If we were very astute, we might have picked up a hint of this development from the *adulescens*' claim that Planesium was just about as untouched as if she were his sister. That, however, would be a false hint, because this is not *Epidicus*, where the beloved does indeed turn out to be the *adulescens*' sister. Rather, she is redeemed for the *adulescens* by turning out to be someone else's sister (rather than someone's daughter, which is the more common means of such redemption). The play has now had a second try at ending, with a recognition-scene resolution to follow the 'cheat a prostitute out of a pimp' resolution that it offered first. But it is not over yet, because we now have a second round of chaos when the pimp enters, to be attacked by the soldier, who has now changed sides in the comic economy. This time the situation is resolved by an arbitration scene, with the lover Phaedromus as judge. He – naturally – decides in favour of the captain, that the money must be refunded. It looks like there will be another fight – and suddenly it's

[68] Marshall (2006: 210). See also his p. 221, where he describes the end of *Am.* as 'a bonus "scene" affirming the play's closure'.

all over. The pimp gives the money, and the rivals, now brothers-in-law, go to dinner. The end: *plaudite.* After all those false ends, the real one is deceptively simple.

Theatrical trickery may be divided into two kinds, depending on the audience's state of prior information. *Captiui* also has a premature ending, but in this case the audience is in a position of superior knowledge, and can enjoy seeing that the apparent first ending is not in fact the end. That secure position is somewhat undermined, however, when the ending does finally come, because loose ends are left hanging which might, if we stopped to think about it, make us uncomfortable. The false hint at an ending occurs when Hegio's captive son returns home, bringing with him not only Philocrates, who had been sent to ransom him, but also – rather unexpectedly – the runaway slave Stalagmus who had kidnapped his other son (Tyndarus) many years previously. After a lot of comic horseplay over giving Hegio the necessary information,[69] from the internal point of view the play is complete, since the initial problem (the loss of Philopolemus, the captive son) has been resolved. Tyndarus is just about to be released and closurally forgiven even before Hegio realises he is his long-lost son. At this point, only we – and Stalagmus – know that this cannot be the end. The play still has a recognition to achieve, which it duly does. This seems neatly, fittingly final, and the characters go in to take the chains off Tyndarus and put them on Stalagmus.[70] Despite the apparent completion, however, the play is left with at least one factual uncertainty (what happens to Stalagmus? Tyndarus speaks of the executioner, though Hegio had said that if he told the truth his sentence would be remitted) and a rather uncomic close brush with real pain. Only at the very end does a hole appear in the audience's position of divine omniscience.

Neat, tight plotting is not, in any case, something we tend to associate with Plautus. As I have suggested several times, it is okay for comic endings to be messy, and the descent into generic mess is always a possibility for a Plautine play. On the other hand, we do tend to associate Terence with neat plotting, which might make us expect decorous, Aristotelian endings to his plays. Terence is certainly neat, tightly structured, careful and balanced in his plots, but the plotting is sometimes most creative when it is not so neat, and this can be seen particularly at endings, which, as I have suggested,

69 For a good metapoetic reading, see Frangoulidis (1996a).

70 I am not as convinced as Konstan is about the tidiness of the ending: '[t]he conclusion to the *Captivi* thus obliterates the ironic perspective on the communal ethos of the city-state which the secret of Tyndarus' identity had made possible' (1983: 71). But perhaps we both agree in the next sentence: 'this is only to be expected in comedy'.

tend towards the farcical. The *Heauton timorumenos* is a double-plotted play, with nicely balancing halves, one love story involving a citizen girl, the other a prostitute. The old fathers neatly interchange their original roles of angry and indulgent; the slaves plot. This looks like a recipe for tidiness, for a precise sort of ending which puts everything where we expect it. But in the closing moments of the play, Chremes, originally the 'wise adviser' but now the angry father, suddenly insists, quite out of the blue, that his erring son should marry if he wants to be forgiven for his prostitute plot. This, I suggest, is not a sign of incompetent dramaturgy or incomplete transfer of details from a Greek play, but rather it is a joke on us, as audience.[71] 'You thought you knew that a double plot like this ends with the citizen girl married, and the prostitute-beloved enjoyed, but we've done that [unusually, Clitipho and Bacchis have had their pretty explicit ending in the back room] and this play is going to end differently.' It ends quite unexpectedly with a double marriage, and Chremes thus surprisingly gets the last laugh.

AND FINALLY . . .

ESTRAGON: Well? Shall we go?
VLADIMIR: Pull on your trousers.
ESTRAGON: What?
VLADIMIR: Pull on your trousers.
ESTRAGON: You want me to pull off my trousers?
VLADIMIR: Pull ON your trousers.
ESTRAGON: (*realizing his trousers are down*). True.
He pulls up his trousers.
VLADIMIR: Well? Shall we go?
ESTRAGON: Yes, let's go.
They do not move.
Curtain. (Samuel Beckett, *Waiting for Godot* (finis))

Momentary delaying of the end is a closural device. One character stops another just as they are about to go in, as Lysimachus does when he fears to go in (end the play/face the wife) at the end of *Mercator*; or Messenio's request to be allowed to declare the auction at the end of *Menaechmi*; or Parmeno's attempt to get at some knowledge of the situation at the end of *Hecyra*.[72]

[71] For such a reading of Terence's double plots, see Levin (1967).

[72] There is a famous case in popular British culture where a football commentator, Kenneth Wolstenholme, said at the end of England's 1966 World Cup victory: 'they think it's all over; it is now'. The

Perhaps the most spectacular example of comic ending with a Big Bang is in Plautus' *Amphitruo*, the play that pushes back the boundaries of comedy with its gods and battles and tragic intertexts. It is also the play, we should remember, which celebrates the supreme power of Jupiter by enacting (for a second time) the double night which facilitates and signifies his omnipotence. It would be hardly surprising, then, if the ending were also doubled up.

Towards the end of the play, the manuscript tradition colludes with the comic mess into which Mercury/Plautus has thrown the plot, when a mutilated passage makes still more confused the consummate chaos of mistaken identity.[73] Amphitruo's friend Blepharo has been brought in to support him, but is completely fazed by the farce. As the manuscripts come back into focus, Blepharo recognises that the play has got stuck, and goes off in disgust, proclaiming that he has no idea how to resolve the situation, or how the play should end. Jupiter – who of course does know – gives the plot a push, by going inside, proclaiming: *Alcumena parturit* ('Alcumena is giving birth', 1039). Now we know the end is nigh. From this point on, the play needs several spectacular endings, lurching from tragedy to comedy, in order to contain so great a plot. Amphitruo, left alone, soliloquises on his unfortunate situation, and whips himself up into a tragic madness: he threatens to rush in and kill everyone – slaves, wife, adulterer, father, grandfather. This is not just an offence against *pietas*, but perhaps also an allusion to Euripides' *Herakles*, where the great hero (in our play just being born) in madness kills his wife and sons and tries to kill his earthly father (Amphitruo himself). But before this tragic plan can be put into action, there is a massive thunderclap – and Amphitruo is knocked right out of the play for the moment, just as Euripides' Heracles is supernaturally knocked out just before he can kill Amphitruo. The aptly named servant-woman Bromia[74] comes out to deliver a tragic messenger speech, telling us of the crashes and bangs, the divine voice and the miraculous birth that have gone on inside. She reports the *deus ex machina* help of Jupiter with the birth,[75] gets as far as the birth of the boys, and we think it's all over. This, after all, was the ending we were promised. As she finishes her narrative, she trips

phrase passed into common parlance, and reflects not only the excitement of victory but also the tantalising power of delay.

73 Christenson (2000: 296) gives a clear account of the situation.

74 Stewart (1958: 351) links her name to his persuasive interpretation of the play as strongly intertextual with Euripides' *Bacchae*, where Dionysus is several times called *bromios*.

75 The tumbling house looks Bacchic: see Stewart (1958). Slater (2000: Appendix IV) develops the connection into a masterly reading of *Am.* as metatheatre.

over the body of Amphitruo, and the play comes back down to comedy with a bump.

Comedy parodying tragedy, that is, for Amphitruo at first can't get up. Plautus offers us a new beginning when we thought he was ending, but one that has trouble getting off the ground. So then we have a second try at the ending, a second messenger speech. This is, indeed, the classic play of doubles. Bromia and Amphitruo first engage in some comic nonsense about recognition, then the messenger retells the birth narrative she has just given, and suddenly brings in the totally unprepared-for and unexpected (though of course well known) story of the strangling of the serpents by the baby Hercules. Amphitruo is pacified by what he hears, and sends her inside to prepare for appropriately terminal sacrifices. But Amphitruo is still not quite done with tragedy: he says he will summon Tiresias, the tragic prophet, and ask him what he ought to do, as if about to set up a sequel. Theban tragedies are again resonating strongly. But then, just when we thought it was all over – *sed quid hoc?* (1130), says Amphitruo, 'what's all this?' Haven't we finished this play? More thunder, and a *deus ex machina* in person. Jupiter comes in to tell Amphitruo that everything's okay, and foretells the greatness of Hercules, as a tragic *deus* should. His Mightiness is the only one with the power to end the play, which he does with a divine version of the closural formula of 'going in' at the end of the play: 'Now I am going back to heaven', he says. Okay, says Amphitruo, and I'll go in to my wife, and forget about old Tiresias. Then he calls for applause. This last scene then finally ends the ending of this play and returns it to the proper path of comedy, when Amphitruo dismisses tragedy along with Tiresias. The call for applause for the sake of Jove – *Ioui' summi caussa* (1146) – is comic, but also ritual and affirmative of the god and the play.

> Or say that the end precedes the beginning,
> And the end and the beginning were always there
> Before the beginning and after the end.
>
> (T. S. Eliot, *Burnt Norton* v 10–12)

Bibliography

Abel, K. (1955) *Die Plautusprologe*. Mülheim-Ruhr.

Adams, J. N. and Mayer, R. G. (eds.) (1999) *Aspects of the Language of Latin Poetry*. Oxford.

Ahl, F. (1985) *Metaformations: Soundplay and Wordplay in Ovid and Other Classical Poets*. Ithaca, NY.

Andersen, Ø. and Haarberg, J. (eds.) (2001) *Making Sense of Aristotle: Essays in Poetics*. London.

Anderson, W. S. (1993) *Barbarian Play: Plautus' Roman Comedy*. Toronto.

(2002) 'Resistance to recognition and "privileged recognition" in Terence', *CJ* 98: 1–8.

(2003–4) 'Terence and the Roman rhetorical use of the *Andria*', *LICS* 3, 2. www.leeds.ac.uk/classics/lics/200304/20030402.pdf

(2004) 'The invention of Sosia for Terence's first comedy, *The Andria*', *Ramus* 33: 10–19.

Andrews, N. E. (2004) 'Tragic re-presentation and the semantics of space in Plautus' *Casina*', *Mnemosyne* 57: 445–64.

Arnott, W. G. (1972) 'Targets, techniques and tradition in Plautus' *Stichus*', *BICS* 19: 54–79.

(1985) 'Terence's prologues', *Papers of the Liverpool Latin Seminar* 5: 1–7.

(1992) 'Ancora sulle scene di apertura della commedia', *Aevum(ant)* 5: 115–27.

(1995) 'The opening of Plautus' *Curculio*: comic business and mime', in Benz, Stärk and Vogt-Spira (1995): 185–92.

(1996) *Menander*. Volume II (edn and tr.). Cambridge, MA and London.

(2001) 'Plautus' *Epidicus* and Greek comedy', in Auhagen (2001a): 71–90.

Astin, A. E. (1978) *Cato the Censor*. Oxford.

Atkinson, J. E. (1992) 'Curbing the comedians: Cleon versus Aristophanes and Syracosius' Decree', *CQ* 42: 56–64.

Auhagen, U. (1999) 'Elemente des Stegreifspiels im *Amphitruo*-Prolog', in Baier (1999): 111–29.

(2001a) *Studien zu Plautus'* Epidicus (ScriptOralia 125). Tübingen.

(2001b) 'Epidicus im Dialog mit sich: zur Selbstanrede bei Plautus und Menander am Beispiel des *Epidicus*', in Auhagen (2001a): 205–18.

(2004) 'Das Hetärenfrühstück (*Cist.* 1 1) – Griechisches und Römisches bei Plautus', in Hartkamp and Hurka (2004): 187–210.

Baier, T. (ed.) (1999) *Studien zu Plautus'* Amphitruo (ScriptOralia 116). Tübingen.

Bain, D. (1977) *Actors and Audience: A Study of Asides and Related Conventions in Greek Drama*. Oxford.

Barns, J. W. B. and Lloyd-Jones, H. (1964) 'A fragment of New Comedy: P.Antinoop.15', *JHS* 84: 21–34.

Barsby, J. A. (ed.) (1986) *Plautus:* Bacchides (with tr. and comm.). Warminster.

(1990) 'The characterisation of Parmeno in the opening scene of Terence's *Eunuch*', *Prudentia* 22: 4–12.

(1993) 'Problems of adaptation in the *Eunuchus* of Terence', in Slater and Zimmermann (1993): 160–79.

(1995) 'Plautus' *Pseudolus* as improvisatory drama', in Benz, Stärk and Vogt-Spira (1995): 55–70.

(ed.) (1999a) *Terence:* Eunuchus (with comm.). Cambridge.

(1999b) 'Love in Terence', in *Amor Roma: Essays Presented to E. J. Kenney on his Seventy-Fifth Birthday*, ed. S. M. Braund and R. Mayer. Cambridge: 5–29.

(2000) 'Donatus on Terence: the *Eunuchus* commentary', in Stärk and Vogt-Spira (2000): 491–513.

(2001) *Terence*. Volume 1 (edn and tr.). Cambridge, MA and London.

(2002) 'Terence and his Greek models', in Questa and Raffaelli (2002): 251–77.

Baske, J. A. (1884) *De alliterationis usu Plautino particula prior* (inaugural dissertation). Königsberg.

Beacham, R. C. (1991) *The Roman Theatre and its Audience*. London.

(2001) 'Playing around with Plautus, or "how can I be expected to act in front of these people"', *Didaskalia* 5:1. www.didaskalia.net/issues/vol5no1/beacham.html

Beard, M. (1990) 'Priesthood in the Roman republic', in *Pagan Priests: Religion and Power in the Ancient World*, ed. M. Beard and J. North. London: 17–48.

(2003) 'The triumph of the absurd: Roman street theatre', in *Rome the Cosmopolis*, ed. C. Edwards and G. Woolf. Cambridge: 21–43.

Beard, M., North, J. and Price, S. (1998) *Religions of Rome*. Volume 1: *A History*. Cambridge.

Beare, W. (1934) 'The date of the *Casina*', *CR* 48: 123–4.

(1959) '*Contaminatio*', *CR*, n.s. 9: 7–11.

(1964) *The Roman Stage: A Short History of Latin Drama in the Time of the Republic*, 3rd rev. edn (1st edn 1950). London.

Bearn, G. C. F. (2000) 'Differentiating Derrida and Deleuze', *Continental Philosophy Review* 33: 441–65.

Benz, L. and Lefèvre, E. (eds.) (1998) *Maccus barbarus: Sechs Kapitel zur Originalität der* Captivi *des Plautus* (ScriptOralia 74). Tübingen.

Benz, L., Stärk, E. and Vogt-Spira, G. (eds.) (1995) *Plautus und die Tradition des Stegreifspiels: Festgabe für Eckard Lefèvre zum 60 Geburtstag* (ScriptOralia 75). Tübingen.

Bergson, H. L. (1900) 'Le rire', *La Revue de Paris. 1894. Janv.-févr.*: 512–44, 759–90; *Mars-avr.*: 146–79.

(1913) *Laughter: An Essay on the Meaning of the Comic* (authorised tr. C. Brereton and F. Rothwell). New York. (This translation originally published 1911, London.)

Bermel, A. (1990) *Farce: A History from Aristophanes to Woody Allen*, repr. with new preface. Carbondale and Edwardsville, IL. (Originally published 1982, New York.)

Bertini, F. (1981) 'Anfitrione e il suo doppio: da Plauto a Guilherme Figueiredo', in Ferroni (1981a): 307–36.

(1983) 'Les ressources comiques du double dans le théâter de Plaute (*Amphitryon, Bacchides, Ménechmes*)', *LEC* 51: 307–18.

Bettini, M. (1982) 'Verso un'antropologia dell'intreccio: le strutture semplici della trama nelle commedie di Plauto', *MD* 7: 39–101.

(1991) 'Sosia e il suo sosia: pensare il doppio a Roma', in *Plauto:* Anfitrione, ed. R. Oniga. Padua: 9–51.

(2002) 'I *Witz* di Gelasimus', in Questa and Raffaelli (2002): 227–49.

Bispham, E. and Smith, C. (eds.) (2000) *Religion in Archaic and Republican Rome and Italy: Evidence and Experience*. Edinburgh.

Blänsdorf, J. (1978) 'Die Organisation des Theaterwesens', in *Das römische Drama*, ed. E. Lefèvre. Darmstadt: 112–25.

(1982) 'Die Komödienintrige als Spiel im Spiel', *A&A* 28: 131–54.

Bond, R. P. (1999) 'Plautus' *Amphitryo* as tragi-comedy', *G&R* 46: 203–20.

Bourque, N. (2000) 'An anthropologist's view of ritual', in Bispham and Smith (2000): 19–33.

Boyle, A. J. (2004) 'Introduction: Terence's mirror stage', *Ramus* 33: 1–9.

(2006) *Roman Tragedy*. London.

Brink, C. O. (1971) *Horace on Poetry: The* Ars Poetica. Cambridge.

(1982) *Horace on Poetry:* Epistles *Book 2*. Cambridge.

Brothers, A. J. (1980) 'The construction of Terence's *Heautontimorumenos*', *CQ*, n.s. 30: 94–119.

(ed.) (2000) *Terence*: The Eunuch (with tr. and comm.). Warminster.

Brotherton, B. (1978) *The Vocabulary of Intrigue in Roman Comedy*. New York.

Brown, P. (1990) 'The Bodmer Codex of Menander and the endings of Terence's *Eunuchus* and other Roman comedies', in *Relire Ménandre*, ed. E. Handley and A. Hurst. Geneva: 37–61.

(1992) 'Menander, Fragments 745 and 746 K–T, Menander's *Kolax*, and parasites and flatterers in Greek comedy', *ZPE* 92: 91–107.

(1993) 'Love and marriage in Greek New Comedy', *CQ*, n.s. 43: 189–205.

(2002) 'Actors and actor-managers at Rome', in Easterling and Hall (2002): 225–37.

(2006) *Terence: The Comedies* (tr., intr. and notes). Oxford.

Buck, C. H., Jr (1940) *A Chronology of the Plays of Plautus*. Baltimore.

Calderan, R. (ed.) (1982) Vidularia*: Introduzione, testo critico e commento*. Palermo.

Cameron, A. (1995) *Callimachus and his Critics*. Princeton, NJ.

Carey, S. (2003) *Pliny's Catalogue of Culture: Art and Empire in the* Natural History. Oxford.

Cave, T. (1988) *Recognitions: A Study in Poetics*. Oxford.

Charney, M. (1987) *Comedy High and Low: An Introduction to the Experience of Comedy*. New York. (Originally published 1978, Oxford and New York.)

Chiarini, G. (1983) *La recita: Plauto, la farsa, la festa*, 2nd edn with addenda (1st edn 1979). Bologna.

Chiaro, D. (1992) *The Language of Jokes: Analysing Verbal Play*. London and New York.

Christenson, D. M. (ed.) (2000) *Plautus*: Amphitruo. Cambridge.

Cohee, P. (1994) '*Instauratio sacrorum*', *Hermes* 122: 451–68.

Coleman, R. G. G. (1999) 'Poetic diction and poetic register', in Adams and Mayer (1999): 21–93.

Connors, C. (2004) 'Monkey business: imitation, authenticity and identity from Pithekoussai to Plautus', *ClAnt* 23: 179–207.

Conte, G. B. (1996) *The Hidden Author: An Interpretation of Petronius'* Satyricon, tr. Elaine Fantham. Berkeley, CA and London.

Cooper, L. (1922) *An Aristotelian Theory of Comedy: With an Adaptation of* The Poetics, *and a Translation of* The Tractatus Coislinianus. New York.

Courtney, E. (1999) *Archaic Latin Prose*. Atlanta, GA.

Csapo, E. (2000) 'From Aristophanes to Menander? Genre transformation in Greek comedy', in *Matrices of Genre: Authors, Canons and Society*, ed. M. Depew and D. Obbink. Cambridge, MA: 115–33.

Csapo, E. and Slater, W. J. (1995) *The Context of Ancient Drama*. Ann Arbor, MI.

Damen, M. L. (1992) 'Translating scenes: Plautus' adaptation of Menander's *Dis Exapaton*', *Phoenix* 46: 205–31.

(1995) '"By the gods, boy... Stop bothering me! Can't you tell Menander from Plautus?" or how *Dis Exapaton* does not help us understand *Bacchides*', *Antichthon* 29: 15–29.

Damon, C. (1997) *The Mask of the Parasite: A Pathology of Roman Patronage*. Ann Arbor, MI.

Danese, R. M. (1997) 'Alta cucina e cibo "mortuale". La polemica culinaria nello *Pseudolus*: un problema socio-poetico', *Atti della Accademia Nazionale dei Lincei* 9: 499–533.

(2002) 'Modelli letterari e modelli culturali del teatro plautino', in Questa and Raffaelli (2002): 133–53.

D'Angour, A. (2006) 'Conquering love: Sappho 31 and Catullus 51', *CQ* 56: 297–300.

Dawe, R. D. (2006) *Sophocles:* Oedipus Rex, rev. edn. Cambridge.

Del Corno, D. (2002) 'Raccontare il "fuoriscena"', in Questa and Raffaelli (2002): 121–32.

De Meo, C. (1983) *Lingue tecniche del latino*. Bologna.

Dentith, S. (2000) *Parody* (New Critical Idioms). London.

Dér, K. (1987) '*Vidularia*: outlines of a reconstruction', *CQ* 37: 432–43.

(1989) 'Terence and Luscius Lanuvinus', *AAntHung* 32: 283–97.

Dessen, C. S. (1977) 'Plautus' satiric comedy: the *Truculentus*', *PhQ* 56: 145–68.
(1995) 'The figure of the eunuch in Terence's *Eunuchus*', *Helios* 22: 123–39.
Deufert, M. (2002) *Textgeschichte und Rezeption der plautinischen Komödien im Altertum*. Berlin.
Dobrov, G. W. (ed.) (1995a) *Beyond Aristophanes: Transition and Diversity in Greek Comedy*. Atlanta, GA.
(1995b) 'The poet's voice in the evolution of dramatic dialogism', in Dobrov (1995a): 47–97.
Douglas, M. (1999) *Implicit Meanings: Selected Essays in Anthropology*. London and New York.
Dover, K. J. (1972) *Aristophanic Comedy*. Berkeley, CA.
DuBois, P. (1995) *Sappho is Burning*. Chicago and London.
Duckworth, G. E. (ed.) (1940) *T. Macci Plauti* Epidicus (with app. crit. and comm.). Princeton, NJ.
(1943) Review of C. H. Buck, Jr, *A chronology of the plays of Plautus*, *AJPh* 64: 348–52.
(1994) *The Nature of Roman Comedy: A Study in Popular Entertainment*, 2nd edn (with foreword and bibliographical appendix by R. Hunter). Norman, OK. (1st edn 1952, Princeton, NJ.)
Duncan, A. (2006) *Performance and Identity in the Classical World*. Cambridge.
Dunn, F. M. (1996) *Tragedy's End: Closure and Innovation in Euripidean Drama*. Oxford and New York.
Dunsch, B. (1999) 'Some notes on the understanding of Terence, *Heauton Timorumenos* 6: *comoedia duplex, argumentum simplex* and Hellenistic scholarship', *C&M* 50: 97–131.
Dupont, F. (1976) 'Signification théâtrale du double dans l'*Amphitryon* de Plaute', *REL* 54: 129–41.
Dutsch, D. (2008) *Feminine Discourse in Roman Comedy: On Echoes and Voices*. Oxford.
Easterling, P. and Hall, E. (eds.) (2002) *Greek and Roman Actors: Aspects of an Ancient Profession*. Cambridge.
Ebrard, W. (1882) *Die Allitteration in der lateinischen Sprache*. Bayreuth.
Eco, U. (2005) 'Innovation and repetition: between modern and postmodern aesthetics', *Daedalus* 134: 191–207.
Ehrman, R. K. (1985) 'Terentian prologues and the parabases of Old Comedy', *Latomus* 44: 370–6.
Else, G. F. (1957) *Aristotle's* Poetics*: The Argument*. Cambridge, MA.
Elsner, J. (1995) *Art and the Roman Viewer: The Transformation of Art from the Pagan World to Christianity*. Cambridge.
Enck, J. J., Forter, E. T. and Whitley, A. (eds.) (1960) *The Comic in Theory and Practice*. New York.
Enk, P. J. (ed.) (1953) *Plauti* Truculentus: *cum prolegomenis, notis criticis, commentario exegetico* (2 vols.). Leiden.
Erasmo, M. (2004) *Roman Tragedy: Theatre to Theatricality*. Austin, TX.

Evans, W. J. (1921) Allitteratio Latina, *or Alliteration in Latin Verse Reduced to Rule.* London.

Faller, S. (2001) 'Soldaten aus Euböa und Rhodos', in Auhagen (2001a): 249–57.

Fantham, E. (1972) *Comparative Studies in Republican Latin Imagery.* Toronto.

(1981) 'Plautus in miniature: compression and distortion in the *Epidicus*', *Papers of the Liverpool Latin Seminar* 3: 1–28.

(1984) 'Roman experience of Menander in the late republic and early empire', *TAPhA* 114: 299–309.

(2001) 'Roman tragedy and the teaching of Aristotle's *Poetics*', in Andersen and Haarberg (2001): 109–25.

(2002) 'Orator and/et actor', in Easterling and Hall (2002): 362–76.

(2004) 'Terence and the familiarisation of comedy', *Ramus* 33: 20–34.

Fantuzzi, M. and Hunter, R. (2004) *Tradition and Innovation in Hellenistic Poetry.* Cambridge. (Originally published in Italian 2002, Rome.)

Fedeli, P. (2000) 'Il *remedium amoris,* fra commedia ed elegia', in Stärk and Vogt-Spira (2000): 251–66.

Feeney, D. C. (1991) *The Gods in Epic: Poets and Critics of the Classical Tradition.* Oxford.

(1993) 'Epilogue: towards an account of the ancient world's concepts of fictive belief', in Gill and Wiseman (1993): 230–44.

(1998) *Literature and Religion at Rome: Cultures, Contexts and Beliefs.* Cambridge.

(2007) *Caesar's Calendar: Ancient Time and the Beginnings of History.* Berkeley, CA.

Ferroni, G. (ed.) (1981a) *La semiotica e il doppio teatrale.* Naples.

(1981b) 'Il sistema comico della gemellarità', in Ferroni (1981a): 353–64.

Fitzgerald, W. (2000) *Slavery and the Roman Literary Imagination.* Cambridge.

Flaucher, S. (2003) *Studien zum Parasiten in der römischen Komödie.* Mannheim.

Flickinger, R. C. (1931) 'Terence and Menander', *CJ* 26: 676–94.

Fontaine, M. (2004) '*Agnus* κουριῶν (Plautus *Aulularia* 561–64)', *CPh* 99: 147–53.

(2006) '*Sicilicissitat* (Plautus, *Menaechmi* 12) and early geminate writing in Latin (with an appendix on *Men.* 13)', *Mnemosyne* 59: 95–110.

(2007) 'Freudian slips in Plautus: two case studies', *AJPh* 128: 209–37.

Fortier, M. (2002) *Theory/Theatre: An Introduction* (1st edn 1997). London.

Fraenkel, E. (1942) 'The stars in the prologue of the *Rudens*', *CQ* 36: 10–14.

(1960) *Elementi plautini in Plauto,* tr. F. Munari. Florence. (Originally published in German as *Plautinisches im Plautus,* 1922, Berlin; English tr. T. Drevikovsky and F. Muecke, *Plautine Elements in Plautus,* Oxford, 2007.)

(1961) 'Two poems of Catullus', *JRS* 51: 46–53.

Frangoulidis, S. A. (1993) 'Modes of metatheatre: theatricalisation and detheatricalisation in Terence, *Eunuchus*', *LCM* 18: 146–51.

(1994a) 'The soldier as a storyteller in Terence's *Eunuchus*', *Mnemosyne* 47: 586–95.

(1994b) 'Performance and improvisation in Terence's *Eunuchus*', *QUCC* 48: 121–30.

(1996a) 'Food and poetics in Plautus' *Captivi*', *AC* 65: 225–30.
(1996b) 'A prologue-within-a-prologue: Plautus, *Miles Gloriosus* 145–153', *Latomus* 55: 568–70.
Franko, G. F. (1995) '*Fides*, Aetolia and Plautus' *Captivi*', *TAPhA* 125: 155–76.
(1999) 'Imagery and names in Plautus' *Casina*', *CJ* 95: 1–17.
(2004) 'Ensemble scenes in Plautus', *AJPh* 125: 27–59.
Frédéric, M. (1985) *La répétition: étude linguistique et rhétorique*. Tübingen.
Freud, S. (1960) *Jokes and Their Relation to the Unconscious*, tr. J. Strachey. London. (Originally published in German 1905, Vienna.)
Frost, K. B. (1988) *Exits and Entrances in Menander*. Oxford.
Frye, N. (1957) *The Anatomy of Criticism*. Princeton, NJ.
Gaiser, K. (1970) 'Die plautinischen *Bacchides* und Menanders *Dis Exapaton*', *Philologus* 114: 54–87.
Garton, C. (1971) 'The *Thesaurus*: a comedy of Luscius Lanuvinus', *AJPh* 92: 17–37.
(1972) *Personal Aspects of the Roman Theatre*. Toronto.
Gelhaus, H. (1972) *Die Prologe des Terenz: Eine Erklärung nach den Lehren von der* inventio *und* dispositio. Heidelberg.
Gentili, B. (1979) *Theatrical Performances in the Ancient World: Hellenistic and Early Roman Theatre*. Amsterdam.
Gerick, Th. (1998) 'Der trochäische Septenar in den *Captivi*', in Benz and Lefèvre (1998): 127–50.
Gill, C. (1993) 'Plato on falsehood – not fiction', in Gill and Wiseman (1993): 38–87.
(1996) *Personality in Greek Epic, Tragedy and Philosophy: The Self in Dialogue*. Oxford.
Gill, C. and Wiseman, T. P. (eds.) (1993) *Lies and Fiction in the Ancient World*. Exeter.
Gilula, D. (1978) 'Where did the audience go?', *SCI* 4: 45–9.
(1979–80) 'Terence's *Hecyra*: a delicate balance of suspense and dramatic irony', *SCI* 5: 137–57.
(1980), 'The concept of the *bona meretrix*: a study of Terence's courtesans', *RFIC* 108: 142–65.
(1989) 'The first realistic roles in European theatre: Terence's prologues', *QUCC* 33: 95–106.
(1991) 'Plots are not stories: the so-called "duality method" of Terence', in *Reading Plays: Interpretation and Reception*, ed. H. Scolnicov and P. Holland. Cambridge: 81–93.
Glasgow, R. D. V. (1995) *Madness, Masks and Laughter: An Essay on Comedy*. Madison, WI.
Gold, B. (1998) '"Vested interests" in Plautus' *Casina*: cross-dressing in Roman comedy', in James (1998a): 17–29.
Goldberg, S. M. (1978) 'Plautus' *Epidicus* and the case of the missing original', *TAPhA* 108: 81–91.
(1981–2) 'The dramatic balance of Terence's *Andria*', *C&M* 33: 135–43.

(1983) 'Terence, Cato and the rhetorical prologue', *CPh* 78: 198–211.
(1986) *Understanding Terence*. Guildford and Princeton, NJ.
(1995) 'Improvisation, plot and Plautus' *Curculio*', in Benz, Stärk and Vogt-Spira (1995): 33–41.
(1998) 'Plautus on the Palatine', *JRS* 88: 1–20.
(2000) 'Catullus 42 and the comic legacy', in Stärk and Vogt-Spira (2000): 475–89.
(2004) 'Plautus and his alternatives: textual doublets in *Cistellaria*', in Hartkamp and Hurka (2004): 385–98.
(2005a) 'The early republic: the beginnings to 90 BC', in *A Companion to Latin Literature* (Blackwell Companions to the Ancient World), ed. S. Harrison. Oxford: 15–30.
(2005b) *Constructing Literature in the Roman Republic*. Cambridge.
Golden, L. (1992) *Aristotle on Tragic and Comic Mimesis*. Atlanta, GA.
Goody, J. (1997) *Representations and Contradictions: Ambivalence Towards Images, Theatre, Fiction, Relics and Sexuality*. Oxford.
Gowers, E. (1993) *The Loaded Table: Representations of Food in Roman Literature*. Oxford.
(2004) 'The plot thickens: hidden outlines in Terence's prologues', *Ramus* 33: 150–66.
Gratwick, A. S. (1982) 'Drama', in *The Cambridge History of Classical Literature. Volume* II, *Part* I: *The Early Republic*, ed. E. J. Kenney and W. V. Clausen. Cambridge: 77–137.
(ed.) (1987) *Terence:* Adelphi (with tr. and comm.) (2nd edn 2000). Warminster.
(ed.) (1993a) *Plautus:* Menaechmi (with comm.). Cambridge.
(1993b) 'The "true" Plautus?' (review of Zwierlein 1990), *CR*, n.s. 43: 36–40.
Green, W. M. (1932–3) 'The ritual validity of the *ludi scaenici*', *Classical Weekly* 26: 156–7.
Greene, E. (ed.) (1996) *Re-reading Sappho: Reception and Transmission*. Berkeley, CA and London.
(1999) 'Re-figuring the feminine voice: Catullus translating Sappho', *Arethusa* 32: 1–18.
Gruen, E. S. (1990) *Studies in Greek Culture and Roman Policy*. Leiden.
(1992) *Culture and National Identity in Republican Rome*. Cornell, NY.
Guggenheimer, E. H. (1972) *Rhyme Effects and Rhyming Figures: A Comparative Study of Sound Repetitions in the Classics with Emphasis on Latin Poetry*. Paris.
Habinek, T. N. (1998) *The Politics of Latin Literature: Writing, Identity and Empire in Ancient Rome*. Princeton, NJ.
(2005) *The World of Roman Song: From Ritualised Speech to Social Order*. Baltimore, MD.
Halkin, L. (1948) 'La parodie d'une demande de triumphe dans L'*Amphitryon* de Plaute', *AC* 17: 297–304.
Halliwell, S. (1991) 'Comic satire and freedom of speech in Classical Athens', *JHS* 111: 48–70.

(2001) 'Aristotelian mimesis and human understanding', in Andersen and Haarberg (2001): 87–107.

(2002) *The Aesthetics of Mimesis: Ancient Texts and Modern Problems*. Princeton, NJ.

Halporn, J. (1993) 'Roman comedy and Greek models', in Scodel (1993): 191–213.

Handley, E. W. (1968) *Menander and Plautus: A Study in Comparison* (an inaugural lecture delivered at University College, London, 5 February 1968). London.

(1975) 'Plautus and his public: some thoughts on New Comedy in Latin', *Dioniso* 46: 117–32.

(1985) 'Comedy', in *The Cambridge History of Classical Literature.* Volume 1: *Greek Literature*, ed. P. E. Easterling and B. M. W. Knox. Cambridge: 355–425.

(2002) 'Theme and variations', in Questa and Raffaelli (2002): 105–20.

Hardie, P. R. (1991) 'The Janus episode in Ovid's *Fasti*', *MD* 26: 47–64.

(2002) *Ovid's Poetics of Illusion*. Cambridge.

Hardy, C. S. (2005) 'The Parasite's daughter: metatheatrical costuming in Plautus' *Persa*', *CW* 99: 25–33.

Hartkamp, R. and Hurka, F. (eds.) (2004) *Studien zu Plautus'* Cistellaria (Script Oralia 128). Tübingen.

Harvey, D. and Wilkins, J. (eds.) (2000) *The Rivals of Aristophanes: Studies in Athenian Old Comedy*. London.

Heath, M. (1990) 'Aristophanes and his rivals', *G&R* 37: 143–58.

Henderson, J. G. W. (1998) *Fighting for Rome: Poets and Caesars, History and Civil War*. Cambridge.

(1999) *Writing Down Rome: Satire, Comedy and Other Offences in Latin Poetry*. Oxford.

(2004) 'Terence's Selbstaussöhnung: payback time for the Self (*Hautontimorumenus*)', *Ramus* 33: 53–81.

(2006) *Plautus* Asinaria*: The One About the Asses*. Madison, WI.

Hesk, J. (2000) *Deception and Democracy in Classical Athens*. Cambridge.

Highet, G. (1942) 'The shipwrecked slaver', *AJPh* 63: 462–6.

Hofmann, J. B. and Szantyr, A. (2002) *Stilistica Latina*, tr. C. Neri, ed. A. Traina *et al.* (originally published in German as part of Leumann, Hofmann and Szantyr 1971, 1st edn 1965). Bologna.

Hofmann, W. (1995) 'Die körpersprache der Schauspieler als Mittel des Komischen', in Benz, Stärk and Vogt-Spira (1995): 205–18.

Hokenson, J. (2006) *The Idea of Comedy: History, Theory, Critique*. Madison, NJ.

Hubbard, T. K. (1991) *The Mask of Comedy: Aristophanes and the Intertextual Parabasis*. Ithaca, NY.

Huizinga, J. (1949) Homo Ludens: *A Study of the Play Element in Culture*. London.

Hunter, R. (1981) 'The *Aulularia* of Plautus and its Greek original', *PCPhS* 27: 37–49.

(1985) *The New Comedy of Greece and Rome*. Cambridge.

(2006) *The Shadow of Callimachus: Studies in the Reception of Hellenistic Poetry at Rome*. Cambridge.

Hurka, F. (2004) 'Die beiden προλογίζοντες der *Cistellaria*', in Hartkamp and Hurka (2004): 29–49.

Isager, J. (1991) *Pliny on Art and Society: The Elder Pliny's Chapters on the History of Art*. London and New York.

James, H. (1934) *The Art of the Novel: Critical Prefaces* (with intr. by R. P. Blackmur). New York and London.

James, S. L. (ed.) (1998a) *Gender and Genre in Roman Comedy and Elegy*. *Helios* 25: 1 (special edn).

(1998b) 'Introduction: constructions of gender and genre in Roman comedy and elegy', in James (1998a): 3–16.

(1998c) 'From boys to men: rape and developing masculinity in Terence's *Hecyra* and *Eunuchus*', in James (1998a): 31–47.

Janko, R. (1984) *Aristotle on Comedy: Towards a Reconstruction of* Poetics II. London.

Jenkins, T. E. (2005) 'At play with writing: letters and readers in Plautus', *TAPhA* 135: 359–92.

Jocelyn, H. D. (1966) 'Plautus: *Rudens* 83–88', *CR*, n.s. 16: 148.

(1967) *The Tragedies of Ennius: The Fragments* (with comm.). Cambridge.

(1969a) '*Imperator Histricus*', *YClS* 21: 97–123.

(1969b) 'Chrysalus and the fall of Troy (Plautus, *Bacchides* 925–978)', *HSPh* 73: 135–52.

(2001) 'Gods, cult and cultic language in Plautus' *Epidicus*', in Auhagen (2001a): 261–96.

Johnston, M. (1933) *Exits and Entrances in Roman Comedy (Plautus and Terence)*. Geneva.

Karakasis, E. (2005) *Terence and the Language of Roman Comedy*. Cambridge.

Kermode, F. (1967) *The Sense of an Ending: Studies in the Theory of Fiction* (2nd edn 2000). Oxford.

Kern, E. (1980) *The Absolute Comic*. New York.

Ketterer, R. C. (1986) 'Stage properties in Plautine comedy II', *Semiotica* 59: 93–135.

Knapp, C. (1919) 'References to literature in Plautus and Terence', *AJPh* 40: 231–61.

Konstan, D. (1976) 'Plautus' *Captivi* and the ideology of the ancient City-State', *Ramus* 5: 76–91.

(1983) *Roman Comedy*. Ithaca, NY.

(1986) 'Love in Terence's *Eunuch*: the origins of erotic subjectivity', *AJPh* 107: 369–93.

(1995) *Greek Comedy and Ideology*. New York and Oxford.

Kris, E. and Kurz, O. (1979) *Legend, Myth and Magic in the Image of the Artist: A Historical Experiment*, tr. A. Laing, rev. L. M. Newman. New Haven, CT and London.

Kruschwitz, P. (2002) 'Ist Geld die "Wurzel allen Übels"? Zur Interpretation von Plautus' *Aulularia*', *Hermes* 130: 146–63.

(2004) *Terenz*. Hildesheim.

Kujore, O. (1974) 'A note on *contaminatio* in Terence', *CPh* 69: 39–42.

Kümmel, M. J. (2004) 'Zu einigen seltene Wörtern in der *Cistellaria*', in Hartkamp and Hurka (2004): 347–62.

Lada-Richards, I. (2004) 'Authorial voice and theatrical self-definition in Terence and beyond: the *Hecyra* prologues in ancient and modern contexts', *G&R* 51: 55–82.

Laird, A. (1999) *Powers of Expression, Expressions of Power: Speech Presentation and Latin Literature*. Oxford.

Langslow, D. R. (1999) 'The language of poetry and the language of science: the Latin poets and "medical Latin"', in Adams and Mayer (1999): 183–225.

(2005) '"Langues réduites au lexique"? The languages of Latin technical prose', in *Aspects of the Language of Latin Prose* (Proceedings of the British Academy 129), ed. T. Reinhardt, M. Lapidge and J. N. Adams. Oxford: 287–302.

Lape, S. (2004) 'The Terentian marriage-plot: reproducing fathers and sons', *Ramus* 33: 35–52.

Leach, E. W. (1969a) 'Ergasilus and the ironies of the *Captivi*', *C&M* 30: 263–96.

(1969b) '*De exemplo meo ipse aedificato*: an organizing idea in the *Mostellaria*', *Hermes* 97: 318–32.

(1974) 'Plautus *Rudens*: Venus born from a shell', *Texas Studies in Literature and Language* 15: 915–31.

Leeman, A. D. (1963) Orationis ratio*: The Stylistic Theories and Practice of the Roman Orators, Historians and Philosophers* (2 vols.). Amsterdam.

Lefèvre, E. (1969) *Die Expositionstechnik in den Komödien des Terenz*. Darmstadt.

(1978a) 'Plautus-Studien II: die Brief-Intrige in Menanders *Dis exapaton* und ihre Verdoppelung in den *Bacchides*', *Hermes* 106: 518–38.

(1978b) *Der* Phormio *des Terenz und der* Epidikazomenos *des Apollodor von Karystos*. Munich.

(1984) 'Plautus-Studien IV: die Umformung des Ἀλαζών der Doppel-Komödie des *Miles gloriosus*', *Hermes* 112: 30–53.

(1995) *Plautus und Philemon* (ScriptOralia 73). Tübingen.

(1997) *Plautus* Pseudolus (ScriptOralia 101). Tübingen.

(1998) 'L'*Anfitrione* di Plauto e la tragedia', in Amphitruo (Lecturae Plautinae Sarsinates 1), ed. R. Raffaelli and A. Tontini. Urbino: 13–30.

(1999a) *Terenz' und Apollodors* Hecyra (Zetemata 101). Munich.

(1999b) 'Plautus *Amphitruo* zwischen Tragodie', in Baier (1999): 11–50.

(2001) *Plautus* Aulularia (ScriptOralia 122). Tübingen.

(2004) 'Plautus' *Cistellaria* zwischen Menanders *Synaristosai* und italischem Stegreifspiel', in Hartkamp and Hurka (2004): 51–88.

Lefèvre, E., Stärk, E. and Vogt-Spira, G. (1991) *Plautus barbarus: Sechs Kapitel zur Originalität des Plautus* (ScriptOralia 25). Tübingen.

Leigh, M. G. L. (2004a) 'The *Pro Caelio* and comedy', *CPh* 99: 300–35.

(2004b) *Comedy and the Rise of Rome*. Oxford.

Leo, F. (1912) *Plautinische Forschungen zur Kritik und Geschichte der Komödie*, 2nd edn. Berlin.

Leumann, M., Hofmann, J. B. and Szantyr, A. (1972) *Lateinische Grammatik: Syntax und Stilistik* (1st edn 1965). Munich.

Levin, R. (1967) 'The double plots of Terence', *CJ* 62: 301–5.

Lloyd, R. B. (1963) 'Two prologues: Menander and Plautus', *AJPh* 84: 146–61.
Lowe, J. C. B. (1983) 'The *Eunuchus*: Terence and Menander', *CQ* 33: 428–44.
(1985a) 'Plautine innovations in *Mostellaria* 529–857', *Phoenix* 39: 6–26.
(1985b) 'The cook scene of Plautus' *Pseudolus*', *CQ* 35: 411–16.
(1988) 'Plautus *Poenulus* 1.2', *BICS* 35: 101–10.
(1989) 'The *virgo callida* of Plautus, *Persa*', *CQ* 39: 390–9.
(1999) 'Pseudolus' intrigue against Simo', *Maia* 51: 1–15.
(2001) 'Greek and Roman elements in Epidicus' intrigue', in Auhagen (2001a): 57–70.
(2007) 'Some problems of dramatic space in Plautus', *CQ* 57: 109–16.
Lowe, N. J. (1987) 'Tragic space and comic timing in Menander's *Dyskolos*', *BICS* 34: 126–38.
(2000) 'Comic plots and the invention of fiction', in Harvey and Wilkins (2000): 259–72.
Luppe, W. (2000) 'The rivalry between Aristophanes and Kratinos', in Harvey and Wilkins (2000): 15–21.
MacCary, W. T. (1969) 'Menander's slaves: their names, roles and masks', *TAPhA* 100: 277–94.
MacCary, W. T. and Willcock, M. M. (eds.) (1976) *Plautus:* Casina. Cambridge.
MacDowell, D. M. (1995) *Aristophanes and Athens: An Introduction to the Plays*. Oxford.
Mahoney, A. (2001) 'Alliteration in Saturnian Latin verse', *NECJ* 28: 78–82.
Marouzeau, J. (1946) *Traité de stylistique latine*. Paris.
Marshall, C. W. (2006) *The Stagecraft and Performance of Roman Comedy*. Cambridge.
Marx, F. (1928) *Plautus:* Rudens (with comm.). Leipzig.
Mattingly, H. B. (1959) 'The Terentian *didascaliae*', *Athenaeum* 37: 148–73.
(1960) 'The first period of Plautine revival', *Latomus* 19: 231–5.
Maurach, G. (1988) *Der* Poenulus *des Plautus*. Heidelberg.
(2005) *Kleine Geschichte der antiken Komödie*. Darmstadt.
Mauron, C. (1964) *Psychocritique du genre comique*. Paris.
McCarthy, K. (2000) *Slaves, Masters and the Art of Authority in Plautine Comedy*. Princeton, NJ.
(2004) 'The joker in the pack: slaves in Terence', *Ramus* 33: 100–19.
McElduff, S. (2004) 'More than Menander's acolyte: Terence as translator', *Ramus* 33: 120–9.
Meisel, M. (2007) *How Plays Work: Reading and Performance*. Oxford.
Milnor, K. (2002) 'Playing house: stage, space and domesticity in Plautus' *Mostellaria*', *Helios* 29: 3–25.
Moi, T. (ed.) (1986) *The Kristeva Reader*. New York.
Moore, T. J. (1991) '*Palliata togata*: Plautus, *Curculio* 462–86', *AJPh* 112: 343–62.
(1994) 'Seats and social status in the Plautine theatre', *CJ* 90: 113–23.
(1998a) *The Theatre of Plautus: Playing to the Audience*. Austin, TX.
(1998b) 'Music and structure in Roman comedy', *AJPh* 119: 245–73.
(2001) 'Music in *Epidicus*', in Auhagen (2001a): 313–34.

(2005) '"*Pessuli, heus pessuli*": la porta nel *Curculio*', in Raffaelli and Tontini (2005): 11–36.
Morales, H. L. (1996) 'The torturer's apprentice: Parrhasius and the limits of art', in *Art and Text in Roman Culture*, ed. J. Elsner. Cambridge: 182–209.
Morgan, L. (2003) 'Child's play: Ovid and his critics', *JRS* 93: 66–91.
Morgan, M. G. (1990) 'Politics, religion and the games in Rome, 200–150 BC', *Philologus* 134: 14–36.
Most, G. W. (1996) 'Reflecting Sappho', in Greene (1996): 11–35.
Muecke, F. (1982) 'A portrait of the artist as a young woman', *CQ* 32: 41–55.
(1986) 'Plautus and the theatre of disguise', *ClAnt* 5: 216–29.
Murray, G. (1943) 'Ritual elements in the New Comedy', *CQ* 37: 46–54.
Nelson, T. G. A. (1990) *Comedy: An Introduction to Comedy in Literature, Drama and Cinema*. Oxford.
Nesselrath, H.-G. (1995) 'Myth, parody and comic plots: the birth of gods and Middle Comedy', in Dobrov (1995a): 1–27.
Newsom, R. (1988) *A Likely Story: Probability and Play in Fiction*. New Brunswick, NJ.
Norwood, G. (1923) *The Art of Terence*. Oxford.
Nuttall, A. D. (1992) *Openings: Narrative Beginnings from the Epic to the Novel*. Oxford.
O'Bryhim, S. (1989) 'The originality of Plautus' *Casina*', *AJPh* 110: 81–103.
(2001) 'Dance, Old Man, Dance! The torture of Knemon in Menander's *Dyskolos*', in *Greek and Roman Comedy: Translations and Interpretations of Four Representative Plays*, ed. S. O'Bryhim. Austin, TX: 96–109.
Olson, E. (1968) *The Theory of Comedy*. Bloomington, IN.
Oniga, R. (2002) 'I modelli dell'*Anfitrione* di Plauto', in Questa and Raffaelli (2002): 199–225.
Orr, L. (1996) 'Narrative repetition, repetitive narration: a taxonomy', *Neohelicon* 23, 2: 203–21.
Otto, A. (1890) *Die Sprichwörter und sprichwörtlichen Redensarten der Römer*. Leipzig.
Owens, W. M. (2000) 'Plautus' *Stichus* and the political crisis of 200 BC', *AJPh* 121: 385–407.
Palmer, L. R. (1954) *The Latin Language*. London.
Parker, H. N. (1989) 'Crucially funny or Tranio on the couch: the *servus callidus* and jokes about torture', *TAPhA* 119: 233–46.
(1996) 'Plautus vs. Terence: audience and popularity re-examined', *AJPh* 117: 585–617.
Pearson, J. H. (1997) *The Prefaces of Henry James: Framing the Modern Reader*. University Park, PA.
Penwill, J. L. (2004) 'The unlovely lover of Terence's *Hecyra*', *Ramus* 33: 130–49.
Petersmann, H. (1973) *Plautus:* Stichus, *Einleitung, Text, Kommentar*. Heidelberg.
Petrone, G. (1983) *Teatro antico e inganno: finzioni plautine*. Palermo.
(2001) 'Il rischio della punizione: scherzi e drammaturgia nell'*Epidicus*', in Auhagen (2001a): 179–90.

Philippides, K. (1995) 'Terence's *Eunuchus*: elements of the marriage ritual in the rape scene', *Mnemosyne* 48: 272–84.
Pohlenz, M. (1956) 'Der Prolog des Terenz', *SIFC* 27/8: 434–53.
Purdie, S. (1993) *Comedy: The Mastery of Discourse*. Hemel Hempstead.
Questa, C. (1995) *Titi Macci Plauti Cantica*. Urbino.
Questa, C. and Raffaelli, R. (1984) *Maschere prologhi naufragi nella commedia plautina*. Bari.
(eds.) (2002) *Due seminari plautini: la tradizione del testo; i modelli*. Urbino.
Rabinowitz, P. (1998) *Before Reading: Narrative Conventions and the Politics of Interpretation*. Columbus, OH. (1st edn 1987, Ithaca, NY.)
Radice, B. (1976) *Terence: The Comedies* (with tr. and intr.). Harmondsworth.
Raffaelli, R. (1984a) 'Narratore e narrazione nei prologhi di Plauto', in Questa and Raffaelli (1984): 69–83.
(1984b) '*Animum advortite*: Aspetti della communicazione nei prologhi di Plauto (e di Terenzio)', in Questa and Raffaelli (1984): 101–20.
(2000) 'C'è del comico in quella follia', in Raffaelli and Tontini (2000): 49–65.
Raffaelli, R. and Tontini, A. (eds.) (2000) Aulularia (Lecturae Plautinae Sarsinates III). Urbino.
(eds.) (2005) Curculio (Lecturae Plautinae Sarsinates VIII). Urbino.
Rawson, E. (1993) 'Freedmen in Roman comedy', in Scodel (1993): 215–33.
Reeve, M. D. (1983) 'Terence', in Reynolds (1983): 412–20.
Reynolds, L. D. (ed.) (1983) *Texts and Transmission: A Survey of the Latin Classics*. Oxford.
Roberts, D. H., Dunn, F. and Fowler, D. P. (eds.) (1997) *Classical Closure*. Princeton, NJ.
Rogers, R. (1987) 'Freud and the semiotics of repetition', *Poetics Today* 8: 579–90.
Rosen, R. M. (1997) 'Performance and textuality in Aristophanes' *Clouds*', *YJC* 10: 397–421.
Rosenmeyer, T. G. (2002) '"Metatheatre": an essay on overload', *Arion* 10: 87–119.
Ruffell, I. (2002) 'A total write-off: Aristophanes, Cratinus and the rhetoric of comic competition', *CQ* 52: 138–63.
Russell, D. A. (1979) '*De imitatione*', in *Creative Imitation and Latin Literature*, ed. D. West and A. Woodman. Cambridge: 1–16.
Said, E. W. (1975) *Beginnings: Intention and Method*. New York. (2nd edn 1998, London.)
Sandbach, F. H. (1982) 'How Terence's *Hecyra* failed', *CQ*, n.s. 32: 134–5.
Scafoglio, G. (2005) 'Plautus and Ennius: a note on Plautus, *Bacchides* 962–5', *CQ* 55: 632–8.
Schlegel, C. (1999) 'Horace *Satires* 1.7: satire as conflict irresolution', *Arethusa* 32: 337–52.
Schmitz, T. A. (1999) '"I hate all common things": the reader's role in Callimachus' *Aetia* prologue', *HSPh* 99: 151–78.
Scodel, R. (ed.) (1993) *Theatre and Society in the Classical World*. Ann Arbor, MI.
Scullard, H. H. (1981) *Festivals and Ceremonies of the Roman Republic*. London.
Seaford, R. (ed.) (1996) *Euripides:* Bacchae (with tr., intr. and comm.). Warminster.

Sedgwick, W. B. (1927) 'Parody in Plavtvs [Parody in Plautus]', *CQ* 21: 88–9.

Segal, C. (1997) *Dionysiac Poetics and Euripides'* Bacchae, expanded edn (1st edn 1982). Princeton, NJ.

Segal, E. (1987) *Roman Laughter: The Comedy of Plautus*, 2nd edn. Oxford. (1st edn 1968, Cambridge, MA.)

(2001a) *The Death of Comedy*. Cambridge, MA.

(ed.) (2001b) *Oxford Readings in Menander, Plautus and Terence*. Oxford.

Serpieri, A., Elam, K., Gulli Publiatti, P., Kemeny, T. and Rutelli, R. (1981) 'Toward a segmentation of the dramatic text', *Poetics Today* 2: 163–200.

Sharrock, A. R. (1994) *Seduction and Repetition in Ovid's* Ars Amatoria *2*. Oxford.

(1996) 'The art of deceit: *Pseudolus* and the nature of reading', *CQ* 46: 152–74.

(2002) 'An a-musing tale: gender, genre and Ovid's battles with inspiration in the *Metamorphoses*', in *Cultivating the Muse: Power, Desire and Inspiration in the Ancient World*, ed. E. Spentzou and D. P. Fowler. Oxford: 207–27.

(2008) 'The theatrical life of things: Plautus and the physical', *Dictynna* 5: 171–89.

Sharrock, A. R. and Morales, H. (eds.) (2000) *Intratextuality: Greek and Roman Textual Relations*. Oxford.

Sheets, G. A. (1983) 'Plautus and early Roman tragedy', *ICS* 8: 195–209.

Sidnell, M. J., Conacher, D. J., Kerslake, B., Kleber, P., McDonough, C. J. and Pietropaolo, D. (1991) *Sources of Dramatic Theory 1: Plato to Congreve*. Cambridge.

Sidwell, K. (1995) 'Poetic rivalry and the caricature of comic poets', in *Stage Directions: Essays in Ancient Drama in Honour of E. W. Handley*, ed. A. Griffiths. London: 56–80.

Silk, M. S. (2000a) *Aristophanes and the Definition of Comedy*. Oxford.

(2000b) 'Aristophanes versus the rest: comic poetry in Old Comedy', in Harvey and Wilkins (2000): 299–315.

Simon, M. (1961) '*Contaminatio* und *furtum* bei Terenz', *Helikon* 1: 487–92.

Skafte Jensen, M. (1997) 'The fall of Troy in Plautus' *Bacchides*', *C&M* 48: 315–23.

Skutsch, O. (1937) 'New words from Plautus', *CR* 51: 166.

(1957) 'Der Zweite Schluss der *Andria*', *RhM* 100: 53–68.

(1967) 'Plautus: *Rudens* 86', *CR*, n.s. 17: 11–12.

(1968) *Studia Enniana*. London.

(1985) *The* Annals *of Quintus Ennius*. Oxford.

Slater, N. W. (1988) 'The fictions of patriarchy in Terence's *Hecyra*', *CW* 81: 249–60.

(1992a) 'Plautine negotiations: the *Poenulus* prologue unpacked', in *Beginnings in Classical Literature* (*YClS* 29), ed. F. M. Dunn and T. Cole. Cambridge: 131–46.

(1992b) 'Two republican poets on drama: Terence and Accius', in Zimmermann (1992): 85–103.

(1995) 'The fabrication of comic illusion', in Dobrov (1995a): 29–45.

(2000) *Plautus in Performance: The Theatre of the Mind*, 2nd edn. Amsterdam. (1st edn 1985, Princeton, NJ.)

(2001) 'Appearance, reality and the spectre of incest', in Auhagen (2001a): 191–203.

Slater, N. W. and Zimmermann, B. (eds.) (1993) *Intertextualität in der griechisch-römischen Komödie*. Stuttgart.

Smith, C. (2000) 'Worshipping *mater matuta*: ritual and context', in Bispham and Smith (2000): 136–55.

Smith, J. A. (2004) 'Buy young, sell old: playing the market economies of Phormio and Terence', *Ramus* 33: 82–99.

Smith, L. P. (1994) 'Audience response to rape: Chaerea in Terence's *Eunuchus*', *Helios* 21: 21–38.

Sommella, P. (2005) 'La Roma plautina (con particolare riferimento a *Curculio* 467–85)', in Raffaelli and Tontini (2005): 69–106.

Stanford, W. B. (1983) *Greek Tragedy and the Emotions: An Introductory Study*. London.

Stärk, E. (1989) *Die* Menaechmi *des Plautus und kein griechisches Original* (ScriptOralia 11). Tübingen.

(1991) '*Mostellaria* oder *Tubare* statt *sedare*', in Lefèvre, Stärk and Vogt-Spira (1991): 107–39.

(2001) 'Zwei Vermutungen zum Original des *Epidicus*', in Auhagen (2001a): 91–104.

Stärk, E. and Vogt-Spira, G. (eds.) (2000) *Dramatische Wäldchen: Festschrift für Eckard Lefèvre zum 65 Geburtstag* (Spudasmata 80). Hildesheim.

Stewart, Z. (1958) 'The *Amphitruo* of Plautus and Euripides' *Bacchae*', *TAPhA* 89: 348–73.

(2000) 'Plautus' *Amphitruo*: three problems', *HSPh* 100: 293–9.

Stockert, W. (1982) 'Zur sprachlichen Charakterisierung der Personen in Plautus' *Aulularia*', *Gymnasium* 89: 4–14.

(1983) *T. Maccius Plautus:* Aulularia (with comm.). Stuttgart.

Strong, H. A. (1906) 'Note on Plautus' *Mostellaria*: Act III Scene II', *AJPh* 27: 67–9.

Sutton, D. F. (1993) *Ancient Comedy: The War of Generations*. New York.

(1994) *The Catharsis of Comedy*. Lanham, MD.

Taliercio, A. (1988) '*Imitatio-aemulatio* nei rapporti fra l'"Hecyra" di Terenzio e l'"Ἑκυρά" di Apollodoro di Caristo', *Orpheus* 9: 38–54.

Tarrant, R. J. (1983) 'Plautus', in Reynolds (1983): 302–7.

Taylor, L. R. (1937) 'The opportunities for dramatic performances in the time of Plautus and Terence', *TAPhA* 68: 284–304.

Taylor, L. R. and Holland, L. A. (1952) 'Janus and the *Fasti*', *CPh* 47: 137–42.

Telò, M. (1998), 'La scena di riconoscimento nello *Ione* di Euripide e Plauto, *Rudens* 1134', *SCO* 46: 909–17.

Thalmann, W. G. (1996) 'Versions of slavery in the *Captiui* of Plautus', *Ramus* 25: 112–45.

Thomas, R. F. (1979) 'New Comedy, Callimachus and Roman poetry', *HSPh* 83: 179–206.

Traill, A. (2005) 'Acroteleutium's Sapphic infatuation (*Miles* 1216–83)', *CQ* 55: 518–33.

Traina, A. (1977) *Forma e suono*. Rome.

Usener, H. (1901) 'Italisches Volksjustiz', *RhM* 56: 1–28.

Vahlen, J. (ed.) (1903) *Ennianae poesis reliquiae*, 2nd edn (1st edn 1854). Leipzig. (3rd edn Amsterdam, 1963, *non vidi*)

Victor, B. A. (1989) 'The *alter exitus Andriae*', *Latomus* 48: 63–74.

Vogt-Spira, G. (1991) '*Asinaria*, oder Maccus vortit Attice', in Lefèvre, Stärk and Vogt-Spira (1991): 11–69.

(1995) 'Traditionen improvisierten Theaters bei Plautus: einige programmatische Überlegungen', in *Griechisch-römische Komödie und Tragödie*, ed. B. Zimmerman. Stuttgart: 75–93.

von Albrecht, M. (1989) *Masters of Roman Prose from Cato to Apuleius: Interpretative Studies*, tr. N. Adkin. Leeds.

Watling, E. F. (1965) *Plautus:* The Pot of Gold *and Other Plays*. Harmondsworth.

Webb, R. (2005) 'The protean performer: mimesis and identity in late antique discussions of the theatre', in *Performing Ecstasies: Music, Dance and Ritual in the Mediterranean*, ed. L. del Giudice and N. van Deusen. Ottawa: 3–11.

Wessner, P. (1962–3) *Aeli Donati Commentum Terenti* (3 vols.). Stuttgart.

White, R. S. (1981) *Shakespeare and the Romance Ending*. Newcastle upon Tyne.

Whitehorne, J. (1993) 'The rapist's disguise in Menander's *Eunuchus*', in Slater and Zimmermann (1993): 122–32.

Whitman, C. (1964) *Aristophanes and the Comic Hero*. Cambridge, MA.

Wiles, D. (1991) *The Masks of Menander: Sign and Meaning in Greek and Roman Performance*. Cambridge.

Wilkinson, L. P. (1963) *Golden Latin Artistry*. Cambridge.

Willcock, M. (1987) *Plautus:* Pseudolus (with comm.). Bristol.

(1995) 'Plautus and the *Epidicus*', *Papers of the Leeds International Latin Seminar* 8: 19–29.

Wills, J. (1996) *Repetition in Latin Poetry: Figures of Allusion*. Oxford.

Wilson, R. F. (1990) *Shakespeare's Reflexive Endings*. Lewiston, NY.

Wimmel, W. (1960) *Kallimachos in Rom: Die Nachfolge seines apologetischen Dichtens in der Augusteerzeit* (Hermes Einzelschriften 16). Wiesbaden.

Wiseman, T. P. (1998) *Roman Drama and Roman History*. Exeter.

Wohl, V. (1998) *Intimate Commerce: Exchange, Gender and Subjectivity in Greek Tragedy*. Austin, TX.

Wright, J. (1974) *Dancing in Chains: The Stylistic Unity of the* comoedia palliata. Rome.

(1975) 'The transformations of Pseudolus', *TAPhA* 105: 403–16.

Zagagi, N. (1994) *The Comedy of Menander: Convention, Variation and Originality*. London.

Zanker, G. (2003) *Modes of Viewing in Hellenistic Poetry and Art*. Madison, WI.

Zeitlin, F. I. (1981) 'Travesties of gender and genre in Aristophanes' *Thesmophoriazousae*', *Critical Inquiry* 8: 301–27.

(1985) 'Playing the other: theatre, theatricality and the feminine in Greek drama', *Representations* 11: 63–94.

Zimmermann, B. (ed.) (1992) *Antike Dramentheorien und ihre Rezeption*. Stuttgart.

Zwierlein, O. (1990) *Zur Kritik und Exegese des Plautus*. Volume I: Poenulus *und* Curculio. Stuttgart.

(1991a) *Zur Kritik und Exegese des Plautus*. Volume II: Miles gloriosus. Stuttgart.

(1991b) *Zur Kritik und Exegese des Plautus*. Volume III: Pseudolus. Stuttgart.

(1992) *Zur Kritik und Exegese des Plautus*. Volume IV: Bacchides. Stuttgart.

General index

Index locorum

Lightning Source UK Ltd.
Milton Keynes UK
UKHW012317060122
396755UK00003B/17